About the Editor

Christopher Chapple holds a doctorate in the History of Religions from Fordham University and is currently Associate Professor of Theology at Loyola Marymount University in Los Angeles, where he has taught since 1985. From 1980 to 1985 he served as Assistant Director of the Institute for Advanced Studies of World Religions at the State University of New York at Stony Brook. He is the author of *Karma and Creativity* and *Nonviolence to Animals, Earth and Self in Asian Traditions* and co-translator of the *Yoga Sutras* of Patanjali. In 1990 he organized "The Jesuits: Education in World Perspective" as part of a series of annual conferences named in honor of the late Rev. Charles S. Casassa, S.J., president of Loyola Marymount University from 1949 to 1969.

The Jesuit Tradition
in Education and Missions

The Jesuit Tradition in Education and Missions

A 450-Year Perspective

Edited by
Christopher Chapple

Scranton: University of Scranton Press
London and Toronto: Associated University Presses

Associated University Presses
440 Forsgate Drive
Cranbury, NJ 08512

Associated University Presses
25 Sicilian Avenue
London WC1A 2QH, England

Associated University Presses
P.O. Box 338, Port Credit
Mississauga, Ontario
Canada L5G 4L8

The paper used in this publication meets the requirements of the American National Standard for Permanence of Paper for Printed Library Materials Z39.48-1984.

Library of Congress Cataloging-in-Publication Data

The Jesuit tradition in education and missions : a 450-year
  perspective / Christopher Chapple, editor.
      p.   cm.
    Includes bibliographical references.
    ISBN 0-940866-17-X (alk. paper)
    1. Jesuits—History. 2. Jesuits—Education—History. 3. Jesuits—
Missions—History. 4. Jesuits—Spiritual life—History.
BX3706.2.J465   1993
271'.53—dc20
                                                              91-67638
                                                              CIP

PRINTED IN THE UNITED STATES OF AMERICA

Contents

Introduction

CHRISTOPHER CHAPPLE

In the year 1540 a new religious order gained official recognition from Pope Paul III. This order, the Society of Jesus, established by Ignatius of Loyola, has left an indelible mark on the history of education and scholarship. Members of the Society, also referred to as Jesuits, established schools, colleges, and universities throughout the world. They also became some of the first Europeans to venture forth to Asia, the Americas, and Africa. In addition to bringing European technology and the Roman Catholic faith to such faraway places as China, the American Southwest, Africa, and Peru, they themselves were transformed in the process, learning the languages and cultural ways of the lands they entered and laying the foundation for later crosscultural study.

The Society of Jesus began in Paris with the pronouncement of vows by companions of Inigo of Loyola in 1534. Pope Paul III granted canonical status to the new religious order in 1540. Shortly thereafter, members of the Society began a twofold mission: to educate and to evangelize. In addition to serving as missionaries, Jesuits in Asia and the Americas became some of the first Europeans to contact and document nonwestern cultures.

During its first century, the Society of Jesus played an important role in the Counter Reformation, bringing new vigor to the Roman Catholic Church in Europe. One of its principal means of doing so was through education. In 1579 the Jesuits administered 144 colleges; by 1749 this number had grown to 669 colleges and 24 universities. The curriculum emphasized rhetoric and communication skills, in addition to philosophy and theology.

Individual Jesuits in Europe made important contributions to a wide range of disciplines in the early period, pioneering in such fields as moral and ascetical theology, historical studies, and the sciences, especially mathematics, astronomy, and geography. The Jesuits also promoted the arts, architecture, drama, and dance.

Within months of the founding of the order, Francis Xavier, one of the close companions of Ignatius, travelled to Asia. He remained there for twelve years, organizing and preaching from India to Japan. Jesuits were welcomed to the courts of India's Akbar the Great in 1579. Robert de Nobili, Mateo Ricci, and others were noted for their studies of indigenous cultures in Asia, laying the foundation for later academic study.

In 1549, the first Jesuits arrived in the Americas, ministering first to Europeans, slaves, and indigenous peoples of Brazil. A mission was established in Peru in 1567 and in Mexico in 1572. Beginning in the early seventeenth century, villages of Catholic Indians known as reductions were established in the area known as Paraguay; by 1731 such Guarani communities flourished, as documented in the motion picture *The Mission*.

French Jesuits arrived in North America in 1611, working with and recording ethnographies of the indigenous peoples of the northeast woodlands. The first school in French Canada was established by Jesuits in 1635. Jacques Marquette gained fame exploring the Mississippi River with Louis Joliet in 1673. Eusebio Kino established the first permanent Jesuit mission in what is now the United States at the beginning of the eighteenth century in southern Arizona.

Due to complex theological and political disputes, the Society of Jesus was suppressed beginning in 1759 when Portugal seized all of the Society's properties within its domain. In 1764 France declared the Jesuits to be illegal, with Spain following suit in 1767. In 1773 Pope Clement XIV mandated the dissolution of the order. A small branch of the Jesuits survived in Poland and Russia under the protection of Empress Catherine II. In 1814 the order was fully restored.

The first Jesuit institution of higher education in the United States, Georgetown University, was established in 1789 by John Carroll, the Bishop of Baltimore, who had been a Jesuit before the suppression. Today there are ten colleges and eighteen universities founded by Jesuits in the United States.

In commemoration of the 450th anniversary of the Society's founding and in acknowledgment of the many challenges faced by Jesuits currently engaged in the educational process at all levels, the 1990 annual Casassa Conference of Loyola Marymount University took Jesuit education in world perspective as its theme. Two primary aspects were highlighted during the three-day gathering: the development of the Jesuit educational tradition in Europe and America and the contact of Jesuits with nonwestern cultures. Over twenty papers were presented on these topics. The present volume includes several of these, grouped into two sections. The first deals with the formation of the Jesuit philosophy of education and with Jesuit education in Europe and America from its inception to the present. The second surveys little-studied areas of Jesuit presence in the New World, Asia, and Africa. Many of the papers deal with concerns that transcend these categories, focusing on how the Jesuit traditions of spirituality, education, and formation interface with the status of women, the challenge of modernity, and the renewed quest for authentic spirituality.

The paper opening the first section examines the inception and application of Jesuit education and scholarship in Europe. Francesco Cesareo provides a summary of the early years, noting that, like today, Jesuit education at its origins enjoyed a symbiotic relationship with secularism.

In the next article, Antonio T. deNicolás provides a hermeneutic for the *Spiritual Exercises* of Saint Ignatius de Loyola that renders them readily accessible to the uninitiated. DeNicolás asserts that authentic education takes place through the imaginative processes and not through the accumulation of data. True knowledge is not "fed by external images" but is fostered by an emptying of the will that allows insight to be revealed. New and eminently readable translations of specific *Exercises* are included, with special emphasis on the cultivation of creative memory and the active dismemberment of destructive habits from the past.

John Willis analyzes the use of scripture by Alfonso Salmerón, a close companion of Ignatius, underscoring early Jesuit interest in scholarly endeavor. Lawrence Wolff then provides a provocative look at the sermons of seventeenth-century Jesuit Louis Bourdaloue that deal with the issues of faith and family life.

Moving into the late nineteenth and early twentieth centuries, Peter McDonough offers a comprehensive assessment of nontraditional models for Jesuit lay education in and around New York City. Thomas Faase probes the issues of inculturation and social justice, themes that have dominated the past three General Congregations and have led to a new emphasis on "solidarity and identification with lower rather than higher social classes." This new focus within the order has accompanied a diminishment of Jesuit presence within the teaching faculties at Jesuit institutions.

Joseph A. O'Hare, S.J., President of Fordham University, began his presentation of the fourth Casassa Lecture with acknowledgment of the life and work of the late Charles S. Casassa, S.J., former President of Loyola Marymount University, for whom these annual conferences are named. He noted that Ernest Boyer, President of the Carnegie Foundation, has stated that Father Casassa "was one of the most revered mentors in my life." In the written essay included here, O'Hare challenges the notion that Jesuit education can be easily characterized, preferring instead to emphasize "the need to develop the imagination and a sense of history," facilitated by the model provided in the *Spiritual Exercises.* He states that "education must focus not only the whole person but on each person," and that "openness to innovation and adaptability" informed by religious values and insight plays a central role in the Jesuit approach to education. He asserts that the growing presence of non-Jesuits within Jesuit institutions requires collaboration, dialogue, and change.

Paul Crowley, S.J., suggests that changes in the Jesuit system of education must be accompanied by continued and increased emphasis on theological study within the university. The suggested source for a Jesuit approach to theology is the *Spiritual Exercises,* which Crowley claims cultivate "an apostolic ardor to remake the world, and be remade ourselves, for the reign of God."

Allan Figueroa Deck, S.J., critiques the problem of modernity facing Latin American culture and summarizes the solution of Marcello Azevedo, S.J., which advocates awareness of the structural injustices inherent in modern organizational models and a willingness to rethink this model, replacing it with insights from basic ecclesial communities.

The presence of women in Jesuit universities creates continuing challenges for the Society of Jesus and for the process of Jesuit education. Margaret Gorman, R.S.C.J., having conducted an extensive survey of women's teaching orders in the United States, concludes that the Sisters of Providence, Congregation of the Incarnate Word, the Ursulines, the Sisters of Saint Joseph, the Religious of the Sacred Heart, and many others have been particularly influenced by the *Spiritual Exercises*. Hers is one of the many essays in this collection that refer to the *Spiritual Exercises* as the primary formative document for the development and continued maintenance of Jesuit education.

The second portion of this volume explores Jesuit missions, history, and cultural insights. It focuses primarily on interactions with native peoples of the Americas, Africa, and Asia. Rather than emphasizing Jesuits as teachers, this section highlights notable cases not previously studied where Jesuits function primarily as learners and pioneers. Two significant areas that have been impacted by early Jesuit interaction are not included in this volume: the northeast woodlands of North America and China. A great deal of fine scholarship is available for the study of Jesuit presence in these areas.[1]

The first region examined in this section is South America, where Jesuits have had a continuing presence for nearly half a millenium. Luis Martín presents a compelling portrait of José de Acosta and Pablo José Arriaga, two Jesuits in sixteenth century Peru who struggled to preserve the dignity of New World Indians, regarding them as "being of flesh and blood shaped through the centuries by a unique physical and cultural environment," identical in nature to the European. Like their more well known counterparts in Asia, Acosta and Arriaga were convinced that European Jesuits must themselves become fluent in indigenous languages and cultures before attempting to present the Christian message. In the second essay of this section, T. Frank Kennedy, S.J., narrates the inception and development of European music and art in the Jesuit Reductions of Paraguay, postulating that self-respect was fostered among the many Indians who came to excel at musical performance and the production of artistic creations.

We next turn to the American Northwest and Southwest. Charles W. Polzer, S.J., Curator of the Arizona State Museum, chronicles the sacrifices made by Eusebio Kino and Juan Maria Salvatierra in their benevolent devotion to the Pima Alta peoples of modern-day Sonora and Arizona and their authentic quest to establish equal justice for native peoples. Gerald McKevitt, S.J., explores the study of indigenous languages by Jesuits in the vast region extending from Montana westward. Less than ten percent of these Jesuits were born in the United States; most of them had learned multiple langauges as children and hence were well equipped to master

Indian linguistics. They produced numerous dictionaries and grammars that continue to serve as basic reference tools for modern linguistics.

The Jesuits in Africa have received scant attention from historians and other scholars. John Orr Dwyer's essay, "The Jesuits in Africa," drawing from both primary and secondary sources, helps to correct this oversight. Frances Xavier visited Mozambique in 1541; significant Jesuit involvement has spanned a 450-year period, including missions in Abyssinia (Ethiopia), the Congo (Zaire, Kwango, Angola), the Zambezi (Zimbabwe), the Sudan, and elsewhere. Of particular interest is Dwyer's description of Loyola Secondary School in Wau, Southern Sudan, which operated from 1983 until civil war prompted its closure in 1987.

Issues of crosscultural interpretation are addressed in the essay entitled "Translating the Good: Roberto de Nobili's Moral Argument and Jesuit Education Today," by Francis X. Clooney, S.J. Clooney offers a probing assessment of deNobili's understanding of Hindu religion and suggests that modern, pluralistic approaches to ethical issues must include "crossreligious theological conversation."

This collection of essays provides a representative sampling of the richness and depth of the Jesuit educational tradition from its aristocratic origins through its ministry through education to post-Reformation Catholics, its work at conversion in newly explored lands, its education of the European immigrants who came to America in search of a better life, and its current emphasis on the promotion of social justice worldwide. Although many aspects of Jesuit history are neglected in this volume, such as the Jesuit contributions to art, architecture, and science, as well as the years during which the order was suppressed, two basic themes are explored: the pervasive commitment to the process of formation and education, as well as a willingness by individual Jesuits to be educated by the very people to whom they ministered.

As we move toward the sixth century of Jesuit education, new challenges emerge: increased reliance on lay participation at all levels in the many schools and colleges established by Jesuits, a continued grappling with the forces of modernity, and the drive to improve the lot of the disadvantaged masses worldwide. Hopefully this volume will help foster a greater understanding and appreciation of this dynamic and fascinating legacy with a glimpse of how this history can help inform current and future changes.

Several persons contributed to the formation of this volume. Anthony B. Brzoska, S.J., Loyola Marymount University's former Dean of Liberal Arts, suggested the topic for the conference that gave rise to this collection of papers. Thomas P. Rausch, S.J., my colleague in the Theology Department and Rector of the Jesuit Community at Loyola Marymount University, urged that the papers be gathered together for publication. He served on the steering committee for the conference, along with Michael O'Sullivan, S.J., Carroll C. Kearley, Michael Engh, S.J., and Loretta Morris, all of Loyola

Marymount. Thomas E. Buckley, S.J., and Ernest S. Sweeney, S.J. of our history department also lent considerable support. I wish to also express appreciation to Benjamin Braude of Boston College, James Gaffney of Loyola University in New Orleans, David E. Mungello of Coe College, Joseph Prabhu of California State University, Los Angeles, Fernando A. Storni, S.J., former President of Catholic University of Cordoba, and Paul J. Weithman of Notre Dame University who all presented papers at the event. Last but not least, Carole Keese, the Conference Coordinator, and Susan Burgerman, my research assistant, devoted long hours to the conference and its proceedings; without them this volume would not have been possible.

Note

1. For information on Jesuits in colonial northeast North America, see Anthony F. C. Wallace's *The Death and Rebirth of the Seneca,* James Axtell's *The Enemy Within: The Contest of Cultures in Colonial North America,* and James T. Moore's *Indian and Jesuit: A Seventeenth Century Encounter,* to name just three. For China, consult *Generation of Giants: The Story of the Jesuits in China in the Last Decades of the Ming Dynasty,* by George Dunne, S.J., Jonathan D. Spence's *The Memory Palace of Matteo Ricci,* David E. Mungello's *Curious Land: Jesuit Accommodation and the Origins of Sinology,* and *East Meets West: The Jesuits in China, 1582–1773,* edited by Charles E. Ronan, S.J., and Bonnie B. C. Oh.

The Jesuit Tradition
in Education and Missions

Part One
The Jesuit Order: Formation and Education

Quest for Identity: The Ideals of Jesuit Education in the Sixteenth Century

FRANCESCO C. CESAREO

The place, role, and identity of Jesuit education in society has been a constant source of debate and inquiry. In the final years of this century, this search for meaning seems to have taken on a greater urgency as the influences of the secular world have become more apparent. Today, Jesuit colleges and universities are trying to delineate clearly who they are and what they stand for vis-à-vis other institutions of higher learning.

If one looks back to the earliest foundations of Jesuit schools, one is struck by the similarity of the situation. The era of Saint Ignatius was the age of the new humanist schools of the Renaissance. The Latin schools and vernacular schools that emerged sought to teach practical skills. The former taught the Latin that allowed students to advance to university studies in preparation for careers in civil service or the church. Those who attended the vernacular schools were taught skills necessary in commerce. Despite the difference in purpose, both schools shared a pedagogical approach. "The subject matter, whether beginning reading, Latin grammar, advanced rhetoric, or abbaco, had to be divided into very small individual bits of knowledge. Teachers and textbooks taught by breaking a skill down into its smallest components, drilling them intensively, and then assembling the bits to make the whole."[1]

It is against this background that one must examine early Jesuit education. When Ignatius died in 1556 he had personally approved the opening of thirty-nine colleges and universities. The number of colleges had grown to 293 in 1607 and by 1750 these institutions peaked at 669. The number of students enrolled in these institutions averaged between 300 and 1500. The Jesuit schools of the sixteenth century were in the mainstream of their time. The curriculum of the Jesuit school was the Latin curriculum, based on the same texts and exercises employed by the humanist educators of the Latin schools. The only noticeable difference was that the Jesuits added more structure to the humanist curriculum by introducing a systematic chronological progression of classes based on ability and age.[2] The similarity that existed between the Latin and Jesuit schools often led to competition and rivalry. As a result, Ignatius and the Jesuits who founded schools had to have a clear understanding of the identity of their schools and the role they would play in society.

This essay will examine how the early Jesuit schools envisioned their mission in light of the accepted pedagogical methods of the day. Focusing on Ignatius's letters on education, the Constitutions of the Society of Jesus, and the regulations of the first Jesuit schools, it will show how Jesuit education added a new impulse to Renaissance education—the desire to provide a religious vision to the academic endeavor that would benefit not only the individual, but society as well. This religious dimension gave meaning and identity to the educational program of the Society of Jesus.

To understand the educational theories developed by Ignatius it is necessary to look at his own educational experience. Ignatius himself gives us an insight into his view of education in his autobiography. Speaking of himself and his studies in the third person, Ignatius said: "After the pilgrim realized that it was not God's will that he remain in Jerusalem, he continually pondered what he ought to do. At last he inclined more to study for some time so he would be able to help souls. . . ."[3] It is clear that Ignatius did not pursue learning for its own sake. Education was to serve a greater end as it assisted humanity in its quest for God.

Realizing his own need for an education, Ignatius began classes in elementary Latin under Jerome Ardevoll, a regent of the University of Barcelona. After two years of study Ardevoll advised him to go to the University of Alcalá (1526). He studied here for sixteen months, trying to assimilate as many subjects as possible. From Alcalá he went to Salamanca, but soon went to the University of Paris (1528), where he remained for seven years. Ignatius first entered the College of Montaigu studying Latin grammar. In the fall of 1529 Ignatius entered the College of Sainte-Barb, where humanism had taken root. Here, "there was a remodeling of the curriculum in order to make the classics in very fact the foundation of the higher studies."[4] Ignatius's own educational experience introduced him to both the scholastic method of the Middle Ages and the humanist method of the Renaissance. In his own educational outlook he attempted to bring together those elements from both methods he felt would be useful and beneficial. This led him to adopt a middle way when he began to organize the Jesuit educational system.[5]

In 1540 Pope Paul III formally approved the Society of Jesus. Even though Ignatius did not intend to found a group of educators, he had formulated some basic convictions in regard to eduation. This is evident in Paul III's bull of approval, *Regimini militantis ecclesiae*. Concerning the work of the Society, the bull states:

> Whoever shall desire to bear the arms of God under the banner of the Cross, and to serve the one God and the Roman Pontiff, His Vicar upon earth, in our Society, which we wish to be called by the name of Jesus, having made a solemn vow of perpetual chastity, must purpose to become a member of a society principally instituted to work for the advancement of souls in Christian life and doctrine, and for the propagation of the faith by public preaching and the ministry of God's Word, by spiritual exercises and works of charity, more particularly by grounding in Christianity boys and unlettered persons, and by hearing the confessions of the

faithful, aiming in all things their spiritual consolation. He must also act so as to have always before his eyes, first God, and then the plan of this Institute which is a definite path that leads to Him.[6]

Later in the bull, a similar idea is expressed: "Above all things let them have at heart the instruction of boys and ignorant persons in the knowledge of Christian doctrine, of the Ten Commandments, and other such rudiments as shall be suitable. . . ."[7] As in the autobiography, one sees the idea of education being linked with the spiritual progress of souls. This is the guiding principle for every task undertaken by Ignatius, as he makes clear in the First Principle and Foundation of the *Spiritual Exercises:* "Man is created to praise, reverence, and serve God our Lord, and by this means to save his soul. The other things on the face of the earth are created for man to help him in attaining the end for which he is created."[8] This idea was the nucleus around which Ignatius developed his educational outlook.

Until 1546 the Society of Jesus did not concern itself with running schools for those outside the order.[9] However, according to Ignatius's secretary, Father John de Polanco, S.J., this should not be interpreted as Ignatius being adverse to opening schools for externs. Polanco contends that Ignatius always had a strong inclination for the task of educating youth in piety and letters.[10]

The first influence on Ignatius in establishing schools for externs was the description of Francis Xavier of the college of Goa (1543), where members of the Society taught Christian doctrine and the humanities to Indian and Portuguese youth. "Later Ignatius referred to the college at Goa as a type of the schools he was anxious to see established by the Society of Jesus."[11] The year 1546 marked a significant step in the Society's involvement in education. In the previous year, a college had been established in Gandia for the training of young Jesuits. In 1546 externs were invited to attend the school, giving rise to the mixed college comprised of both Jesuit and lay students. As early as 1548, the Jesuits began to open colleges intended chiefly to teach lay students who did not envision priesthood.[12] The significance, then, of the College of Gandia lies in the fact that it gave impetus to the teaching apostolate of the Jesuits.

In an era when education was undergoing changes and expansion, the involvement of the Jesuits in this work meant developing a clear understanding of the goals and purposes they hoped to attain through their schools. Foremost in Ignatius's mind in accepting education of the laity was his belief that this would promote the salvation and perfection of the students, as they penetrated their world with Christian doctrine and spirit. "This outlook of Ignatius was one which was highly social and patriotic, for he thought that the lives of citizens in a state would be happy and worthwhile in proportion to the extent to which they were imbued with the Christian spirit."[13] To accomplish this, he fused together those elements from the diverse educational methods of the day which he felt were best and transformed them into a system which would accomplish his purpose. Whether the students who attended the Jesuit colleges were lay or clerical, Ignatius's aim was the same—to prepare leaders for society. However, the training of an elite group of able leaders was not the sole or primary purpose of education. Ignatius was concerned with the formation of a "citizen of Christ's kingdom in this world, steadily earning his way to the eternal happiness achieved by glorifying God."[14]

On the surface, the educational program of Jesuit schools in the sixteenth century resembled other Renaissance educational programs. Yet, despite their common elements, the first Jesuit schools early acquired an individual tradition and identity. The Constitutions of the Society of Jesus make it very clear that the Society of Jesus undertakes the work of education from an apostolic motive since it believes that sound schooling can help conduct men to salvation. Ignatius indicates this in the section of the *Capitoli* entitled *De mostrar muchachos,* which states that the task of education was not to be literary, but only the inculcation of Christian doctrine and good customs.[15] To accomplish this, Ignatius added to the humanist educational program the study of philosophy and theology, to serve as the foundation of a "theistic philosophy of life—a philosophy which gives true significance and worthwhile meaning to the life of man both in this world and the next. There is constant encouragement of the student not only to moral and sacramental living but also to the exercise of all the supernatural virtues which lead to the highest union with God."[16] Thus, Ignatius's objective in education seems to have been twofold: to form a good, solid Christian leader who could exert a positive influence on the social, political, and cultural environment in which he lived and, by means of this, to allow for the spiritual progress of one's soul on its pilgrimage toward salvation.

The spiritual orientation of education as envisioned by Ignatius can be seen in the earliest of the Society's educational ventures. In a letter written in 1547 to Jesuit scholastics at the College of Coimbra, Ignatius calls attention to the worthiness of their studies and their importance in the attainment of virtue:

> You are serving God's honor and glory in many ways.
> First, by your present labor and the intention with which you undertake and regulate everything for your neighbor's edification, just as soldiers waiting to get supplies of arms and munitions for the operation about to be launched cannot say that their labor is not in the service of their king.
> The second way is to attain a high degree of virtue, because you will thus be able to make your neighbor such as you are yourselves. . . . You are preparing an instrument that is not less, but better, fitted to confer grace by leading a virtuous life than by leading a learned one, although both learning and virtue are required if the instrument is to be perfect.[17]

This twofold aim is apparent in the founding of the College of Messina. When the people of this city petitioned Ignatius to establish a college there, they envisioned the work of the college to advance not only learning, but also knowledge and love of God. They asked Ignatius to send learned and religious men, who would teach letters and piety, as they worked for the intellectual and spiritual welfare of the community.[18] The Jesuits at Messina developed a curriculum that brought together practices of piety with exercises of learning, based on the *"modus et ordo Parisiensis."* The phrase *modus et ordo Parisiensis* signified to Ignatius and the early Jesuit educators a foundation in classical Latin grammar, an emphasis on Cicero and Vergil, the speaking of Latin, and a method based on repetition, constant review, memorization, disputation, and composition exercises. The course of study at Messina included Latin grammar, rhetoric, philosophy, mathematics, Greek, Hebrew, and theology.[19] Although this course of study was similar to that found in other humanist schools, the ultimate aim differed. As indicated in the Constitutions of the College of Messina, these studies were to be pursued to assist the community at large.[20] In addition, all studies were to be directed toward the salvation and good of souls.[21]

This fusion of intellectual and character formation is seen in the *Libellus Quo Initia Scholarum Collegii Messanensis Annuntiantur* (1548), which states:

> Above all else, attention must be given to assisting the souls in spiritual matters through the reading of some good instruction concerning Christian doctrine, that is, that which needs to be known and observed by all faithful Christians. These lessons should be adapted for both the old and the young.
>
> In this way, with divine assistance, all of the lessons and exercises, will be conducted with great care and diligence, according to the method of Paris, which is the most useful and exact. This will quickly result in good habits and spiritual profit, allowing for the greater glory of God and usefulness and consolation for the souls of the faithful.[22]

This distinctive spiritual tone found at Messina made this college the prototype of other Jesuit schools.

The spiritual dimension of the general humanistic education of lay students was made clearer by the papal bull of Julius III *Exposcit debitum* (21 July 1550). One of the ends of the Society according to this bull was to strive for the defense and propagation of the faith and for the progress of souls *(profectum animarum)* in Christian life and doctrine by means of the education of children and unlettered persons in Christianity.[23]

A similar notion is expressed by Father Jerome Nadal, S.J., in his treatise *De Studiis Societatis Iesu* (1552). He opens this treatise with a statement that any rule of studies must have two divisions, one relating to the professors, another to the students, but both directed primarily toward spiritual advancement.[24] With this in mind, a general rule is advanced stating that authors must first be purged of anything that might poison the boy's soul while perfecting his Latin. Ignatius, in a letter written in June 1549, indicates why such care was so important. He contends that a boy's first impressions are the strongest and remain for many years. Since these impressions have a positive or negative influence on his afterlife, the books he is exposed to must exert a good influence.[25]

The spiritual efficacy of studies is given further support by Father Polanco in the *Industriae* of 1548. He indicates that, even before one approaches his studies, a certain interior disposition need be present. Polanco uses the imagery of the old self dying before one can yearn for spiritual things. In this context, studies are a means of divine service and should not be pursued out of curiosity, for one's honor, or for their own sake. If studies are founded upon these principles, they do not serve the end for which the Society engages in education, namely, the greater glory of God and the assistance of souls.[26] Education, therefore, becomes a holy enterprise.

These early ideas on the mission and scope of education in the Society were given a firm foundation by Ignatius in the Constitutions of the Society of Jesus. After 1551, the Constitutions were the guiding spirit of the educational work of the Jesuits. Part 4 of the Constitutions deals with the educational ministry of the Society. The principles elaborated here must be understood in light of the overall aim of the Society, as stated by Ignatius at the outset of the Constitutions: "The end of this Society is to devote itself with God's grace not only to the salvation and perfection of the members' own souls, but also with that same grace to labor strenuously in giving aid toward the salvation and perfection of the souls of their fellowmen."[27] One of the ways to achieve this end was through education, as the Preamble to part 4 of the Constitutions states:

> The aim which the Society of Jesus directly seeks is to aid its own members and their fellowmen to attain the ultimate end for which they were created. To achieve this purpose, in addition to the example of one's life, learning and a method of expounding it are also necessary. . . . Toward achieving this purpose the Society takes charge of colleges and also of some universities.[28]

By colleges Ignatius meant schools where grammar, the *litterae humaniores,* and rhetoric were taught, while universities conducted classes in the arts and theology.[29]

The identity envisioned by Ignatius for the Society's educational apostolate is most evident in chapters 8 and 11 through 17 of part 4 of the Constitutions. Several recurring principles and objectives are expressed in these chapters that capture the ideals of Jesuit education in the sixteenth century. Four key themes emerge that will serve as the focus of the remainder of this essay. First, the objective of the educator to stimulate the student to relate studies to his final end—that is, the knowledge and love of God and the salvation of his soul; second, the goal of the curriculum in the formation of a Christian outlook on life, enabling the student to live well and meaningfully for this world and the next; third, the moral and intellectual formation of students; fourth, the preparation of capable and influential leaders for society.

One of the principal tasks of the educator for Ignatius was to relate studies to the knowledge and love of God and the salvation of one's soul. In chapter 16 of the Constitutions, Ignatius makes this clear: "The masters should make it their special aim, both in their lectures when occasion is offered and outside of them too, to inspire the students to the love and service of God our Lord, and to a love of the virtues by which they will please Him. They should urge the students to direct all their studies to this end."[30]

Since this was the aim toward which studies were directed, it was also the factor that determined the branches of learning in Jesuit schools. According to the Constitutions, those subjects most helpful in achieving this aim are: humane letters, logic, natural and moral philosophy, metaphysics, scholastic and positive theology, and Sacred Scripture.[31] Among these, Ignatius gave a prominent place to theology since it is the means most suitable in assisting men to the knowledge and love of God and to the salvation of their souls. Thus, "principal emphasis" and "diligent treatment" should be given to theology and Sacred Scripture in the universities of the Society.[32]

Out of these basic directives, various treatises and regulations were drawn up to implement the principles put forth by Ignatius. In an exhortation entitled *Protrepticon ad Magistros Scholarum Inferiorum Societatis Iesu,* Father Francesco Sacchini, S.J., writes: "Among us the education of youth is not limited to imparting the rudiments of grammar but extends simultaneously to Christian formation."[33]

This idea is also expressed in the *Regulae Rectoris Collegii Romani* (1551). This document states that the rector should concern himself with four areas in the life of his students. First and foremost, he should be concerned with the cultivation of Christian virtues and spiritual perfection among the students.[34] To accomplish this, the rector needs to remind students constantly that their studies are pursued for one end, to give glory to God and to assist their souls toward perfection. For this reason they should be diligent in their studies so as to profit spiritually.[35] Although this is the principal concern for the rector, he also must see to it that his students are proficient in letters.[36] Here is seen a fusion between exercises of piety and learning. The regulations state that students should read not only those authors who would present them with solid doctrine, but also those who would ensure a firm foundation in grammar.[37] This academic program was conducted in the midst of regular exercises of devotion: daily Mass, daily examination of conscience, daily prayer hour, weekly confession and communion—further highlighting the religious dimension of the educational enterprise.

In 1555–56 a series of regulations was issued for Jesuit schools in Italy indicating the responsibilities of the prefect, teachers, and students. The importance of relating studies to the knowledge of God and the salvation of one's soul is once again apparent. However, what was merely implicit in earlier documents is made more explicit here, namely, the spiritual ramifications of study for the broader social community. At the outset this document indicates that study is undertaken for God's greater glory and the universal good of one's neighbors.[38] In light of this, the prefect of studies must be diligent in advancing those branches of learning which would be beneficial in teaching good letters, assisting the community, and inculcating a desire for those virtues proper to Christians.[39]

The responsibility of teachers, according to these regulations, was to teach youth "buone lettere et buoni costumi" for the greater glory of God, the perfection and salvation of their students, and the spiritual welfare of society.[40] To accomplish these goals, they must be knowledgeable in their field so that they can instruct students in the best authors. However, the regulations warn that the study of these authors is undertaken not for the sake of letters themselves but to implant the love and fear of Jesus in the hearts of students. In addition, through example, instructors are to grasp from these authors those values and customs which ought to direct the lives of Christians.[41] Therefore, they must always point out the spiritual fruits that will sustain their students in the living out of their Christian life, which in turn will advance the salvation of the world.[42]

As for the students themselves, the regulations state that they must be conscious of the overall end of studies in the Society of Jesus. Aware of these goals, students must pursue their studies with the purpose of becoming instruments in glorifying God by serving their neighbors.[43] The document warns that studies pursued without a spiritual dimension and without humility would quickly bring ruin and perdition on those who cultivate learning. To protect against this, study should not be pursued as an end in itself, or it would be a source of distraction and crush its spiritual benefits.[44] Rather, God must always be the sole source and object of studies, allowing the very act of study to be a prayer to God's honor.[45]

Therefore, one of the significant ideals around which Ignatius developed his educational outlook was the knowledge of God and the cultivation of the soul. This was the end of the Society and was logically the goal of the educational apostolate. Yet, if his schools were to draw students and compete with the existing Renaissance schools, they also had to prepare the student for life in the world of his day. Students emerging from Jesuit schools had to be able to compete with their counterparts in the secular schools. Ignatius did not ignore this dimension. Concerning himself with the practical goals of education, Ignatius fused together his spiritual aims with more mundane concerns, as he developed a curriculum conducive to preparing students for life in this world.

In line with the first ideal upon which Jesuit education was based, Ignatius was concerned that the branches of study should contribute to the goal of the curriculum as a whole, namely, the formation of a Christian outlook on life, enabling the student to live well and meaningfully for this world and the next.

For Ignatius, this meant an outlook in which the "student has thought through to his own personal conviction, in contrast to the memorized knowledge which is characteristic of a child. The outlook was the focus of integration for all the other elements in his system. It was what would enable, as well as inspire, the students to perfect themselves and to contribute intelligently and effectively to the welfare of society."[46] In preparing students to live in their contemporary society, Ignatius wished to mold the nature and actions of his students in the image of Christ. "In other words, Ignatius desired to give him on earth a happy life beneficial to society, and afterwards everlasting joy proportionate to the service he had given to God and man."[47]

The formation of this Catholic outlook was based on the curriculum employed. The nucleus of this curriculum was theology. In this case, Ignatius was concerned with a practical theology, one that would allow for the cultivation of piety and the achievement of the Society's end, assisting people to the "knowledge and love of God and to the salvation of their souls."[48] Thus, both students and teachers alike were to grasp from their studies ideas that would inspire service of God and neighbor.[49]

In line with his third ideal, Ignatius envisioned an educational system that concerned itself with the intellectual and moral formation of the individual. By intellectual education Ignatius meant the imparting of knowledge and the inducing of a man to act according to the intellectual virtues; moral education induces a man to develop the moral habits referred to as virtues.[50] These two aims of Ignatius's educational system were found throughout all the faculties in the university.

The Constitutions clearly outline how this ideal was to be realized. In chapter 8 Ignatius states: "While lecturing, in addition to giving the interpretation, they ought to keep alert to touch upon matters helpful for habits of conduct and for Christian living."[51] Further on, in chapter 16 he states: "Very special care should be taken that those who come to the universities of the Society to obtain knowledge should acquire along with it good and Christian moral habits. It will help much toward this if all go to confession at least once every month, hear Mass every day and a sermon every feast day when one is given."[52]

Those subjects most suited to intellectual and moral formation were philosophy and theology. While both involved intensive intellectual training, they also motivated one toward moral virtues, good conduct, and the practice of piety.[53] Even in the explanation of grammar or the classical authors instructors should use every opportunity to inculcate moral lessons that would be profitable for the students.[54]

Given the end of the Society and its studies, one would expect that character formation would hold a prominent place in the educational schema. In a letter written to Father Antonio Araoz, S.J., on 1 December 1551, Ignatius described the benefits and advantages of the Society's educational program and indicated that moral formation goes hand in hand with intellectual growth. Writing about extern students, Ignatius points out that in the Jesuit schools they "reap great fruit of letters." Further on in the letter he writes: "They profit in spiritual matters, through learning Christian doctrine and grasping from the sermons and customary exhortations that which is conducive to their eternal salvation. They make progress in purity of conscience and consequently in all virtue through confession every month, and through the care taken that they be decent in their speech and virtuous in their entire lives."[55]

The ideals discussed thus far all contribute to the formation of a well-rounded person inspired by a Christian vision. This vision, always focused on God and salvation, allows for a process of inner renewal leading toward the perfection of the self. Once this has been achieved, the individual seeks to promote a similar perfection in his neighbor, thereby improving the social order. Thus, another significant element in the formation of Ignatius's educational vision was the hope that the Society would offer capable and zealous leaders to the social order.

In the Constitutions Ignatius indicates that universities are among the most important undertakings of the Society, because they are a means of producing the leaders and citizens influential for good who are necessary in ecclesiastical and civil society.[56] To achieve this end, Ignatius encourages students to perfect their Latin style and pronunciation. This was essential in an era when such eloquence was an opening to those who wielded power and influence. In addition, they also were to speak in a simple manner for the population at large. This is seen in chapter 8 of the Constitutions: "They will exercise themselves in preaching and in delivering [sacred] lectures in a manner suitable for the edification of the people, which is different from the scholastic manner, by endeavoring to learn the [vernacular] language well, to have, as matters previously studied and ready at hand, the means which are more useful for this ministry, and to avail themselves of all appropriate means to perform it better and with greater fruit for souls."[57]

The curriculum adopted by Ignatius for his schools had a twofold purpose: first, to teach students how to live meaningful Christian lives while exerting influence upon their society and, second, to prepare students to earn a living so that they would be in a position to play a significant role in society. "He showed no interest in a curriculum helpful towards the livelihood alone; but into the curriculum which in his era was in fact helpful towards gaining a livelihood, Ignatius injected much training which imparts the theistic outlook that gives a meaning to life. He wanted his lay graduates to prepare themselves to be capable and influential for good in their countries."[58] In a letter to Father Antonio Araoz, S.J. (1 December 1551), Ignatius spells out how nations would benefit from the educational program of the Society. He states that the nation would have among its citizens those who would assist in good works, such as hospitals. Furthermore, future leaders would emerge. Ignatius writes: "From among those who are at present merely students, in time some will depart to play diverse roles—one to preach and carry on the care of souls, another to the government of the land and the administration of justice, and others to other occupations. Finally, since young boys become grown men, their good education in life and doctrine will be beneficial to many others, with the fruit expanding more widely every day."[59] Similar ideas are also put forth by Ignatius's secretary Father Polanco, S.J., in *De Collegiis Externis* (1551).[60]

In a letter to Father Mercuriano, S.J. (June 1552), Ignatius further indicates the importance of the social dimension of his schools. He writes that the Society desires that the nation or province in which a college is located receive intellectual and spiritual benefits from the example and learning of the students, who should cultivate their knowledge in order to be of service to the nation.[61] In addition, two or three priests should be assigned to the college for the care of souls through the celebration of the sacraments and the teaching of Christian doctrine.[62] Thus, the Jesuit application of the study of the liberal arts contributes to the welfare of both Church and State.[63]

That Ignatius envisioned educational institutions as having a social purpose by exerting influence on society at large is evident in his aspirations for the Collegio Romano (1551). In a letter that has no date or name, Ignatius enumerates certain motives that might convince someone to found this college. Although there is no direct mention of the Collegio Romano in the letter, from the context one can conclude that this is the college being referred to by Ignatius. Ignatius writes:

> If he is zealous for the common good and the help of souls and the spread and increase of the Catholic faith, this is a work which is especially destined to such an end. For not only will the youth of Rome be taught and trained in learning and good morals, but in time students can come from all parts of Italy and beyond for the same purpose. . . . Likewise, a large number of apostolic workers of our own Society will be educated there, with their studies directed solely to the same end of the common good. . . . Thus this college will be a never failing nursery of ministers of the Apostolic See for the service of holy Church and the good of souls.[64]

The hope Ignatius placed in the Collegio Romano can also be seen in his aspirations for the Collegio Germanicum to be founded in Rome. In a series of letters concerning the Germanicum, the social dimension is at the forefront. Writing to Father Claude Le Jay, S.J., in July 1552, Ignatius states that the German College would undertake the education and moral training of young men who showed promise in piety, learning, and virtue. Once they had progressed in these areas, they would be sent back to Germany, where they "by the example of a life of study and the influence of their solid learning will preach the word of God, and by their lectures, or at least by their personal influence, will be able to open the eyes of their fellow countrymen to the light of the true faith and tear down the veil of ignorance and vice."[65] Ignatius concludes the letter by placing the work of the German College in the context of the overall aim of the Society's educational work—the glory of God and the salvation of souls.

What conclusions can be drawn about the identity of Jesuit academic institutions in the sixteenth century? On the surface, Jesuit schools resembled any other Renaissance school. The basic curriculum was similar to that employed by the Renaissance humanist schools of the era: training in the humanities, skills for written and oral communication, the study of classical languages. Pedagogically too, Jesuit schools followed the methods of the Renaissance Latin schools: lectures, disputations, compositions, as a means of allowing the students to progress in their knowledge of letters. True, Jesuit schools had highly structured the curriculum, but the content was the same.

The identity and uniqueness of the Jesuit schools lies in the way the curriculum was used to further the ultimate goal Ignatius hoped to attain through the educational program. Education during the Renaissance was secular, concerning itself with inculcating civic morality for the ruling class and others who served the state. The emphasis was on classical moral virtues rather than Christian religious doctrine and practices.[66] During the era of the Catholic Reformation, a new impulse was added to education—the desire to provide basic religious instruction in order to reform morals and save souls. It was this religious dimension that gave identity to the schools of the Society of Jesus. In the context of the one single aim of the Society, Ignatius infused the existing educational curriculum and structure with a religious vision beneficial to the individual and society as a whole. Ignatius's concept of education was the harmonious development of the whole man, spiritual and intellectual. By fostering a Catholic outlook on life, Ignatius saw his academic institutions as playing an influential role in the shaping of his world. For Ignatius, education was to mold leaders who would be beneficial to the Church and State. But equally and perhaps more importantly, education was to assist men in achieving the goal to which all are called—eternal salvation. The foundation and object of Jesuit education for Ignatius was God and, through this work, giving Him greater glory. This same ideal and objective gave these schools their unique character and identity in the sixteenth century.

Can the initial quest for identity offer any assistance or insights into the present struggle for identity among Jesuit schools? As in Ignatius's day, on the surface Jesuit institutions are similar to their secular counterparts. Curriculums are basically the same; graduate programs and professional schools compete with other similar programs. In these respects, Jesuit institutions have taken the injunction of Ignatius found in the Constitutions that the regulations concerning education "ought to be adapted to places, times, and persons"[67] quite literally. In allowing for the adaptation of structure and curriculum, did Ignatius also leave room for the adaptation of the basic inner principles which animated Jesuit schools and from which arose their identity? Did the adaptation that took place in the 1960s and 1970s bring the vision of Ignatius to near extinction?

The current concern and debate over identity would seem to affirm such a view. The challenge today is to animate these institutions with the ideals and vision of Ignatius by making these values the heart and soul of the institution's life. This can no longer be accomplished through mandatory practices of religious devotion as a means of fusing together the spiritual and intellectual life. Yet the goal toward which those religious practices pointed can still penetrate the educational mission of Jesuit schools. Just as Ignatius took the curriculum of his day and injected it with a higher dimension, so too today the curriculum should spur questions in the minds of students concerning the values and morals of their world. Students should be made to see the greater purpose of their education. Peter-Hans Kolvenbach, S.J., the Father General of the Society of Jesus, recently reminded American Jesuits of the Ignatian vision that must animate their schools: "The Society of Jesus has always sought to imbue students with values that transcend the goals of money, fame, and success. We want graduates who will be leaders concerned about the society and world in which they live, desirous of eliminating hunger and conflict in the world, sensitive to the need for more equitable distribution of God's bounty, seeking to end sexual and social discrimination, and eager to share their faith and love of Christ with others."[68]

Just as in Ignatius's day, indeed more so, Jesuit institutions have an opportunity to bring a spiritual and moral dimension to a world dominated by secular values. They can only do this if they stand apart from the world and challenge it with a genuine Catholic Christian outlook. This may cause a feeling of uneasiness for many, but not to do this is to abandon the vision of Ignatius and to remove any reason for the existence of Jesuit schools. As in the sixteenth century, the identity and uniqueness of Jesuit schools must rest on their spiritual heritage. Ignatius used education as a means to a religious end. In 1555 he wrote: "For ourselves, theology would do well enough with less of Cicero and Demosthenes. But as St. Paul became all things to all men in order to save them, so the Society in its desire to give spiritual assistance seizes upon the spoils of Egypt to turn their use to God's honor and glory."[69] The circumstances may be different, but the goal today is the same as in the sixteenth century—to train leaders who will make a positive difference in the world by bringing to it a Christian outlook, thereby giving greater glory to God.

Notes

1. Paul F. Grendler, *Schooling in Renaissance Italy: Literacy and Learning, 1300–1600* (Baltimore: The Johns Hopkins University Press, 1989), p. 409.

2. Ibid., p. 379. Grendler points out that the Italian pedagogical theorists did not insist on a single pattern of studies. However, all of the Jesuits taught the same texts and authors in a methodical progression of classes. The innovation in the Jesuit

curriculum is also treated by Aldo Scaglione, *The Liberal Arts and the Jesuit College System* (Amsterdam: John Benjamins, 1986).

3. *The Autobiography of St. Ignatius Loyola,* edited and translated by Joseph F. O'Callaghan and John C. Olin (New York: Harper and Row, 1974), p. 54.

4. Allan P. Farrell, S.J., *The Jesuit Code of Liberal Education: Development and Scope of the Ratio Studiorum* (Milwaukee: The Bruce Publishing Co., 1938), p. 41. Also see George E. Ganss, S.J., *St. Ignatius' Idea of a University* (Milwaukee: The Marquette University Press, 1954), pp. 9–17.

5. Ganss, p. 17.

6. John C. Olin, *The Catholic Reformation: Savonarola to Ignatius Loyola, Reform in the Church 1495–1540* (Westminster: Christian Classics, 1969), p. 204.

7. Ibid., p. 205.

8. Louis J. Puhl, S.J., *The Spiritual Exercises of St. Ignatius* (Chicago: Loyola University Press, 1951), no. 23, p. 12.

9. Farrell, p. 13.

10. "Res Ignatio placuit, qui, ad iuventutis bene instituendae in spiritu et litteris rationem, semper fuit valde propensus." *Chronicon Societatis Iesu auctore Ioanne Alphonso de Polanco,* 6 vols. (Madrid, 1894–98), 2:195.

11. Farrell, p. 16.

12. Ganss, pp. 21–23.

13. Ganss, p. 18.

14. Ibid., p. 175.

15. *Monumenta Ignatiana, ser. III: Constitutiones Societatis Iesu,* 4 vols. (Rome, 1934–48), 1: 43. Subsequent references to this text will appear as *Mon. Ign. CSI.*

16. Ganss, p. 176.

17. William J. Young, trans., *The Letters of St. Ignatius Loyola* (Chicago: Loyola University Press, 1959), pp. 128–29.

18. "Havendo l'illustrissimo signor Gioan di Vega, vicerè di questo regno di Sicilia, la cura per il suo grande e vero christiano animo di tenere governato il detto regno, e accomodato non solamente del temporale, ma ancora del spirituale, mettendo con la sua molta prudentia per l'uno et per l'altro mezzi convenienti e necesarii; a supplicatione delli spettabili giurati della nobile cità di Messina, pochi mesi fa, ha fatto venire in essa città certi padri della compagnia e congregation di Giesu . . . persone molto notabili così in lettere come in religione, vita e costumi, a li quali è stato designato per stantia sua la chiesa e casa di S. Nicola acciochè a gloria d'Iddio e per l'utilità comune della gioventù e delli huomini studiosi, leggano le lettioni infrascritte." *Monumenta Paedagogica Societatis Iesu,* 4 vols., ed. Ladislaus Luckacs, S.J. (Rome, 1965–81), 1: 383–84. Subsequent citations of this text will appear as *Mon. Paed.*

19. *Mon. Paed.* 1: 94–106. The Parisian system adopted at Messina and other Jesuit schools was based on a five-class system in ascending order. See Ganss, pp. 107–9.

20. "Las facultades que todos ordinariamente deben apprender son: letras de humanidad, lógica, philosophía natural; y ubiendo aparejo, algunas mathematicás y moral, metaphísica y theología scolástica y la Scrittura; y si sobrase tiempo, algo de lo positivo, como de concilios, decretos, doctores sanctos, y otras cosas morales, que para ayudar el próximo son más necessarias." *Mon. Paed.* 1: 41.

21. *Mon. Ign. CSI* 1: 57.

22. *Mon. Paed.* 1: 386.

23. ". . . proponat sibi in animo se partem esse Societatis ad hoc potissimum institutae, ut ad fidei defensionem et propagationem et profectum animarum in vita et doctrina Christiana, per publicas praedictiones, lectiones et aliud quodcunque verbi Dei ministerium, ac spiritualia exercitia, puerorum ac rudium in Christianismo institutionem, Christifidelium in confessionibus audiendis ac caeteris Sacramentis ad-

ministrandis spiritualem consolationem, praecipue intendat"; Julius III, *Exposcit debitum, Mon. Ign. CSI* 1: 376.

24. Farrell, p. 55.

25. Ibid., pp. 55–56.

26. "Pareze que antes que al studio se ynbiasen, se debría ver en ellos alguna mortificatión del hombre viejo y algún gusto de las cosas spirituales, y que se inclinasen a tomar los studios como medios del divino servitio, no por otro algún diseño de curiosidad, honra o interesses; porque si las letras no se edificassen sobre tal fundamento, no servirían para los fines que pretiende la Compañía, de la divina gloria y ayuda de las ánimas, y del mesmo que studia." *Mon. Paed.* 1: 31.

27. *The Constitutions of the Society of Jesus,* trans. George E. Ganss, S.J. (St. Louis, The Institute of Jesuit Sources, 1970), General Examen, chap. 1, no. 3, p. 77. Subsequent references to this text will appear as *Const. SJ.*

28. *Const. SJ,* part 4, preamble, pp. 171–72.

29. Farrell, p. 145.

30. *Const. SJ,* part 4, chap. 16, no. 486, p. 224.

31. *Const. SJ,* part 4, chap. 5, no. 351, pp. 187–88.

32. *Const. SJ,* part 4, chap. 12, no. 446, p. 213.

33. "Non enim apud nos tenerae aetatis disciplina circumscribitur unis grammaticae rudimentis, sed ad christianam simul institutionem se porigit." Francesco Sacchini, *Protrepticon ad Magistros Scholarum Inferiorum Societatis Iesu,* as quoted in John W. Donohue, S.J., *Jesuit Education: An Essay on the Foundation of Its Ideas* (New York: Fordham University Press, 1963), p. 159.

34. "Prima. Tutti si sforzino di haver la intentione recta non cercando le lettere per altro fine che della divina gloria et aggiuto delle anime, et così si risolvino de studiare da vero con grande diligentia per conseguire il fino detto, et satisfare alla santa obedientia, et nelle sue orationi dimanderanno gratia di aggiutarsi e fare profetto nelle lettere." *Mon. Paed.* 1: 66.

35. Ibid.

36. Ibid.

37. ". . . et in ogni facultá si legga la dottrina più solida et autori più approbati che in quella siano et specialmente li sia raccommandato che tutti siano ben fundati nella grammatica avanti che passino oltra." *Mon. Paed.* 1: 76.

38. "Et perchè l'assunto che ha tolto la Compagnia d'insegnare non procede se non da charità, et da desiderio del maggior honor di Dio, et maggior bene universale delli prossimi, mirarà bene et che lui et che li altri mastri procedino con questo santo zelo, usando tutta la diligenza nelli studii loro, per poter più aiutar li prossimi, et insegnar le miglior lettere, facendo soleccitudine; et si sforzerà in Giesù Christo nostro Signore di darli buono odore et edificatione di se medesimo, et con parole et con vivi esempii della vita propria indurli al desiderio di quelle virtù che proprio sonno di christiani." *Mon. Paed.* 1: 329.

39. Ibid.

40. *Mon. Paed.* 1: 331.

41. *Mon. Paed.* 1: 332.

42. *Mon. Paed.* 1: 332 and 337.

43. "Essendo ch'l fine di nostra Compagnia in tutti gl'essercitii et ministerii suoi è il maggior honor di Dio N.S. et la salute et edificatione commune delli prossimi, quelli che sonno destinati al studio hanno d'haver l'occhio molto intento a questo fine, acciochè volentieri s'affatigano per imparare, et usino tutta la diligenza loro per acquistare buone lettere, donde poi con quelle siano instrumenti di glorificare il nome santo di Dio et di servire alli prossimi in Giesù Christo N.S., come si costuma nella Compagnia." *Mon. Paed.* 1: 345.

44. "Et perchè le lettere senza spirito et senza humiltà sonno più presto roina et

perditione di quelli che le sanno, ch'altrimente: non tanta cura si deve haver delle lettere et delli studii che si smenticano di procurar l'augmento dello spirito et della devotione loro; però il primo conto faranno delle orationi et essercitii spirituali." *Mon. Paed.* 1: 345.

45. "Et acciochè li studii loro siano fondati in Dio, si ricorderanno che non studiano per altro, se non per l'obbedienza et per maggior honore di Dio; donde, se in questo saranno sinceri, non solamente li studii non gli saranno causa di distrattione, ma gli deventarenno vera oratione, e gli verranno in augmento et di spirito et di devotione, come sogliono fare tutte le cose che veramente si fanno per obbedienza e per amor di Dio." *Mon. Paed.* 1: 346.

46. Ganss, pp. 185–68.

47. Ibid., p. 186.

48. *Const. SJ,* part 4, chap. 12, no. 446, p. 212.

49. *Const. SJ,* part 4, chap. 16, no. 486, p. 224.

50. Ganss, p. 59.

51. *Const. SJ,* part 4, chap. 8, no. 403, p. 201.

52. *Const. SJ,* part 4, chap. 16, no. 481, p. 223.

53. Ganss, p. 60.

54. See Father Hieronymus Nadal, S.J., *Ordo Studiorum Germanicus* in *Mon. Paed.* 2: 83–106.

55. "Que en las cosas spirituales se ayuden, aprendiendo la doctrina christiana, y entendiendo en los sermones y exhortationes sólitas lo que conuiene para su eterna salud. En la puridad de la conscientia se aprouechan, y consiguientemente en toda virtud, con las confessiones de cada mes, y con el cuydado que se tiene de que sean honestos en el hablar, y virtuosos en su vida toda." *Monumenta Ignatiana, Sancti Ignatii de Loyola Epistolae et Instructiones,* 12 vols., ser. 1 (Madrid, 1903–11), 4: 8. Subsequent references to this text will appear as *Mon. Ignat. EP.*

56. *Const. SJ,* part 4, preamble, no. 308, p. 172; part 7, chap. 2, no. 622, pp. 274–75; part 10, resume, no. 815, p. 333.

57. *Const. SJ,* part 4, chap. 8, no. 402, p. 201.

58. Ganss, p. 166.

59. "Que de los que solamente son al presente studiantes saldrán con tiempo diversos, quién para predicar y tener cura de las ánimas, quién para el gouierno de la tierra y administratión de la justitia, quién para otros cargos; y finalmente, porque de los niños se hazen los grandes, la buena institutión en vida y doctrina destos aprouechará a otros muchos, estendiendose cada día màs el fructo." *Mon. Ignat. EP* 4: 9.

60. *Mon. Paed.* 1: 418–19.

61. "Quello che la Compagnia pretende nelli collegii soi se reduce a doi capi. Primo, che la terra o prouincia doue si fa detto collegio sia aiutata nelle lettere e cose spirituali con l'essempio e dottrina e ogni industria delli collegiali; il secondo, che li scolari della Compagnia si facciano idonei nelle lettere per essere operarii nella vigna de Dio N.S., il che etiam redunda in utilità della terra; perchè, oltre che dànno buona edificatione con la uita e conuersatione buona, dopoi, come si fanno literati, potranno in legere, predicare, sentire confessioni et altre opere di charità, giouare il ben comune, essendo come un seminario nelli tali collegii, del quale nascono simili frutti continuamente." *Mon. Ignat.* EP 12: 309–10.

62. "Hora, risguardando detto fine, si sogliono mandar'nelli principii a detti collegii alcuni che attendano propriamente ad aiutare l'anime per mezzo delli sacramenti et exhortationi et dottrina christiana et altri mezzi spirituali, come sarebbeno doi o tre sacerdoti che attendano a cio." *Mon. Ignat. EP* 12: 310.

63. This is clear in the *Tractatus de Religione Societatis Iesu* of Francisco Suarez, S.J.: "Generalius autem loquendo, studia et universitates honestarum artium, non

solum propter ecclesiasticam, sed etiam propter civilem communitatem et utilitatem, necessaria sunt, et ita in omnibus regnis et provinciis recte institutis, hujusmodi generalia studia floruerunt." (Brussels, 1857), p. 285.

64. Young, p. 437.

65. Ibid., p. 259.

66. Grendler, pp. 409–10.

67. *Const. SJ,* part 4, chap. 13, no. 455, p. 216.

68. Father Peter-Hans Kolvenbach, S.J., excerpts from address in Washington, D.C. on the occasion of the Bicentennial of Jesuit Education in the United States, June 1989, in *The Catholic Standard,* 21 September 1989, p. s9.

69. ". . . quanto a noi, la theologia ci potria bastare senza tanto Cicerone et Demostene. Ma come santo Paulo omnia omnibus factus est ut omnes lucrifaceret, cosi la Compagnia nostra per desiderio de aiutare le anime piglia questi spogli de Egipto per uotarle in onore e gloria di Dio." *Mon. Ignat. EP* 8: 618.

Mysticism as Biology and Educational Foundation in Ignatius de Loyola

ANTONIO T. DE NICOLÁS

Imagination is more important than knowledge.

—Einstein

Introduction

A new model emerging from recent studies on human cortical information-processing, as provisionally advanced by perceptual psychology, brain-chemistry, brain evolution, brain development, ethology, and cultural anthropology[1] has replaced older and simpler models of the same process such as the unextended rational substance of Descartes, the *tabula rasa* of Locke, the association-matrix of Hume, the passive, reinforcement-driven animal of Skinner, and the genetically hard-wired robot of the sociobiologists. Though the elements of these earlier models are included in the new one, the conversation about human experience has changed dramatically, and so have the possibilities of education. The practical observations in physics and the practical comprehension of observations in neurology—the "how" questions rather than the "why" questions—have forced us to develop new techniques for dealing with the material of human experience that have yet to find a place in education.

This change in style has been forced on science by the epistemological importance of the conditionality of the experience of "I-ness," our homuncular experience of self identity as the ground of, or fixed viewpoint, determining all our objectivity. In other words, objectivity is being questioned or is in question and so is the method of transmitting this objectivity in the classroom.

This new revolution has been formulated in the following postulates:

1. What we call "nature" consists of "arrays" on which human mentation imposes structure.
2. Phenomena, which are our only contact with these arrays, are exactly

what their name implies, namely "appearings" in which structure has been so imposed.

3. In some instances what appear to be phenomena—time is an example— may turn out to be wholly structures: wholly consequences, that is, of a particular manner of intuitivist data-processing.[2]

These postulates are not derived from some Eastern philosophy, or some mystical sayings, but from our own cultural source of sacramental knowledge, the observation of objective reality by controlled experimentation.

Because of the semblance of these postulates with the "wisdom" models of the past, Plato's cave, for example, or Sankara's descriptions of the world through mental "superimpositions"[3] or, principally, because of the efforts of "mystics" to manipulate experience as to be able to feel the world without the viewpoint of the I-ness and claim an aperspectival experience of the not-I, or That,[4] a descriptive hermeneutics of mystical practice as exemplified by Ignatius de Loyola should be interesting. Not because mystical practice produces euphoria or bliss or some such trivialities, but because it sheds light on human experiencing, on objectivity, on habit forming, on our neural inheritance. The justification for concentrating on those experiences that bypass I-ness or homuncularity is not the pursuit of some kind of nonrational source of knowledge, but the fact that, while science, starting from naive objectivism, has been able, by the force of experiments and mathematical analysis, to develop a counterintuitive model of perception empirically, a large human tradition arrived at the same counterintuitive model without any physical experimentation by cultivation of mental states in which it was not inferred but actually *experienced*. And this should be the task of education.

It would seem perfectly rational therefore to ask if a description of mystical experience might not greatly increase our capacity for further inference, in retrospect if not while it is actually going on. More important, it might actually lead to the incorporation of a new model of ontology into ordinary experience by making it felt as well as inferred. Ignatius comes to the forefront of the conversation since it was his model of education that included these elements in his liberal curriculum.

The study of mystic experience from its biological base has several advantages. It separates religious practice from religious theology. The first is biologically based, the other socially based. The first is the legitimate gift of a free education, the second is manipulative. It separates religious experience from other somatic pathologies, like schizophrenics, shamans, ascetics, masochists, or drug-induced experiences, for mystics, as opposed to the rest of the fauna of "oceanic"[5] states, leaves us epistemologies that therefore can be taught. The others do not. Very few career mystics of any persuasion, and very few individuals who have had one or more oceanic experiences spontaneously, are clinically psychotic by any intelligent criteria, but many psychotics engage in cult formation based on hallucinatory experiences. Mystic experience is always a delimiting case of various I-delimiting concerns, and so is science, but in science scientists are also "I"s and must pass all their observational input and interpretative output through the circuitry involved in the human identity experience. Even computers bear the mark of Adam because his descendants programmed and targeted them. Plato, of course, must be brought in to join this dialogue. Why did he, out of which experience, call in his divided line all the knowledge of science "the shadow of knowledge"? Was he right when he divided the line so that Chaos could not be studied independent from Cosmos? Is not Cosmos a superimposition on Chaos?[6]

The Primacy of Images.
Desires Are Images and Will Their Act.

Mystics center their spiritual practice on a maxim that to them is self evident: Desires are images and Will their act.[7] If desires are images—all perception is primarily an image—then the practice of the mystic is a deliberate concentration to build only those images that will cancel out gratification of the self—the shadow—and in general those images coming to him/her from the outside. This nameless field of original creation has been named Chaos, nirvana, moksa, the will of God. In short, the project of the mystic is to reverse the normal process of sensation—sensation for an I-observer, an agent—fed by external images through a process of emptying the senses from all sensation coming to them from the outside, including the memory of sensation, and sensitizing the body only from the inside. That this life project is possible is remarkable, the more so since it has been the best kept secret of the human species and the followers of such tradition have been persecuted or marginized all through history. Since this feat, however, has left us an epistemology, it may be reflected upon and articulated so that inferences may be drawn and other humans may repeat it.[8]

Mystics base their practice on the discovery, promotion, and execution through repetition and dedication of those faculties, and only those, capable of achieving such a feat. Cognitive skills have been developed late in culture, but the ancients fought fantasy as the enemy of their spiritual quest. Fantasy to them—in Sanskrit, the I-maker *ahamkara*—was an act that could not be performed unless it started, developed, and ended in the benefit of the subject, the *ahamkara*, I-maker. It was the same with cognitive skills. The faculty the mystics used was and is the imagination, as it builds absolute backgrounds to give light and meaning to the acts of the foreground. The acts of the mystics are measured against the background they build. If this background is not built properly the mystics are at the mercy of the enemy: the self, the flesh, and exteriority. But images as background are not possible unless they are willed. But how to distinguish outside and inside, signs from one or another origin? The life of the mystic is an agonic reading of signs, those coming from outside and those from the inside. Mystics are masters at showing the steps leading to the building of those technologies—soft ware— that build human interiority and give light and meaning to ordinary acts. But they also know that these technologies are human devices, and thus they ready themselves to empty themselves of them and of the attachment that might come through the use of such technologies. Spiritual practice in the mystic is as much a construction of structures as it is a de-construction of them and of the feelings accrued in their use.[9]

Mystics differ in the use they make of their internal signs—bliss, tears, visions, voices, and the rest. Some, like Teresa of Avila[10] and Ignatius de Loyola, used them to form communities and make decisions; others, like Saint John of the Cross,[11] used them simply to know they were on the right path and to get rid of them. Though mystics differ in the use they make of the signs of spiritual practice, they all use the same technologies—biological structures—to manipulate experience. This applies to the mystics of Christianity as well as Judaism, Islam, Hinduism, Buddhism, Taoism, and the rest. Furthermore, the mystics from all these traditions agreed that these technologies will not *cause* the experience of not-I to appear, but they also agree that without them the not-I experience will not take place.[12]

Our universities are populated by faculty opposed to a total education of habits of mind. The enemies of mystical practice have been the social orthodoxies of theology and scientism. While theology claims a base in experience, in practice it devalues the manipulative control mystics have over the building of such religious experience. Scientism, on the other hand, denies the experience itself by relegating it to the realm of the pathological. Both forms of social orthodoxies, however, appear late in human history and, while they appropriate meanings belonging to earlier traditions and practices, like faith, belief, revelation, charisma, prophesy, voice, preaching, hearing, and so on, at their hands these terms have a totally new base of meaning and action.

Orthodoxies, theological or scientistic, are ideologies for the simple reason, as Sankara noted, that they cannot function without the sense of I, that is, of a superimposition of themselves over the undifferentiated arrays of perception. They are literary shadows of knowledge; they can hardly qualify as relevations.

The Neural Chain

Mysticism is not a literary style, nor is there a literary *genre* that can be identified as mystical, as there is in poetry, stories, novels, theater. Mysticism is built on the building of an interior experience, or in mysticism experience comes first. It is only later that one may see its expression through some literary *genres*. But if one is going to use literary categories then one may say with accuracy that in the mystical experience the *body* of the mystic is the **primary text** for in it the mystic inscribes the primary acts, technologies, through which the signs of those acts can be articulated and become public.[13]

For the mystic the human body is not a fact, but the repository of a multitude of technologies reaching in and out of itself to extend as far as the technologies will allow. In so far as these technologies are humanly built they are not causal of experience, but the type of experience that appears through those constructs would not occur without the development of these technologies. Educators should bear in mind an integral education.

Using Ignatius de Loyola as our example we see that the internal mechanisms he builds are geared to produce a particular kind of experience: a union of two separate wills, the mystic's and God's. In educational terms this is equivalent to a program to educate the will. This kind of experience, according to Ignatius's writings, proceeds by the use of a faculty other than the intellectual technologies we are familiar with, or fantasies, or the borrowing of images from the outside, or the following of the necessities of thought. The mystic's practice focuses exclusively on the building of original images not present in the world until he/she makes them up. In building these original images the mystic listens to signs of affection and movements of the will. In this search the familiar world of the mystic is reduced to insensibility while a new world with different sensations emerges. There is darkness of the senses in the bereaved sensorium; there is doubt about the origins of these signs; there is divestment of beliefs; there is loss of hope, at times even of love. This is the journey where only faith travelling in the dark succeeds. And the manifestation of that success is the experienced union of two wills, but only after the individual self-will has died and the mystic has been able to survive his/her own dark burial. The mystics have expressed this union mostly in poetry, some in prose, the majority in silence—the silence of the union of love, of two lovers united, sexual language to express the birth of "God" in the human flesh, sexual language to express the duration of eternity. For in this union the mystics experience the immortality of the not-I, an experience owned by no subject and therefore indestructible, even when there is the witness as individual mystic experiencing it. In the not-I experience the body is the instrument, not the agent, of such experience.[14]

A) PREPARATION: THE TRAINING OF THE WILL.

The training of the mystic is an agonic path. Ignatius is our best guide here. Those who succeed often forget how hard it was to start. Though some mystics talk of the beginnings with condescension, without these beginnings there would not be a dark night of the soul, nor mystical experience, nor a way for the rest of us to reflect upon it. The beginnings are a time of trial, of meandering about, of disorientation, of aridity. They are also a time of direct assault upon the bodily habits of the initiate, a time of violence on those habits. He/she is asked to look for a "place," (*Exer.* 20) a new place to perform those exercises of the soul away from the ordinary place, the ordinary habits, away from the familiar: the cave of Manresa, a place in the mountains, a lonely room, a solitary place, a room in the country, an unaccustomed place with controlled lighting and temperature, a place where the mystic-to-be is forced to invent new body habits and where he/she is immune to the outside communications system. Instead of the old external communications system a new and willed system is introduced: new habits of light (*Exer.* 79), of temperature, a new time table, a new distribution of time, of hours, of half hours, of the morning, of the afternoon, of the night. This new time table is forced on the body to sharpen a new will and will the new habits, the new diet, the new sleeping hours, the sharp changes of the time table, the constant exercise of the will (*Exer.* 74, 75, 76, 77).

The body is forced into a new environment. It is asked to learn new positions, positions dealing with preparations for the body to be able to endure hours of meditation, hours of violence to previous habits, to learn how to stand, how to walk, how to sit, how to lower one's eyes, how to raise them, how to close out sounds, how to listen to signs from inside (*Exer.* 81, 258). All gestures, facial expressions, bodily movements must be painstakingly examined as in slow motion so that the body becomes a repellent to the outside world and begins to habituate itself to the technologies of facing within and gathering inside in order to proceed to meditation. While the new habits of the body are only means to an end, the end has already been partially achieved, the initiate has learned to sharpen his/her will, and this is what she/he really needed in order to proceed with meditation.

The will of the initiate is turned inward, remodelling the inside. The will of the initiate is used as a surgical knife to cut openings into the interior world. The life of the initiate is sliced into separate segments for examination, (*Exer.* 24, 25, 26, 27, 33, 34, 38, 42, 43) into years, days, half days, hours. He/she must follow the trails of these surgical cuts and give to them a new language emerging from the inside, new emotions, new feelings: ugliness of sin, of selfishness, pain and tears at evil, self-pity, gratitude, amazement, disgust, consolation, desolation (*Exer.* 57, 59, 62). Almost unnoticed, a language of the will emerges relating the initiate to the new background, and an interior time table begins to chime. This is the sound of the clock of the "solitary region." This time table determines from now on the **real** acts of the day: (*Exer.* 74) waking up, the time and kind of meditation, conversations with the guide, examination of conscience, (*Exer.* 43) meditation on previous meditations, changing of diet, keeping the same diet, changing the hours of sleep or keeping them, preparing the coming meditation—in short covering the inside and outside of the mystic-to-be with a whole language-technology that immunizes him/her to other previously held body habits and technologies.

Prayer may take various forms; it may be light and relax the emotions

(*Exer.* 238), or it may focus on the seven deadly sins (*Exer.* 244) or on the three powers of the soul (*Exer.* 246). It may become a meditation that considers every word pronounced (*Exer.* 249) or that concentrates only on those points of meditation "where I felt the most intense spiritual feeling" (*Exer.* 62). And, of course, one must not forget, a new diet has to be included (*Exer.* 84), and one should sleep with less comfort than one is used to and cause sensible pain to the body (*Exer.* 85). Even while going to sleep there is no stopping this clock; one should prepare oneself for the coming day by going over the memory-points of the meditation one is going to make in the morning (*Exer.* 73). Upon awakening, one should bring to mind what one is about to meditate on. The clock of the "solitary region" does not allow any external language to come in; there are no cracks between exercises: "no dando lugar a unos pensamientos ni a otros" (not making room for these kind of thoughts or any other) (*Exer.* 74).

But soon the drama unfolds, even at this preparatory stage. The initiate experiences the excitement of the new and also the bereavement of the old and familiar. The initiate knows from experience that the exercises do not guarantee the divinity will enter the "solitary region," while the familiar no longer feels as it used to. The initiate can not anticipate what is about to happen, or even if it will happen at all. And yet, he/she needs to give up everything without the guarantee that the empty spaces are going to be filled. This journey needs raw human faith. And this is only the beginning; it will certainly get worse, before it gets better, if it ever does. There are only two things going for the initiate: the initiation exercises themselves that keep opening horizons of language; and the fact that the initiate knows that he/she is chasing after an experience which has already happened, absolutely or to others, and that therefore its predictability rests on this memory.[15]

B) MEMORY

For the initiate, the student, or even the mystic, memory is the mediating ground between the liberation from the I-maker, the shadow-I, and the absolute background or not-I experience. In general it is the memory of the experience that has already happened: The Trinity in Christianity, nirvana in Buddhism, the first sacrifice in the Rg Veda, liberation in general. It is precisely because this experience has already taken place that it is already outside of the time of the shadow-I. Remembering the manifestations of such an original experience is a return to the original ground. This means that the first act of meditation for a mystic is to remember, to turn all things into memory. Meditation proper begins with the ability to bring all things into remembrance. These memories are then turned into imaginings.

It is the shared ground of common memories that joins people into communities. Without shared memories communities have no way to recognize themselves. Christ had stated this internal law on which the mystics stand: "Do this in remembrance of me," (Luke 22:19). And even the arrival of the Spirit is so that He "brings all things to your remembrance" (John 14:25). To be a mystic is to live on memory, for only the mystic sets the technology of memory into spiritual practice, turning memory around, storing memories, turning every sign, whatever its origin, into a memory-point, and thus being able to articulate memories so that they become active. Through memory they, the mystics, set the will of the origin—God, the gods, forces, energies— into motion. This is the return trip of the act of creation when the One dismembered itself and became creation. Memory is the mediation for meditation to start as creation, fall, redemption, providence, restoration, angels, Adam, Eve, the life of the world to return to the lost unity, the image of unity, the memories of the acts of a dismembered God, or One, or simply Chaos. It is this predictability of memory that carries the mystics through dark nights of the soul, and it is this predictability that allows the mystic to organize and manipulate the present in view of the future. Memory mediates all human action: it is human language, and it is also divine manifestation. Images in memory become the starting point of meditation proper.[16]

Strictly speaking, the *Spiritual Exercises* are a string of memories, of memory-points. Even the exercises as written are not to be read for information or edification or content. Each and every word is slowly and carefully chiselled out so that it becomes a memory-point for action, or for making memory.

The journey of the retreatant's will dividing his/her life into the search for sins, the day divided into exercises of the will to discover flaws, to remove flaws—these exercises are primarily exercises in memory: memories that travel back and forth, up and down, within the perimeter of a human life. Meditation begins by "bringing to memory" the first sin of the angels (*Exer.* 51); "by bringing to memory" our sins (*Exer.* 52), all the sins of my lifetime (*Exer.* 56), year by year, place by place, looking at the places I have lived, conversations I have had, work done (*Exer.* ibid.); by bringing to memory in order to instruct the intellect in it, "so that the intellect, without meandering, may reason with concentration going over the reminiscences (memories) of the things contemplated in past exercises" (*Exer.* 64). Ignatius literally means, through the *Exercises,* "to bring all things into remembrance."

To bring all things into remembrance, however, demands from us certain shifts in technologies. In every case human effort is needed.

Ignatius de Loyola shared with the other mystics of his time habits of reading different from ours. Early in his *Autobiography* (6 and 7) he lets us know how he used reading in order to fix memory points and visualize the things that the Saints did and that he could also do. With these memories he would then dream of doing greater things for the service of God. In this manner Ignatius kept his mind well occupied. Ignatius's knowledge came through the experience of meditation, not through reasoning out the mysteries of Christianity. It is true that the *Exercises* use the three potencies or faculties of the soul, but it is through memory that they are held together, or by turning all things into remembrance. The flight of the soul will eventually take place through imagining.

Turning all things into remembrance is not an easy task, however. The memories of Christianity are not factual history, are not deeds humans did to humans or nature. In order to turn all things into remembrance one must perform a radical hermeneutical act. How does one remember "the souls in hell," or the Trinity before Creation, or angels sinning, or how Christ used his five senses, or even one's own sins without a radical reinterpretation of those cognitive cyphers in the light of the experience that already happened? Those are living memories to a Christian, and are therefore recoverable. To recall them is to call them, and therefore they may be articulated in language. They are the language in which imagining takes place. On these memory-units imagining will act. This memory bank is the only security the retreatant has that the system works; it is the language of Christianity, its communications system. It is in this sense, of memory in use, that memory acts with an element of predictability in the system. Memory, by turning back, vivifies the retreatant and guarantees the future. Memory mediates all human action: it is language and it is divine human life.

C) DISMEMBERING THE ONE: THE ACT OF IMAGINING.

Mystic manipulation of experience may be scientifically illuminating precisely at that point where they part company. Science presupposes the I-experience and therefore reinforces the formation of such experience. Mysticism desensitizes the experience organized for and by the I in order to gain the aperspectival not-I experience.

Contrary to contemporary practices in psychology and education where imagining is guided so that individuals and groups share in imagining the same image, or where archetypal images are the object and goal of the act of imagining, the mystics in general and Ignatius in particular, astonishingly enough, leave the initiate and the curious almost completely to their own devices (*Exer.* 18) as to which images to use or how to make them in the act of meditation.

Actual imagining is the retreatant's exercise. This may be understood because Ignatius cannot draw on any existing reservoir of images in order to correct mistaken identities. He cannot draw from any subjective field of images with which the subject may be more or less familiar, because through some of those images individuals have already experienced transformations, even creations. Ignatius displaces the retreatant from any subjective or objective pool of images and vigorously transplants him/her to an imageless field where the absence of images will force the exercise of creating them.

This kind of imagining is the more powerful because it does not rest on images anyone ever before created. Neither the exercitant nor the world has the images of the exercises of imagining. The images to be born are of a sheer power of imagining that includes not only the act of imagining, but the act of creating the images.

This strategy of Ignatius is so demanding that it rests more on the actual technologies of imagining than on any images. Thus his insistence on the technologies of concentration in order to bring out the pure image, the uncontaminated image, the image in perfect solitude, the original image, the divine image. The image created in meditation is the only image that will gain currency in meditation. One cannot borrow it, one must create it. In this creation all other images are automatically excluded. The whole technology developed in the *Exercises* has one aim: the perfect image, for it is in it and through it that God's signs will appear. The image will turn to language and return to the public domain.

The pure image, the original image, will penetrate the public domain if first it penetrates the material body of the retreatant. This material body is always set facing the scene, the image, to be imagined. But this material body is a fluid body through imagining: a slave in the Nativity, a knight in the Two Kingdoms, a sinner facing the Cross; it may change sizes if compared to other men, the angels, God (*Exer.* 58); it may become a vermin worth "many hells" (*Exer.* 60) or the temple, image of God, animated by God, sensitized by Him (*Exer.* 235).

Today's acts of imagining are closer to fantasy for they are acted out for the sake of a subject. Older traditions confirm that it is up to the mystic to make originally the images of their meditation, that, in fact, meditation consist in just making images. The guide was content with providing memory-points, and then, after meditation, he would help the mystic in the reading of the signs. But meditation proper consists in making images. In this meditation there is no subjective or objective reservoir of images to borrow. Making images is the proper spiritual exercise. The mystic stands by himself or herself on an imageless field with their store of memories, one at a time, and it is this absence itself of images that will force the mystic into exercises of making them. Thus the actual act of imagining rests mostly on technology, manipulation, rather than on the images themselves: concentration, a guided and directed will, the closing of external worlds, the memories of origin, finally, the uncontaminated, the original, the divine image. This image cannot be borrowed; it must be created. For it is only to the degree that this image resembles the original act of creation that signs will appear. It is only through the creation of the pure image that sensation will flow from imagining to the biology of the mystic. Unless this pure image penetrates with sensation the mystic it will not, in turn, affect either the public domain or the common neurology.

The imagining of the mystic is peculiar in that it has features absent in other forms of using the imagination. The main feature is that of dismemberment.

As the body of the mystic faces in meditation the frame of the memory upon which he/she is going to exercise imagining—the birth of Cosmos from Chaos, the birth of angels, of evil, a scene of the life of Christ, and such—the body of the mystic undergoes a radical dismemberment. Before meditation the mystic has a set or sets of habits through which he/she feels the world. After meditation this original set or sets of habits has been broken so as not to feel as it originally felt. Instead, the mystic is sensitized to new objects and signs he/she knew nothing about before meditation. In between these two stages the mystic has performed an act of dismembering worth a second look.

The retreatant is placed in front of a scene and asked to make his/her own "contemplación viendo el lugar" (contemplation seeing the place). With exhausting detail, he/she is asked to make up the scene—the road: how long, wide, flat, running through valleys or hills; the cave: how big, small, how high, how low, how furnished (*Exer.* 112). Imagine hell, the width and depth and length (*Exer.* 65), or imagine the synagogue, villages, and castles (*Exer.* 91) or the Three Divine Persons (*Exer.* 102), or Mary riding a donkey or Joseph pulling an ox (*Exer.* 110). But for Ignatius the image alone is not the source of signs. The image on recall is to call it to memory. The actual birth of the signs or the system of signs does not take place until the retreatant proceeds, through imagining, to "read" the image through his own dismembered sensorium. The perfect image, the solitary image, the divine image is set into motion through the sensuous motion of the retreatant's senses as he or she runs them, one at a time, through the image. It takes the "reading" of the image by each sense so that it becomes a mediation of signs. The efficacy of the image is made possible on condition that the subject be kept elusively absent, as a fixed unity, in the act of imagining. What he or she is asked to do instead is to lend sight, sound, smell, touch, movement to the image. He or she vitalizes the image through his or her dismembered sensorium. Each sense must read the image separately; each sense must sensitize the image separately; each sense must read/write its separate movement on the image separately. What is done through visualization must be repeated through hearing, smelling, touching, moving. This applies to the exercises on hell, the Nativity, the Cross, Resurrection—in short, to any exercises where images are to be imagined.

The experience of not-I appears as the experience of I disappears, at least for the time being. But the mystic destroys nothing: the body has been trained to receive larger doses of sensation and to hold them—larger than the unities the body held at the start of meditation.

What takes so long to describe, and even longer to practice, suddenly becomes a habit and the initiatory moments are almost forgotten and steps initially considered essential are skipped over for new exercises. The technology of the mystic has taken over and become a habit. Some cultures seem to come equipped with the habit, and "oceanic" experiences appear almost natural. Other cultures need to be reminded that their neural inheritance guarantees that the performance of such practices is simply a matter of recalling past memories buried under modern technologies.

There is a moment, however, in the path of mystical practice when all striving—the careful, agonic concentration to sharpen the will; the powers of imagining—accumulate on the mystic with such force that all the habits of the past, all the expectations of the familiar, seem to be about to collapse completely. Fear, death seem to invade every corner of the mystic's body and soul. This is the time of the total death of the "old man." The total darkness of the soul. The time to live only on the power of faith. Sadly enough, it is at this time when most initiates and practicing mystics stop on their path. Only a few true mystics continue. This is the most brutal episode to happen in the life of any human being. And many are careful not to burn all the boats, just in case. At its most successful, this death is a complete death of all the habits of ordinary human life organized under the direction of the I-shadow image. And this is a painful bereavement for the body and the soul of even the strongest. For the body and the soul have no guarantee that the sensations of meditation are there to stay. In the dawn of this new possible way of life there is not enough light to know if life as we once knew it will happen again, and it is even less clear that what happened while doing meditation will happen again, in or outside of its practice. This is the ultimate dark night of the soul, the most horrible and desolate tunnel through which all spiritual, mystical life must pass. And it shows clearly the manipulating ability the body holds over sensation for in this dark night of the soul the dark night is doubled. The senses are empty of sensation, but so is the internal sensory mechanism already enticed to feel things spiritual. It is also dry.[17]

Some Consequences of the Biology of Religion on Education

The first victim of this approach I have outlined is the claim by science that only the world created by science is real. The fact of the matter is that science makes reality in so far as it superimposes on chaos its own cognitive structures. The answers we receive as reality are only the fish we are able to catch in our cognitive nets. The whole range of scientific objectivity rests on the assumption of an I-shadow observer that scientific objectivity has not been able to shake. This means that the structures of knowledge through which we know scientifically, though they determine some of the superimpositions we place on chaos, neither exhaust knowledge nor exhaust reality. There are other forms of knowing that belong with the same legitimacy in the classroom. These structures are what we have described here as the structures of knowing in a mystical manner, or of possessing the experience of the not-I. If for no better reason than to shift the models of knowledge of science, these structures should be part and parcel of scientific study and the curriculum. We possess, as it were, a certain domineering and arrogant quality in our dealings with sensory information, and our "brain" listens only to replies to its own inquiries. Ambiguity is not our bag. Since science, however, is the product of philosophy, it should be searching for models that include both types of experiences, of the I and the not-I. Such a model is present in Plato, in his divided line, where all the faculties needed for both experiences are described and where reality is discussed in terms of both cosmos—the shadow of knowledge—and chaos—wisdom.

Human biological systems process information in a determinative manner. There is little tolerance in these systems for doubt, and they insist on certainty and unambiguity. This determinative character is more a matter of the structures imposed on reality than a feature of the elements of such a reality. Thus systems endure and survive.[18] Thus shifts in education are not easy to come by.

This determinative way of processing information leads the human nervous system to habituation. It forms habits of perception, and so it ignores repeated and expected stimuli and answers only to new and unexpected ones.[19]

For biological systems are more active than passive. They form unities of perception even where there are none—perceptual mistakes—and try scenarios of reality to be tried and destroyed when unconfirmed.

For biological systems to function freely it is a prerequisite that their worlds be not fully determined. Or the fact that human biological systems have memory is a sign that their worlds are not fully determined. Memory serves the future because all futures share a common past, but not the same future.[20]

But memory is only useful in systems of perception that include memory to link the same agent to all his/her perceptions. It is not a prerequisite in systems of perception where past, present, and future meet as common present, as in the experiences of not-I.

Though it is common knowledge that human biological systems have the ability to reward themselves, the hierarchy of these rewards is not clearly understood. The larger the experience, the larger the reward. In other words the reward is proportional to the size of the image holding the experience together. Perception is always a perception through image. Experiences of the self for the self receive much smaller reward than experiences of not-I or for no one. The discrepancy in our brain structure itself between left and right brain perception, as it has been conveniently described, does not do much to explain knowledge, but it serves to separate two different ways of knowing and, perhaps, it accounts also for them.

It is common knowledge that the I-shadow does not form part of our equipment at birth. The child discovers this self later. It is this I-shadow, this I-ness experience that is the most problematic. It is not part of reflection. It sits on reflection. It is earlier than memory, it is presupposed by memory. It is not part of any empirical observation, it observes the observer. The question is, how does it come into being?

For Plato this I-shadow was the true fall. He placed this shadow in the region between knowledge through imagination and knowledge of science and art. No one I know has been bothered by this question. But I have learned to trust the intuition of the ancients rather than to ignore them. And Plato was right.[21]

For a system of interpretation like his that placed side by side the experiences of I and not-I this revelation of the birth of the I-shadow was commonplace. He included it in his system. Others reduced the system and deified the shadow. In actual practice as envisioned by Plato, it works like this.

The not-I experience not only includes the arresting of chaos into an "oceanic" human experience, but carries with it other features not present in cosmos. Time for example moves very slowly, and, even when the experience is about or includes the surrounding environment, there is a noncoincidence of time, at least in the brain, between the happening in the oceanic trance and in the ordinary world. In other words, the same event happens twice to the brain, once in the oceanic state and again in the normal state. This means that between the two experiences there is a delay, enough time for the shadow to appear and appropriate to itself that section of experience it controls, or may control. The ancients, and Plato reinforces this, solved the problem by repeated trips to the upper part of the divided line and the cultivation of oceanic experiences. Our modern humans seem at a loss, for the upper part of the divided line has been removed as a possibility and all that is left is feeding the shadow with the type of knowledge it generates. (This might explain also why modern biological systems, and science for that matter, lack direction, images of direction, and therefore any justification for doing what they are doing except that they can and it works.)

Human biological systems move within social and cultural groupings. The danger is that the social and the cultural may also interfere with the overall well-being of the systems. Science and religion, for example, may stop being what they are experientially and become ideological systems to promote their own interests, not those of the global community. Science, for example, may become social scientism, an ideology to treat all phenomena, persons included, as objects; while religion may become theology, an imposition of its own knowing systems on the religious practice of humans. Where science and religion unite is in the neural connection and legacy they have left to the rest of us to develop; where they separate is in the social and cultural ideologies they independently serve. Neither ideology produces science nor religion. The decent behavior of humans even in the absence of religious belief is guaranteed by the neural impression decent people left for all of us in our common, neural inheritance.

Conclusion

This study was undertaken to enlarge the understanding of both science and religion by placing their findings on one common level: biology as the ground of educational possibilities. The biological inheritance of the species is primarily determined by our experiences of I and not-I, normal and oceanic. If in fact there are large resources of body manipulation that could be explored through a better comprehension of the structure of identity, and if this study needs to address primarily the practices of mystics like Ignatius for its success and implementation in education, then there is no single finding today that could be compared with this to force us to focus on inner space. If not, identity and its structure will retain only philosophical interest while we learn to modify it pharmacologically—and in all probability, to judge by the record of technology for its own sake, to our disadvantage and hurt. The study of oceanic experiences, of mystical practice, is by its very nature religious and bound to modify our social style and our educational system by qualifying the limited intuitions of old-type scientific objectivism, as Einsteinian insights qualified Newtonian without contradicting them.[22] What occurs in a change of cultural style is that the universe of discourse is expanded, and this affects its institutions. And every such explanation, in that it alters our sensibilities to the experiences of I and not-I, is by the terms of our inquiry religious or spiritual in its contents. In its social and educational aspect the discussion is even more urgent, for what we call America today is the gathering of many people from cultures other than the European—cultures that promoted and cultivated experiences of the not-I type and that should be represented in our discourse, at least. It is this expansion of social discourse that will constitute our own awareness of the religious within our human environment, rather than a return to the numinous and the mysterious upon which the theological religions and social sciences built their case and our human separateness. Let us go back to the basics, to the *Spiritual Exercises* as the foundation of education.

Notes

1. My remarks are based mostly on the following authors: William R. Uttal, *The Psychobiology of Mind* (Hillside, N.J.: Lawrence Erlbaum Associates, 1978); C. D. Laughlin Jr. and E. G. d'Aquili, *Biogenetic Structural Analysis* (New York: Columbia University Press, 1974); E. G. d'Aquili, C. D. Laughlin Jr., and J. MacManus, eds., *The Spectrum of Ritual: A Biogenetic Structural Analysis* (New York: Columbia University Press, 1979); D. E. Berlyne and K. B. Madsen, eds., *Pleasure, Reward, and Preference: Their Nature, Determinants, and Role in Behavior* (London: Academic Press, 1973); A. Routtenberg, ed., *Biology of Reinforcement: Facets of Brain Stimulation Reward* (London: Academic Press, 1980); J. Olds, *Drives and Reinforcements: Behavioral Studies of Hypothalmic Functions* (London: Ravens Press, 1977);

C. Blackemore, *Mechanics of the Mind* (Cambridge: Cambridge University Press, 1977); Frederick Turner, *Natural Classicism: Essays on Literature and Science* (New York: Paragon House Publishers, 1985).

2. This formulation does not belong to a mystic but to a hard-nosed scientist; Alex Comfort, *I and That: Notes on the Biology of Religion* (New York: Crown Publishers, 1979), p. 16.

3. Sankara (A.D. 788–820) developed in detail the concept of superimposition. See my essay "The Unity and Indivisibility of the Self (Brahman)" in *Main Currents in Modern Thought,* vol. 29, no. 4, March–April 1973, p. 130–37.

4. "That" is found in Hinduism as the not-I experience from the Upanisads down.

5. The term "oceanic" experience has been attributed to Freud when in fact it was first used by Romain Rolland in a letter to Freud of 5 December 1927:

> I am myself familiar with this (oceanic) feeling. All my life I have never been without this feeling. . . . In this way I can say that I am deeply religious. This constant state (like a sheet of water that I can feel under the bark) does no harm to my critical faculties and my freedom to exercise them, even against the immediacy of this interior experience. Thus I lead at the same time, without discomfort or pain, a "religious" life (in the sense of this prolonged sensation) and a life of critical reason (which is without illusion). I add that this "oceanic" feeling has nothing to do with my personal aspirations.

6. See my *Powers of Imagining: Ignatius de Loyola* (Albany, N.Y.: State University of New York Press, 1986), chap. 5.

7. This statement is the epistomological epigram of mysticism in its many practiced varieties. It stresses the primacy of images in perception, their link to the will and affections, and their possible transformation by the manipulation of images and through the mediation of images.

This epistomological base in contrary to theology, which deals with propositions, concepts, their relations, their link to the intellect, and the immutable truths of intellectual principles.

Some theologies accept mystical experience as the ground of religion; others take the written word as such a ground. It should be noted that a democratic society should give legitimacy to all these varieties of religious experience, not because they are religious but because they are representative of the whole range of mental acts Americans perform.

8. See my *Powers of Imagining,* Preface and Introduction.

9. For details on *ahamkara* and *anahamvadin,* see my book *Avatara: The Humanization of Philosophy through the Bhagavad Gita* (York, Maine: Nicolas-Hays, 1978), chap. 4.

10. See Victoria Lincoln, *Teresa: A Woman* (Albany, N.Y.: State University of New York Press, 1984).

11. See my essay "Mystic Experience and Technologies of Transformation," in A. de Nicolas and E. Moutsopoulos, eds., *God: Experience or Origin* (New York: Paragon House, 1985).

12. Here are some notes on Teresa de Avila's description of imagining and meditation:

"God is not a product of the imagination: but it is through the imagination that God becomes present" (*Life* 28:10). She also reminds us with her Castillian irony that "the toad does not fly" (*Life* 23:13).

On the difficulty of meditation, principally at the beginning she writes: "And very often, for many years, I was more anxious for the hour I had determined to spend in prayer to be over than I was to remain there . . . and so unbearable was the misery I felt on entering the oratory, that I had to master all my courage" (*Life* 8:7).

On the transformation of the soul in meditation she writes: "The soul undergoes a change; it is always absorbed. . . . the intellectual vision is represented to the imagination so that in conformity to our weakness this presence may last in memory and keep the mind well-occupied" (*Life* 28:9).

On the use of the faculties in meditation she writes: "The faculties are like wild horses, they run in all directions; meditation proper begins with the technologies that gather them within. . . . There the faculties are not lost, nor do they sleep. . . . Only the will is occupied. . . . Not knowing how, it becomes captive; it merely consents to God allowing Him to imprison it as one who well knows how to be captive of its lover" (*Life* 14:2).

"This experience does not seem to be anything else but the almost total death to all earthly things. . . . It seems to me the soul is crucified since no consolations come to it from heaven, nor visits from heaven; neither does it desire any from the earth, nor is the soul on the earth. . . . it is as though one were crucified between heaven and earth. . . . the intense pain takes away sensory consciousness . . . and this experience resembles the AGONY OF DEATH, with the difference that the suffering bears along with it great happiness . . . it is arduous, delightful martyrdom" (*Life* 20:11).

13. For a detailed study of primary and secondary text, primary and secondary technology, see my *Powers of Imagining,* Preface, Introduction, and chap. 1.

14. See for more details my *Powers of Imagining,* chaps. 1 and 2.

15. See for more details my *Powers of Imagining.*

16. See above.

17. On meditation technologies of dismemberment see for more details my *Powers of Imagining,* chap. 1 especially. See also my book, *Meditations through the Rg Veda* (York, Maine: Nicolas Hays, 1976).

18. Matter, for example, is a condition of energy that severely limits the probabilistic waywardness of its elementary particles; large clumps of organized matter, like crystals, have overcome much of the vagueness and unpredictability of their primary constituents (they, however, pay for this certainty by becoming liable to entropic decay). See F. Turner, *Natural Classicism,* p. 63.

19. A classical example is "reading" and how the soft-ware of a technology became neural hard-ware to the point of transparency.

20. A very interesting new book on memory that does not describe this use of memory by the mystics but includes almost everything else memorable is Ed Casey, *Remembering: A Phenomenological Study* (Bloomington, Ind.: Indiana University Press, 1987).

21. It would make an interesting study to compare the difference between the *shadow* of knowledge in Plato and Socrates' *daimonion.* The latter is much like an "oceanic" experience, the former the experience of the I or of the observer. It is important to note that the Greek *daimonion* is a neuter grammatical form, and not a noun, like *daimon* as it is usually translated. It does not indicate it is a daimon-person, personal being—angel, muse, or ghost; it is rather a divine event, a "sign" a "divine voice":

> But the reason for this [Socrates not being involved in politics], as you have heard me say many times and at many places, is that something *divine and daimonionic comes to me,* . . . I have had this from my childhood; it is a sort of voice that comes to me, and when it comes it always holds me back from what I am thinking of doing, but never urges me forward. (*Apology,* 20D–E).

22. Contemporary philosophy of science is finally addressing the pertinent questions. Semantic analysis reduced to the studies of meaning has produced constitution

analysis concerned with the study of the *origins* of meaning. In this manner a deeper understanding of the perspectival structure of objects is being produced, as well as an awareness of the fundamental question of how are the objects-for-knowing generated by theoretical strategies. As a consequence the second important question arises: Which one counts for reality? See Patrick A. Heelan, "Experiment and Theory: Constitution and Reality," in *The Journal of Philosophy,* 85, no. 9 (September 1988).

A Case Study in Early Jesuit Scholarship: Alfonso Salmerón, S.J., and the Study of Sacred Scripture

JOHN D. WILLIS

Introduction

Alfonso Salmerón was born 6 September 1515, in Toledo, Spain, the same year in which Desiderius Erasmus completed for publication his critical edition of the Greek New Testament, his *Novum Instrumentum,* the year in which Martin Luther initiated his course of lectures on Saint Paul's Letter to the Romans. Whether or not his parents had heard about the changes to the northeast of Spain in 1515, they never could have connected the future of their newborn son with controversial Germans and Dutchmen, nor could they have done anything in 1515 except scorn a twenty-one-year-old Basque rowdy named Iñigo López de Loyola as a future role model for their little boy.

Yet little Alfonso's future would be bound up with the changing world of northern Europe. He not only would be drawn into its swirling maelstrom, but also would help change the speed and direction of its chaotic forces. He would become one of the most ardent disciples of one of Christianity's greatest spiritual masters—a Spanish compatriot who, before his submission to God, formerly had been master of the duel and skirt. Salmerón would become one of the founders of and leading members in a religious order that has been called "the most dynamic element in the Roman Church between 1550 and 1650."[1]

His parents, Maria and Alfonso, Sr., did their part to ensure a good foundation for their son's career, whatever it might be. They sent him to school, first in Toledo, then on to the new University of Alcalá.[2] The money invested in his education expressed their hope that their son, once educated, would one day add honor and riches to the family name. Alfonso Salmerón, Jr., would grow up to fulfill the fondest dreams of pious parents, for he would bring a wealth of spiritual and intellectual honor and riches into the household of God, not the least of which came through his many years of scripture study, lecturing, and preaching.

Education

He was enrolled at Alcalá when thirteen years old, "at the moment of Erasmus's highest popularity," according to Salmerón's sole biographer in this century, the late William V. Bangert, S.J., of Fordham University.[3]

> Salmerón found himself completely at home in the study of the Latin and Greek classics. He had an exceptional memory. To the wonder of his fellow students, he could recite entire orations of the classical authors. Recognized as one of the outstanding students of the university, he took the top prizes with ease.[4]

While at Alcalá, Salmerón met and became close friends with Diego Lainez, who was three years older than he. Lainez took his master's degree at Alcalá at age twenty[5] and desired further study at the University of Paris so, sometime in 1533, the two friends set out for Paris.

As they told the story, when pilgrim scholars Salmerón and Lainez dismounted upon arriving in the Parisian Latin Quarter, the first *compatriote d'Espagne* they met was none other than Iñigo de Loyola, the man whose visionary spiritual leadership would change their lives. He quickly obtained lodging for his two countrymen at the Collège Ste.-Barbe, "where they met Iñigo's close friends, Favre, Bobadilla, and Rodrigues."[6] Salmerón received the Master of Arts degree on 3 October 1536, "under the tutelage of Master Francis Xavier,"[7] three and a half years after Iñigo had obtained the Licentiate of Philosophy degree on 13 March 1533.[8] During this period of Alfonso's education and spiritual formation, the intellectual and religious climate in Paris was quite diverse.

Stimulating intellectual breezes were fanned in Paris by savants like the celebrated Hellenist Guillaume Budé or the poet Jean du Bellay,[9] men who could inspire King Francis I to build the Collège de France in 1530. But while salty breezes blew in some parts of town, the *fulmen censurae* (lightning of censure) crackled through the cloudy halls of the Sorbonne attempting to strike dead the literary careers of any innovators in scripture study. For example, Jacques Lefèvre d'Etaples's commentaries on the Gospels, published in 1522, were condemned the next year in 1523. Erasmus's *Paraphrases in Novum Testamentum,* published from 1517 to 1524, were censured in 1531.[10]

Salmerón undoubtedly knew some students and professors in the Collège de France, along with their bibliographies and methods, just as he also undoubtedly knew students and professors in the Sorbonne, with their concerns to preserve Catholic truth and the correct interpretation of tradition. So while he had developed a taste for Greco-Roman literature at Alcalá, at Paris he learned the methods—and dangers—of the latest techniques in the study of the scriptures.

Throughout the 1530s at both Alcalá and Paris, Salmerón was repeatedly reminded in the daily news of the dangers of willful, petulant scripture interpretation, as the hydra of heresy reared its many heads throughout Europe. The Diet of Augsburg in 1530, the formation of the Schmalkaldic League in 1531, Francis I's Letter to the French Parliament concerning heretics on 10 December 1533,[11] and the whole series of shocking developments in England throughout the 1530s[12] must all have combined to horrify the young Catholic leaders filling Europe's classrooms—including Salmerón, his comrades, and their charismatic leader, Ignatius.

Years later, Salmerón's own creative intellect would blend the direct and indirect lessons learned at Alcalá, the Sorbonne, and the Collège de France. On the one hand can be seen his education in every page of his commentaries, as he used the fullest range of research methods and topics known to him. Yet it is hardly surprising that he would write his voluminous commentaries out of two concerns: to preserve the *sensus catholicus* of sacred scripture and to refute the interpretations of the innovators.

In 1549, thirteen years after the conferral of his Master of Arts degree, Salmerón received the doctoral degree, but under rather unusual circumstances. Ignatius needed three scholars with doctorates for an assignment at the University of Ingolstadt in Bavaria, and Salmerón was one of the three chosen for the job, along with Claude Jay and Peter Canisius. Here is Bangert's description of what happened.

> Ignatius Loyola gave high priority to the assignment he entrusted to Jay, Salmerón, and Canisius. By now he realized the vast influence that scholarship was to have in the conflict of religions in Germany, and he wanted three Jesuits equipped with a doctorate in theology before they put foot inside the lecture halls of Ingolstadt. He spoke to Cardinal Marcello Cervini about the problem. On 9 August 1549 Cervini wrote to Cardinal Giammaria del Monte, recommending that the three Jesuits be granted the doctorate. Del Monte arranged, therefore, that the three stand for the doctoral degree at the University of Bologna. He recommended to the Dominican bishop of Minori, Ambrozio Catarino, that he obtain the services of two other Dominican doctors of theology and with them compose the examining board. Catarino enlisted the help of Vincenzo Villa Placentinus, the dean of the theology faculty at Bologna, and Vincenzo de Quintano, a master in the university.
>
> On 2 October the three Jesuits faced the three questioning Dominicans. The examination was a stiff one. Salmerón's diploma spoke of his subjection to a "difficult, severe, and awesome examination" (**arduo, rigoroso ac tremendo examini**). Angelo Massarelli noted that Jay, Salmerón, and Canisius lived up to the expectations of a brilliant performance. Catarino and his fellow examiners saluted in a special way the display of learning they had just witnessed. On 4 October the three Jesuits received their doctoral degrees in theology.[13]

The description of this event indicates, on the one hand, how the Dominicans diligently applied themselves to their assigned role as examiners for the members of the fledgling *Societas Iesu*. On the other hand, their—shall we say—zealous execution of their task also shows how, as representatives of the *Ordo Praedicatorum,* they combined their collective talents to assure themselves—beyond the shadow of a Dominican doubt—that the three Jesuits had *earned* their triple stripes through firm acquaintance with their theological curriculum. At any rate, the examiners were impressed by the examinees, and the degrees were conferred.

The three new doctors went on to the University of Ingolstadt where each received his schedule of assigned lectures and then met his first students— fourteen pupils, "ten of whom," Bangert wrote, "presented the blank and uninspiring faces of disgruntled illiterates who were in class against their will."[14] Disheartening as this situation was for freshly minted scholars, Salmerón began his assigned inaugural lecture series on Saint Paul's Epistle to the Romans, a good beginning for a long career in the study of the scriptures.

Career[15]

CHARTER MEMBER AND LEADER OF THE SOCIETY OF JESUS

Alfonso Salmerón was a charter member of the Society and remained vitally involved in critical decisions throughout its early years. At Vicenza in 1538, he was one of those who voted to call the order the *Compañia de Jesús*. He helped elect Ignatius the Society's first superior general in April of 1541. He began to guide persons through the *Spiritual Exercises* in 1540, and so well that Ignatius judged him "second only to Favre as an effective retreat master." Salmerón was one of the most important editors of the *Constitutions*. Along with others in his generation, as well as so many afterwards, he was a founder of Jesuit colleges.[16] He served as Vicar General for the Society for a brief period[17] and as the provincial of Naples for eighteen years.[18] Although twenty-one years his senior, Ignatius was capable of soliciting and accepting Salmerón's advice on moral questions,[19] as well as ones concerning the Society.[20]

PAPAL LEGATE

Pope Paul III instructed Salmerón and Bröet to go to Ireland in 1541 to strengthen the position of the Church there, although the mission proved unsuccessful.[21] On 27 July 1555, Pope Paul IV assigned him to a papal mission under the supervision of Luigi Lippomano. Salmerón went by way of Augsburg, briefly attended the Diet being held there, assisted the Jesuits in attendance, and then went on to Poland. In May of 1556, he was assigned to Cardinal Scipione Rebiba's diplomatic trip to Brussels to see Philip II of Spain, who was there. Pope Paul IV again called on him to join the staff of Cardinal Carafa's embassy to Brussels in September of 1557. Salmerón first stopped along the way to assist brothers Peter Canisius and Nicholas Goudanus at the Colloquy at Worms, and finally arrived at Brussels in December.[22]

While his influence during these assignments has yet to be determined, Salmerón's expertise was believed valuable enough to include him in affairs of such importance.

PAPAL THEOLOGIAN AT THE COUNCIL OF TRENT

When Ignatius received orders from Pope Paul III to send three members of the Society to the Council of Trent, Diego Lainez and Pierre Favre were chosen, along with Salmerón, who was not to go until he had preached the Lenten series at Bologna.[23] Once at the council, Cardinal Cervini assigned to Salmerón the task of opening each day's session with an explanation of the material to be discussed and to Lainez the duty of closing with a summation. According to a letter written around 10 July 1546 from Salmerón to Ignatius, these duties were assigned to ensure an orderly, orthodox direction to the proceedings.

> It is also helpful that—alas, because of diseased doctrine among some theologians—the cardinal has rendered judgment that one of us first speak among them to explain the material; the other being entrusted with the end, at that time giving his opinion, especially to refute everything which was said badly.[24]

In the same letter, Salmerón indicated how the little band of Jesuits was having strong influence behind the scenes. They were being asked constantly by the prelates for their opinions on the theological issues being debated, and even to provide verbatim statements to be read to the council by other theologians.[25]

Salmerón had a major impact upon the council when the Tridentine fathers debated the question of justification. His speech on 23 June 1546 is one of only two preserved entire in the council records,[26] which fact Bangert explained as due to Cardinal Cervini's "special predilection for Salmerón."[27] He spoke again on justification on 28 September and 16 October,[28] from which speeches he wrote two tracts on justification that circulated during the council.[29] He lost the friendship of Girolamo Seripando on account of the Augustinian's adherence to the theory of *duplex iustitia,* a concept that Salmerón vigorously opposed in person and through others at the council.[30]

His remaining work at the first session dealt mainly with sacramental theology. Bangert observed how Salmerón's addresses on 18–19 August 1547 on the Sacrifice of the Mass "made a deep impression."

> The wide erudition, especially in Scripture and patristics, as recorded by Massarelli, was massive, a demonstration of Salmerón's especially retentive memory and clarity of presentation. He clearly moved in the current of religious humanism. In the long intervention on . . . 18 August he quoted Scripture at least twenty-nine times; twelve times he cited theologians and fathers of the Church.[31]

When the second session was planned, Pope Julius III requested that Salmerón and Lainez again be papal theologians—not surprisingly, given their previous success and experience. Most of their work at that session pertained to the theology of the Eucharist, Penance, Extreme Unction, the Sacrifice of the Mass, and orders.

Their performance at the second session earned them the renewed confidence of successor Pope Pius IV, who wanted both men back for the third and final gathering in 1562. A week after Salmerón had given his opening three-hour address on 10 June 1562, Canisius wrote to Francis Borgia. "It is the general opinion here that Father Alfonso ranks, and deservedly so, as the number one man among the theologians of the council. He has brought great honor to the Society."[32] Honor he may have brought for his work on sacramental theology,[33] but there were complaints about Salmerón's longwindedness.[34]

PREACHER

Salmerón was approved to preach publicly in August of 1537 and was ordained to the priesthood "sometime in late October or early in November" of 1538, after his twenty-second birthday.[35] He was committed to the proclamation of the Word, and his many successful preaching tours indicate that he enjoyed this part of his ministry. Preaching was the natural means used to assist local parishes in fighting inroads made by Protestant preachers and to foster basic Christian adult education.[36] Salmerón was vitally involved in both aspects throughout his career.[37]

The marchesa of Pescara, Vittoria Colonna, who was an intimate friend of Michaelangelo, requested a Jesuit preacher for her church of Sant' Anna de' Folgenami in Rome. As a tribute to his skill in the pulpit, Salmerón was assigned the task by Ignatius in the fall of 1545.[38] A little over a year later, on 27 December 1546, the feast day of St. John the Evangelist, Salmerón was at the Council of Trent when he delivered a sermon to the assembled fathers. His colleagues at Trent were so moved by this homily's lofty emphasis (on a reformed pastorate)—drawn almost solely from biblical motifs—that they had it published at Rome and Paris the next year.[39] It is noteworthy that, throughout his labors as papal theologian at the Council at Trent, Salmerón's preaching and pastoral work with the poor also continued.[40]

During 1548 and 1549, he preached across northern Italy, an area then undergoing spiritual renewal.[41] His itinerary included Bologna, Venice, Padua, Verona, back to Venice and Padua, Belluno, Venice, back to Belluno, Saravalle, back to Venice and Padua, Ferrara, and finally, Bologna again. Salmerón stressed everywhere the importance of the sacraments to his hearers, and these preaching tours produced significant success.[42] In one letter to Ignatius, he noted how his sacred oratory had been compared by the Bellunoese to that of Saint Bernardino de Siena.[43] The comparison would suggest that Salmerón's sermons emphasized personal morality and devotion.

> Salmerón spoke with compelling power. He mobilized a wide array of scriptural texts strategically placed, skillfully maneuvered, and clearly paraphrased. He honed a trick of rhetorical conceits that sustained protracted reflections on scriptural images. He sketched vivid vignettes of daily life in the streets, the shops, the home. Salmerón's oratory had a significance that extended far beyond a show of personal talent. He was but one voice in a large Jesuit chorus that was giving fire to a mighty force of preaching in the Catholic Reform.[44]

Surely one reason Salmerón was such a successful preacher (and Ignatius's frequent first choice to fill special requests for Jesuit homileticians) was that he enjoyed it. Ever busy with a myriad of duties and details in his life as a Jesuit leader, he never tired of his pastoral contact with the people and seeing the changes his sermons accomplished. Salmerón was the kind of leader whose activities gave living marrow, bone, and sinew to the reforms enacted at Trent. He knew the potential power of preaching and fully exploited it when he was in the pulpit.

> Sacred oratory ran like a thread through [Salmerón's] life. His sermons with their distinctly scriptural cast reflected two major influences, academic and ascetical: the Biblical Renaissance at Alacalá and the *Spiritual Exercises* of Ignatius. At Alcalá, as has been seen, Salmerón became fired with a life-long enthusiasm for scriptural studies. And in the *Spiritual Exercises* of Ignatius he encountered, of the fifty-two meditations and contemplations of the last three weeks of the *Exercises,* forty-eight episodes that are in the Gospels. This background he cast into apostolic form in his sermons.[45]

Bangert is unquestionably correct in linking Salmerón's biblical preaching with his spiritual formation and scriptural education. That he was asked throughout his career to lecture upon the Bible also reinforced his acquaintance with the sacred page. At least some of Salmerón's sermons were later published.[46]

LECTURER ON SCRIPTURE

Salmerón's first experience as a scripture lecturer came in 1540 at the Sapienza, the University of Rome, and then again for an interval from 1543 to 1546. "In the fall of 1545 he delivered scriptural lectures three times a week on St. Paul's Epistle to the Ephesians at the Jesuit church of Santa Maria della Strada." Four years later at the University of Ingolstadt (29 November 1549), Salmerón delivered his first lecture in a series there on the pauline literature, beginning with the Letter to the Romans. Nearly a year later (early October 1550), he was in Verona where he began a course of lectures on the Gospel of Matthew. Within less than six months in 1551, he was in his beloved Naples for his Lenten series of lectures on the Epistle to the Galatians, given four to five times per week in the Church of Diva Maria.[47]

A number of these Lenten lecture series—which probably combined both academic lecture and sermon—gave Salmerón opportunity for serious work in the scriptures, and he became well-known for his effectiveness. During the Lenten series of 1554, Polanco observed how "men were in awe of Salmerón's teaching 'to the point of wonder' [ad stuporem usque]."[48]

The *Commentarii:* Salmerón's Intellectual Contribution

DATES OF COMPOSITION AND PUBLICATION

On 3 February 1566, though only fifty-and-a-half years old, Salmerón wrote to Francisco Borgia of his deteriorating physical condition, reporting "a loss of vision and hearing, loss of principal teeth—and others are likewise loosening—and that which is most important, a lack of physical energies."[49] Borgia noted Salmerón's physical condition, suffered in great part because he had given the best years of his health in service to his order, Church, and God. Probably hoping to spark the failing and discouraged Salmerón as well as to preserve the mature fruit of a lifetime of study for the Order, Borgia asked his ailing brother to write. That request eventually would result in Salmerón's commentaries on the New Testament.

In June of 1569, Salmerón tried to beg off from this assignment.[50] He began to write sometime during the next year, however, for he wrote Borgia of his frustrated progress of "writing, striking out, and erasing" by May of 1570.[51] With the intermittent help of a series of assistants—Robert Bellarmine, Diego Paez, and Bartolomé Pérez—and encouraged by minister generals Mercurian and Acquaviva (both of whom occasionally sent books for the project), Salmerón worked on his publishing project with the same selfless intrepidity that characterized his earlier years of active service for the Society.

The physically waning scholar worked from 1570 until 1585, the year of his death. As he lay on his deathbed "frequently uttering passages from scripture, especially the psalms,"[52] Salmerón undoubtedly thought of his lengthy writing project. His last assistant, Bartolomé Pérez, kindly pledged to see the commentaries through the press before Salmerón died on 13 February 1585, as Bangert noted, with his "eyes fixed on the crucifix."

Salmerón's brethren would try to bury him the next day, but the crowds demanded to see their beloved pastor. They clamored for relics, cutting off bits of clothing, hair and beard—even trying to saw off a foot. He was buried late that night. Loved and esteemed by his own generation, he soon, however, would be forgotten by posterity.

Pérez kept his word and worked to achieve the publication of the *Commentarii,* a task that took several years. The first edition of twelve volumes (the Gospels and Acts of the Apostles) appeared in Madrid between 1597 and 1601 from the press of Ludovici Sánchez. The remaining four volumes on the epistolary literature appeared in 1601 in Brescia, at the expense of Mathius Colosini and Bacotius Barecio. In 1602, volumes 1 through 9 were issued in Cologne by the firm of Heirat and Gymnicum, which also produced volumes 10 through 16 in 1604. The last edition of sixteen volumes was published by the latter house from 1612 to 1615[53] and is the one used in this study.

PURPOSES OF THE COMPOSITION

In his Preface to the *Commentarii,* Salmerón noted that the formal occasion for his having written was the duty of religious obedience to Borgia's order, cited above.[54] He bemoaned being given such a task at such a late stage in life by quoting a passage from Ecclesiasticus: "When a man has been exhausted, then he must begin; and when he has rested, then he will work."[55] Salmerón sought the reader's sympathetic sigh of pity as he wrote of his "bad eyesight, rough handwriting and inelegant style."[56] Though he was unquestionably sincere, the aged Salmerón forgot that his protestations of inadequacy preceded over 7,834 double-column folio pages of text. He believed what he wrote about himself, but his self-doubts were overcome by his conviction that his scholarly project was important to his order, Church, and God.

Salmerón disclosed his primary purpose for having written the *Commentarii* when he opened his Preface with a carefully selected quotation from scripture, 2 Timothy 3:14–15:

> Truly, remain in those things which you have been taught and believe, knowing by whom you were taught, and knowing from childhood our sacred scriptures which are able to instruct you unto salvation, through faith which is in Christ Jesus.[57]

Just as the Apostle Paul had instructed his young protégé to abide in the apostolic tradition, so Salmerón commended his readers *ad perseverantiam in Catholica doctrina,* as he wrote only a line before he quoted the scripture above. From his point of view, then, the *Commentarii* represented a dual obedience.

Salmerón was not only carrying out the assignment given by the authority of Minister General Borgia; he was also fulfilling the charge given in the Word of God by authority of the Apostle Paul. Salmerón's primary purpose, therefore, was both positive and apostolic in nature—the transmission of the tradition of Jesus Christ, the Gospel, which he described as "the kernel and compend of all the scriptures, the key unlocking all the hidden and deep secrets of the divine."[58]

Salmerón's second purpose was essentially related to the first, though approached by the *via negativa.* The faithful transmission of the Gospel also required defining and defending its sacred content in contradistinction to false doctrines taught by the heretics, a problem also certainly understood by the Apostle Paul.

Paul had closed his first epistle to Timothy with a warning to protect the apostolic tradition.[59] Interestingly, near the beginning of his second letter to Timothy, he almost repeated the same words: *bonum depositum custodi per Spiritum Sanctum.*[60] Salmerón allowed Vincent of Lérins—historic authority on the relationship between scripture and tradition—to explain the phrase.

> "Guard the deposit." What is the "deposit"? It is that which is committed to you, not invented by you: it is not leading, but following. On account of you, let posterity be grateful for the deposit understood, which antiquity formerly venerated without understanding it. In the same way, teach only the things which you have learned, so that you always speak in a new way, without speaking something new.[61]

For Salmerón, Vincent's arguments to "follow not lead" and to "teach in new forms not substance"[62] supported the Pauline injunction to protect the Gospel, or apostolic tradition. That Salmerón had the Protestants in mind when he cited Vincent cannot be doubted, for he immediately observed how "writers in his day" had neglected the Vincentian wisdom and departed from orthodoxy.[63] Protestant principles like *sola scriptura* were used to criticize the Catholic tradition; yet, as Salmerón suggested through Vincent, such ideas ended up tampering with the Church's historic understanding of the apostolic tradition and, ultimately, in departing from its truth.[64]

In summary, Salmerón's two purposes in writing his commentaries were taken from scripture itself. (1) He sought to perpetuate the faithful transmission of the Gospel and apostolic tradition to new generations of Bible students through interpretations that preserved the Catholic sense. (2) He wanted to protect the deposit of faith given by providing comprehensive attention to the false scriptural interpretations of the Protestants. According to Augustine, these were the tasks of the Christian teacher.[65]

This two-pronged approach very much fit his biographical experiences—his youthful interest in Bible study at Alcalá; his early awareness of the turmoil in Paris and Europe due to heretical innovations; and his wide experience as a biblical lecturer and preacher.[66] Throughout his career spread across Europe, Alfonso Salmerón had tried faithfully to hold to the *traditio Christi,* as well as to protect it from wolves in sheep's clothing. His stated purposes for having written his *Commentarii* were completely natural to him, for he had spent a lifetime of study and apostolic labor in support of them.

FORMAT OF THE *COMMENTARII:* DERIVATIVE OF JESUIT SPIRITUALITY?

The overall structure Salmerón chose for his *Commentarii* conveys some information about his understanding of how scripture should be approached for study. Reflection upon the way in which he shaped the New Testament for commentary suggests the possibility that Salmerón's spiritual formation as a Jesuit contributed to this phase of his methodology.

Volume 1, though it begins the series with its title page describing "commentaries on the evangelical history and the Acts of the Apostles," actually contains "prolegomena on the Sacred Gospels," more about which will be written in the next section on method.

Volumes 2 through 11 develop the life of Jesus from its "beginning in eternity," as stated the Johannine Prologue, until the resurrection and ascension. The subtitles of the volumes (less the phrase "of our Lord Jesus Christ," which was appended to each of them except the second volume) are as follows:

V. 2: "The Word before It Became Flesh"
V. 3: "The Infancy and Boyhood"
V. 4: "The History, up to the Lord's Supper"
V. 5: "The Sermon on the Mount"
V. 6: "The Miracles"
V. 7: "The Parables"
V. 8: "The Disputations"
V. 9: "The Discourse Given to the Apostles during the Supper"
V. 10: "The Passion and Death"
V. 11: "The Resurrection and Ascension"

Volumes 12 through 16 bear titles and subtitles markedly different from the preceding volumes (perhaps reflecting Pérez's editorial decisions after Salmerón's death[67]), though they return to the general canonical order of the New Testament. Volumes 13 through 16 were described on the title page of volume 13 as "commentaries on all the epistles of the blessed Paul, and the canonical epistles, divided into four volumes," and they stand together. Volume 12 on the Acts of the Apostles stands on its own, the traditional line of demarcation between "history" and "doctrine." Volumes 12 through 16 contain the following:

V. 12: "The Founding and Beginning of the Church in the Acts of the Apostles"

V. 13: "Commentaries on All Epistles of Blessed the Paul, and the Canonicals," vol. 1
Book 1: Prolegomona to the Pauline Letters, in 3 Parts
Books 2–4: Disputations on the Letter to the Romans
V. 14: "Exposition on Epistles Corinthians," vol. 2 [Book 5]
V. 15: "Disputations on the Epistles of the Holy Paul," vol. 3
Book 6: Disputations on Galatians-Thessalonians
Book 7: Disputations on 1 Timothy-Philemon
Book 8: Disputations on Hebrews
V. 16: "Disputations on the Canonical Epistles & the Apocalypse," vol. 4, ["and Some Appended Letters in Which the Author Answers Some Sacred Questions"]

Even though the *Commentarii* were not finished at the time of his death and were taken over by Pérez, the volume and book titles still reveal Salmerón's orientation toward the materials of the New Testament. The full titles to all the commentaries, including their dates of publication in the third edition, appear in the Appendix to this paper. What does the structural format for all sixteen volumes suggest?

First, Salmerón approached the Gospels with an overt historical concern, unhesitatingly rearranging their testimonies into a chronological, synoptic[68] *historia Iesu Christi*. This approach was at least as ancient as Tatian's *Diatessaron* so it comes as no surprise, even though it was never very popular as a framework for interpretation in the history of exegesis. That Salmerón used this method is less puzzling, however, when his personal spiritual formation as a Jesuit is taken into consideration.

He used the *Spiritual Exercises* throughout his life and guided many novices through them over the years, gaining notice and approbation by Ignatius himself for his excellence as a retreat master, as noted above. But the central structure of the *Exercises* is the incarnation, life and ministry, death, burial, resurrection, and appearances of Jesus, upon and through which develops the process of systematic, imaginative contemplation.[69] Salmerón had seen the *Exercises* repeatedly work their power in others, and given the fact that he was accustomed to their synoptic, chronological method, would it not be completely natural that he should have chosen it for his own approach to the life of Jesus?

In any case, the structures of both the *Commentarii* and the *Exercises* emphasize the kerygmatic nature of the Gospel story. Salmerón's orientation to the New Testament clearly was didactic, as seen in his superstructure for the Gospels and the epistolary literature. Recalling his two purposes for writing the commentaries—to continue the apostolic deposit of faith given in the scriptures and to assist this process by marking it off from heretical innovations—Salmerón's didactic approach is even more pronounced in the particular genres used within and throughout the commentaries.

GENRES AND METHOD IN THE *COMMENTARII*

Salmerón used three genres in his commentaries to carry out his purposes: *prologomenon, tractatus,* and *disputatio.* Each served a distinct function in his didactic scheme, and each represented his unique appropriation of methods used by biblical scholars throughout the exegetical tradition.[70] Through his adaptations of them, he was able to blend his dual purposes in composition with his understanding of native literary forms within the New Testament canon.

The *prolegomenon* format served to introduce the main topics, issues, and difficulties for study of the New Testament.[71] Some of the issues raised by Salmerón in this exegetical genre—the veracity of the Vulgate, for example—arose from newer disciplines such as the rise of textual criticism rather than from traditional questions. To revert to scholastic categories of biblical interpretation, many of Salmerón's introductory points covered in his *prolegomena* were more *questiones quodlibetales* than they were *questiones disputatae.*

His use of the tractatus parallels the medieval *lectio* or *expositio* in function, not form, in that by it he sought to exposit the positive meaning of the text. Each *tractatus* was headed by an abbreviated quotation of the scripture under study, sometimes followed by one or two references to gospel parallels for comparison. This genre was Salmerón's primary vehicle for expositing the Catholic sense of scripture, and he used it solely for his expositions of the Gospels and Acts of the Apostles in volumes 2 through 12.

Salmerón's use of the *disputatio* for his interpretations of the remainder of the New Testament canon after the Book of Acts also is a reflection of his appropriation of scholastic exegetical methodology. Since the literature in the Pauline corpus particularly was of a didactic, dogmatic nature and since the *disputatio* traditionally had its primary focus on the dialectical-dogmatic phase of scripture interpretation, the New Testament materials after the Acts of the Apostles were naturally amenable to this format. Additionally, Protestant preoccupations with Pauline theology made the epistolary literature a natural territorial battleground wherein Salmerón carried out his second primary purpose: to establish the Catholic sense over against the innovations of the heretics. It was under the *disputatio* genre, used throughout volumes 13 through 16, that he most often and severely broached the issues raised by Protestants.

Beyond their functions, however, the three genres all drew upon the same set of theological, historical, philosophical, linguistic, and hermeneutical disciplines. Consequently, the developmental *style* of any given *prolegomenon, tractatus,* or *disputatio* often appears nearly identical to discussions under the other two literary genres, even though the overarching viewpoints differed. How Salmerón used his wide-ranging erudition through the three genres follows.

As a rule, Salmerón investigated any given topic or scripture along the following lines. As he developed his line of exposition, he would depend upon other passages of scripture to elucidate the meaning of the text at hand through quotations within the discussion, as well as by cross-references in the margins. This was one of his most common sources of interpretation: scripture interpreting scripture.

But as a theologian knowing the history of exegesis and dogma, he also adduced evidence from church fathers'[72] biblical commentaries, theological treatises, and letters, again quite frequently through quotations within the text. Scholastic theologians (particularly Thomas Aquinas) were explicit favorites for understanding biblical theology—to be sure, an Ignatian pre-dilection.[73]

Salmerón's exegesis was reflective of some of the methodological changes in his century, however, in his copious use of any pertinent lingistic, grammatical, and syntactical points raised by the scripture being considered. His early training in the classics at Alcalá and his remarkable memory were evident throughout the *Commentarii* in his frequent parallels from Greco-Roman history, philosophy, theology, poetry, and lexicography scattered throughout both text and margins.

Finally, whenever pertinent (and usually in the *disputationes* in volumes 13 through 16), he cited book, chapter, and verse, from an extraordinarily wide and deep bibliography of Protestant writers.[74] This practice seems quite uncommon among Catholic exegetes of the day. Still, he wanted to enable his readers to check his criticism against the arguments of his opponents. If he ever quoted their actual words—and it seems he never did—it is clear from his practice that he was unwilling to take up valuable space (or to invite unnecessary questions) with lines from the innovators.

As a result of these combined factors—his own purposes carried out through a creative reappropriation of scholastic exegetical methods[75] within the context of his education and the questions of his time—Alfonso Salmerón wrote biblical commentaries that have no parallel in the history of exegesis, at least up to his own day.[76] Arguably, he produced what can be called the first interdisciplinary commentaries on the Bible in the modern era. Even William Bangert (who oddly referred to Salmerón's method as "basically simple") noted how the *Commentarii* bear a " 'modern' impress."[77]

Salmerón's Adequacy as an Exegete

Since the bulk of the *Commentarii* were written during Salmerón's retire-ment years at Naples and since they were published after his death, little contemporary testimony exists as to his success as an exegete. Borgia's personal request that Salmerón write the commentaries, plus the regular

assistance afforded him during the process, only imply his contemporaries'
positive judgments about the quality of his work. Aside from this are only
isolated remarks by persons who heard his sacred oratory or scripture
lectures. Even those are uneven, however, ranging from the unbridled adula-
tion of a Bernardino Realino[78] to the chastened praise of a Cardinal Fre-
derico Borromeo, nephew of the famed Charles Borromeo.[79]

In the twentieth century, scholarship has made little progress from cacoph-
ony to euphony, that is, from uniform disagreement to a critical consensus.
Because scholars have disagreed so widely as to the quality of Salmerón's
exegetical work, the enduring value of the *Commentarii* still remains very
much open to question. Most of his critics seem not to have read Salmerón's
New Testament commentaries for themselves at all. Some[80] apparently have
relied on the few uneven judgments alluded to above, while others[81] have
based their views mainly on the analysis of one scholar, Fernand de Lanversin,[82] who may or may not have read Salmerón very deeply.

De Lanversin's criticism, published in 1939 and apparently accepted in its
main lines by every subsequent historian interested in Salmerón's scripture
studies, can be summed up as follows.

Viewed in a positive light, the *Commentarii* were "a fortunate reaction
against the abuse of a theology too abstract, dialectical, and too loosely
grounded to scripture."[83] Likewise, Salmerón showed himself "open to all
the allied disciplines which aid in establishing the text and meaning of
scripture."[84] Perhaps most important, Salmerón

> had the credit of cutting the path towards a theology more profoundly and largely
> based in scripture and tradition, pursuing his adversaries on their own turf, in this
> way preparing the way for the great controversialists and patristic studies.[85]

The *Commentarii*, therefore, were mainly notable for their reaction against
unscriptural theology and for their transitional contribution to apologetics
and patristics.

De Lanversin's more detailed criticisms appeared when he discussed the
"general traits locating Salmerón in the exegetical tradition." Some of his
remarks seem more to reflect twentieth-century exegetical standards than
sympathetic comparison of with what Salmerón did with the traditions
available to him. In general, the methodology chosen for the *Commentarii*
was a mistake in judgment, producing a kind of bastardized scholarship,
neither good exegesis nor good biblical theology.

> One may regret, in the work he has left to us, an overly analytical style, a mass of
> evidence of very unequal worth, and a lack of perspective. By desiring to hold the
> middle ground between a scripture commentary and theological treatise, the entire
> work bears an indecisive character: the commentary feels overloaded, while the
> theological exposition appears fragmentary.[86]

Aside from this fundamental criticism, Salmerón's approach to scripture interpretation was "too conservative, even backwards at times"[87]—apparently compared with today's standards. Compared to his Jesuit contemporary at Paris, Juan Maldonado, Salmerón was "inferior." His work may have been impressive in its "bulk, seriousness, and penetration," but it was undistinguished, even bland, compared to Maldonado's "decisiveness and occasional boldness."

> Less personal, Salmeron, after having acted as reporter, lets the reader judge, only hesitatingly indicating his preference. He is not open to fresh avenues, preferring an exegesis that is a little difficult to any positions so much as even a little adventurous.[88]

In short, Salmerón was accused of having been overly liberal in the selection of his materials, overly objective in not leading the reader to a conclusion, and overly conservative in his explanations of the text.

Was de Lanversin correct in these appraisals that Salmerón's method was a mistake, producing an unwieldy, unbalanced, overwrought, too conservative, and overly objective product, neither good exegesis nor good theology?

First, if one compares the *Commentarii* to the bulk of scripture studies in the sixteenth century or even to those written in the medieval period, one can answer, "Yes, Salmerón's work is open to many of the charges." Perhaps only Bonaventure's commentary on the Gospel of Luke bears some similiarity in its combination of textual exposition and scholastic theology. Commentators like the often-touted Maldonado usually only gave a sentence or two, or perhaps a paragraph on passages of extraordinary interest to him, and so Salmerón's average treatment of five to ten pages would seem excessive.

Yet Salmerón's *Commentarii* are interesting precisely because he broke away from the traditional methodologies being followed in his day (with a few exceptions, like Erasmus's *Paraphrases* on the New Testament).[89] His plan introduced discussions, quotations, and marginal notes pertaining not only to the internal questions of the text, but also to the historic, theological questions surrounding it. A reader today can pick up one of Salmerón's prolegomena, tractates, or disputations and become intellectually engaged precisely because of the expanse of textual, biblical, historical, and theological, even apologetic, points that he felt it important to admit into the discussion.

In fact, the material that specifically took on the Protestants aside, Salmerón's *Commentarii* resemble Fortress Press's *Hermeneia* series more than anything else on today's shelves. Granted that he was less original and independent than an Erasmus (in, for example, the *Annotations*), and less theologically creative than a Luther (in, for example, his commentary on the Book of Romans), but which of *their* writings bear real methodological comparison to today's biblical exposition? And while Salmerón truly was more conservative than Erasmus and Luther whenever there was a prior established *consensus fidelium,* neither the Dutch humanist nor the German reformer had much interest in interference with their interpretations from either the exegetical or theological traditions. Granted that their independence helped to earn them a place in the history of theology (and the history of Europe), why should Salmerón's attempt to bridge the pre-Reformation, even precritical era be ruled merely "too conservative" when he was pursuing a more complex and difficult methodology?

Also, Salmerón *recognized* that his attempt to compose commentaries that (1) upheld the *sensus Catholicus* and (2) refuted the Protestants would effect an imbalance in the evidence he would adduce for some of his interpretations, an imbalance that would invite criticisms from his readers.[90] He anticipated the charges of critics that his *Commentarii* were "overloaded and imbalanced," yet he was unwilling that an exegetical Occam's Razor shave off any discussions of faith or orthodoxy in such an uncertain period of the Church's history. Therefore, even if the charge can be sustained throughout the monumental work (as it surely can be sustained in places), at least Salmerón was conscious of what he was doing. He was not, that is, guilty of a lapse in perspective.

Last, it is fallacious to evaluate the intellectual quality of the *Commentarii* along the lines drawn by de Lanversin, wherein Salmerón's work purportedly suffers from a lack of boldness and independence, and from general inconclusiveness, compared to Maldonado. Standards have changed by which sixteenth century exegetes are evaluated. Today, historians of exegesis are more interested in Desiderius Erasmus's *Annotationes* and *Paraphrases* than Maldonado's works precisely because Erasmus was more intellectually independent and theologically daring than his colleague at Paris—indeed, than most Catholic scholars of that epoch. Nevertheless, if one reverts to the exegetical tradition before or contemporaneous with him for the standard by which he ought to be measured, then Erasmus must be judged too bold, too independent and, considered by most pre-Vatican II Catholic scholars, treacherously inconclusive!

Similarly, why should Salmerón be criticized for having been faithful to his purposes: an intentional lack of boldness, an intentional dependence upon the *consensus fidelium?* Likewise, it seems rather remarkable that a Tridentine leader so dedicated to a conservative approach should have presented his material so fully as to trust the persuasive power of the Catholic tradition itself, rather than that he should have felt himself forced to impose his own individual distillation of it on the reader. Additionally, his extensive quotation of Protestant exegetes and theologians shows not only his own willingness to take seriously the fledgling Protestant intellectual tradition, but also reflects his faith in himself and his peers. His judgments of Protestantism were open to critical scrutiny, a tribute to his scholarship and fair play.

But this objectivity also is a reflection of his faithfulness to his Jesuit spirituality. The Presupposition of the *Spiritual Exercises* reads:

. . . [I]t is necessary to suppose that every good Christian is more ready to put a good interpretation on another's statement than to condemn it as false. If an orthodox construction cannot be put on a proposition, the one who made it should be asked how he understands it. If he is in error, he should be corrected with all kindness. If this does not suffice, all appropriate means should be used to bring him to a correct interpretation, and so defend the proposition from error.[91]

It is possible that Salmerón's extensive compilation of evidence, coupled with his unwillingness to impose his own opinions, may have been a uniquely Jesuit attempt to lead his readers to their own informed decisions. This explanation proposes that Salmerón's method may have reflected another appropriation of his spirituality, rather than a simple failure to have had more controlled conclusions.

Finally, when one remembers that many scholars today often choose to persuade more by the preponderance of evidence than by rhetorical device, Salmerón's so-called "over-objectivity" looks surprisingly modern.

Salmerón's Value as an Exegete for Historical Theology

Salmerón stands as a bridge between the medieval and modern worlds of biblical interpretation. On one side, he was an heir to scholastic methods of exegesis that he drew upon for their precision in treating theological issues arising out of the biblical texts. On another, he was educated during a period in which biblical study was undergoing significant change.

He was a scholar who knew the methods and intellectual questions being addressed to and arising from sacred scripture in his own day, and so he was led beyond the scholastic tradition to include every discipline that helped to establish the meaning of the text. In addition, he was a leading member of the Society of Jesus, and an active churchman in a variety of tasks—legate, theologian, lecturer, and priest. Salmerón knew the needs of his Church, having become well-acquainted with the influence of the Protestants, whose arguments and persuasiveness depended so much upon their interpretation of sacred scripture.

Salmerón, in writing his *Commentarii,* was therefore cognizant of a wide range of responsibility to the exegetical tradition, to the multiple developments in biblical scholarship in his day, to the Society of Jesus (and the Magisterium it supported), and to the thousands of Roman Catholics who might indirectly benefit from his work on sacred scripture.

Salmerón also was one of the very first Jesuit exegetes in a long and distinguished line of biblical interpreters in the Society of Jesus. His Jesuit spirituality has been discussed here as one possible formative element in the way he set up the structure, genres, and overall approach of the *Commentarii.* His chronological-synoptical structure in the commentaries covering the Gospels, his use of scholastic categories to carry out his Pauline dual purposes,[92] his concern to accumulate the facts,[93] and his overall objectivity[94] whether in dealing with Protestant literature or in allowing his readers to draw their own conclusions from his evidence—all these characteristics of the *Commentarii* were probable products of a peculiarly Jesuit way of thinking about scripture and tradition, a way of thinking that developed in Salmerón over a period of years and had become second nature to him.

The eminent historian Jean Delumeau has included Salmerón's *Commentarii* among examples of the new "positive theology" in the sixteenth century.[95] Salmerón himself witnesses how the Society of Jesus, with its demanding educational standards and its equally demanding method of spiritual formation shaped its men into living examples of positive theology.

Appendix

Salmerón's *magnum opus* was issued under the following titles in the 1612–15 edition. The title page to the first volume reads:

Alfonsi   1
Salmeronis
Toletani,
e societate Iesu
Theologi Praeclarissimi,   5
COMMENTARII
in evangelicam historiam,
Et in Acta Apostolorum:
Nunc primum in lucem editi.
Addita est Auctoris Vita, per R. P. Petrum   10
Ribadeneiram conscripta.
Cum duplici Indice locupletissimo.
Ad Reverendiss. & Illustriss.
D.D. Julium, Episcopum Herbipolensem, Franciae
Orientalis Ducem, et S.R. Imperii Principem, &c.   15
Coloniae Agrippinae
Apud Atonium Hierat, et Ioan. Gymni.
Anno M. DCXII.
Cum gratia et privileg. S. Caesarcem Maiestat.

Volumes 2 through 12 retained the first eight lines only, plus the standard publication information, but each contained a separate subtitle, as follows:

Tomus Secundus,
QUI INSCRIBITUR DE VER-
bi ante Incarnationem gestis.
(1612)

Tomus Tertius,
QUI INFANTIA ET PUERI-

tia Domini nostri Iesu Christi inscribitur.
(1612)

Tomus Quartus,
DE HISTORIA VITAE DOMINI
nostri Iesu Christi, usque ad Do-
minicam Coenam.
(1612)

Tomus Quintus,
DE SERMONE DOMINI NO-
stri Iesu Christi in Monte.
(1612)

Tomus Sextus,
DE MIRACULIS DOMINI NOSTRI
Iesu Christi.
(1613)

Tomus Septimus,
DE PARABOLIS DOMINI NOSTRI
Iesu Christi.
(1613)

Tomus Octavus,
QUI DE DISPUTATIONIBUS
Domini inscribitur.
(1613)

Tomus Nonus,
QUI DE SERMONE IN COENA
ad Apostolos habito inscribitur.
(1613)

Tomus Decimus,
QUI DE PASSIONE ET MORTE
Domini nostri Iesu Christi inscribitur.
(1613)

Tomus Undecimus,
QUI DE RESURRECTIONE, ET
Ascensione Domini inscribitur.
(1614)

Tomus Duodecimus,
QUI DE ECCLESIAE NASCENTIS
exordijs, & in acta Apostolorum,
inscribitur.
(1614)

Volumes 13 through 16 contain the remainder of the New Testament canon and bear different general headings, beginning with volume thirteen in which is Salmerón's commentary on the Letter to the Romans:

COMMENTARII IN OMNES
Epistolas B. Pauli, & Canonicas; in quatuor tomos di-
stributi, quos versa pagina invenies; quorum hic
est primus, in ordine autem
TOMUS DECIMUS TERTIUS
(1614)

COMMENTARIORUM IN
Epistolas P. Pauli Tomus II. in ordine autem,
Tomus Decimus Quartus;
CONTINENS EXPOSITIONEM
in utramque B. Pauli Apostoli Epistolam
ad Corinthios.
(1614)

DISPUTATIONUM IN EPISTO-
las Divi Pauli tomus TERTIUS; in ordine autem
tomus xv.
In quo alii tres Libri continentur.
SEXTUS IN EPISTOLAS AD GA-
latas, ad Ephesios, ad Philipp. ad Colossenses, &
in utramq; ad Thessalonicenses. Septimus
in utramq; ad Timotheum, ad Titum,
& Philemonem. Octavus in Epistolam ad Hebraeos.
(1615)

DISPUTATIONUM IN EPISTOLAS CANONICAS,
& Apocalypsim TOMUS QUARTUS, ac omnium operum
postremus, in ordine autem
TOMUS XVI.
Apponuntur in fine aliquot Epistolae eiusdem Authoris,
quibus ad nonnulla sacra interrogata
respondet.
(1615)

The shift in styles and wording suggests that Pérez's editorial work effectively began at least after the Book of Acts.

Notes

1. Jean Delumeau, *Catholicism between Luther and Voltaire: A New View of the Counter-Reformation,* trans. Jeremy Moiser, intro. John Bossy (London: Burns and Oates, 1977) p. 35. Trans. from *Le catholicisme entre Luther et Voltaire,* 1971.
2. Though other efforts at founding a university had proceeded as far back as 1293, the plan for the University of Alcalá was proposed by Archbishop Francisco

Jiménez de Cisneros to Pope Alexander VI, who issued a bull approving its foundation on 13 April 1499. "On 24 July 1508, Cisneros went to Alcalá with a scholastic
colony recruited in Salamanca to found his College of San Ildefonso, "according to
The Catholic Encyclopedia, s.v. "Alacalá, University of," by Ramón Ruiz Amado.

3. William V. Bangert, S.J., *Claude Jay and Alfonso Salmerón: Two Early Jesuits*
(Chicago: Loyola University Press, 1985), p. 154 [hereafter cited as "Bangert"].
Salmerón's first biographer was Pedro de Ribadeneira, S.J., *La Vida y muerte del
padre Alonso Salmeron* (Madrid, 1595) [hereafter cited as *"Salmeron"*]; reprinted in
Ribadeneira's *Historias de la Contrarreforma,* with introduction and notes by Eusebio Rey, S.J., (Madrid: Biblioteca de Autores Cristianos, 1945), pp. 582–99 [here-
after cited as *"Contrarreforma"*]. For the later editions of this in Latin (1604) and
French (1695), see Auguste Carayon, *Bibliographie historique de la Compagnie de
Jésus, ou Catalogue des ouvrages relatifs a l'histoire des Jésuites, depuis leur origine
jusqu'à nos jours* (Paris: August Durand, Libraire, 1864), p. 345 (pt. 4: Biographies
particulières, entries 2554–55). Sixteen years after the publication of Carayon's bibliography appeared the second biography of Salmerón, Giuseppe Boero, S.J., *Vita del
Servo di Dio P. Alfonso Salmerone* (Florence, 1880) [hereafter cited as "Boero"].
Bangert's biography surpasses these works in its scope, though it depends upon them
for many details.

4. Bangert, p. 587. Notes 27, 28 (Bangert, p. 396), cite Ribadeneira, pp. 587–88.

5. Henry D. Sedgwick, *Ignatius Loyola: An Attempt at an Impartial Biography*
(New York: The Macmillan Company, 1923), p. 111 [hereafter cited as "Sedgwick"].

6. Bangert, p. 155. James Brodrick, S.J., *The Origin of the Jesuits* (London:
Longmans, Green and Co., 1940), p. 40, n. 2, cited the *Monumenta Historica Societatis Jesu* [hereafter "MHSJ"], *Monumenta Xaveriana* 1:227, and wrote of this
meeting: "[Ignatius] was the first person they encountered in the streets of Paris when
they arrived there in 1533, still little more than boys, with not enough French to order
their dinners."

7. Bangert, p. 156.

8. Leonard von Matt and Hugo Rahner, S.J., *St. Ignatius of Loyola: A Pictorial
Biography* (Chicago: Henry Regnery Company, 1956), p. 59. Rahner noted that on 13
March 1533, "after a stiff examination, [Iñigo] was solemnly promoted to the Licentiate of Philosophy in the Calvary Chapel of Sainte Geneviève. This gave him the right
to receive the title of Master of Philosophy in a further public ceremony. However, as
this involved a considerable outlay, Inigo postponed the ceremony until [14] March
1535." Sedgwick, p. 35, stated that Ignatius received the master's degree "in Lent of
1533," while Brodrick, *Origin of the Jesuits,* p. 41, put the conferral of the master's at
"1534, at Easter." This was not a typographical error, since Brodrick repeated it in his
Saint Francis Xavier, 1506–1552 (Garden City, N.Y.: Image Books, 1957), p. 28.

9. Du Bellay would become Bishop of Paris in 1532 (keeping that office until 1551)
and was elevated to the cardinalate in 1535.

10. Erasmus answered these charges in his *Declarationes ad censuras lutetiae
vulgatas sub nomine facultatis theologiae parisiensis,* in the Leiden edition (LB)
9:814E ff.

11. See B. J. Kidd, ed., *Documents of the Continental Reformation* (Oxford:
Clarendon Press, 1911), no. 270, pp. 526–28.

12. In 1534 alone, the following were enacted: the Submission of the Clergy and
Restraint of Appeals; the Ecclesiastical Appointments Act; Act Forbidding Papal
Dispensations and the Payment of Peter's Pence; the First Act of Succession; the
Supremacy Act; the Second Act of Succession; the Treasons Act; and the Abjuration
of Papal Supremacy by the Clergy. Then followed the Act for the Dissolution of the
Smaller Monasteries (1536), the Royal Injunctions of Henry VIII (first, 1536; second,

1538), Act for the Dissolution of the Greater Monasteries (1539), all capped by the Six Articles (1539). See Henry Gee and William John Hardy, *Documents Illustrative of English Church History, Compiled from Original Sources* (London: Macmillan and Co., 1910; reprint, New York: Kraus Reprint Co., 1972), pp. 195–319.

13. Bangert, pp. 109–10.

14. Bangert, p. 112.

15. The late William Bangert, S.J., spent the final months of his life editing the galleys of a full-length biography of Claude Jay and Alfonso Salmerón. Readers interested in more than the elliptical sketch given here are pointed to *Claude Jay and Alfonso Salmerón: Two Early Jesuits* (Chicago: Loyola University Press, 1985), upon which this paper draws heavily for its biographical details.

16. See Bangert, p. 164 ff.

17. Eight months during 1561–62, according to Bangert, p. 294. See pp. 259–63 for a discussion of this.

18. Bangert, p. 294. Also see chaps. 9, 10, pp. 296–352.

19. Bangert, p. 224.

20. For example, Ignatius once wrote the fathers at Trent of his desire to have the council officially sanction the Society. Salmerón wrote back on behalf of the others, noting that no order had ever sought conciliar approval; that no council had ever done so; that the *Constitutions* were not in shape to present to the fathers; and, last but not least, that other orders would take offense at such a move. Ignatius accepted the suggestion and did not pursue the matter. See Bangert, p. 215.

21. Bangert, p. 167. They went by way of Scotland, landing in Ulster on 23 February 1542 (p. 169). They stayed only a little over thirty-four days, shocked at the widespread treachery and violence, and returned to Scotland by 9 April 1542 (p. 171).

22. Bangert, pp. 224–36.

23. Bangert, p. 175. Claude Jay, S.J., also was present at Trent as "procurator, or deputy with vote" of the archbishop and cardinal of Augsburg, Otto Truchsess von Waldburg, said James Brodrick, *The Origin of Jesuits* (Garden City, N.Y.: Image Books, 1960), p. 187. Bangert, p. 68, explained von Waldburg's appointment of Jay as due to the cardinal's desire to attend the Diet of Regensburg (the Conference of Ratisbon) in 1541.

24. Alphonso Salmeron, *Epistolae*, 2 vols., Monumenta Historica Societatis Jesu, nos. 31–32 (Madrid: Gabriel Lopez, 1906–7; reprint, Rome: Institutum Historicum Societatis Jesu, 1971–72), No. 9 (Trent, ca. 10 July 1546), 1:26–27 [hereafter cited as ["Epistolae"].

25. Ibid., *Epistolae*, no. 9, 1:27. "Después, assi' por este buen odor como por el conversar, podemos dezir que quasi todos los perlados de todas tres naciones, italianos, espagñoles y françeses, nos tienen special amor, y tienen zelos si no son de nosotros visitados; y esto tanto, que los que más eran contrarios entre los spagñoles, agora son públicos pregoneros en loar y dezir bien y conbidarnos á comer y comunicarnos lo que an de dezir en las congregationes etc. [par.] Después desto ay muchos perlados doctos, etiam en las cosas sagradas, que, primero que digan, nos muestran sus votos para que sobrellos les digamos nuestro pareçer; y otros que, aunque sean doctos en otras facultades, no lo son en theologia, quieren ser primero informados á boca, y después que de verbo ad verbum les digamos lo que an de dezir." Cited in Bangert, pp. 178–79. The *contrarios* probably were the same Spanish prelates who—according to Graf Paul von Hoensbroech, *Der Jesuitenorden: eine Enzyklopädie aus den Quellen,* 2 vols. (Bern: Paul Haupt, 1927), s.v. "Konzil von Trient," 2: 87—scorned the patchwork clothing of their countrymen: ". . . [K]uehler war die Aufnahme bei den Bischoefen; die Spanier schaem sich fast der zwei jugendlichen, armselig gekleideten Landsleute."

26. The text is in *Concilium tridentinum, diariorum, actorum, epistularum, trac-*

tatuum, nova collectio, 13 vols, ed. Stephen Ehses and Göres Gesellschaft (Freiburg-im-Breisgau: Herder, 1901–61), 5²:265–72 [hereafter cited as "CT"]. This was translated in an appendix to a doctoral dissertation by John C. Hughes, "Alfonso Salmerón: His Work at the Council of Trent," (Ph.D. diss., University of Kentucky, 1973), appendix 2, pp. 221–35 [hereafter cited as "Hughes"]. Critical discussion of Salmerón's teaching on justification can be found in Hanns Rückert, *Die Rechtfertigungslehre auf dem tridentinischen Konzil* (Bonn: A. Marcus and E. Weber, 1925), pp. 100–106, 134–42, and 144–49.

27. Bangert, p. 180.

28. Parts of the speech delivered on 16 October were published only in this century, as noted by Bangert, p. 403, n. 19. See "De Imputativa Justitia," in "En el IV centenario de un voto tridentino del Jesuita Alfonso Salmerón sobre la doble justicia," Jesús Olazaran, S.J., ed., *Estudios Eclesiasticos* 20 (1946): 211–40.

29. CT 12:658–62, "Doctrina iustificationis conscripta ab Alfonso Salmerone [Mense septembri 1546]," and CT 12:727–36, "Ex epistola B. Pauli apostoli ad Romanos. Quid sit iustificari per fidem et gratis, sine operibus. Quid sit non imputari peccatum."

30. Hubert Jedin, *Papal Legate at the Council of Trent: Cardinal Seripando,* trans. Frederic C. Eckhoff (St. Louis: B. Herder Book Co., 1947), p. 355, noted Filheul's use of Salmerón's and Lainez's suggestions in his speech. Also see Bangert, p. 189.

31. Bangert, p. 194.

32. Bangert, p. 269.

33. See the following references in CT for Salmerón's work on penance (CT 6, pt. 3¹, pp. 84–85, 278); orders (ibid., pp. 110–12), and the eucharist (ibid., pp. 375–78, 380–82). CT 6, pt. 3³, is composed of summaries and responses by Salmerón and Lainez to the session at Bologna on the Eucharist, Penance, Extreme Unction, orders, matrimony, purgatory, indulgences, and the Sacrifice of the Mass. According to Joseph de Guibert, S.J.—*La Spiritualité de la Compagnie de Jésus, esquisse historique,* Bibliotheca Instituti Historici S. I., vol. 4 (Rome: Institutum Historicum S. I., 1953) [hereafter cited as "Guibert"], chap. 9, "Mouvements spirituels et controverses," p. 370—Salmerón and Oviedo were ordered by Ignatius to prepare a eucharistic directory in 1554. Salmerón fulfilled this duty, probably drawing upon his materials from Trent, and his manuscript circulated for several years in Rome until it appeared in print at Naples in 1556.

34. Jedin, *Seripando,* p. 631, referred to the "obstructionism of the first papal theologian, Salmeron," who "consumed four times the period allotted to him and stubbornly refused to shorten his address in any way. By an unforgivable weakness on their part, the legates allowed themselves to be intimidated."

35. Bangert, pp. 163–64.

36. E.g., A. Lynn Martin, *The Jesuit Mind: The Mentality of an Elite in Early Modern France* (Ithaca: Cornell University Press, 1988), chap. 4, "The Salvation of Souls," esp. pp. 69–71.

37. For example, Cardinal Giovanni Morone had requested Jesuit help against "Lutheranizers" in Modena during 1543. Salmerón was assigned, but apparently emphasized the efficacy of good works more than made Morone comfortable. After four months the Jesuit was shuttled back to Rome, courtesy of the *spirituli*—but he would clash with Morone again. Years later, Morone would be jailed for heresy. His lawyer would argue that Salmerón had been dismissed not for doctrinal reasons, but for an objectionable habit of naming names from the pulpit! (This homiletical practice was allowed to die a quiet death by later preachers in the Society, though it was revived by some eighteenth-century Puritans, with equally memorable results.) Still, Salmerón was favored by others outside the Morone circle. Bangert, pp. 239–40.

38. Bangert, p. 175.

39. "Oratio Alphonsi Salmeronis theologi de societate Jesu in concilio Tridentino habita, die festivitatis divi Joannis evangelista, ann. M. D. XLVI," preserved in Johannes Dominicus Mansi, *Sacrorum conciliorum, nova et amplissima collectio,* 60 vols. (Paris: Huberti Welter, 1901–27), 33:1117–1127. Jean-François Gilmont, S.J., *Les Écrits Spirituels des Premiers Jésuites, inventaire commenté* (Rome: Institutum Historicum S. I., 1961) [hereafter cited as "Gilmont"], p. 156, lists the original title that was changed by Mansi. The sermon has been translated by Hughes, appendix 3, pp. 236–52. For Salmerón's emphasis on the need for episcopal residence, one of the more hotly debated issues for the council concerned with reform, see *Alphonsi Salmeronis Doctoris Toletani atque in Concilio Tridentino Theologi Doctrina de Jurisdictionis Episcopalis Origine ac Ratione,* J. B. Andries, ed. (Mainz, 1871). Salmerón was displeased to learn of this sermon's publication, however, for he did not believe, at least in 1547, that publishing was part of the Jesuit way of "simplicity, modesty, and a total charity to our neighbor," according to Bangert, p. 188.

40. Bangert, p. 190.

41. H. Outram Evennett, *The Spirit of the Counter-Reformation,* ed. with a postscript by John Bossy (Cambridge: Cambridge University Press, 1968; reprint, Notre Dame: University of Notre Dame Press, 1970), pp. 16–17, 26–27 [hereafter cited as "Evennett"]. Would the records of this region indicate that Salmerón's preaching played a direct role in the renewal?

42. For example, on Christmas Day in 1547 about five hundred received communion, along with a number of reconciled Protestants. Bangert, pp. 196–97.

43. Salmerón, *Epistolae,* no. 32 (Venice, 27 April 1549, to Ignatius), 1:74.

44. Bangert, pp. 294–95, and pp. 324–28, connecting early Jesuit preaching with the revival of sacred oratory. On this topic see the major work by John W. O'Malley, S.J., *Praise and Blame in Renaissance Rome: Rhetoric, Doctrine, and Reform in the Sacred Orators of the Papal Court, c. 1450–1521,* Duke Monographs in Medieval and Renaissance Studies, no. 8 (Durham, N.C.: Duke University Press, 1979), esp. chaps. 4 through 6, pp. 123–237. For the decades that followed, see Frederick J. McGinness, "Preaching Ideals and Practice in Counter-Reformation Rome," *The Sixteenth Century Journal* 11 (1980):109–27.

45. Bangert, p. 198.

46. Constancio, Gutierrez, S.J., *Españoles en Trento,* with a Prologue by Joaquín Pérez Villanueva, [in series] Corpus Tridentinum Hispanicum, no. 1 (Valladolid: Valencia, 1951), pp. 62–63 [hereafter cited as "Gutierrez"]. Gutierrez noted the sermons at Trent, and also the publication of his *Sermones in Parabolam [-as] Evangelicam [-as] totius anni,* issued at Cologne in 1612 (along with his New Testament commentaries), by the firm Hierat and Gymnicum.

47. Bangert, pp. 174–208.

48. Bangert, p. 220.

49. Salmerón, *Epistolae,* no. 269 (Naples 3 February 1566, to Borgia), 2:72. "Yo no puedo dezir otro con verdad, sino que siento falta de vista y de oyr, y falta de dientes principales, y otros están como de partida, y lo que importa más, falta de fuerças corporales." Translated in Bangert, p. 324.

50. Salmerón, *Epistolae,* no. 317 (Naples 3 June 1569, to Borgia), 2:187. Cited in Bangert, p. 329. Borgia replied quickly eight days later in *Epistolae,* no. 317a (Rome 11 June 1569), 2:188–89.

51. Salmerón, *Epistolae,* no. 324 (Naples 19 May 1570, to Borgia), 2:202. "Agora me resuelo de no saber nada, y do no tener parte ninguna; y esto sin figura de hypérbole: hago, y deshago, y borro, aunque por este conoçimiento no e dexado de trabajar." Bangert, p. 329.

52. Bangert, p. 350. "One phrase he recited was: 'I shall be satisfied when your glory shall appear.'" This was likely drawn from Psalm 102:16–17.

53. Gutierrez, pp. 62–63. Compare Gilmont's explanation of the publication history, pp. 157–58.

54. *Commentarii,* praefatio, **4.

55. *Commentarii,* praefatio, p. **3, verso, cited Ecclesiasticus 18:6.

55. *Commentarii,* praefatio, **4. "Cogor oculos claudere ad infantiam meam, ruditatem in scribendo, ac impolitum stylum."

57. *Commentarii,* praefatio, **3.

58. *Commentarii,* praefatio, p. **6.

59. 1 Timothy 6:20a, "O Timothee depostium custodi, devitans profanas vocum novitates et oppositiones falsi nominis scientiae."

60. 2 Timothy 1:14.

61. *Commentarii,* praefatio, p. **4, verso. " 'Depostium custodi. Quid est,' inquit, 'depositum? Id est, quod creditum est, non quod à te inventum: non ducens, sed sequens. [. . .] Per te posteritas gratuletur intellectum, quod ante vetustas non intellectum venerabatur. Evadem tantùm quae didicisti, doce, ut cùm dicas novè, non dicas nova.' " This is an abbreviated quotation from Vincent of Lérins's *Commonitorium primum,* chap. 22, which can be found in PL 50:667. Salmerón's quotation skipped Vincent's somewhat repetitious elaboration of the *non ducens, sed sequens* idea. The bracket and ellipsis dots in the quotation show where the deletion occurred.

62. E.g., C. S. Lewis, *The Discarded Image: An Introduction to Medieval and Renaissance Literature* (Cambridge: Cambridge University Press, 1964), p. 192, quoted Geoffrey de Vinsauf's principle of *expolitio,* "Its formula is 'Let the same thing be disguised by variety of form; be different yet the same'—multiplice forma Dissimuletur idem; varius sis et tamen idem."

63. *Commentarii,* praefatio, p. **4, verso.

64. Vincent's statements on the relation between scripture and tradition suggested the difficulties Protestants later would experience. For example, in a consistent application of the *sola scriptura* principle, Protestants could only leave the simple words of the Bible unreconstructed and uninterpreted, or else *sola scriptura* itself would prevent their negative criticisms of the Catholic theological tradition, as well as their own positive insights, from being passed on to a second generation. Why? Even though Protestants believed their biblical interpretations were true, and therefore the marrow of divinity for future generations, once they desired to transmit their truth to others (without simply repeating the words of the Bible), they would have formed their *own* tradition. Yet their ruling idea of *sola scriptura* would again have to come into effect, ultimately questioning and destroying their "true tradition" which by definition was based on extrapolations from scripture. It was impossible that a principle developed apart from tradition, indeed developed as an antitradition, could become tradition itself. Part of Protestantism's own subsequent history bears out the seriousness of this problem.

65. E.g., Augustine, *De doctrina christiana,* book 4, chap. 4.

66. See Salmerón, *Epistolae,* nos. 28 (Verona, ca. Nov–Feb 1548–49) and 29 (Verona, ca. 10 Feb 1549), both to Ignatius, 1:71–72. This quotation was cited in French in the *Dictionnaire de la Bible,* 5 vols. (Paris: Letouzey et Ané, 1895–1912), 3:1403–21, s.v. "Jésuites (travaux des) sur les Saintes Écritures," by August Durand, p. 1405 [hereafter cited as "Durand"].

67. See the appendix above, which shows the shift in style between volumes 1 through 11 and 12 through 16, the latter perhaps reflecting Pérez's editorial work. The titles and substitles to volumes 12 through 16 are uneven, at times seeming typeset almost in haste, or at least with less care than in preceding texts. This may reflect either Pérez's control, or his absence when the publisher's typesetter did his job.

68. "Synoptic" here is used not to refer to the first three gospels, but according to

its literal Greek meaning.

69. E.g., *The Spiritual Exercises of St. Ignatius: A New Translation Based on Studies in the Language of the Autograph,* trans. Louis J. Puhl, S.J. (Chicago: Loyola University Press, 1951) [hereafter cited as *"Spiritual Exercises"*]. The second through the fourth weeks, plus "The Mysteries of Our Lord: (nos. 261–312), illustrate this point.

70. For the medieval methods of scripture study see Pierre Riché and Guy Lobrichon, eds., *Le Moyen Age et la Bible,* vol. 4 in *Bible de tous les temps* (Paris: Éditions Beauchesne, 1984), sec. "Étudier la Bible," chaps. 1–3, pp. 147–231 [hereafter cited as "Riché and Lobrichon"]; also, the succinct discussion by M.-D. Chenu, O.P., *Nature, Man, and Society in the Twelfth Century,* preface by Etienne Gilson; trans. Jerome Taylor and Lester K. Little (Chicago: University of Chicago Press, 1957; trans. from *La théologie a douzième siècle,* Paris: J. Vrin, 1957), pp. 146,291–300 [hereafter cited as "Chenu"].

71. The *prolegomenon* genre naturally appeared at the head of the actual commentaries themselves, comprising all of volume 1's nearly 550 pages. Salmerón used an essentially deductive approach, beginning with discussions of the nature and veracity of the sacred scriptures (*prolegomena* 1–2) and then descending to more particular questions about them. Some of the more important *prolegomena* treated were: the German, Greek, Septuagint, and Vulgate editions of the biblical text (3–6); *canones* for grasping the literal sense (9–10); *regulae* for properly approaching the Gospels (11); the need for Latin, Greek, and Hebrew, following his order (13); Hebrew and Greek idioms and phrases, verbs, and participial constructions (14–16); the place of humane studies and of scholastic theology for the exegete (17–18); the differences between the Old and New Testaments (22); the name, reality, dignity, etc. of the *Evangelion* (24); why Jesus did not write but spoke his Gospel (25); why Jesus wanted only his disciples to write his story, not secular historians and profane authors (27); and whether the Apostles amplified Jesus' story and doctrine, as asserted by unbelievers (28). These introductory topics are among the more important in Salmerón's first volume, though many other *prolegomena* of equal significance have been ommitted in this brief précis. Indeed, even the topics mentioned above disguise the complexity within some of them; for example, there were 150 canons discussed pertaining to the appropriation of the literal sense of scripture.

72. In *Commentarii* 1:438B he cited ". . . ex Graecis quidem Origenes, Hippolytus Martyr, Theophilus Antiochenus, Theodorus Heracleota, Apollinarius Laodicenus, Didymus Alexandrinus, Chrysostomus, Cyrillus, Theophylactus, Leontius, Euthymius, Nonnus Panopolitanus: ex Latinis verò, Hilarius, Victorinus, Fortunatianus, Ambrosius, Hieronymus, Augustinus, Gregorius, Beda, Remigius, Anselmus, Haymo, Rupterus Tuitensis."

73. In *Commentarii* 1:335B–339A, "Prolegomenon XVIII. An studium Scholasticae Theologiae opem & adiumentum adferat ad sacras literas faciliùs percipiendas, & aliis interpretandas," Salmerón listed the following luminaries (p. 336A): "B. Thomas, & B. Bonaventura, Albertus Magnus, & Alexander Halensis, Petrus Lombardus, qui primus sententias Theologicas compilavit, & denique B. Augustinus, & Damascenus: ex quorum fontibus omnes scholastici potârunt, ut videri possint omnium eorum qui Theologiam profitentur, parentes." Also see *Spiritual Exercises,* Rules for Thinking with the Church, no. 363, which expresses preference for the scholastics.

74. In *Commentarii,* praefatio, 1:**6–7, he noted, "Fateor enim me ad hoc opus moliendum vehementer fuisse permotum, ex quo in manus nostras recentiorum Haereticorum, id est, Theodori Bezae, & Augusti Malorati . . ." and then he listed the following heretics whose works he also would cite: "Lutheri, Buceri, Zuinglii, Oecolampadii, Melanchthonis, Calvini, Brentii, Musculi, Bullingeri, & aliorum huius farinae."

75. John W. O'Malley, S.J., "Erasmus and the History of Sacred Rhetoric: The Ecclesiastes of 1535," (Inaugural Bainton Presidential Lecture) *The Erasmus of Rotterdam Society Yearbook* 5 (1985), p. 5, noted the "three tasks the scholastics considered peculiarly their own: *legere, disputare, praedicare.*" Salmerón's dedication to preaching has been shown and his commentaries' genres also expressed his labors at reading *(tractatus)* and defending *(disputatio)* the meaning of the scriptural text.

76. This statement is made after having consulted the writers contained in Migne's PG and PL, as well as other sixteenth century authors given in Migne's *Scripturae sacrae cursus completus, ex commentariis omnium perfectissimis ubique habitis, et a magna parte episcoporum necnon theologorum europae catholicae, universim ad hoc interrrogatorum, designatis, unice conflatus, plurimis annotantibus presbyteris ad docendos levitas pascendosve populos alte positis,* 28 vols. (Paris: Migne, 1837–41) [hereafter cited as "Migne, *SS*"]. Included among these were Bellarmine, Erasmus, Maldonado, Cajetan, Calvin, Masius, Piscator, Sà, Van den Steen (à Lapide), Vatable, and others. Luther can also be included in this generalization.

77. Bangert, p. 337.

78. E.g., Francis Sweeney, S.J., *Bernardine Realino: Renaissance Man* (New York: Macmillan, 1951), p. 80. Also see some additional quotations (translated into French) in Durand, p. 1406.

79. See Guttiérrez, p. 58, n. 84.

80. I.e., *Dictionnaire de la Bible* (1903), s.v. "Jésuites (travaux des) sur les Saintes Écritures," by Auguste Durand; *The Catholic Encyclopedia* (1912), s.v. "Salmeron, Alphonsus," by Walter Drum, S.J.

81. The following scholars basically depend on the work of Fernand de Lanversin, S.J.: Victor Baroni, *Le Contre-Réforme devant la Bible: la question biblique* (Lausanne: Imprimerie la Concorde, 1943), p. 246; Gilmont, *Les Écrits spirituels des premiers Jésuites* (1961), p. 157, n. 14; John C. Hughes, "Alfonso Salmerón: His Work at the Council of Trent" (Ph.D. diss. University of Kentucky, 1974), pp.30–35; William Bangert, S.J., *Jay and Salmerón* (1985), pp. 341–42; and, recently, Guy Bedouelle and Bernard Rouseel, eds., *Le temps des Réformes et la Bible,* vol. 5: *Bible de tous les temps* (Paris: Éditions Beauchesne, 1989), p. 362.

82. I.e., *Dictionnaire de théologie Catholique,* s.v. "Salmeron, Alphonse," by Fernand de Lanversin, S.J. (14, pt. 1:1040 ff.), written in 1939.

83. De Lanversin, p. 1041, par. 3.

84. Ibid., p. 1042, par. 5.

85. Ibid., p. 1047, par. 3.

86. Ibid., p. 1047, par. 4.

87. Ibid., p. 1042, par. 6.

88. Ibid., p. 1043, par. 3.

89. Erasmus's *Paraphrases,* too, have been neglected for centuries as basically insignificant until recently. While his stature and influence certainly explain part of this exploration into his "complete" corpus, there is no doubt that a new openness to what constitutes "commentary" and "theology" also have played a role here. See, for example, Jacques Chomarat, "Grammar and Rhetoric in the Paraphrases of the Gospels by Erasmus," *The Erasmus of Rotterdam Society Yearbook* 1 (1981):30–68, and the very important book by Friedhelm Krüger, *Humanistische Evangelienauslegung: Desiderius Erasmus von Rotterdam als Ausleger der Evangelien in seinen Paraphrasen,* Beiträge zur historischen Theologie, no. 68 (Tübingen: J. C. B. Mohr, 1986).

90. *Commentarii,* praefatio, **5. "[par.] Caeterùm cùm duplex possit contingere in citandis Patrum testimoniis extremum: nam quidam immodicè, ac densè hoc faciunt, & interdum ubi minimè est opus, cùm res qua de agitur, in aperto sit atque conspicua, nullisque probationis aut testimonii indiga: alii verò etiam in locis ab obscurissimis, &

ad intelligendum difficillimis, atque adeò antiquorum Doctorum expositiones exigentibus, hoc tam ieiunè ac parcè faciunt, ut cogitare in illis iudicum desiderare, & maiorem antiquitatis cognitionem: nos viam mediam amplectemur, ita ut neque prolixitas, neque parcitas, ut existimo, reprehendi valeat: quanquam ubi cum Haereticis congredimur, aut dogma fidei aliquod confirmamus, densiores atque longiores consultò esse voluerimus."

91. *Spiritual Exercises,* presuppositions, no. 22.

92. *Spiritual Exercises,* nos. 261–363.

93. Spiritual Exercises, no. 2, but also the whole Ignatian framework for approaching the religious life with its attention to detail, organization, and reflection.

94. *Spiritual Exercises,* no. 22.

95. Delumeau, p. 42. "The New Testament commentaries of the Jesuit Salmerón, the patristic publications of the Benedictines of Saint-Maur, the *Annales Ecclesiastici* of Baronio, among many other works, bear witness to this rapid rise of positive theology."

Parents and Children in the Sermons of Père Bourdaloue: A Jesuit Perspective on the Early Modern Family

LAWRENCE WOLFF

During Lent in 1671 the Jesuit Louis Bourdaloue gave a series of tremendously successful sermons in Paris at Notre Dame. Mme de Sévigné was regularly in attendance, and her famous letters to her beloved daughter in Provence were punctuated with exclamations on Bourdaloue. "Bourdaloue preached this morning beyond all the most beautiful sermons he has ever done," she wrote in one letter.[1] At another sermon her daughter was virtually present in spirit: "I dreamed twenty times of you, and wished you every time by me. You would have been ravished to hear it, and I still more ravished to see you hearing it."[2] That the sermons of Bourdaloue assumed such a tortuously intense mediating position between mother and daughter is all the more interesting for the fact that family relations were addressed as a delicate and important subject in his moral theology. His carefully and lengthily reasoned exhortations to moral and spiritual improvement touched upon relations between parents and children at precisely those points rendered sensitive by the evolutionary development of the family in early modern society and culture. Bourdaloue was the most celebrated Jesuit preacher in France in the reign of Louis XIV, delivering his sermons to "ravished" audiences in Paris and at court during the last three decades of the seventeenth century.[3] With Jesuit schools at the height of their prestige, the Jesuits immensely successful as educators of children, Bourdaloue offered an important Jesuit perspective on changing ideas about childhood itself.

Historiographical controversy over the early modern family was stimulated by the publication in 1960 of the trailbreaking work of Philippe Ariès on the history of childhood and family life. Ariès argued for a "discovery of childhood" dating from the Renaissance, a new level of attention to children that accompanied a new emphasis on the family in its nuclear and patriarchal form.[4] This attention was not necessarily benign, for, although it sometimes manifested itself in the more articulate expression of parental sentiment, as in the letters of Mme de Sévigné, it simultaneously stimulated increasingly attentive forms of discipline. Children became the targets of both sentiment

81

and discipline, generated within the newly focused family and the newly organized school. The Jesuits, in fact, played a prominent role in these developments, according to Ariès, who saw in the Jesuit college, its organization meticulously expressed in the *ratio studiorum,* the model institution for producing disciplined children.[5] Bourdaloue was a preacher, not a teacher, and his sermons were given to parents, not to children. He addressed both the sentimental and disciplinary issues of contemporary families. His reflections reveal that the Jesuit order was involved not only institutionally through its schools in the shaping of early modern childhood; within the order there was also a theological engagement with the social complications created by changing family values.

"Charity to Orphans"

The sermon on "Charity to Orphans" was delivered to an audience addressed as *Mesdames* at the Paris Hospital for Abandoned Children, which had been founded earlier in the seventeenth century by Saint Vincent de Paul. Bourdaloue began with Saint James: "Pure religion is this: to visit the orphans in their affliction." Asserting as his premise that God was the father of orphans, Bourdaloue argued that his audience, in helping them, might become "the cooperators and coadjutors" of God himself.

> He is their father, and when you enter into their needs by a beneficient charity, you take the place of their mothers in Jesus Christ. I say more than that: it is thus that you become, in a sense that is both true and honorable, like the mothers of Jesus Christ himself.[6]

Bourdaloue thus adapted his subject to seventeenth-century devotion to the child Jesus, which parallelled the growing secular attention to contemporary children. This devotion was especially cultivated by Berulle and the Oratorians. The reasoning of one Oratorian, P. Pierre Floeur, showed how forcefully these parallel devotions could reinforce each other.

> If the infancy of men has allurement for us, shall not the infancy of the God-Man have it too? May we not grant the charms of human childhood to this Divine Child? If children whose origin is tainted have yet a certain empire over our hearts, must we not give the same power to the Divine Child, whose conception is so pure?[7]

The "allurement" of infancy and the "charms" of childhood reflected a vocabulary of heightened sentimentality, and Bourdaloue could count on a complex sentimental response in inviting his audience to become mothers of Jesus Christ himself.

That Bourdaloue was following a rhetorical strategy of sentimental appeal was most evident in his evocation of an image of children within the sermon: "Here *(Voilà)* are the children for whom God charges you today, you and me."[8] From the text the historian cannot determine whether children of the hospital were actually present to provide a direct visual appeal to senti- ment—*Voilà*—or whether the children were to be seen only in the imagina- tion of the audience. The latter possibility of imaginative evocation would have brought to the Bourdaloue sermon something of the Ignation spiritual exercises, the envisioning of religious subjects, of the child Jesus Christ. Certainly Bourdaloue did not hesitate to color the children's image vividly, to color it red, and to add an aural evocation of children crying.

> If you fail them, the blood of these innocents will demand justice of God. For their blood, like that of Abel, has a voice that makes itself heard by God, and cries from earth to heaven. It is for you, *Mesdames,* of the utmost interest that the voice of this blood should never cry out against you.[9]

Bourdaloue played upon contemporary consciousness of children, aware that screaming babies are very loud indeed, and he endowed that mundane observation with a religious dimension: crying from earth to heaven. One must suppose that this rhetorical flourish was merely imaginative, for, if the children of the hospital had been present and crying, their voices would have seriously disrupted the sermon.

Present or absent, the children were in any case addressed by the preacher, who challenged them directly before returning to *Mesdames* in conclusion:

> And you, unfortunate troop, children whom crime caused to be born without rendering you criminal, even in your misfortune bless God the sovereign, the Father of mercies: *Laudate pueri, Dominum.* If you are the refuse of the world, there is in heaven a Creator who interests himself in your conservation, and to whom you are as dear as the rest of men. He is at the highest point of glory; but from that high point of glory, he does not disdain to lower his regard to your misery. . . . It is he who teaches the great ones of this century, and the greatest ones, themselves to descend, even to you; he who makes them go out from their palaces, from their rich and magnificent apartments, to range themselves beside you. . . . Lift up to him your voices to pay him the just tribute of your praises. It is the praise of children, and of children at the breast *(des enfans à la mamelle),* that pleases him above all others. . . . Along with your voices, lift up your hands still pure, and serve as intercessors for this whole assembly. *Mesdames,* you could not have more power- ful ones, to open for you the treasury of divine graces, and to obtain for you the happy eternity that you desire.[10]

The sentimental appeal reached its highest pitch as the children themselves were addressed, rhetorically evoked as a choir of uplifted voices and hands, envisioned even at the breast. Again the "charms" of human children were endowed with a specifically religious power, the sentimental appeal of chil- dren to adults reconceived as a purposeful appeal in prayer from children to God.

Bourdaloue was the better able to exploit the sentimental power of chil- dren since he obviously believed in their fundamental innocence. Religious attention to children in early modern Europe stimulated controversy over whether they were innocent or wicked creatures, with Protestants generally, and Puritans in particular, tending to take the latter view. Contemporary Puritan wisdom was emphatic: "The young child which lieth in the cradle is altogether inclined to evil."[11] Bourdaloue had no such reservations about the children of the foundling hospital. Though doubly tainted, by original sin and by presumed illegitimacy, he declared them to be "innocents"—"whom crime caused to be born without rendering you criminal." From that premise he could conjure with their images and cries all the more effectively.

The core of the sermon's argument, however, in which Bourdaloue explained why Saint James defined "pure religion" as visiting the orphans, was interestingly unsentimental, even antisentimental. According to Bourdaloue it was because visiting orphans revealed true love of one's neighbor (amour du prochain): "this supernatural love (amour surnaturel), this Christian love, pure love, which detached (dégagé) from all the interests of the world, regards the neighbor in God, and comforts him in God."[12] The emphasis on "detachment" clearly indicated that love for orphans was pure and supernatural precisely because it was not the "natural" love for one's own children. It was more pure, more Christian, to love the foundlings in the hospital than the children in one's own home. Bourdaloue underlined this with an odd reference to the Old Testament. In Deuteronomy the Israelites were enjoined by God to adopt orphans, to bring them into their families. Of Christians, however, God asked both more and less:

> In the new law, which is a law of love and mercy, in place of all that, God relies upon your charity; he does not oblige you to gather the orphans into your homes, or to have them eat at your tables, but is content that your charity should efficaciously provide for their establishment.[13]

It was domestically more convenient, but sentimentally more rigorous, requiring Christian love in the hospital establishment rather than the family home. Thus, while Bourdaloue obviously appreciated the sentimental power of childhood in his own century and sought to harness that power to his rhetorical strategies, he purposefully "detached" that sentiment from its "natural" context in the family. This was no accidental argument for the hospital occasion. It was consistent with his view of family relations, for he understood the potency of sentiment excited by children well enough to find it religiously suspect.

"The Love of God"

The sermon on "The Love of God" (L'Amour de Dieu) was a Lenten exhortation to love God properly. The first point of the sermon was that the love of God had to be "a love of preference" *(un amour de préférence)*, which meant, according to Saint Thomas, that "I prefer Him to all other creatures of the world," that is, to all that is not God."[14] Bourdaloue developed this point in a sort of syllogism:

> For in the end, if there was a creature who could be loved as much as God, it would be no longer a creature, but it would be God; and thus, if I love a creature as God, I love God as a creature: I do not love God as God, and therefore commit against him a very obvious outrage.[15]

In the sermon on "Charity to Orphans" Bourdaloue emphasized detachment and disinterestedness as qualities of Christian love for one's neighbor, loving "the neighbor in God." In the sermon on "The Love of God" he explicitly named the danger of an insufficiently disinterested love: it compromised one's love for God. He insisted on the strictest logic and clarity in sorting out the possible confusions of love and its objects—loving God as a creature, loving a creature as God.

This concern may be related to the general problem of passion in Baroque art and literature, its dangerous intensity, its potential misdirection toward wrong objects, its confusion of secular and religious sentiments. Bourdaloue himself expertly played upon that confusion when he promiscuously mixed his secular and religious signals in sympathetically presenting the orphans. The danger of competing loves for God and creature was not an abstract theologian's dilemma, and in the case of Mme de Sévigné it was frankly articulated as a psychological fact of seventeenth-century motherhood. She went on religious retreat during Holy Week in 1671, possibly the week after hearing Bourdaloue preach in Paris on "The Love of God," and wrote to her daughter about how her retreat was going awry.

> I mean to pray to God and give myself up to a thousand meditations. I intend to fast for all sorts of reasons, walk for as long as I have been in my room, and altogether be bored to death for the love of God. But, poor dear, what I shall do far better than all that is think about you.[16]

That was the story of her retreat: she began by praying to God and ended up writing letters of love to her daughter. It was just the kind of confusion that Bourdaloue feared when he preached on "love of preference."

There are some variations in different texts of the "The Love of God," especially in the discussion of "love of preference." In one version Bourdaloue concluded that section with an injunction to prefer God to one's honor. In another version there was added a passage that ended the argument more appropriately, by returning to the initial distinction between love of God and love of creature and then raising explicitly the issue of parents and children.

Love of preference, that is what will condemn so many worldly souls, who because they attached themselves to fragile and vile creatures, have loved them, adored them, served them, even to the point of forgetting the essential obligations that the charity due to the Creator imposed upon them. Let us not even speak of certain shameful passions. Love of preference, that is what will condemn so many fathers and mothers, who, because they idolized their children merited that God should reproach them as he did the high priest Héli: "Magis honorasti filios tuos quam me": Because you have made more state of your children than of me, I will reprove you.[17]

That this passage existed as a variation suggests that it was a point at which Bourdaloue's moral theology was still in development, unfixed. This was entirely appropriate to a century in which ideas about the family were changing significantly. Again, the case of Mme de Sévigné underlines Bourdaloue's sensitivity to the issues of his age. In 1671 she was reproached by the Jansenist Robert Arnauld d'Andilly for making her daughter into "an idol," was warned that "this sort of idolatry was as dangerous as any other."[18] The agreement between Jesuit and Jansenist was complete: excessive parental love was a form of idolatry, an offense against God. Such rigorousness on the part of Bourdaloue was consistent with his sermon at the foundling hospital, where charity to orphans was sustained by a more detached sentimental relation to children.

Religious concern about family attachments was already an issue within the Catholic Counter-Reformation during the century before Bourdaloue began to preach. Saint Ignatius saw the *Spiritual Excercises* as valuable for liberating oneself from "any inordinate attachment."[19] Saint Teresa in *The Way of Perfection* addressed the problem of family connections, with chapter 8 on "the great benefit of self-detachment, both interior and exterior, from all things created" and chapter 9 on "the great blessing that shunning their relatives brings to those who have left the world."[20] With perhaps unintended wit, she warned against visits from relatives: "A nun who wishes to see her relatives in order to please herself, and does not get tired of them after the second visit, must, unless they are spiritual persons and do her soul some good, consider herself imperfect."[21] Giving up visits from relatives was not enough, though, for "we must keep them out of our minds as much as we can, as it is natural that our desires should be attached to them more than to other people."[22] Saint Teresa, writing about the general category of "relatives" in the sixteenth century, seemed to suggest a more extended family and certainly was more concerned about nuns' attachments to their parents than to children of their own. In seventeenth-century France, however, there were two celebrated cases of nuns who triumphantly abandoned their children, Saint Jeanne de Chantal, who left behind a fourteen-year-old son in 1610 to found the Order of the Visitation, and Marie de l'Incarnation, who left an eleven-year-old son in 1631 and went overseas to establish the Ursulines of Quebec.[23]

These famous examples of holy abandonment dramatized the competing claims of piety and parenthood in the seventeenth century, but both mothers, like the nuns addressed by Saint Teresa, were women with religious vocations. What was striking about the message of Bourdaloue, later in the seventeenth century, was that he brought the same standard to bear upon the sentiments of lay parents who lived with and cared for their children in family domesticity. This may be partly attributed to the increasingly rigorous religious values of the Counter-Reformation, an extreme rigor sustained by the Jansenists in particular and sometimes matched by the Jesuits, who were otherwise accused of laxity. In part, however, Bourdaloue's ambivalence toward the family must be viewed in the context of increasingly articulated domestic attachments in early modern society, which inevitably provoked a religious response.

"The Duty of Fathers"

Family attachments were not only sentimental, for the early modern family was viewed more and more as a unit of disciplinary relations, in which an ideal of patriarchal authority subordinated wives to husbands and children to parents, especially to fathers. Bourdaloue addressed this issue in his sermon on "The Duty of Fathers with Regard to the Vocation of their Children." Just as the religious response to family sentiment started with the cases of parents with vocations, so the response to family discipline and paternal authority was first attentive to the problem of children with vocations. In fact, Bourdaloue began with the scriptural instance of Jesus Christ himself, at the age of twelve, lost and found by Mary and Joseph in the temple of Jerusalem, according to the gospel of Saint Luke:

> And his mother said unto him, Son, why hast thou thus dealt with us? Behold, thy father and I have sought thee sorrowing. And he said unto them, How is it that ye sought me? wist ye not that I must be about my Father's business? And they understood not the saying which he spake unto them.[24]

Bourdaloue supposed that, if Mary and Joseph had failed to understand Jesus Christ, it was still less likely that contemporary parents understood their duties to their children. He therefore proposed to explain "to fathers and mothers what they owe to their children, and to children what they owe to their fathers and mothers, in one of the greatest affairs of life, which is that of vocation and estate." He denied any intention of interfering in "the interior of your families" and claimed to restrict his domain to those aspects of family "government" in which "religion and conscience are interested."[25] Nevertheless, just by stipulating the affairs of both "vocation and estate," he easily extended his argument from the case of Jesus Christ to children with religious vocations, to all other children and their worldly estates. Thus

Bourdaloue delivered a sermon on the rights of children in an age that was generally much more attentive to the powers of parents.

He spoke, of course, to an audience of parents, and imposed upon them obligations of parenthood while denying them absolute authority over their children.

> I say it is not for you to dispose of your children with regard to their vocation and their choice of estate. And I add that you are nevertheless responsible to God for the choice your children make and the estate they embrace. . . . God does not want you yourself by your own full authority to determine for your children the estate in which they must become engaged. However, God demands of you an accounting for the estate in which your children become engaged.[26]

This restriction of authority undermined the patriarchal family and was potentially deeply subversive. For the ideological power of patriarchy in early modern Europe was founded on a widely trumpeted analogy between the omnipotence of God, the authority of the king in his kingdom, and the authority of the father in his family. These analogies were developed by such seventeenth-century theorists of absolute monarchy as Robert Filmer, author of *Patriarcha* in Stuart England, and Jacques-Bénigne Bossuet, court theologian to Louis XIV.

Counter-Reformation Catholicism was not immune to the attraction of triply reinforced authority, and in another sermon also entitled "The Duty of Fathers" the French Oratorian Jean Lejeune delivered a very different message from that of Bourdaloue.

> If you do not punish your children they profane the churches . . . if you knew the evil which would result for them . . . you would prefer to break their arms and legs.[27]

Ariès emphasizes the importance of corporal punishment in defining the disciplinary subordination of children in early modern France. It was essential to Jesuit schools with their famous discipline, but also to other schools and within families, throughout Europe, Protestant and Catholic. The historian Lawrence Stone, examining "The Reinforcement of Patriarchy" in this period, pointed to Puritan Massachusetts, where a child's disobedience to parents was sometimes punishable by death.[28] Bourdaloue, however, in the matter of children choosing their estates, allowed parents to employ advice and exhortation, but denied them the right to force and violence.[29] One observes an unexpected resemblance, in this matter of family affairs, between Bourdaloue and his exact contemporary John Locke. Both men were born in 1632, though the French Jesuit appears as a figure of the Counter-Reformation, while the English philosopher has been historically interpreted as a herald of the Enlightenment. Yet Bourdaloue's contractual approach to paternal duty—preaching "to fathers and mothers what they owe to their children, and to children what they owe to their fathers and mothers"—was certainly in the spirit of Locke. It was Locke who rebutted Filmer's *Patriarcha* in the treatises on government of 1689, arguing that a father's authority was only temporary, that children grow up to be free, that a family contract between parents and children was analogous to the political contract between governments and peoples. It was Locke, in *Some Thoughts Concerning Education* of 1693, who rejected the pedagogy of beating, the violent corporal authority of parents and teachers over children.[30] Thus he signaled a turning point in the culture of disciplinary patriarchal authority, marking the beginning of an ideology of liberation for children that would be most fully articulated by Rousseau in the eighteenth century. Yet there stood the Jesuit Bourdaloue, an orthodox Catholic of the late seventeenth century, preaching in strange agreement with Locke, across the cultural and ideological chasm that separated them. It was agreement on one distinct issue, but that issue, by virtue of contemporary analogies, was relevant to the whole nature of authority in early modern Europe.

Bourdaloue preached that fathers might dispose of the education and property of their children, but not of their "persons" *(personnes)* which left them free to choose an estate.[31] He spoke of the "injustice" committed against children by parents who violated this "natural right" *(droit naturel)*. He defended "the liberty of children" and denounced "the false pretensions of fathers and mothers" who assaulted that liberty.[32] The resemblances to Locke were not just of argument, but even of language, in Bourdaloue's vocabulary of persons and rights, liberty and injustice. Allowing all children to choose their worldly estates, he was especially concerned that those with religious vocations should have the "liberty" to enter the Church. Yet he emphatically condemned parents who forced their children to enter, describing indignantly the situation of a daughter pushed into the convent.

> One conducts this victim into the temple, feet and hands bound. . . . In the middle of a ceremony, brilliant for the spectators, but funereal for the person who is its subject, one presents her to the priest, and makes of her a sacrifice, which, far from glorifying and pleasing God, becomes execrable in his eyes. Oh! Christians! What an abomination![33]

Here Bourdaloue went beyond Locke to strike a chord of resemblance to Diderot and his scandalously anticlerical eighteenth-century vision of convent life. Interestingly, Bourdaloue did not reserve his disapproval only for the coercion of daughters in matters of religion. He also rejected forcing a daughter into marriage against her will: "If she must be bound, isn't it just that you allow her at least the power to choose herself the chain."[34] Such a bitter, even ironic, comment suggests that Bourdaloue fully understood, with grave misgivings, the parallel positions of wives and children in patriarchal society.

Bourdaloue's advocacy of children's rights may appear all the more unexpected since he was so suspicious of parental love as a form of idolatry.

Certainly he never counseled parents to respect children's liberty out of love. In fact, his reasoning was far from sentimental. He argued that God was the first father of all men, the father of all fathers, and therefore human fathers merely administered their families on God's behalf. So when such fathers assumed the power to dispose of their children's vocations and estates, they attributed to themselves the power of God. Bourdaloue composed and delivered the reproachful monologue of God himself.

> Where is the mark of my sovereign paternity, if other fathers dispute it, and if I dispose no more of those to whom I gave being, to place them in the rank and condition of life that would please me? You undertake, oh man! to do it: who gave you the power? In a family of which I entrusted you only the simple administration, you act as the master, and you order everything according to your will.[35]

Bourdaloue thus rendered God's indignation in the phrases of a father indignant at his children's presumption. The preacher assaulted patriarchy by mocking the presumption of fathers themselves. A father who chose his child's estate presumed both to know the future and to read the heart of the child, which only God in his omniscience could do.

> For upon the knowledge of all that, is founded the right to assign vocations to men; and when God calls someone he employs the knowledge of all that. But where is the father on earth who possesses the least of that knowledge? Is it not therefore an insupportable temerity in a father to want to make himself master of vocations and estates in his family? Is it not, either to attribute to himself the wisdom of God, which is a crime; or to undertake, with the wisdom of man, that which demands a superior and divine wisdom: an enterprise that one can only treat as madness.[36]

For Bourdaloue "injustice" to children was curiously unrelated to children themselves. It was, above all, a "crime" against God.

Yet precisely such crime, this crime of paternal presumption, was "what happens every day in Christendom," reported Bourdaloue, describing the patriarchal society in which he lived. The power of the father was rooted in "custom," even in "a kind of law."[37] Bourdaloue's dissent from that law was all the more remarkable since he himself did not expect other clergymen to subscribe to his position.

> A law recognized universally in the world, and against which ministers of the Church and preachers are scarcely permitted to stand up. A law commonly tolerated by those who should act with most zeal to abolish it, by the spiritual directors who are most reformed in appearance and the most rigid, by the doctors who are most severe in their morality, and who affect more to be so or to seem so.[38]

Clearly Bourdaloue regarded his own view as that of a suppressed minority even among churchmen, expecting to find ranged against him ministers, preachers, spiritual directors, and doctors of the Church. This suggestion of conflict over family affairs within the Church was appropriate to a period in which patriarchal domestic authority was becoming more and more ideologically irresistible.

Interestingly, Bourdaloue's dissenting position on patriarchy became a table-turning strike against the Jansenists, that is, against those who affected to be most reformed, most rigid, most severe in their morality. It was they, and not the Jesuit Bourdaloue, who were making accommodations and abusing moral theology. For paradoxically it was the stern patriarch, so seemingly appropriate to religious standards of severity and rigidity, who gave offense to God, while the liberated child was theologically correct. In fact, another sermon of the late seventeenth century, in full agreement with Bourdaloue about parents and children, vocations and estates, was the work of another Jesuit, Pierre-Joseph d'Orléans. In his "Christian Instruction to Persons Engaged within Marriage upon the Education of their Children," d'Orléans warned parents that God had certain claims upon those children: "The function which He reserves to Himself is to assign them an estate; it is an unjust usurpation if, in that sphere, you dare to thwart the commands of Providence."[39] The historian Jean-Louis Flandrin has concluded that "the respect which the Church professed for paternal authority," in this period, was both "ambiguous" and "artificial."[40] Bourdaloue's sermon on "The Duty of Fathers" cut through the artificial professions of respect and labeled paternal presumption as "crime" and "madness." The concurrence of d'Orléans suggests that Bourdaloue may have helped to formulate a dissident Jesuit perspective in resistance to the pretensions of patriarchy.

Conclusion: "What Happens Every Day in Christendom"

In "The Duty of Fathers" and "The Love of God" Bourdaloue analyzed closely related theological dilemmas. In the latter sermon he argued that parents who loved their children too much, idolatrously, made their children into gods and compromised their own love for God. In the former, he suggested that parents who claimed too much authority over their children were making themselves into gods, attributing to themselves authority that belonged rightly to God. Thus, the two crucial arenas of family development in early modern Europe, sentimental and disciplinary, were both fraught with religious dangers. Excessive sentiment and excessive discipline gave offense to God. These were the same bonds, of both love and authority, that related parents and children and defined the early modern family. In "Charity to Orphans" Bourdaloue showed that he could more easily be sentimental about children in the hospital than in the home. With children already detached from their parents there was no need to eschew or denounce sentimentality, and he pitched his appeal in terms of children's blood and cries, not theological syllogisms. Rhetorical sentiment, like religious mysticism, apparently exercised a certain fascination upon him, and sometimes crept into his sermons, complicating his more often strictly reasoned moral theology. The religious historian Henri Bremond labeled Bourdaloue "a mystic in spite of himself," though his "terrible sermon" on prayer in 1688 was the leading denunciation of mystical Quietism in France.[41] Following Bremond, one might also view Bourdaloue as sentimental about children in spite of himself, susceptible after all to the "charms" of the orphan child.

These Bourdaloue sermons also suggest more complex ways of interpreting the "repressive" character of the Catholic Counter-Reformation. His championship of children's rights against patriachal power hinted at a kind of liberation, even pointed toward eighteenth-century ideas about childhood. In rejecting the affected severity of other preachers and spiritual directors he sought to undercut at once both Jansenist standards of rigor and conventional ideas about authority. Jean-Jacques Duguet, a Jansenist of the late seventeenth century, formulated thus the primacy of piety for a contemporary Christian woman.

> Religion is everything, enters everywhere, has control over everything; it is religion that should rule everything, sacrifice everything, ennoble everything. Salvation is not only the most important business, but the only one. One must work towards it independently of everything else, and only apply oneself to other matters with reference to that great purpose. Everything must be adjusted to it, everything respond to it; but it must never be adapted to fit our other purposes. A husband, children, friends, and all just associations, are only for salvation.[42]

This insistence on the ruling, controlling role of religion expressed certain absolute ambitions of the Counter-Reformation, and Bourdaloue seemed to pursue the same priority when he showed family attachments detracting from God's due; he even described God's supposed indignation. He recognized that religion was indeed being "adapted to fit other purposes," when children were worshipped idolatrously, when parents justified their authority by reference to that of God. Yet God in the sermons of Bourdaloue, while "entering everywhere," did not necessarily wield "control over everything." Instead God was invoked as a sort of check and balance to powerful forces in early modern society, a counterweight to excessive parental love, to overweening parental power. Bourdaloue was not a churchman of unrealistic rigorism; he could not have expected to achieve the repression of family feeling and the destruction of domestic order in early modern France. His sermons suggest that the Counter-Reformation could also pursue a policy of containment when faced with a social phenomenon as successful as the family. The historian Robin Briggs has concluded that "the contest between church and family"—considering bonds of marriage as well as those of parenthood—was in any event "a hopelessly unequal one."[43] In spite of Bourdaloue, parents would continue to love their children in varying degrees of intensity and would try to determine their futures as well.

Bourdaloue's sermons were not preached in that spirit of absolute abstraction that sometimes rendered rigorous theology remote and irrelevant. Though spiritually demanding, he resembled the Jesuit casuists at least in his direct engagement with early modern society. He attended to "what happens every day in Christendom." His theological arguments followed the figures of crying children, idolatrous mothers, and dictatorial fathers. Socially attuned, his variations and illustrations showed that he was sensitive to the crucial developments occurring in the early modern family. That Bourdaloue was so suspicious of the family, of the sentimental bonds and disciplinary order that constituted it, was perhaps also related to his Jesuit perspective. As a member of an order famous for its schools, committed to its educational mission, Bourdaloue could hardly allow to the family an exclusive claim upon the Catholic children of early modern Europe.

Notes

1. Mme de Sévigné, *Correspondance,* ed. Roger Duchêne, (Gallimard, 1972), 6 March 1671, 1:179.
2. Mme de Sévigné, 13 March 1671, p. 183.
3. On Bourdaloue see Emile-Antoine Blampignon, *Étude sur Bourdaloue: avec quelques documents inédits, suivie d'un choix de sermons* (1886; Geneva: Slatkine, Reprints, 1972); and P. M. Lauras, *Bourdaloue: sa vie et ses oeuvres* (Paris: Librairie Catholique, 1881), 2 vols.; and René Daeschler, *La Spiritualité de Bourdaloue: Grâce et Vie unitive* (Museum Lessianum, 1927); and Daeschler, *Bourdaloue: Doctrine Spirituelle* (Paris, 1932); and Henri Bremond, "La Spiritualité de Bourdaloue," *Histoire Littéraire du Sentiment Religieux en France,* (1928; Paris: Librairie Armand Colin, 1968), 8: 310–60; and R. B. Meagher, "Louis Bourdaloue," *New Catholic Encyclopedia,* 2:732–33.
4. Philippe Ariès, *Centuries of Childhood: A Social History of Family Life,* trans. Robert Baldick (New York: Vintage Books, 1962), "The Discovery of Childhood."
5. Ariès, "A New Institution: The College."
6. Bourdaloue, "Exhortation sur la charité envers les orphelins" ("Charity to Orphans"), *Oeuvres complètes de Bourdaloue de la Compagnie de Jésus,* (Besançon: Chez Ant. Montarsolo, 1823), 8:91.
7. Henri Bremond, *A Literary History of Religious Thought in France, The Triumph of Mysticism,* "The Spirit of Childhood and the Devotion of the Seventeenth Century to the Child Jesus" (1921; London: Society for Promoting Christian Knowledge, 1936), 3:444.
8. "Charity to Orphans," p. 94.
9. "Charity to Orphans," p. 96.
10. "Charity to Orphans," p. 98.
11. Lawrence Stone, *The Family, Sex, and Marriage: In England 1500–1800* (New York: Harper & Row, 1977), p. 175.
12. "Charity to Orphans," p. 87.
13. "Charity to Orphans," p. 94.
14. Bourdaloue, "Sur l'Amour de Dieu" ("The Love of God") *Sermons Choisis,* ed. Louis Dimier (Paris: Librairie Garnier Frères, 1936), p. 287.
15. "The Love of God," p. 288.
16. Mme de Sévigné, *Selected Letters,* trans. Leonard Tancock (Penguin, 1982), 24 March 1671, p. 77.

17. "The Love of God." Compare *Oeuvres complètes de Bourdaloue,* ed. P. Bretonneau (Paris: Mellier Frères, Librairie Religieuse, 1846), 1:40; and *Sermons Choisis,* ed. Dimier, p. 292 and p. 433 (n. 112). On texts of Bourdaloue see Dimier, "Avant Propos," pp. i–viii.

18. Mme de Sévigné (ed. Duchêne), 29 April 1671, p. 238.

19. Saint Ignatius of Loyola, *The Spiritual Exercises,* trans. Anthony Mottola (Image Books, 1964), p. 47.

20. Saint Teresa of Avila, *The Way of Perfection,* trans. E. Allison Peers (Image Books, 1964), pp. 81–87.

21. Saint Teresa, p. 83.

22. Saint Teresa, p. 86.

23. Henri Bremond, *Histoire littéraire du sentiment religieux en France,* (1923; Paris: Librairie Armand Colin, 1967), 6:49–71; Jean Delumeau, *Catholicism between Luther and Voltaire: A New View of the Counter-Reformation,* trans. Jeremy Moiser (London: Burns & Oates, 1977), p. 45.

24. Bourdaloue, "Sur le Devoir des pères par rapport a la vocation de leurs enfants" ("The Duty of Fathers"), *Choix de Sermons de Bourdaloue* (Paris: A. Roger et F. Chernoviz, 1899), p. 215; trans. King James Version.

25. "The Duty of Fathers," pp. 216–17.

26. "The Duty of Fathers," p. 217.

27. Robin Briggs, *Communities of Belief: Cultural and Social Tensions in Early Modern France* (Oxford: The Clarendon Press, 1989), p. 247.

28. Stone, p. 175.

29. "The Duty of Fathers," p. 220.

30. Peter Gay, ed., *John Locke on Education* (New York: Teachers College, Columbia University, 1964).

31. "The Duty of Fathers," p. 219.

32. "The Duty of Fathers," p. 227.

33. "The Duty of Fathers," p. 223.

34. "The Duty of Fathers," p. 228.

35. "The Duty of Fathers," p. 218.

36. "The Duty of Fathers," p. 221.

37. "The Duty of Fathers," p. 222.

38. "The Duty of Fathers," p. 222.

39. Jean-Louis Flandrin, *Families in Former Times: Kinship, Household, and Sexuality,* trans. Richard Southern (Cambridge University Press, 1979), p. 135 and p. 251, n. 52.

40. Flandrin, p. 134.

41. Bremond, "La Spiritualité de Bourdaloue," *Histoire littéraire,* 8:315.

42. Briggs, p. 238.

43. Briggs, p. 276.

Social Order, Social Reform, and the Society of Jesus

PETER McDONOUGH

In Europe no valid claim can be made for a definite Jesuit style, its canons precisely laid down in Rome, and in the Americas there is even less justification for such a statement. The various regions adapted certain stylistic features, according to the exigencies of the time and place and the abilities of the builders, and out of them they created something original.

—Pál Kelemen, *Baroque and Rococo in Latin America*

1

The involvement of the Society of Jesus in social movements and political causes since the 1960s has received considerable publicity.[1] Yet the decades preceding the surge of social awareness and activism—from the turn of the century, when Jesuits began to respond to papal admonitions about working class movements, through the postwar era of prosperity in the United States and Western Europe—were also important years in the development of social and political Catholicism. They witnessed the downfall of the *ancien régime* in the Hapsburg empire, the coming to power of communism in Russia and later in Eastern Europe and China, the rise and defeat of fascism, the rise and more gradual decline of authoritarian governments in Latin Europe, the advent of the *Pax Americana,* the demographic ascendancy of Latin America in world Catholicism, and the onset of the Second Vatican Council. As the leading religious order in the church, the Society of Jesus had important

The research connected with this paper was funded mainly by the National Endowment for the Humanities and the German Marshall Fund of the United States. The Social Science Research Council, the Fulbright Commission, the Horace H. Rackham School of Graduate Studies, and the Institute for Social Research at the University of Michigan also provided generous support. Robert Mester gave invaluable help in bibliographical searches. Special thanks are due to the nearly two hundred Jesuits on three continents who participated in the study with interviews, advice, and feedback on provisional interpretations such as the present one. The paper is dedicated to the memory of Philip A. Carey, S.J.

stakes in these events. In some of them Jesuits played significant roles.

A pivotal change demarcating the pre- and postconciliar eras involved the globalization of Catholicism: the shift from a Eurocentric to a culturally more pluralistic perspective. A major antecedent of this change had been underway long before the sixties, however. It encompassed a pair of transformations unfolding over time and across regions: the migration of European Catholics to the United States and the participation of the immigrant community in the industrialization of the young nation. Industrialization spurred the development of Catholic social doctrine. The diaspora of European Catholics was promising but also threatening to a centralized church. Together, these changes raised ideological and institutional challenges.

The organizational manifestations of a social doctrine that was rather equivocal to begin with made preconciliar Catholicism more variegated than a history-of-ideas reading of the period might suggest.[2] Local circumstances encouraged adaptation on the part of traditionally flexible Jesuits. Differences within the American branch of the Society of Jesus—in the experimentation with educational formats beyond the liberal arts model, such as labor schools and schools of social work, for example—were as important as the gap between the intellectual and organizational styles of European and American Jesuits.

The chief concern of this paper is with the evolution and diffusion of these experiments during the years prior to Vatican II. The dual focus is on variation in social ideas and practice over time and across regions. The intellectual and organizational responses of the Jesuits to social challenges building up over half a century are of interest not only in their own right, as symptoms of the operational diversity behind the dogmatic monolith, but also as indicators of tensions that eventually came to the surface with the Second Vatican Council.

The economic and demographic transformations that accelerated after the Second World War strained the capacity of the Jesuits to master their environment. By the beginning of the sixties some Jesuits were uneasy with the emergence of social and political conditions that were incomprehensible on the basis of habitual categories of thought. After a period of achievement that coincided roughly with the New Deal era, the social bases of Jesuit activities in the United States began to waver. The Catholic subculture attained virtual assimilation and headed for the suburbs. The Catholic working class yielded to prosperity.[3]

The thinning of the class and communal constituencies of Catholicism had several repercussions on the social apostolate of the Jesuits. The thrust of domestic activism shifted from labor relations to racial discrimination. And such intellectual excitement as social ministry engendered focused on the international arena: on North-South relations generally and on Latin America in particular. The vanguard of American Catholicism turned toward globalization.[4]

So, interest in interracial and international ventures arose partly out of success. The principal constituents of American Catholicism had arrived. As the contribution of the Jesuits to assimilation reached the point of diminishing returns, they sought new fields to explore. But modifications in the social programs of American Jesuits were not simply a reaction to the slackening of class and communal ties. Changes in these areas may account for the overall direction but not the intensity that Jesuits brought to their new undertakings, in particular for a radicalism that was turned against the Church itself as often as against social injustice.

This component of the upheaval was generational. The cultural equivalent of the achievement of the Jesuits in the institutional sphere, of their infrastructure of schools, parishes, and retreat houses, was an intellectual system that claimed to be essentially perfect but that was anomalous in its stress on stasis, hierarchy, and completeness in the midst of societal change and, perhaps even more ruinously, inadequate to the psychic need of young Jesuits to make the social *magisterium* their own. Once the institutional challenges of American Catholicism had largely been met, Counter-Reformation triumphalism left Jesuits little room to stretch and prove themselves either organizationally or intellectually. Many of them were bored and anxious. Then, suddenly, with the evaporation of the Tridentine synthesis, they had little to test themselves against. A fairly common reaction was to move between alienation and anomie directed both at the church and against the world outside.

The institutional commitments of the Jesuits in the United States were concentrated in education. As providers of services—in particular, of training in the skills required for white-collar mobility—their schools were successful. The labor schools and the schools of social work, as well as the schools of commerce and finance, were variations on the skills-for-mobility model of education. The efficiency of the schools in facilitating achievement had the effect of shrinking their erstwhile clientele. By the 1960s their capacity for organizational innovation and for the retention of the same clientele was nearly exhausted.

In addition, even during their days of greatest success as centers of instruction, the Jesuit schools were not at the cutting edge of creativity in social thought. Their intellectual mission did not keep pace with their competence in professional training. The Jesuits found themselves adrift between one goal that they had more than met and another that they could not attain. The service goal no longer generated the challenge it once did; in the realm of education-as-instruction the Jesuits were overachievers. The other goal was influence over social policy; in the absence of fresh ideas this was out of reach. The static and hierarchical vision inherited from Europe was inadequate as a theoretical guide to the dynamism and relative democracy of the American experience. By the 1960s this intellectual framework had become plainly incongruous, just as the apostolic apparatus of the order—the management of "the works," as they were called—had become a routine burden. As American Catholics became more mobile, Jesuits became less so.[5]

This study is devoted to the changes and nonchanges in social ministry that preceded Vatican II. The first section situates the experience of the American Jesuits relative to influences emanating from their peers in Europe. The key themes are, on the one hand, the misapprehensions of the Europeans regarding the activities of the American Jesuits and, on the other, the selective reception and indeed tacit rejection accorded the ideological priorities the Europeans urged upon their junior partners.

The next section sets the temporal context. The main part of the analysis falls in the period of immigrant- and postimmigrant industrialization, from about the turn of the century to the mid-sixties. Earlier Jesuit critiques of industrialization itself are passed over, and the analysis stops short in the mid-sixties, before the effects of the Council took hold.

A baseline model of Jesuit education, derived from in-house speculations about the ideal college envisioned for the postwar era, is then described. It represents the starting point from which, to one degree or another, the educational vehicles designed for social ministry departed. It serves to introduce the variations on the classical paradigm represented by the Jesuits' schools of social work, their labor schools, and their grand experiment in the think-tank genre, the Institute of Social Order.

Then comes an analysis of contemporary reflections on the social ministry of the postwar years, during the fading days of the preconciliar period, when the conceptual and institutional apparatus that Jesuits had used with a measure of success began to falter amid the scope and rapidity of change. The paper concludes with a retrospective assessment of the strategies of social analysis and education employed by the American Jesuits from the turn of the century onward.

2

At the time that the social *magisterium* received its initial formulation with the encyclical *Rerum Novarum* in 1891, North America was still mission territory in the eyes of the Roman curia. The Catholic population of the United States was smaller than that of Europe, and the attainment of economic hegemony on the part of the United States was some decades in the future. The cultural domination of the Roman authorities remained firm. Theological currents flowed from Europe to the United States.[6] Social doctrine, crystallized in 1931 in *Quadragesimo Anno,* propagated a corporatist ideal in terminology alien to the North American experience.[7]

After two world wars, the demographic and economic bases of Catholicism had altered drastically. The American Catholic subculture had expanded and was on the verge of assimilation. Corporatist prescriptions had lost their luster because of their link with the discredited regimes of Latin

Europe, much as Marxist ideals were tainted by Stalinism, and the Southern and Eastern European provenance of both schools of thought offended the sensitivities of Anglo-American liberalism.[8] In theology and philosophy American Catholic intellectuals continued to be shaped in the European, particularly the French and German, mold. But on economic and social questions American and European Catholicism followed separate paths. Confessional parties and labor unions of Christian Democratic inspiration were as foreign to the American political landscape as were socialist ideologies and organizations. Conversely, the almost transcendental bountifulness of the United States and the relentless optimism of its citizens baffled the leaders of European Catholicism, including those responsible for managing the Society of Jesus.

American exceptionalism failed to arouse grave alarm so long as the acceptance of democratic and capitalist values by the faithful did not jeopardize their allegiance to the spiritual core of Catholicism. If proof of fidelity were needed, it could be found in the growth of religious vocations coming from the American branch of the church. If it seemed intellectually laggard, the American context was nonetheless innocent of the ideological polarization and anticlericalism that plagued the church in Europe.[9]

By the mid-1950s there were inklings that influence might be flowing the other way around, from North American to European Catholicism. It was then that the financial and manpower resources of the American Jesuits caught up with and exceeded those of their counterparts across the Atlantic. Concurrently, on the intellectual plane, the advocacy of religious toleration and political pluralism by the American Jesuit theologian John Courtney Murray began to attract attention. He was temporarily silenced but eventually, with Vatican II, vindicated.[10]

Murray's triumph represented a breakthrough in Catholic thinking about politics. In rejecting the standard of religious monopoly, he brought the political theory of Catholicism more in line with American practice and at least implicitly called into question the nostalgia for a preindustrial steady state that lay behind much of Catholic social theory. Pluralism was no longer a second-best system of borderline legitimacy. His innovation is also significant for what he left untouched. He said virtually nothing about the economic and social environment of democracy, and he did not advocate change in the moral and sexual teachings of the church. In both of these respects Murray was conservative. Nevertheless, he could not be dismissed in Roman circles as another American devoid of ideas, bent on pushing his way to influence by way of material resources. His theory articulated what was implied by the American experiment, that democracy might not only work but also depend on and cultivate virtue in its citizens.[11]

The increase in American influence presaged by the celebrity of Murray and the impetus given toward a new center of gravity by the numerical growth of membership in the American branch of the Society of Jesus were short-lived. By the early 1960s the population of Latin America had surpassed that of North America, questions of North-South relations had climbed to the top of the strategic agenda of Catholicism, and Jesuit numbers had begun to fall, conspicuously so in advanced industrial societies. The shining moment of American Catholicism corresponded to the brief interlude, no more than a decade, between the Kennedy presidency, the ascendancy of American Catholic money and numbers vis-à-vis the Europeans, and the demographic decline of North American Catholicism relative to Latin America.

On the whole, then, intellectual exchange between Jesuits in the United States and Western Europe during the decades preceding Vatican II was confined to theology and philosophy. Here the European influence was as overwhelming as it was virtually nonexistent in social and political theory; influence ran almost entirely one way in the former domain and was practically absent in the latter.[12] This asymmetry requires explanation.

The distinctiveness that puzzled European Jesuits was founded on several features of the American condition: a relatively flexible structure of economic opportunity, a comparatively open system of political participation, and a certain though far from complete separation of religious from economic and political power. This distinctiveness was compounded by another factor, the weight of the Irish heritage, that can be viewed as a special extension of the European experience—one that I shall consider momentarily.

In contrast to North America, the countries of Southern, Latin Europe were characterized by rigid class hierarchies, closed political systems, and proximity between Catholic ecclesiastics and political and economic elites. These groups were united on the need to maintain social order. The identification of the church with the defense of economic hierarchy and political exclusion in Latin Europe reinforced intransigent reaction on one side and anticlericalism on the other.[13]

Economic, political, and religious-versus-secular lines of conflict were less strictly superimposed in other parts of Europe. Especially toward the North, in the Netherlands, Germany, and Belgium, for example, where Catholicism did not exercise a near-monopoly over religious affiliation, the church kept its distance from national, usually Protestant elites and encouraged the formation of Catholic labor organizations and political groups. The preservation of moral order was not identified with the defense of the economic status quo, and moderate social reform was promoted.[14]

From the beginning of the century to the late fifties, the Latin strain in Catholic thought predominated in the United States. Yet while the Latin influence was unsurpassed in scholastic philosophy and theology, it existed in a quarantine. This was not only because of the isolation of Thomism from secular philosophical currents. American Catholics remained largely untouched by corporatist thinking on political and social matters. Italian and Spanish Jesuits found it difficult to conceive of a social environment, virtually bereft of class consciousness, like the one inhabited by working-class Catholics in America.[15] The corporatist formulae that had been elaborated to avert class confrontation, and the neo-medievalism associated with such categories, passed almost unoticed in the United States, in which (outside of the South) a feudal past was lacking and where issues of class conflict seemed rather remote in the first place. The Europeans saw themselves on the frontline of the communist assault. The Americans, by contrast, seemed to be on the frontier of a social and political landscape that defied ideological classification. The unfamiliarity of the Americans with Marxism, not to mention with conservative continental idealism, increased their reputation for provincialism and lack of intellectual depth.

The Northern European current in Catholic social thought seemed less exotic in the American setting. The Catholic subcultures of Austria and Germany bore some resemblance to the religious enclaves of their counterparts in the United States. German immigrants settling predominantly in the Midwest brought over elements of moral traditionalism and working class mutualism. The intellectual features of the reform tradition were incidental to the pragmatic legacy of Catholic unionism and associationalism in the old country.[16] In contrast, while the Italian immigrants cherished ritual and popular liturgy, they brought nothing in the way of Catholic social thought—a construct that, if it caught their attention at all, they almost certainly associated with the defense of the upper classes. The aesthetics of the liturgy, along with the institutional infrastructure—the schools and the parishes—of the Catholic subculture, outweighed the intellectual content of Catholicism for most of the laity and, probably, for clergy and religious as well.[17]

It was a third stream in European Catholicism, however, that washed over and came close to obliterating the Northern and Southern continental currents. Some of the historical memories borne by the Irish—for example, the struggle against landlordism—had parallels in the background of other Catholic immigrant groups, and in their sexual morality they were thought to be "more Catholic than the Pope." But the Irish were distinct from the rest of European Catholics and fortuitously close to earlier American settlers, by reason of their experience with colonialism. Their precocious expertise in mass political organization, before the onset of industrialization, was reminiscent of the sequence of political mobilization undergone by Americans since the Jacksonian era. The devotion of the Irish to democracy was of the meat-and-potatoes kind. It was neither anticlerical nor class-consciously revolutionary. A republicanism fueled by resentment of the British crown was balanced by a skepticism regarding the beneficence of Manchester liberalism.[18]

The mainstream of American Catholicism during the decades of immigrant absorption was Irish. Nativist animosity was strong; discrimination reinforced a measure of working-class solidarity in the Irish-American ghettoes.

Nevertheless, there was a genuine commonality between the host and the transplant cultures, manifest in the appeal of nationalist sentiment and patriotism over class identification and in the facility of the Irish in mass politics.[19]

The cultural affinities of the Irish with Catholics of continental European origins were not close, whatever their ambivalence regarding the United States. Intellectual ties were loose, and the historical trajectories of political mobilization were divergent. The Irish and the Roman authorities shared an understanding in the area of sexual morality, however much they may have differed in practice, one leaning toward a strict and the other toward an indulgent reading of the moral code.[20] This ascetic connection aside, the political institutions and the social ethos of a largely Irish-American Catholicism remained a mystery to European Catholics, including most Jesuit observers.[21]

On balance, the energies of immigrant Catholics went into institution-building. The reputation of the Europeans was for cultivating the life of the mind. This division of labor contributed to the notoriety of American Catholicism for intellectual underachievement. What bound them together, besides a doctrinal modicum regarding sexual behavior and family practices, was a liturgy in a language that was native to none but common to all. It was not so much that the Americans rejected social theories from Europe and replaced them consciously with ideas of their own as that in the press of problem-solving they ignored ideas of any provenance and concentrated instead on the demands of brick-and-mortar administration. This was both a blessing and a curse. The Americans were immunized against the schematic abstractions of continental social and political theory even when they took, on occasion more enthusiastically than the Europeans themselves, to ponderous moralisms or (in the case of Freudianism) sexual nostrums.[22] On the downside, the pragmatism of immigrant and second-generation Catholics did not equip them for critical insight into the American dream, especially when they engaged in superpatriotism and success-mongering to vouchsafe their Americanism. Suspicion of alien ideologies was inclined to translate into antiintellectualism.[23]

Two other factors distinguished American from European Catholicism. One pertained with special force to the Jesuits and to the emphasis they gave to education. While the Society of Jesus ran a modest number of elite *collèges* in Europe, Jesuit energies in the United States were taken up almost entirely with the task of running a vast network of high schools, colleges, and universities for the immigrant constituency. Few resources were left over for experiments in other areas.[24]

Jesuits in the United States did not have the organizational slack available to their European brethren for sustaining a program of social analysis and action. Their efforts in this field were marginal to the institutional responsibilities of the order, and they were short on intellectual distinction. The "social apostolate" was only sporadically a corporate endeavor. The American Jesuits who engaged in it got the leftovers of both worlds: scant organizational resources and little intellectual prestige.

Then there was the question of race. The issue began to claim attention in Europe during the late thirties, as antisemitism in the guise of Aryan eugenics gained prominence. But the American problem of interracial relations between blacks and whites was barely visible in Europe and only slightly more so to the faithful in the United States, since blacks made up an exiguous proportion of Catholics. No doctrine had been formalized. The issue seemed peculiarly American rather than Catholic. The silence of Catholic teaching in this area would later converge with the increasing salience of the issue in the United States to embolden some American Jesuits to take courageous stands in favor of racial integration.[25]

3

For Catholics and other minorities, the land of opportunity meant social mobility and the possibility of assimilation into the American way. The process was reflected in and driven by not only structural change—increasing education, the realignment of the occupational distribution, and the like—but also by the growth of governmental action to contain the hardships wrought by industrialization.

The responses of Jesuit social observers to this twofold transformation ranged from outright rejection to ambivalence. Purists attacked capitalism for abuses that would lead inexorably to communism and moral laxity, and they warned against the encroachment of a swelling public bureaucracy. They advocated a return to agrarian simplicities and dreamed of the restoration of a medieval/manoral way of life, economically self-sufficient and decentralized like the feudal demesne that stymied the state-building ambitions of monarchs.[26] This fantasy enjoyed a certain vogue from the beginning of the century through the thirties. Outside of an appreciation of Gregorian chant and Neo-Gothic stained glass, it did not resonate among the majority of American Catholics, who were city dwellers. It had no social or political consequences.[27]

Ambivalence was more common among Jesuits than revulsion. Industrialization was assumed to be irreversible, as was the development of democracy in the American case. The task, practical rather than transcendental, was not merely to come to terms with economic and political innovations but to welcome what was desirable in them. The posture was more one of outsiders looking in, gazing through the shop window, than of prophets turning their backs on modernization.

Part of the task of cultural absorption was taken up by John Courtney Murray, who proposed a working compatibility between Catholicism and pluralism. Yet, while Murray focused in characteristically American fashion on the liberalization of the political order, he neglected to deal with two questions related to the preservation of the good *polis* in the midst of secularization that struck Europeans as being of at least equal importance: the social-structural—that is, the class—concomitants of industrialization, and the burgeoning role of central governments in fostering and monitoring capitalism. The fact that the neomedievalists advocated escapist remedies for these trends did not render the problems themselves unreal.

Murray was not alone in these limitations. The prosperity that followed the Second World War enabled Catholics and most Americans to sidestep such questions. Postimmigrant generations of Catholics had few quarrels with New Deal legislation or with the abundance of the postwar years.[28] For the most part, such changes were seen as beneficial, and they appeared to leave traditionally private values intact. It was only when cumulative societal transformations began to restructure the authority patterns of everyday life— in particular, familial hierarchies, through the increasing education and participation of women in the work force—and when the government assumed greater responsibility in areas previously beyond the public sphere, that mild ambivalence turned to a reevaluation of the place of American Catholicism in the political and social order.[29]

Mirages of agrarian harmony, invocations of the principle of subsidiarity against the depredations of an intrusive state, and paeans to the family differed in detail, and they mattered to some sectors of American Catholicism more than to others. But each in its way was a metaphor for a way of life, a collective identity, that seemed threatened by the temptations of a multiplicity of life styles. Awareness of profound transition bred one fallacy and one dilemma. The fallacy consisted of a penchant for glorifying preindustrial society and for demonizing the consumerism of modernity. The dilemma lay in the difficulty of understanding the dynamics of this transition on the basis of a view of society that was both hierarchical and static. Like their European colleagues, American Jesuits lacked a theory of social change. Their thinking was categorical rather than dynamic. The resulting diagnoses were long on condemnation but short on analytical power.

The following discussion is bounded by two eras that stand outside the time frame of this essay. The agrarian vision that enjoyed some popularity in the twenties and thirties was more of an esthetic than a social ideal for American Catholics, and it was peripheral to the programs that Jesuits developed to deal with the consequences of industrialization. It posited a preindustrial paradise.[30] At the other end, anxiety over the changing role of women and the fate of the family did not become paramount until after the Second Vatican Council. Issues such as these have typified postindustrial Catholicism. It is the middle years, starting in the thirties and culminating in the sixties, when the position of Catholicism vis-à-vis American political and social normalcy was worked through, that constitute the focus of this essay.

There is one thread, however, that binds together the preindustrial, industrial, and postindustrial eras in Jesuit social thought. Even though the theme assumed supreme significance only a decade or more after Vatican II, and although the functions attributed to it have varied over time, the preservation of the hierarchical family and, by extension, the designation of the role of women and the management of sexuality as pinions of social order have been central to the thinking of Jesuits about social change. These are subterranean motifs that surface occasionally in the present analysis; they are given prominence in the concluding section.[31]

The family and related concerns have been matters that few Jesuit social observers have failed to comment on. Issues such as these have been of interest not only on their own but also as emblems of a traditional way of life, a broader social order, dislocated by modernity. Thus, the pastoral musings of some Jesuits in the early decades of the century might more profitably be understood not as renditions of a frictionless polity but as tropes of an idealized domesticity.[32] Similarly, references to the global community prominent in papal encyclicals and pastoral letters of the postconciliar era reflect familial imagery writ large. The imagery is evocative, the organizational design is vague, and it is likely that these moral excursions can be taken more seriously as homely dramas and lessons for character-building than as prescriptions for collective action. They concern the micropolitics of everyday life. In any case the resonance is with esthetic and ethical, rather than conventionally analytical, views of human activity, and within this mindset the message seems less eccentric than it otherwise might.

4

In 1943, more than a decade before he became the editor of *America* magazine, the Jesuits' journal of opinion, Thurston Davis published a brief article entitled "Blueprint for a College." The plan that Davis set forth in the pages of *Jesuit Educational Quarterly* as a model school for the postwar years was drawn up, with some obvious exceptions, along the lines of a seminary. In spite of the anticipated flood of veterans, enrollment at the model school would not exceed one hundred. The student body would be exclusively male. The faculty would be all-Jesuit, "seven priests and two scholastics." It was to be an elite liberal arts college in which "intensity would be the keynote." The aim of the college was

> to prepare young men, by thorough grounding in the classics, philosophy, history, science, and religion, for careers in the following fields: journalism and creative writing, the theater, the radio, social work and labor-union leadership, politics, school and university teaching . . . the 'cultural' professions. . . . The ideal of 'lay vocations' will be instilled into the students. . . . The fathers of the faculty will maintain contact with graduates through a carefully organized alumni society.

After ten years there will thus have been created a small group of active Catholic laymen, placed strategically in the more vital centers of American life within a given area, who by reason of their training and by more or less constant contacts with their Alma Mater will form a very potent instrument of intelligent Catholic action.[33]

Davis's college was very nearly a *collège* in the European sense—what the Jesuits in the United States called a preparatory school—extended through the years of undergraduate education, and his larger ambitions rested on European premises about the role of religion in public affairs. To be sure, his perspective on "the cultural professions" drew on elements from the American Catholic experience. It was not limited to the intelligentsia, still a minuscule part of the Catholic community in the United States. Yet it was not broad enough to encompass business "statesmen," also a small portion of the subculture. Both the academic and entrepreneurial sectors would grow in the postwar years, and in different ways their interests would surpass the mixture of traditional learning and leadership in service that Davis posited as the basis of Jesuit schooling. His vision of scholarly excellence was better suited to a poor, predominantly Catholic country—Ireland, Spain or parts of Latin America—than to the United States of the postwar period. The traditional conditions of clerical influence did not obtain in advanced industrial societies.

Davis stressed education in the liberal arts, the staple of Jesuit schooling, as a preparation "for life and making a living." He also stressed the long-term practicality of his ideal campus for Jesuits who, instead of catering to the crude pragmatism of "vocationalism," as they were called on to do under wartime conditions, could return to teaching what they knew best: literature, classics, philosophy, and religion. Over the years, he believed, this wide coverage would have a greater payoff than narrow specialization in the short run.

Davis invoked, finally, another Jesuit heritage, emphasizing the need to train leaders and gain influence in a world seen as increasingly threatening. He issued a call to arms:

> . . . the coming generation of Catholics faces a showdown, and we Jesuits should attempt to fit them for the battle of the next half-century. it will be a half-century dominated by a monster secular press, class struggle, godless universities, and tremendous technical achievements in many of the means used to form public opinion. These are but a few of the fronts on which battle will be joined, and it will be a battle for the culture and the soul of America. It will be won or lost in the newspaper, the theater, on the radio, in the labor union, the city hall, and the classroom. The Church needs leaders in these storm-centers of American life, leaders in the cultural professions. We are assuming here that intensive liberal training in a small Jesuit college, where the full impact of a zealous Jesuit faculty can be brought to bear on the intellectual and religious formation of each student, will still produce such leaders.[34]

The goal was to multiply among lay cadres the mixture of conviction and versatility, the air of adventure for a cause, that lent grandeur to the Jesuit legend. Davis wanted to form articulate, humanistic conservatives who would set forth to shape public opinion. A small number of Jesuits would be leaven to the world.

Although the rhetoric and some of the spirit of his vision surfaced in parts of the Society's educational system during the following decades, his "blueprint for a college" did not become reality.[35] The idea of establishing a traditional alternative to what Davis would later call the "educational Jacobinism" of mass society, of carving out a niche specializing in the classical humanities, was not implausible.[36] The institutional vehicle of cultural and political influence was of manageable size. The problem came in extrapolating from the tightly controlled setting of a semimonastic world. The objective of shaping the direction and the policies of the larger society in the United States, never far from illusory, grew further and further out of reach in the wake of the Second World War. The flow of influence went the other way around, conditioning the options of the Society of Jesus.

The flaw of the strategy laid out by Davis was that it presupposed historical circumstances that were vanishing in Europe and that never existed in the United States. It had the poignancy of perfection in a vacuum. It was intellectually coherent but socially uprooted. What is remarkable about the scheme is the degree to which a European vision of political Catholicism remained, as late as the 1940s, the norm for American Jesuits who thought about such matters, even if in practice Jesuit educators diverged from the classical prescription. The European ideal was legitimate but, insofar as it envisioned the cultivation of political power, rather unrealistic.

The naiveté of Davis's project as an institutional strategy in the United States went beyond the literalness of its intellectual cloning from a European prototype. The resemblance of the idealized *collège* to a seminary isolated in the countryside evoked not only notions of the mastery and influence associated with the glory days of ecclesiastical power in predominantly Catholic settings but also images of an arcadian innocence untouched by the industrial world it sought to control. Davis was correct in assessing the need for a conceptual architecture that might lend coherence to the Jesuits' sprawling hodgepodge of liberal arts and professional schools in the United States. If the goal was not merely social service but policy influence, then an intellectual agenda had to be shaped. The trouble was that the substance of the theoretical vision set forth by Davis remained antiquated and alien.

Most real-life Jesuit experiments in social instruction and political analysis in the American setting suffered from the reverse problem. They were practical, once their modest goals of providing instructional services to a Catholic clientele in search of upward mobility were recognized. But they lacked the cachet of a liberal education. Undertakings such as the labor schools and the schools of social work did not have the intellectual respectability of the curriculum, requiring classical Latin and Greek and leading to the bachelor of arts degree. Besides, they were not for elites and "leaders of men" who might be taken as seriously for their culture as for their financial success. The difficulty was not only a matter of snobbery or style. The professional schools were not seedbeds of ideas. *Faute de mieux,* the model proposed by Davis served as a guideline according to which Jesuit schools were granted status or relegated to the category of the less-than-prestigious.[37]

5

The beginning of the distinctively American schools of social work and the equally pragmatic schools of commerce and finance can usually be traced to the enthusiasms of one or another enterprising Jesuit responding to a demand for training in the new white-collar occupations as well as to the doctrinal mind of the church. The career of Terence Shealy exemplifies the pattern. He had been brought up "amid scenes of wild grandeur and beauty" in County Cork, had written a poem entitled "To My Mother in Ireland for my First Mass" that made the rounds of the Catholic press, and by the first decade of the twentieth century had established himself in New York as an exceptionally eloquent speaker.[38] He helped organize the law school at Fordham. By 1909 he was directing retreats for "Catholic gentlemen" from the New York area. Many of them were alumni of Jesuit schools and they contributed to a fund that in 1911 enabled Father Shealy to open a retreat house, Mount Manresa, on Staten Island.

Under Shealy's tutelage, the initiative that started out as the "Laymen's Retreat Movement" became "The Laymen's League for Retreats and Social Studies." He had taken to heart the directives of Leo XIII, originating in the final decades of the nineteenth century, about the perils of capitalism and the appeals of communism. He railed against both, though there was little doubt about what was thought to be the greater danger.[39] "The objects of this work," outlined in a statement presented to John Farley, then archbishop and later cardinal of New York, "are to prevent the spread of false doctrines and to combat Socialism, especially among the laboring classes." Archbishop Farley welcomed the undertaking. "The new feature, i.e., Social Studies," he responded, "is highly to be commended for reasons too obvious to the man of the world to call for special mention. Social questions are uppermost in the minds of thinking men today, and calling for solution such as only careful study by the members, and clear exposition by the leaders of your League, can deal with successfully."[40]

In 1911 Shealy inaugurated the Leagues' activities with a series of twelve lectures defending the idea that "Socialism, in its Principles, is Irreligious and Immoral." A columnist for the *Wall Street Journal,* Thomas Woodlock, presented an argument over the course of six lectures in defense of the proposition that "Socialism in its proposals is impracticable and impossible."[41]

The goal of the School of Social Studies was "to promote the study by Catholic men and women of the great social questions which are of vital interest in our time, and thus to train a corps of competent writers and lecturers who will spread among Catholics a sound knowledge of social facts and of the Christian principles in the light of which these facts must be interpreted."[42] The model of enthusiastic laymen operating under the guidance of the clergy was in line with the strategy, officially called Catholic Action, favored by the papacy.[43]

The school—more accurately, a speakers' forum composed of dedicated amateurs—lasted nearly eleven years, ceasing operation with Shealy's death in 1922. It succumbed to the drawing power of the School of Sociology and Social Studies, which Shealy had also founded at Fordham University in 1916. The idea at Fordham was to prepare tuition-paying students for jobs as city or state social workers. Fordham granted professional degrees, certifying its graduates for white-collar positions. This was the institutionally durable outcome of the early Jesuit explorations in social ministry.

Thus, the Jesuit social work schools and the schools of commerce and finance began to emerge about two decades into the new century, slightly after Protestant clerics and activists initiated their attempts to apply the Social Gospel in the urban areas of the United States.[44] The target group of the Jesuits was made up of immigrant Catholics. Their efforts appear to have been driven as much by demography as by dogma. The immigrant community was heterogeneous and displayed a mix of ambitions and abilities. Like the law faculties, the schools of social work and the business schools catered to their clientele by offering night courses in applied topics. They were professional-vocational schools. They became paying propositions by filling a niche in the educational market.

None of the professional schools fit the liberal arts program laid down in the *Ratio Studiorum*, the canonical guide to Jesuit education.[45] The fact that these institutions were incubated at the margins of the order's established operations enabled them to admit women much earlier than the college and university faculties that provided education in the classics. Operational eclecticism went hand in hand with intellectual flexibility. Such doctrine as was provided stressed, in line with corporatist thinking, the need for cooperation between management and labor. The business and social work schools sprung from much the same socioeconomic and intellectual sources. There was no significant ideological or programmable rivalry between them.[46]

6

The labor schools were embryonic in operations like "The Laymen's League for Retreats and Social Studies" that took shape in the early decades of the century, and they came into their own during the Great Depression. In

1936 the superior general of the Society commissioned the American Jesuits
to "marshal forces against communistic atheism and work for the establishment of a Christian social order."[47] The mission of the labor schools, like
that of their predecessors, was educational. But their audience was comprised mostly of working-class men, and they were not degree-granting
institutions. Nor did they pay for themselves. While they were often quar-
tered in space provided by a high school and or college—a basement room,
for example—the labor schools stood apart from the intellectual and social
audience of the Jesuit educational enterprise.

The labor schools did share one feature, however, with mainline Jesuit
institutions. They were launched not merely or even mainly in response to
European directives but to deal with economic and social circumstance in
the United States. By 1935, as the depression deepened, John Lewis, Philip
Murray, and other labor leaders had split from the American Federation of
Labor. The CIO—the Congress of Industrial Organizations—was formed for
the purpose of gathering unskilled and semiskilled laborers into unions that
crossed craft lines. Many of these men were Catholics. Organizational drives
were facilitated by the Wagner Act and the generally supportive New Deal
administration. Competition between radical and moderate currents and
between clean and corrupt factions for domination of this mass of manpower
was intense.[48]

The labor schools departed from the classical model of Jesuit education in
three ways. The audience was overwhelmingly working class, and the content
of instruction was decidedly practical. In addition, the schools furnished an
outlet for Jesuits who were neither at the intellectual vanguard of the order
nor quite fit the grind of parish work. The labor school Jesuits were themselves marginal, and their activities remained a sideshow to the rest of the
Society's operations.[49]

Their students were adult working-class males who came one evening a
week, usually from eight to ten or ten-thirty, for courses in parliamentary
procedure, techniques of public speaking, labor law, and the like. These
vocational classes, rather than the offerings in Catholic social doctrine, were
the drawing cards. Some links with traditional methods remained. Courses in
public speaking were updated versions of instruction in rhetoric out of the
classical curriculum. The strategy of responding to the market for applied
education matched the one that Terence Shealy had hit on decades earlier in
attracting lower-middle-class students to the Fordham School of Social
Work. The applied curriculum represented a time-honored venture in Jesuit
adaptability.[50]

If the propagation of dogma in the form of Catholic social thought was
secondary to the training in practical skills, there was an ideology by default,
and it was anticommunism. The Jesuits saw themselves as rivals of leftist
militants in the labor movement.[51] In New York City they were especially
worried by the hold of the left over the Transport Workers' Union, most of

whose members—trolley car operators, bus drivers, track repairmen—were Irish. This anomaly was compounded by flashes of an anticlericalism that some Jesuits feared bordered on the ferocious resentment harbored by the Spanish working class.[52]

The Jesuit were hard-pressed to compete with leftist union organizers, and they rarely entered into face-to-face debate with their opponents.[53] This failure to engage the opposition on intellectual grounds disappointed the leadership of the Society in Rome. In fact, however, the rank and file of American workers were neither fiercely class-conscious nor anticlerical. Most of the rivalry between leftwing organizers and Jesuit labor priests went on over their heads.[54]

In the United States a major alternative to ideological combat, and a backup to the provision of educational services, was pastoral care. Although the social encyclicals recommended spiritual retreats for working men and counselling of various sorts as measures that might serve as ideological inoculation, the inspiration for such efforts cannot be reduced to anticommunism. They were prompted at least as much by identification with the trials of working-class life that had surrounded almost all of the labor-school Jesuits during their own upbringing, and they afforded the kind of one-on-one contacts that Jesuits who did not consider themselves intellectuals or teachers felt comfortable making.

Philip Carey filled this pastoral slot. The son of a streetcar conductor, in the late thirties he helped set up the labor school housed next to Xavier high school and the Jesuits' parish church on Sixteenth Street in Manhattan, a few blocks northwest of Union Square where soapbox orators, political organizers, and advocates of assorted causes harangued passersby. Much of Carey's work involved lending a sympathetic ear and helping resolve family disputes. He was a master of kindly discretion, adept at knowing what not to do. Sermons on the dangers of communism in the abstract, he perceived, would bore most of the men, who were worn out in any case by the time they came to the weekly get-togethers. When he was not giving classes in labor ethics or attending to cases of personal hardship among his working class contacts, Carey kept busy organizing activities for Catholics of various classes and ages, including businessmen and children.[55]

Another Jesuit, John Delaney, also stressed variations on the pastoral manner. He directed the Xavier labor school from 1940 to 1943. Delaney built on his familiarity with the mores of the American Catholic subculture by channeling the prestige of the priest's role into mediating family troubles. He expanded the counselling of individual workers, which men like Carey had begun in conjunction with their classroom activities, into workshops and retreats in which wives participated with husbands.[56]

Delaney saw family, not class, relations as the foundation of social order. Although he never developed a full-blown rationale for his method of operation, Delaney worked well within the tradition of social concern and practice as understood by American Catholics. He was a case worker rather than a community organizer, and his operation was more of a crisis clinic than a labor school.[57] This division of labor, and the set of priorities implied by it, gave him a measure of fulfillment and pleased his clientele. But it did not satisfy the leadership of the order. It smacked too much of parish work, which Jesuits traditionally attempted to avoid, it lacked a powerful multiplier effect, and it was devoid of ideas recognizable on the other side of the Atlantic. The model of freelance caretaking, as contrasted with corporate leadership, stayed at the periphery of Jesuit work in the United States.

For a decade—between the late thirties and late forties—the labor schools enjoyed some popularity and effectiveness. But intellectual, institutional, and demographic factors limited their success. They never had a share in the academic prestige of the regular Jesuit teaching operations, and their organizational locus was ambiguous. Without intellectual drive, lacking an institutional home, they eventually faded before the rising competence and the shrinking numbers of working-class Catholics.

7

Besides the schools of social work and business and finance, and besides the labor schools, the great venture of the Society of Jesus in the social apostolate during the preconciliar era was the Institute of Social Order. The pedigree of this operation, which lasted roughly from the mid-thirties to the mid-sixties, was European. The organizational precedent for the ISO was *Action Populaire,* a think tank for "social analysis and action" set up by the Jesuits in Rheims in 1904.[58]

In contrast to the labor schools, the Institute of Social Order was to be an intellectual powerhouse, formulating and disseminating policy. The ISO would move beyond the academic boundaries of the instructional, service model followed by the schools of social work and the faculties of commerce and finance. Ideally it was to incorporate basic research that would feed into practical and potentially direct action on social questions. According to this perspective, the strategy was to attain influence—to make a difference in policy—rather than directly to provide services.

The multiplicity of pulls was reflected in the meandering course of the operation. In 1935, the fledging enterprise was put under the direction of Edmund Walsh, better known as the founder of the School of Foreign Service at Georgetown and subsequently confidante of Senator Joseph McCarthy. His celebrity promised success, and his anticommunist credentials suited the views of the Polish aristocrat, Vlodimir Ledochowski, who was superior general of the Jesuits at the time. But Walsh was distracted by commitments in Washington, and initial plans were not followed up.[59]

By the beginning of the 1940s two Jesuits of quite different styles emerged as players in shaping the direction of the ISO. One was John Delaney, whom Ledochowski appointed to direct the ISO but who, as it turned out, converted the New York labor school, which was supposed to be the flagship of the operation, into a venture in family therapy. The other was John LaFarge, scion of a cosmopolitan clan intimate with artistic and literary elites.[60] LaFarge envisioned the ISO as an implantation of *Action Populaire* on American soil. His objective was to elevate the intellectual content of the Institute, and the model he tried to emulate was European.[61]

With the death of Ledochowski in 1943 Delaney lost his patron and was removed as director of ISO. LaFarge was kept busy editing *America*. He functioned as an elder statesman rather than decision-maker, and his influence over the direction of the Institute turned out to be small. In the absence of a clear mandate for the organization, Daniel Lord assumed its direction in 1943. Lord brought enthusiasm and a reputation for getting things done to an amorphous situation. The result was a few years of hectic activity combining sodality-style work in Saint Louis, where Lord was headquartered, with annual roundups of Jesuits from across the country engaged in one way or another in social ministry.[62]

The move to Saint Louis implied a commitment to expand the project to national scope, and this goal was emphasized by the periodic meetings of Jesuits from different regions. But Lord was not a social thinker, and it was beginning to dawn on a few Jesuits that the social *magisterium* itself did not furnish ready answers to the social fluidity of postwar America. By 1947, Lord was replaced by Leo Brown, a Jesuit with a Harvard doctorate in economics. In fact Brown was less of an academic than a labor negotiator and consultant. Nevertheless, the change in leadership was accompanied by a clarification of the functions of the ISO. Now it was to be a research and training center for Jesuit analysts, affiliated with Saint Louis University but without the usual teaching obligations, rather than a miscellaneous network of more or less socially active Jesuit cadres.[63]

The restructuring appeared to be in line with the think-tank format of the *Action Populaire*. But the theoretical rationale of the Institute continued to be confused, the demographic audience that might support the enterprise was dubious, and as an educational hybrid it lacked institutional security. The prolonged boom in the postwar United States made Catholic social doctrine, especially as it came packaged in corporatist formulae, seem even stranger than it had during the 1930s.[64] Besides, there was no haven in Catholic academia for an organization like the ISO that downplayed teaching and gave priority to research. The Institute existed in an intellectual and institutional limbo.

The unsteady course of the Institute of Social Order reflected divergent goals. Devising policy applicable to American social realities was one thing; preserving immutable principles was another. The tension between the timeless and the universal, on the one hand, and the dynamics and pragmatism of the American experience, on the other, was structural as well as intellectual. The viability of the ISO was premised on orderliness or at least strong continuity in two spheres in which changes turned out to occur cumulatively, quickly, and more or less simultaneously. Education and suburbanization eroded the walls surrounding the Catholic ghetto, and the blue-collar occupations on which American Catholicism had been built went into decline. These denominational and class parameters had been receptive to a mentality that prized both stability and social practicality. The imaginative edifice of immigrant Catholicism, an amalgam of medievalism and Counter-Reformation rhetoric imported from Europe, retained the interest of a dialect that persisted in the New World even after it had fallen into disuse in the metropole. But it had lost credibility as an intellectual system, and its social underpinnings were collapsing fast.[65]

Through much of the lifespan of the Institute of Social Order, from 1943 until 1963, the Jesuits published a magazine whose editorial shifts mirrored changes in their institutional and intellectual environment. In the early days *Social Order* treated the theoretical foundations of Catholic social thought as more or less unalterable. This position encouraged cautious reform and calls for getting the facts straight rather than revolutionary ardor or imaginative analysis. The priority given to the pastoral aspects of social ministry in the absence of intellectual rigor drained the field of challenge.[66] As if in recognition of the hazards of popularizing a paternalistic and hierarchical social program that came with alien labeling, a few of the articles in the first issues of *Social Order* affected the peppy manner of Belloc/Chestertonian journalism. Only very rarely did the journal adopt the scientific tone of an academic review.

Toward the end of the fifties, with the appointment of Edward Duff as editor, an effort was made to enliven and improve the quality of the magazine. Duff opened a series of articles on "Catholic social action in the American environment" with the traditional premise that "we have moral theology insights providing clear directives in intra-personal relationships."[67] But, he added, while this core of verities sufficed for issues of personal ethics and "intrapersonal relations"—that is, for "questions of faith and morals"— problems of economic and political policy could not be solved by analogy with dilemmas of individual morality and family life. "My simple argument," Duff wrote, "is that we do not have today [a] developed body of Catholic social teaching, concretely applicable to the American scene."[68]

Duff's comments did not constitute an attack-by-hindsight on the traditions of social Catholicism but a warning against extending into the present time a pastoral approach geared to "the immediate relief of personal distress" that seemed to have worked well enough up through the thirties and forties but that was now suffering from intellectual and institutional fatigue.[69] Catholics had yet to recognize that economic and political disputes could no longer be resolved as they had been in the old neighborhoods, as spats within the family. The disjuncture between private morality and public policy at the national level could not be overcome by exhortations to abandon selfishness.

> If concentration on labor-management issues has in the past marked American Catholic social thinking and if an uncritical acceptance of a middle-class ideology known as the American Way of Life threatens to blur the clarity and particularity of the Catholic vision, it will be apparent why American Catholicism—apart from its impressive range of charitable institutions—has small influence on the direction of American society or the policies of the national government.[70]

Duff pinpointed the difference between the service model of social action, directed at the tribal communities of the Catholic subculture, which he characterized as obsolescent, and a more sophisticated model of political influence, directed at secular policy, which had yet to be attained. Inattention to political ideas encouraged a conservative inertia and petty moralism that diverted American Catholics toward a simplistic anti-Communism wary of newer movements favoring civil liberties, racial justice, and third-world causes.

However, it was not just the paternalistic view of labor-management relations, which many Jesuits agreed could be updated without damaging Catholic teaching, or Cold War shibboleths that got in the way of reform in domestic and international policy. Complacency with the settlement of the management-labor divisions of the thirties and forties and the movement toward global concerns tended to obscure transformations of a subjective nature that were occurring in the values of younger cohorts, and there was as yet no framework to make sense of this latent restlessness. In the abundance of postwar America, modes of personal conduct and interpersonal relations that were once thought to be steadfast came into question on a large scale.[71] The shift was not merely another symptom of the perennial battle between the young and the old but a rearrangement of the terms of the struggle itself, brought on by prosperity and technological advances in the media. In their efforts to situate the Catholic tradition within a modernizing America the Jesuits had come up against a fused combination of generational change and historical transformation.

8

The Institute of Social Order attained its peak manpower in 1951. Including the editor and assistant editor of *Social Order,* the staff totaled ten Jesuits then. By 1960, the number of Jesuits assigned to the ISO had dwindled to five. The next year a subcommittee appointed by the provincials recommended discontinuing publication of *Social Order* and cutting the staff of the ISO further. The downsizing was put off by the general of the order, who would not countenance such a drastic curtailment of the social apostolate on the part of the American Jesuits in the same year that John XXIII had issued *Mater et Magistra* to mark the thirtieth anniversary of the previous social encyclical.[72] Ten years later, the operation was disbanded.

The labor schools set up by the Jesuits and other clerics in the thirties and forties underwent a parallel decline. In 1947, at their peak, Leo Brown was able to count

> no fewer than ninety-eight education programs for workmen conducted under Catholic auspices. Twenty-four labor schools are associated with Catholic colleges or universities; sixty-four schools are sponsored by parishes or diocesan institutions. In addition, there are five forums, which are conducted much in the manner of labor schools, and five labor institutes.[73]

Leftist and middle-of-the-road forces were still fighting for control of the union moment. The internecine battles of the thirties reemerged after the hiatus of the war. The Jesuits still had a service to offer to Catholic laborers who wanted to defend themselves and perhaps make good in these power struggles.[74]

By the end of the fifties most of the labor schools were offering intermittent classes in industrial relations or had shut their doors altogether. The schools folded because the market in which they offered their services had shrunk and been penetrated by able competitors. They were typically one- or two-man shops that had outlived their usefulness as the unions gained competence during the war years and afterwards. Political conditions had also changed. "Preoccupation with the anti-Communist approach," one observer noted, "left the Catholic program without a driving force after Walter Reuther came to office and routed the Communist element of the UAW."[75] Economically and culturally, too, the schools had less to offer. Full employment cut into their appeal, and television provided alternative recreation to the outings with the boys that the night classes had furnished in previous days. Leo Brown issued a postmortem in 1960:

> One of the most successful efforts of ISO in its early years, the labor-schools programs, was of diminishing usefulness. Industrial relations institutes were springing up all over the United States, and state and other secular universities were offering programs which were at least as attractive as our own labor schools. At the same time the need for such schools was rapidly diminishing. The inexperienced labor leaders of the 1930s had acquired experience. The unions, better established, became persuaded that they could provide their own educational programs. The obvious need for Jesuit activity in fields of social action had greatly diminished.[76]

Some of the labor schools, then, died of natural causes. Others changed their clientele to include both management and labor and managed to survive into the sixties and beyond. A very small number of second-wave labor schools came into being in the late fifties and early sixties in the South, focusing on the key domestic issue of racial integration while keeping some attention on tasks related to labor organizing.[77]

The factors that went into the demise of the ISO were more complex. When the Institute was reorganized in 1947 it set its sights not on action but on ideas. Original scholarship was to be the chief product, and influence on policy the eventual result. The Institute was supposed to advance sociological knowledge and to extend the application of Catholic thought to social policy without controverting the received teaching of the church. These presumptions became increasingly difficult to credit. While the norm persisted that the crux of the social *magisterium* should be approximately universal with respect to time and place, this criterion served less as a positive guide than as a stricture on adventurous thinking.[78]

The hope was that hard work and the requisite talent, supplied by Jesuits, would produce something very close to an unassailable synthesis of social thought. The talent was considerable, as was the zeal. By and large, however, the output was pedestrian. The logics of doctrine, scholarship, and problem-solving did not so much collide, either fruitfully or in combat, as go their separate ways. By the end, around Vatican II, the Jesuits were shrewd enough to recognize that the doctrine, far from being immutable, was undergoing substantial renovation. Yet the Jesuits associated with the ISO did not tap into the anomalies between ideas and social realities that provoke intellectual breakthroughs, and their religious and their secular sensibilities remained apart at the wellsprings of creativity.

The schools of social work, then, succeeded on their own terms. They had a clientele of lower-middle-class Catholics striving after upward mobility. Their intellectual ambitions were modest. They were certifying agencies, professional gatekeepers, rather than stimulants of original analysis or creativity. They found an institutional home in the pre-existing Jesuit educational apparatus.

The labor schools laid even less claim to intellectual creativity than the professional schools, nor were they capable of becoming paying or break-even enterprises for the Jesuits. They were probably less crucial to workers than the schools of social work and of commerce and finance were useful to lower-middle-class students. The payoff on both sides of the exchange was uncertain. Nevertheless, for over a decade they served a minor function, and they ceased to exist soon after the demand for their role slackened.

The Institute of Social Order was ambiguous in all aspects of institutional viability. On the one hand, it was supposed to be out ahead of the instructional, service model that was the prototype for both the social work and the labor schools. On the other hand, original ideas were neither easy to come by nor promoted within the topdown structures of Tridentine Catholicism. In addition, the "civilian" constituency for an exercise in distinctively Catholic social thought and policy was uncertain, given the shifting demographics of American Catholicism. Intellectually, organizationally, and demographically, the ISO was orphaned.

9

The fifties were a decade of unprecedented abundance when the labor schools began to wind down and when questions were raised with increasing frequency about whether the Institute of Social Order would find an intellectual compass. Sustained prosperity was disorienting for a world view erected on scarcity and austerity. By the end of the decade, malaise about the scale and complexity of social change became detectable among the American Jesuits. The task of understanding and shaping events was daunting.

Just before Christmas, 1958, Joseph Fitzpatrick delivered an address to the Jesuits at Woodstock College in Maryland, the premier seminary of the American branch of the Society, in which he gave an overview of the trends that were transforming the old parameters of the social apostolate. His theme was the disappearance of the certainty of simpler times and the appearance of doubt in the face of complexity. His presentation was a threnody for the vanished stage of industrialization when Jesuits felt they understood and could influence social change.[79]

> It is indeed a strange shift in the affairs of men. . . . [I]n the depths of the depression, when hunger was a common thing on our city streets; when resources were limited and experience slight, men had a confident optimism about the social apostolate; whereas today, at the height of a prosperous era, when resources are relatively abundant and experiences rich, men are hesitant, doubtful and reluctant. . . . [These are] days of doubt, 1948 to the present, days when the dimensions of our world have been twisted and stretched by extraordinary events, and we have not quite determined how the social apostolate should be related to a changing world of which we know so little.[80]

Formerly, optimism and certainty had been kept up by what appeared to be the starker and smaller, less impersonal proportions of social problems. Innocence might also have been encouraged, although Fitzpatrick did not dwell on the possibility, by the ignorance and parochialism of some of the Jesuit pioneers in labor relations during the thirties.[81] Anticommunism had cast antagonists into bold relief.

> We had the conviction that we knew what social evils were. We could see them, in the exploitation of workingmen; in the lack of social responsibility in business; in the menace of communism. The social apostolate, therefore, was a well-defined task. We were to teach people what communism was; teach workingmen how to organize and manage their unions; teach employers the Catholic principles of social justice. The solution of the problems was being worked out dramatically all around us. The CIO came into its own when Lewis led his followers out of the AFL convention of 1935. The auto workers were organized in the sit-down strikes of 1936. The Wagner act was declared constitutional in 1937. Minimum wage legislation was passed; and social security. The Spanish civil war broke out in July of 1936. Lenin had said clearly that, "The torch of Europe would burn at both ends." Moscow and Madrid were to be the two poles of the relentless axis of communism. Every hour of the conflict became for us a symbol, first of the failure to correct the

social abuses that had led to the conflict; secondly of the struggle of embattled Christians against the communist menace. We felt, as we manifested our interests in the social apostolate, that we were part of a dynamic movement that was doing things and getting somewhere. We were convinced that social justice was in the making.[82]

World War II, Fitzpatrick argued, "put a sudden end to optimism, not only in the social apostolate, but in most other areas of life as well." It was not so much the war itself as the experience of the magnitude of social change that mass mobilization and technological advancement forced on Jesuits. The tidiness of the parochial order had given way to an unmanageable cosmopolitanism.

We realized that the problem that we had defined in measurable terms and for which we thought we had solutions, was actually only one small aspect of a world-wide problem of unbelievable proportions. Men lost all confidence that they had an answer; in fact, they began to realize they did not even know how to define the problem.[83]

"The problem," as Fitzpatrick saw it, was actually a composite of half a dozen transformations in social structure and politics, on an international scale. The first involved the magnification of the potential for destruction in armed conflict, between the Soviet Union and the United States.

Fitzpatrick was a sociologist, not an analyst of world conflict, and he relegated his exposition of the dangers of the Cold War to a single paragraph. He focused instead on developments that were making for realignments between North and South and for shifts in the balance of power within Catholicism itself. One of these was population growth. "Latin America is growing so rapidly and the number of priests is growing so slowly that, if the trend continues, by the year 2000, Latin America may be predominantly pagan, with a few islands of Catholicism."[84] Fitzpatrick understood that the differential growth in population between North and South would contribute to the passing of the era of a predominantly Anglo-Irish-American Catholicism.

Several other structural changes contributed to a weakening sense of control. Urbanization bred a "cultural disorganization" that threatened the communities in which Catholicism thrived. While they helped fortify American leadership of the capitalist world, "technological achievements" also went with an increasing depersonalization and "white-collar way of life." One corollary of this complexity was especially poignant for Jesuits with memories of the thirties:

The labor unions are no longer the struggling campaigners they once were. . . . Many of them are big, well-established, sometimes powerful, and, in an embarrass-ing number of instances, more guilty of injustice than the employers whose in-justices they professed to correct.[85]

Fitzpatrick saw that the "area of dramatic development today," generating the enthusiasm once reserved for the labor movement, was "in the field of integration, interracial relations." This was unknown territory for most Catholics, Jesuits included.

Fitzpatrick turned finally to a traditional focus of Catholic concern, the family. His list of social problems, starting with the global and massively structural, had worked down to the local, "probably the area of most effective social action today." It was here, Fitzpatrick suggested, that the balance between complexity and manageability favored Jesuits with a practical slant on social reform.

The personalism of family relations contrasted poignantly with the emphasis on structural transformations that pervaded the essay and that contributed to the air of melancholy—not characteristic of Fitzpatrick's other writings—and the elegiac review of times passed. Fitzpatrick stressed the importance of social changes in the aggregate partly to remind his audience of the solipsistic perils of the existential currents then fashionable in Catholic intellectual circles. "I believe you are more inclined," Fitzpatrick observed, "to set aside reports about the teamsters and longshoremen in order to follow the latest developments in theology."[86] At the same time, while his observations on the forces underlying recent social changes were sweeping, he did not even hint at a theory of comparably global proportions that might give a clearer sense of their interconnectedness. No grand integration was forthcoming.

Fitzpatrick concluded with a twofold recommendation. He insisted on the importance of humble "tasks of the social apostolate on the local level, the tasks that do not need extensive organization, the tasks that every Jesuit can find all around him if he has the time to give to them . . . the family apostolate, close contact with the poor in order to assist and guide them, interracial and inter-group relations, work with youth." There was a *prima facie* urgency to remedial work in these areas. Jesuits needed motivation, not specialized training, to work effectively or at least to make a start at this level. The other priority was scholarship, for "social action is a dangerous or a futile thing if it is not supported by competent scholarship." Fitzpatrick argued that "large or small, social action will be increasingly effective in so far as it is guided by competent and scholarly knowledge."[87]

. . . I have told you nothing definite that could give you a sense of security; nor have I told you anything inspiring that can fire your enthusiasm. It would be unfortunate if we became too distressed about our doubts, or if we attributed our doubts to our deficiencies. Doubt and uncertainty are the characteristics of the entire world, and our own doubt and uncertainty simply reflect the all-pervading uncertainty of the times in which we live. The doubt and hesitation should not be taken as signs that there is little that we can do, but as signs that the much more to be done will require greater patience, more painstaking scholarship, and a greater daring that has its security in an abiding confidence in God.

Your generation will have a task much more difficult than my generation had.[88]

10

It may be that no more uniformity exists in the development and diffusion of social ministry by the Society of Jesus during the half-century between the Modernist crisis and Vatican II than Kelemen was able to make out in the riot of baroque and rococo art produced by the Jesuits in Europe and Latin America. In reality, whatever its pretensions to universalism and time-lessness, the institutional and intellectual evolution of social ministry is contingent, bound by circumstance and built on exigency; and attempts to find a pattern in the carpet, a Jesuit style, may thus be futile and naive. From this perspective, theory is the part where Harpo plays the harp.

But uniformity is a limiting case of generality. Regularities, in the form of systematic differences, can be discerned. One such middle-range pattern is contained in the distinction between the service, the policy, and the intellectual goals of social ministry among Jesuits during the years leading up to Vatican II.

The schools of social work that the American Jesuits set up in the first half of the century provided a service: training in community organization, in therapeutic intervention, and the like. The service was educational rather than direct; very few Jesuits were social workers or community organizers themselves. At the same time, practical know-how rather than theoretical knowledge was transmitted. The schools broke from the classical, belletristic template of the liberal arts colleges, but they did not pioneer in original thought, as did some of the graduate programs in secular universities. The schools of social work delivered a service—training in skills useful for white-collar occupations. Graduates could do well by doing good.

The labor schools were the second important experiment of the American Jesuits in supplying services relevant to social questions. Like the professional schools, albeit at a more rudimentary level, the labor schools instructed their students in practical techniques. The Jesuits involved in them came closer to direct action, less in political agitation than in the lending of a sympathetic ear to working men burdened with financial and personal worries. Many of the schools had a strong pastoral orientation. The parish was occupationally rather than territorially defined.

In the beginning, the clienteles of the professional and the labor schools alike were drawn mostly from the Catholic subculture. Even then, there were signs of heterodoxy. The professional schools admitted women long before the high schools and liberal arts colleges of the Jesuits. After all, social work faculties trained members of the helping professions, and these professions were largely feminine. The labor schools cultivated a clientele beneath the lower-middle class and the upper fringes of the working class that fed the mainstream schools of the Society. These reforms were inspired by local conditions, not by directives from Rome. In contrast to the presuppositions that burdened the Institute of Social Order, such measures did not depend on the existence of Catholic surroundings.

The professional schools have survived, the labor schools have disappeared. Although the ethnic and denominational composition of the market differs from that of earlier times, there still is a market for training in middle-level service roles.[89] The older Catholic working class that was the backbone of blue-collar unionism shrunk, and the unions themselves took over training in organizational and administrative techniques. The labor schools did not so much fail as fade away, as they ran out of functions to perform.

The Jesuits were less successful in meeting two other goals: that of gaining influence over policy making and that of developing and disseminating fresh ideas on social and political questions. The influence objective, like that of the provision of services, was geared to practice. A crucial difference was that in the United States the arena of influence was predominantly secular and competitive; services, on the other hand, could be delivered primarily to a Catholic constituency. Policy alternatives, no matter how correct they might be in the light of Catholic doctrine, could not be urged upon a large multidenominational audience by fiat or the presumption of familiarity. Success in the policy game required politics: jockeying for power, lobbying, electioneering.

While American Catholics proved no less adept at this than members of other religions, the Jesuits themselves did not bring anything either distinctively Catholic or intellectually novel to debates over social policy. At least until their exodus to the suburbs, graduates of Jesuit professional schools could be found in the city halls, police departments, welfare agencies, and other arms of the civil service in the Northeast and Midwest, forming a reserve of good will that smoothed the path of church interests through the public bureaucracy. But the professional schools were not in the business of training intellectual leaders, and the provision of services affected the formulation of policy at a distant remove. Strategically, the causal flow went in the other direction, from the shaping of policy to its implementation.[90]

Ideas were the missing link between the provision of services and the shaping of social policy. Through the decades leading up to Vatican II, the Jesuits lacked a social theory germane to the American context. It was not only that corporatist ideas were foreign; so were a good many other political and esthetic fashions that were absorbed piecemeal into the American scene. The static and hierarchical features of corporatism did not help. But even these characteristics might not have been crippling. After all, pluralist theory presumed interorganizational democracy but internal hierarchy, and the structural functionalism that dominated American sociology was weak on dynamics.[91] The mortal flaw was that corporatist theory presupposed a predominantly Catholic setting. The terminology made some sense, as did the Latin liturgy, within Catholic enclaves in the United States. Outside of these ghettoes, however, the ideas seemed weird and possibly dangerous.[92]

Jesuits attached to the Institute of Social Order did not confront the

American creed with Catholic social theory. For the most part they concentrated on themes, such as labor relations, of evident practical concern to the American Catholic community. They wrote competent reports. By and large, the few Jesuits who gained national and international reputations in the social sciences stayed clear of the ISO orbit.[93]

Two reasons can be adduced for the failure of the Jesuits to attain eminence in the social sciences. One was material: a lack of financial resources. This problem plagued almost all of the Society's institutions of higher education.[94] Another obstacle was cultural. Outright censorship may have been less of an barrier (although it was always a threat, as the silencing of Murray demonstrated) than the constriction induced by the premise that, at least in what was of genuine consequence, there was nothing new to learn.[95] One effect of this supposition was to channel creative urges into verbal embellishment. Another was to take creativity out of research. Factual description overtook critical interpretation. Ironically, the compartmentalization enjoined by "realistic moderation" provided an escape from testing ideas with data. The results were professional but largely pedestrian.

An exception to this division of intellectual labor, one that winds up proving the rule, was the priority that Jesuits gave to the sociology of the family. In this area the potentially creative friction was only partly between social theory and evidence; the greater tension was between moral concern and social change.

The centrality of the family in the social thought of American Jesuits stems from the belief that gender relations are in effect immutable absolutes transcending transformations in social structures and political ephemera. With this basic position as a given, four different visions of the family come into view, in chronological order and, roughly, in order of sophistication.[96]

The simplest is the image of the paternalistic family as a micromodel of the good society; benevolent government is the family writ large. Treatment of the family as a microcosm of the larger polity was pervasive in the agrarian-medieval depictions of preindustrial utopias. The metaphor corresponded to a triumphalist, Constantinian understanding of church-state relations.[97]

A second-stage model attributes to the family a stabilizing role at the base of a variety of political and social systems. The notion of a narrow congruity between the family and the form of the state is abandoned as unduly literal. The hierarchical family socializes children into the work ethic and helps produce citizens whose values are compatible with a diversity of political forms. It is the universal linchpin of social order.[98]

Both of these perspectives, the first more assertively than the second, claim that the family affects the form of governments or the governability of different political systems. A third approach takes the opposite view, namely, that the traditional family is threatened by the modern state and must be protected as an island of virtue. It is an enclave under siege, like the church itself, rather than a paradigm or positive underpinning of the rest of the social aggregate. The balance of influence has shifted from the family to the forces at large in society—notably, to the interventionist state.[99]

Lastly, since Vatican II, an image of the family of man, of the human community, has evolved to reflect the "catholicity" of Catholic social doctrine. The vision is one of values that transcend political borders, national boundaries, and racial barriers. The stress on culture-specific family patterns as ethical and political paragons is somewhat less insistent.[100]

In all of these perspectives, norms governing the family and the role of women are vital to the proper functioning of society as a whole. In none of them is the angle of vision purely analytical. More typically, the view is, on the one hand, practical and concrete in its concern with a tangible unit of social organization and, on the other, sacramental and esthetic in investing the family and women with a symbolic, quasi-salvific charge. Questions of identity and programs of action tend to be fused. It is this sensibility, more expressive than sociological, that courses through Jesuit thinking on strategic social issues but that rarely found overt release in either the applied or the theoretical ventures in social ministry during the preconciliar period.[101]

Recently, the frustration of progressive hopes in social management has stimulated mutual curiosity about the interconnectedness between this tendency in Catholicism and American liberalism. Earlier efforts by Jesuits and other Catholic intellectuals to engage the American establishment were stymied in part by doubts that they had anything distinctively Catholic to contribute to the dialogue. There was no evident mode of transition from the service to the influence mode. For a variety of reasons such hesitancy has receded. But that is another story.[102]

Notes

1. See among others Thomas Philip Faase, *Making the Jesuits More Modern* (Washington, D.C.: University Press of America, 1981); William VanEtten Casey, S.J. and Philip Nobile, eds., *The Berrigans* (New York, 1971), and John Seidler and Katherine Meyer, *Conflict and Change in the Catholic Church* (New Brunswick, N.J.: Rutgers University Press, 1989).

2. See Richard L. Camp, *The Papal Ideology of Social Reform: A Study in Historical Development* (Leiden, E. J. Brill, 1969).

3. See Andrew M. Greeley, *The American Catholic: A Social Portrait* (New York: Basic Books, 1977) and Irene Woodward, ed., *The Catholic Church: The United States Experience* (New York: Paulist Press, 1979).

4. See Joseph B. Gremillion, ed., *The Church and Culture since Vatican II: The Experience of North and South America* (Notre Dame, Ind.: University of Notre Dame, 1985).

5. Compare Peter Kivisto, "The Brief Career of Catholic Sociology," *Sociological Analysis* 50 (1989): 351–61 and Loretta M. Morris, "Secular Transcendence: From ACSS to ASR," *Sociological Analysis* 50 (1989): 329–49.

6. Gerald A. McCool, S.J., *Catholic Theology in the Nineteenth Century: The Quest for a Unitary Method* (New York: Seabury Press, 1977).

7. See for example Oswald Von Nell-Breuning, S.J., *Reorganization of Social Economy* (Milwaukee, Wis.: Bruce Publishing Co., 1937).

8. Compare John B. Killoran, "Maritain's Critique of Liberalism," *Notes et Documents* 21/22 (1988): 110–22.

9. See Gerald Fogarty, S.J., *The Vatican and the American Hierarchy from 1870 to 1965* (Wilmington, Del.: Michael Glazier, 1985).

10. See Donald E. Pellotte, *John Courtney Murray: Theologian in Conflict* (New York: Paulist Press, 1976) and J. Leon Hooper, S.J., *The Ethics of Discourse: The Social Philosophy of John Courtney Murray* (Washington, D.C.: Georgetown University Press, 1987).

11. John Courtney Murray, S.J., *We Hold These Truths: Catholic Reflections on the American Proposition* (New York: Sheed and Ward, 1960).

12. Gerald A. McCool, S.J., "Neo-Thomism and the Tradition of St. Thomas," *Thought* 62 (1987): 131–46.

13. See Alfonso Alvarez Bolado, S.J., *El Experimento del Nacional-Catolicismo, 1939–1975* (Madrid: Editorials Cuadernos para al Diálogo, 1976) and John D. Stephens, "Democratic Transition and Breakdown in Western Europe, 1870–1939: A Test of Moore's Thesis," *American Journal of Sociology* (1989): 1019–77.

14. See Carl Strikwerda, "The Divided Class: Catholics vs. Socialists in Belgium, 1880–1914," *Comparative Studies in Society and History* 30 (1988): 333–59.

15. See Richard Oestreicher, "Urban Working-Class Political Behavior and Theories of American Electoral Politics, 1870–1940," *Journal of American History* 74 (1988): 1257–88.

16. See David Blackbourn, "Progress and Piety: Liberalism, Catholicism and the State in Imperial Germany," *History Workshop Journal* 26 (1988): 57–78; Alfred Diamant, *Austrian Catholics and the First Republic: Democracy, Capitalism, and the Social Order, 1918–1934* (Princeton, N.J.: Princeton University Press, 1960), and Ralph Gleason, *The Conservative Reformers: German-American Catholics and the Social Order* (Notre Dame, Ind.: University of Notre Dame, 1968).

17. See Mary E. Brown, "Competing to Care: Aiding Italian Immigrants in New York Harbor, 1890s–1930s," *Mid-America* 71 (1989): 37–51 and Gary R. Mormino, *Immigrants on the Hill: Italian-Americans in St. Louis, 1882–1982* (Urbana, Ill.: University of Illinois Press, 1986).

18. See Tom Garvin, *Nationalist Revolutionaries in Ireland, 1858–1910* (Oxford: Oxford University Press, 1987) and Donal McCartney, *The Dawning of Democracy: Ireland 1800–1870* (Dublin: Helicon, 1987); compare Stephen P. Erie, *Rainbow's End: Irish-Americans and the Dilemmas of Urban Machine Politics, 1840–1985* (Berkeley, Calif.: University of California Press, 1988).

19. Timothy J. Meagher, ed., *From Paddy to Studs: Irish-American Communities in the Turn of the Century Era, 1880 to 1920* (Westport, Conn.: Greenwood Press, 1986).

20. See the analysis of "militant respectability" by Hugh McLeod, "Catholicism and the New York Irish, 1880–1910," in *Disciplines of Faith: Studies in Religion, Politics and Patriarchy*, eds. Jim Obelkevich, Lyndal Roper, and Raphael Samuel (London: Routledge and Kegan Paul, 1987).

21. Compare Joel Perlman, *Ethnic Differences: Schooling and Social Structure among the Irish, Italians, Jews, and Blacks in an American City, 1880–1935* (Cambridge: Cambridge University Press, 1988).

22. See Henry Steele Commager, *The Empire of Reason: How Europe Imagined and America Realized the Enlightenment* (Garden City, N.Y.: Anchor Press, 1977).

23. See Nathan Glazer and Daniel Patrick Moynihan, *Beyond the Melting Pot* (Cambridge, Massachusetts: M.I.T. Press, 1964).

24. Manpower was spread so thin that the quality of the schools suffered. The

Jesuits stayed clear of primary education; the task of training in literacy, numeracy, and manners was left to nuns. The Jesuits were most successful in secondary education, where they concentrated on the skills required for white-collar mobility. Their colleges and universities gave credible training in classics and incorporated respectable professional schools, but they were not outstanding as centers of intellectual advancement.

25. See for example John LaFarge, S.J., *The Race Question and the Negro* (New York: Longmans Green and Co., 1932).

26. See Joseph Husslein, S.J., *The World Problem: Capital, Labor, and the Church* (New York: P. J. Kennedy and Sons, 1918) and George G. Higgins, "Joseph Caspar Husslein, S.J.," *Social Order* 6 (1953): 51–53.

27. Michael D. Clark, "Ralph Adams Cram and the Americanization of the Middle Ages," *Journal of American Studies* 23 (1989): 195–213 and Bernard Rosenthal and Paul E. Szarmach, eds., *Mevievalism in American Culture* (Binghamton, N.Y.: Center for Medieval and Early Renaissance Studies, 1989). The neomedieval fad was part of larger movement, not limited to Catholics, with social-utopian as well as esthetic components. Regional art was another offshoot. A judicious overview of the utopian strand is given in Edward K. Spann, *Brotherly Tomorrow: Movements for a Cooperative Society in America, 1820–1920* (New York: Columbia University Press, 1989). The back-to-the-land schemes of the twenties and thirties were precursors of the small-is-beautiful movement that emerged in the sixties: for an update, see Marty Strange, *Family Farming: A New Economic Vision* (Lincoln, Nebr.: University of Nebraska, 1988). Francis Oakley, *The Medieval Experience* (New York: Scribners, 1974) provides an assessment of the medieval period on the basis of modern scholarship rather than nostalgia. Perhaps the major byproduct of the fascination with the medieval, however, was esthetic: see Umberto Eco, *The Middle Ages of James Joyce: The Aesthetics of Chaosmos* (London: Hutchinson Radins, 1989).

28. See Sean Dennis Cashman, *America in the Twenties and Thirties: The Olympian Age of Franklin Delano Roosevelt* (New York: New York University Press, 1989) and David J. O'Brien, *American Catholics and Social Reform: The New Deal Years* (New York: Oxford University Press, 1968).

29. See Robert Wuthnow, *The Restructuring of American Religion* (Princeton, N.J.: Princeton University Press, 1989). The distancing of American Catholicism from the compensatory patriotism of immigrant days was also stimulated by the Vietnam war, which served to mobilize the Catholic left. However, it is the role of government vis-à-vis the family—in particular, the abortion issue—that has galvanized the ecclesiastical establishment.

30. See Luigi G. Ligutti and John C. Rawe, S.J., *Rural Roads to Security: America's Third Struggle for Freedom* (Milwaukee: The Bruce Publishing Co., 1940) and Peter J. Schmitt, *Back to Nature: The Arcadian Myth in Urban America* (New York: Oxford University Press, 1969). The clearest parallel with the pastoral ideal advocated by a handful of Jesuits was the program of the Southern Agrarians; see Paul K. Conkin, *The Southern Agrarians* (Knoxville, Tenn.: University of Tennessee Press, 1988) and Michael O'Brien, *The Idea of the American South, 1920–1941* (Baltimore, Md.: Johns Hopkins University Press, 1979). Not all programs of preindustrial social ministry sponsored by Jesuits in North America were escapist or esthetic. Their work among Native Americans goes back to the period of settlement and continues to the present. See Hiram Martin Chittenden and Alfred Talbot Richardson, *Life, Letters and Travels of Father Pierre-Jean DeSmet, S.J., 1801–1873* (New York: F. P. Harper, 1905) and James P. Ronda, "Black Robes and Boston Men: Indian-White Relations in New France and New England, 1524–1701," in Philip Weeks, ed., *The American Indian Experience, A Profile: 1524 to the Present* (Arlingon Heights, Ill.: Forum Press, 1988).

31. This aspect of Jesuit social thought is treated more fully in Peter McDonough,

"Metamorphoses of the Jesuits: Sexual Identity, Gender Roles and Hierarchy in Catholicism," *Comparative Studies in Society and History* 32 (April 1990).

32. Compare T. Jackson Lears, *No Place of Grace: Antimodernism and the Transformation of American Culture, 1880–1920* (New York: Pantheon Books, 1981).

33. Thurston Davis, "Blueprint for a College," *Jesuit Educational Quarterly* 6 (October 1973): 74.

34. Ibid., 76–77.

35. The ideal was probably most closely approximated by the College of the Holy Cross in Massachusetts.

36. Thurston N. Davis, S.J., "Major Trends in American Non-Jesuit Higher Education," *Jesuit Educational Quarterly* 18 (June 1955): 5–16.

37. Compare Robert F. Harvanek, S.J., "The Changing Structure of the American Jesuit High School," *Jesuit Educational Quarterly* 13 (1960): 69–83 and Harvanek, "The Objectives of the American Jesuit University: A Dilemma," *Jesuit Educational Quarterly* 14 (1961): 69–87.

38. "Obituary of Father Terence J. Shealy," *Woodstock Letters,* 52 (1923): 86–104.

39. When Shealy died, the Brooklyn *Tablet* wrote that "his dramatic denunciation of the sins of capitalism, his vehement attacks on present-day hypocrites, his sarcastic descriptions of milk-and-water Catholics, his mimicry of society personages, his invectives against the orgy of salaciousness that corrupts society, made such impressions on his hearers that they never forgot him." *Ibid.,* 100.

40. Ibid., 90–91.

41. Anonymous, "Laymen's League for Retreats, New York," *Woodstock Letters* 42 (1913): 67–69.

42. Gerald C. Treacy, S.J., "The Beginnings of the Retreat Movement in America," *First Annual Conference* (1928): 13–19.

43. See Giacomo de Antonellis, *Storia dell'Azione Cattolica dal 1867 a Oggi* (Milan, 1987). This was equally true of the model college described by Thurston Davis.

44. See Robert M. Crunden, *Ministers of Reform: The Progressives' Achievement in American Civilization, 1889–1920* (New York: Basic Books, 1982).

45. For an attempt to fit the professional schools in the Jesuit educational tradition, see George Ganss, S.J., "Education for Business in the Jesuit University: A Study in Constitutional Law," *Jesuit Educational Quarterly* 23 (1961): 133–50. A brief account of the growth of the Jesuit business schools is given by Raymond Baumhart, S.J., "Jesuit Topsy: The College of Commerce," *Social Order* 3 (May 1950): 215–18.

46. While the professional schools may not have been progenitors of grand theory, they were adventurous in a number of important ways. The matriculation of women was potentially subversive of Jesuit educational tradition. Unlike the liberal arts colleges, the professional schools—with the possible exception of the law faculties—did not cultivate *eloquentia perfecta,* and they were not likely to be articulate about their institutional innovations. In any case they probably chose to maintain a low profile on issues involving female education.

47. Austin G. Schmidt, S.J., ed., *Selected Writings of Father Ledochowski* (Chicago, Ill.: American Assistancy of the Society of Jesus, 1945): 907.

48. Robert H. Zieger, *American Workers, American Unions, 1920–1985* (Baltimore, Md.: Johns Hopkins University Press, 1986).

49. A higher-than-average proportion of Jesuit labor priests were probably spiritual coadjutors rather than fathers of the fourth vow.

50. Compare Ken Fones-Wolf, *Trade Union Gospel* (Philadelphia: Temple University Press, 1989).

51. The identification of religion with obscurantism by the urban intelligentsia

confirmed the Jesuits in their hostility to academic secularism and little-magazine bohemianism: see Terry A. Cooney, *The Rise of the New York Intellectuals: Partisan Review and Its Circle* (Madison, Wis.: University of Wisconsin Press, 1986). See also Joseph T. Clark, S.J., "Some Lessons Learned from Anti-Communist Activity," *Woodstock Letters* 67 (1938): 245–60 and Philip E. Dobson, S.J., "The Xavier Labor School," *Woodstock Letters* 68 (1939): 266–79.

52. Joshua B. Freeman, "Catholics, Communists, and Republicans: Irish Workers and the Organization of the Transport Workers Union," in *Working Class America: Essays on Labor, Community, and American Society,* eds. Michael H. Frisch and Daniel J. Walkowitz (Urbana, Ill.: University of Illinois Press, 1983).

53. Neil P. Hurley, S.J., "The Catholic Evidence League of New York City," *Woodstock Letters* 82 (1953): 301–16; Philip A. Carey, S.J., typed notes, Xavier Institute of Labor Relations, n.d. (late 1950s?)

54. James J. McGinley, S.J., *Labor Relations in New York Rapid Transit System, 1904–1944* (New York: King's Crown Press, 1949).

55. Joseph P. Fitzpatrick, S.J., "Contact with 'Little People' Formed Xavier's Labor Priest," *National Jesuit News* (April 1978): 18. Sometimes the pastoral and the local-political functions were indistinguishable. The work of Carey's colleague John Corridan inspired the movie "On the Waterfront"; see Allen Raymond, *Waterfront Priest* (New York: Holt, 1955).

56. John P. Delaney, S.J., Bulletin of Institute of Social Order, New York, mimeo, December 1940, 11 pp., Missouri Province archives, and Delaney, "Retreats for Working Men," Service Bulletin, Institute of Social Order, mimeo, December 1941, 18 pp., Xavier Labor School archives.

57. Anthony L. Ostheimer and John P. Delaney, S.J., *Christian Principles and National Problems* (Chicago: W. H. Sadlier, Inc., 1945) and Ostheimer, *The Family: A Thomistic Study in Social Philosophy* (Washington, D.C.: The Catholic University of America, 1939).

58. See Paul Droulers, S.J., *Le Père Desbuquois et l'Action Populaire* (Paris, 1980).

59. See Donald F. Crosby, S.J., *God, Church and Flag: Senator Joseph McCarthy and the Catholic Church, 1950–1957* (Chapel Hill, N.C.: University of North Carolina Press, 1978); Louis J. Gallagher, S.J., "Father Edmund Walsh," *Woodstock Letters* 86 (1957): 21–70; "Plan of Action for the Establishment of a Christian Social Order, Through Jesuit Activity," Chicago, 1 June 1935, 9 pp., Missouri Province archives, and the twenty-one-page pamphlet published as *An Integrated Program of Social Order* (St. Louis, Mo.: Queen's Work, 1935).

60. Henry Adams et al., *John LaFarge* (New York: Abbeville Press, 1987) and Abraham A. Davidson, *The Eccentrics and Other American Visionary Painters* (New York: Dutton, 1978).

61. John LaFarge, S.J., "Scope and Method of the Proposed New York Social Action Institute," 7 pp., n.d. (probably 1939), Missouri Province archives.

62. See *Played by Ear: The Autobiography of Daniel A. Lord, S.J.* (Chicago, 1956) and Joseph T. McGloin, S.J., *Backstage Missionary: Father Dan Lord, S.J.* (New York, 1958).

63. Both Lord and Brown generated considerable income from various outside projects. Most of the revenues that Lord collected came from the sale of inspirational pamphlets; Brown was paid for consulting and arbitration. The capacity to finance at least in part the ISO was almost surely a factor in their appointments by the American provincials as directors of the operation. See Gladys W. Gruenberg, *Labor Peacemaker: The Life and Works of Father Leo C. Brown, S.J.* (Saint Louis: The Institute of Jesuit Sources, 1981).

64. A significant effort at rehabilitation was Bernard W. Dempsey, S.J., *The*

Functional Economy: The Bases of Economic Organization (Englewood Cliffs, N.J.: Prentice-Hall, 1958). Dempsey had studied under Joseph Schumpeter at Harvard, had translated Von Breuning's compendium on corporatism, and at the time of writing his own book was dean of the School of Commerce and Finance at Saint Louis University.

65. See Robert D. Cross, *The Emergence of Liberal Catholicism in America* (Cambridge, Mass.: Harvard University Press, 1958).

66. See also Charles R. McKenney, S.J., *Moral Problems in Social Work* (Milwaukee, Wis.: Bruce Publishing Co., 1951).

67. Edward Duff, S.J., "Social Action in the American Environment," *Social Order* (September 1959): 299.

68. Ibid., 302.

69. Duff, "Catholic Social Action in the American Environment," *Social Order* (September 1962), 302–3.

70. Duff, *op. cit.,* 310.

71. See John Patrick Diggins, *The Proud Decades: America in War and Peace, 1941–1960* (New York: Norton Press, 1988) and Philip Rieff, *The Triumph of the Therapeutic: Uses of Faith after Freud* (New York: University of Chicago Press, 1968).

72. See Joseph N. Moody and Justus George Lawler, eds., *The Challenge of "Mater et Magistra"* (New York: Herder and Herder, 1963).

73. Leo Cyril Brown, S.J., "Catholic-Sponsored Labor-Management Education," *Journal of Educational Sociology* 20 (1947): 510.

74. See Joseph M. McShane, S.J., "The Jesuits and Organized Labor in the City of New York, 1936–1988," paper presented at the Conference on American Catholicism in the Twentieth Century, University of Notre Dame, November 1–3, 1990.

75. Mark A. Fitzgerald, C.S.C., "Labor and Management Go Back to School," *Grail* (October 1954), 22.

76. Brown, "History of ISO," mimeo, Missouri province archives, 1961, 8.

77. Clement J. McNapsy, S.J., *At Face Value: A Biography of Father Louis J. Twomey, S.J.* (New Orleans: Institute of Human Relations, 1978).

78. A significant effort to sort through this problem was made by Philip S. Land and George P. Klubertanz, S.J., "Practical Reason, Social Fact, and the Vocational Order," *Modern Schoolman* 28 (1951): 239–66.

79. Compare David Halle, *America's Working Man* (Chicago: University of Chicago Press, 1986).

80. Joseph P. Fitzpatrick, S.J., "New Directions in the Social Apostolate," *Woodstock Letters* 88 (April 1959): 115–16.

81. See for example William J. Smith, S.J., *Spotlight on Labor Unions* (New York: Essential Books, Duell, Sloan and Peares, 1946).

82. Fitzpatrick, *op cit.,* 117–18.

83. Ibid., 124.

84. Ibid., 126.

85. Ibid., 127–28.

86. Ibid., 115.

87. Ibid., 128–30.

88. Ibid., 130.

89. The School of General Studies at Fordham University is a present-day model for this type of education.

90. See James G. March and Johan P. Olsen, *Rediscovering Institutions: The Organizational Basis of Politics* (New York, 1989).

91. See William Buxton, *Talcott Parsons and the Capitalist Nation State* (Toronto: University of Toronto Press, 1985).

130 PETER MCDONOUGH

92. While the Catholic component of the American working class was large, one reason why corporatism never caught on among American Catholics is that historically the incidence of Catholic businessmen was low in the United States, compared to the size of this group in such countries as Belgium, France, Italy, and Austria, where a formalized corporatism was not entirely bizarre.

93. Aside from John Courtney Murray, the chief figures are Joseph Fitzpatrick and Joseph Fichter. See Fichter, *One-Man Research: Reminiscences of a Catholic Sociologist* (New York, 1973).

94. Paul A. Fitzgerald, S.J., *The Governance of Jesuit Colleges in the United States, 1920–1970* (Notre Dame, Ind.: University of Notre Dame Press, 1984) and Paul Hassenger, ed., *The Shape of Catholic Higher Education* (Chicago: University of Chicago Press, 1967).

95. See Gerald P. Fogarty, S.J., *Nova et Vetera: The Theology of Tradition in American Catholicism* (Milwaukee, Wis.: Marquetta University Press, 1987) and Michael V. Gannon, "Before and after Modernism: The Intellectual Isolation of the American Priest," in *The Catholic Priest in the United States: Historical Investigations,* ed. John Tracy Ellis (Collegeville, Minn.: Saint John's University Press, 1971).

96. Compare Steven Mintz and Susan Kellogg, *Domestic Revolutions: A Social History of American Family Life* (New York: Free Press, 1988).

97. Richard Nuccio, "The Family as Political Metaphor in Authoritarian-Conservative Regimes: The Case of Spain," working paper no. 9, Program in Latin American Studies, University of Massachusetts, Amherst, 1978.

98. John Courtney Murray, S.J., "The Danger of the Vows: An Encounter with Earth, Woman, and Spirit," *Woodstock Letters* 96 (Fall 1967): 421–27.

99. The major work is by John L. Thomas, S.J., *The American Catholic Family* (Englewood Cliffs, N.J.: Prentice Hall, 1956). Compare Alan Wolfe, *Whose Keeper? Social Science and Moral Obligation* (Berkeley, Calif.: University of California Press, 1989).

100. See "Sviluppi metodologici e dottrinale nel magistro della chiesa, "*Civiltà Cattolica* 11 (1989): 3–16 and Peter Hebblethwaite, "The Popes and Politics: Shifting Patterns in 'Catholic Social Doctrine.'" in *Religion and America: Spiritual Life in a Secular Age,* eds. Mary Douglas and Steven Tipton (Boston: Beacon Press, 1983). See also James R. Kelly, "Catholicism and Modern Memory: Some Sociological Reflections on the Symbolic Foundations of the Rhetorical Force of the Pastoral Letter 'The Challenge of Peace,'" *Sociological Analysis* 45 (1984): 131–44.

101. Compare James Terence Fisher, *The Catholic Counterculture in America, 1933–1962* (Chapel Hill, N.C.: Univeresity of North Carolina Press, 1990) and Richard M. Merelman, "On Culture and Politics in America: A Perspective from Cultural Anthropology," *British Journal of Political Science* 19 (1989): 465–94.

102. See Patrick W. Carey, ed., *American Catholic Religious Thought* (New York: Paulist Press, 1987) and John Patrick Diggins, *The Lost Soul of American Politics: Virtue, Self-Interest, and the Foundations of Liberalism* (New York, 1984). A representative critique of liberalism by an American Catholic of the time before the Council is Thomas P. Neill, *The Rise and Decline of Liberalism* (Milwaukee, Wis.: Bruce Publishing Co., 1951). For more recent interpretations see Drew Christiansen, S.J., "On Relative Equality: Catholic Egalitarianism after Vatican II," *Theological Studies* 45 (1984): 651–75 and Avery Dulles, S.J., "Catholicism and American Culture: The Uneasy Dialogue," *America* 162 (27 January 1990): 54–59.

Policies and Predicaments for the Jesuit Educational Mission from the Past Three General Congregations

THOMAS P. FAASE

General Congregations of the Jesuit Order[1] are instances of the formation of culture. In the process of gathering information and postulates from the membership as well as in their deliberations, this worldwide legislature does less to structure the life of Jesuits than it does to stir their reflective capacities. To consider their educational mission in the light of the Congregations, then, is to take note of the very high level of cultural reflectiveness that has always characterized the Jesuits.

It follows that the institutional achievements of the Jesuits, their colleges and universities among other structures, operate in conjunction with an inheritance of values, beliefs, formative experiences, attitudes, and role models. At its best, this culture infuses institutions as breath gives life to flesh; at worst, the culture gets trapped by institutions as self-serving rationalizations of the status quo, ideologies in defense of vested interest.[2]

Structure of the Argument

The policies and predicaments for the Jesuit Educational Mission, as viewed in this inquiry, stem from this conjunction of culture and structures. Simply stated, policies emerge from the past three General Congregations as cultural mandates to stir the reflectiveness and practical deliberations of Jesuit membership. Predicaments emerge from the intransigence of structures to allow rethinking and reshaping of crucial patterns of behavior. The degree of incongruence evidenced between the policies and predicaments is interpreted as a crisis to be resolved.

The substance of what follows is to provide a review of the main themes of the past three General Congregations[3] to heighten the sense of their convergence around the integrating factor of practical action for faith and justice, then to review the impediments to implementation of that action within American Jesuit educational institutions, and then to indicate the vulnerability of that to the point of crisis. Two interpretations of the nature of that crisis are then compared, and prospects of its resolution are discussed.

The policies of these congregations that are under discussion are the concern for faith and justice, the matter of inculturation, the integration of life and works, the practical involvement of mission and world, and Jesuit allegiance to the Pope.

The Concern for Faith and Justice

Delegates to the Thirty-First General Congregation readied to deal with matters of renewal and social justice were stunned to be given the agenda to battle atheism throughout the world. It was dealt with by contextualization so that the document on atheism[4] gave a far more universalistic understanding to the need for fostering the faith among believers and unbelievers alike. The faith and justice theme was born out of this compliance and accommodation to the Holy See. What began in polemics became the most deeply characterizing theme of all three congregations.

In the Thirty-Second General Congregation, this became the Jesuit "priority of priorities" and, in elaboration of the document "Our Mission Today,"[5] this was worked out in terms of poverty and underdevelopment more than in terms of militaristic regimes who prohibited freedoms of religion. The Thirty-third confirmed the centrality, identifying it with the characteristics of integration, universality, discernment, and a corporate nature.[6]

The Matter of Inculturation

The second policy of the three General Congregations is that of inculturation. The Thirty-First General Congregation built upon the Second Vatican Council's document *Ad Gentes* to deal with the topic slightly in its decree on Mission Service. The Thirty-Second General Congregation deliberated arduously on the matter ending up with only a two-paragraph decree. Yet, some members of the Congregation insist that it was the most revolutionary position legislated by that Congregation.[7] It signals a break with the European culture taken as normative and emphasizes by implication the place of a new pluralism and noncolonialism. And, rather than relegating the matter of inculturation to "missionaries," the document insisted that it "deserves the progressively greater concern and attention of the whole Society." The Thirty-Third General Congregation reaffirmed Inculturation saying it "prevents us from absolutizing our perceptions and actions."[8]

The Integration of Life and Works

The third policy is that of the integration of life and works. The Thirty-First General Congregation dealt with many specifics that touch on this from precepts preserving the Institute, the matter of grades, the brothers vocation, to the better choice of ministries. The direction the integration of life and works takes in the Thirty-Second General Congregation is ironic. While it sets the theme for union of minds and hearts, its effect is most practically felt in those deliberations on poverty where the Society set up the distinction between Apostolic Institutes and Communities. This radical step removes the institutions of the Society from common identification with their communities and eventually leads to removing them from the control of the communities as well. In the document "Jesuits Today," a Jesuit comes to be seen as a "man on a mission" coming to the work from outside.

Practical Involvements of Mission and World

The fourth policy of the three congregations is the practical focus that comes from the Thirty-Third General Congregation. It gave a more decidedly wholistic and applied tone to the cultural mandates of the preceding congregations.

The Thirty-Third General Congregation blended all of the foregoing themes. It tied faith and justice more integrally to evangelization and inculturation and called Jesuits to:

> deeper involvement in the lives of the people around us . . . to hear "the joys and the hopes, the griefs and the anxieties of the people of this age, especially those who are poor and in any way afflicted"; a regular exposure to new situations of life and thought which oblige us to question our way of seeing and judging; a gradual assimilation of that apostolic pedagogy of St. Ignatius; a well-informed use of social and cultural analysis; and an inculturation which opens us to the newness of Jesus . . .[9]

There is the strong influence of *praxis* and of appeals for a change of heart in the documents of the Thirty-Third General Congregation. Education and the intellectual apostolates are seen in this light.

> When carried out in the light of our mission today, their efforts contribute vitally to the total and integral liberation of the human person. . . . The opportunities and responsibilities of these apostolates require a change of heart and an openness to human needs around us; they also demand a solid intellectual formation. Jesuits in these fields and our men in more direct social and pastoral ministries should cooperate and benefit from one another's expertise and experience.[10]

Further insistence on practical involvement is seen in its "prerequisites for credibility." Credibility requires collaboration and solidarity with the poor. As the Congregation states:

> The validity of our mission will also depend to a large extent on our solidarity with the poor. For though obedience sends us, it is poverty that makes us believable. So,

together with many other religious congregations, we wish to make our own the Church's preferential option for the poor.[11]

Taken together these policies spell out a new stance for Jesuits in relation to the world around them, a stance that has fundamental implications. I have suggested that it is a movement in the culture of the Jesuit Order that lessens the emphasis on the role of the Society of Jesus as the elite of the Church and opts instead for the position of a minority in the world.[12] This is equivalent to the Jesuits choosing to move from being big fish in a small pond to being little fish in the big pond, by allying themselves with all the other little fish who comprise the majority of the populations of the world. This is an integral and consistent sense of the way in which faith and justice, inculturation, poverty and praxis come together.

Jesuit Allegiance to the Pope

A fifth policy of the three congregations is that of allegiance to the Vatican. It is consistently a hallmark of the Order. It is also consistently troublesome. There were "clouds on the horizon"[13] in the Thirty-First General Congregation. The Pope interrupted the Thirty-Second in disagreement with the deliberations and leveled the most severe imposition of authority between the Thirty-Second and the Thirty-Third General Congregations, when he named his own Delegate to see to the preparation of the next General Congregation and the temporary governance of the Society. The delegate he named had been more contrary to the "priority of priorities" than almost any other delegate at the Thirty-Second General Congregation.[14]

Predicaments of Compromised Policies

Each of the policies of the past three General Congregations is a mandate for social change. There exist in the structures of any organization impediments to change. From these impediments, predicaments arise. The educational mission of the Jesuit Order evidences such impediments. Each of the policies that have been talked about is compromised by the world in which Jesuits maintain institutional and educational commitments.

The social change envisioned by the faith-and-justice posture of the Jesuits is compromised by the solidarity with the affluent that is necessary to support large American educational institutions. College populations of youth who are seeking upward mobility and economic orthodoxy in order to maintain the privileged status that their parents only recently attained pay little heed to faith-and-justice concerns. And government encroachments have affected many programs through the schools' quest for funds, even to the point of actually characterizing many programs within the colleges and universities.

The inculturation policy calls for Jesuits to be exposed to the poor, to be somehow allied with the majority of the world who are poor, who are very unlikely recruits for the Jesuit schools as they are presently set up. But Jesuit universities or colleges have seldom been places where exposure to the poor is available or where serious conscientization is the order of the day. More often, these schools are places where many similar sorts of persons socialize and learn, all the while being sheltered from unsavory influences and unsafe environments. Jesuit, Catholic schools are often the safe havens of families who want to avoid the very contact that inculturation calls for.

The integration of life-and-works policy is compromised by the disintegration of life and works in many senses. Many of the schools experience a lessened effect of Jesuit presence due to dwindling numbers and a lessened control over the schools due to fewer Jesuit administrators working within the institution. Aggravating the predicament are problems in community such as the loss of morale and loss of shared vision.

Closely tied to the predicament of integration of life and works is the predicament of the absence of *praxis* or practical, experientially based involvement on the part of Jesuit educators. Increasingly, younger Jesuits seek pastoral or Third-World apostolates instead of American colleges or universities. This feeds the phenomenon of university and college communities becoming "islands" of academe and quiescence. This predicament is also aggravated by the gulf that exists between Jesuit academics and pastoral Jesuits.

The predicament of allegiance to the Vatican comes about much of the time because of the incongruence between official Church teachings and ecclesiastical entanglements with the power structures. This has occurred between the Vatican and the Jesuit curia and between various bishops and Jesuit activists or "liberals" in their dioceses. Although the culture and teachings of the Church and the culture and policies of the Jesuits are in accord, the teachings and policies are constantly being impeded by institutional arrangements.

The policies of faith and justice, inculturation, integration of life and works along with poverty, and the call to practical, deeper involvement with the world stand over against and contrary to the American cultural ethos of upward mobility, economic success, conspicuous consumption, and freedom to live the good life apart from densely populated, impoverished circles of deprivation. These predicaments stem from institutional arrangements that compel courting wealthy segments of society, tailoring programs to government funding, living apart from ordinary poor folk, and being encircled by the reigning ideologies and pervasive taken-for-granted precepts of people of privilege and status. It is no mere coincidence that nearly every policy discussed here and very many contemporary commentaries on the Jesuit relationship to the world refer to the meditation on the two standards.

The Vulnerability of Implementation

There is a vulnerability that comes as consequence of inserting the policies of the past three General Congregations into established Jesuit institutions and their milieux. It is the likelihood of the loss of social standing and even legitimation. It is a matter of downward mobility and the dismay of former colleagues when confronted with Jesuits becoming countercultural.

What is at stake in suggesting that the Jesuit Order is called to sacrifice existing sources of its prestige, to opt for solidarity and identification with lower rather than higher social classes, and to become a voice for minorities in the world speaking out on behalf of the afflicted and deprived is in a very fundamental sense a loss of present power for the Society of Jesus. In the existing structures of the day and nation, it is to forego authority and the respectability that derives from that.

There are two interpretations, among others, of what is the basis of the Jesuit response to the suggestion of its having to lose power. One interpretation is that the Jesuit response to this loss of power is a crisis of sexual identity and affectivity in both individual and collective spheres. Another interpretation is that the Jesuit response to this loss of power is a crisis of status, a sense of belonging and prestige. The first interpretation is a reflection of the thinking of Peter McDonough; the second is a reflection of the author's position.

A Psychosexual Interpretation of the Crisis

The first interpretation is that which Peter McDonough discusses in his article "Metamorphoses of the Jesuits: Sexual Identity, Gender Roles and Hierarchy in Catholicism."[15] What McDonough builds from is a close link between authority on the one hand and sexual identity and affectivity on the other. He suggests that there has been a three-tiered "progressive unfolding" of changes in the church and the Jesuits, which eventuated in a crisis of psychosocial sexual identity. These tiers are: first, the political changes toward pluralism in governments and religions; secondly, the social and economic movement from a Europe-centered to a global-centered concern, from an East/West concern to a North/South concern; and thirdly, the dissolving patriarchal culture within the Church. He points to this most menacing tier as follows:

A third set of issues touched both the institutional and ideological core of Catholicism. They involved questions of sexuality and authority that are intimately linked in the patriarchal church. Alterations in the church's position regarding political regimes and religious denominations and in its policies on social and economic issues could be treated as matters of opinion. They did not cut to the doctrinal quick. But questions regarding sexuality and affectivity went deeper and in no other areas of the Church were personal and organizational dilemmas so closely linked. . . . The connections between gender inequality, psychosocial identity and organizational authority are, or once were, extraordinarily tight in Catholicism. Change in this area poses a crisis of individual and corporate identity and purpose centered on the working out and sustenance of a male role in opposition to women.[16]

McDonough also seems to argue that the cultural or ideological core of the Jesuits consists, first and foremost, in its intellectual system. Formerly that core was essentially perfect, characterized by stasis, hierarchy, and completeness. But as such, McDonough would argue, it was inadequate to the psychic need of younger Jesuits, gave them little room to move, little to test themselves against intellectually, and thus resulted in alienation and anomie directed both against the church and the world.

McDonough calls upon the views of Walter Ong, S.J., to make his point.[17] From the failure of the intellectual storehouse and heritage of the Jesuit Order to provide authority and accomplishment, the "macho" was lost and "the age-old rhetorical, oral-agonistic world of male ceremonial combat" was abandoned. This loss of something to fight for, to strain against, left younger Jesuits individually and the Order collectively in the throes of a crisis of affectivity and sexual identity.

An Alternative Interpretation

McDonough misses what is most central to the Jesuit ethos and most genuinely characterizes the Society of Jesus. He also underestimates the centrality of the call to faith and justice for the Society of Jesus, for the Church, and for the world. Restoring these elements to their rightful place calls for an alternative interpretation of the crisis the Jesuits face in education in the United States. This interpretation is based on viewing the Jesuits in the light of their past three General Congregations.

Considerations of the past three General Congregations and the predicaments one finds in their implementation suggest the following interpretation of Jesuits in crisis: tying Jesuit higher education in the United States to Jesuit identity does occasion a crisis. But it surely can be argued that it is not a crisis primarily of sexual identity and affectivity. Rather, it is a crisis of prestige, a crisis in the Jesuit's sense of belonging and social status.

While there is clearly a tight link between authority and sexual identity, there is also a link between authority and social standing. Of the three tiers of social change, all of which are well portrayed in McDonough's article, it seems compelling that the tier of social and economic issues is paramount. Surely in the experience of the Church, the movement off the East/West axis to a North/South axis is of immense importance.

Rather than being treated as "matters of opinion," the plight of those in poverty and repression is continuously being brought to consciousness more nearly as a matter of identity. Church positions and policies on social and economic issues *do* "cut to the doctrinal quick." It is argued here that, with a stranglehold as tight as celibacy or gender roles might ever be, the cause of justice and poverty opposed to the status of respectability and wealth creates its own identity crisis for the Jesuit Order collectively as well as for its individual members.

Furthermore, it is patently wrong that the primary cultural equivalent to Jesuit institutional structures is the "macho" intellectual synthesis or lack thereof. Most clearly, the primary cultural equivalent to its institutional structures is its profound spirituality and methodology of discernment. As such, this cultural equivalent is at least as much affective as it is intellectual and more androgynous than "macho."

The cultural primacy of spirituality has been under scrutiny throughout this inquiry. It is evidenced in numerous ways. The deepest roots of Jesuit involvement with education and with the world are those of the First Principle and the *Contemplatio* of the Spiritual Exercises. In its methods of discernment of spirits are found the ingredients of *praxis* and strategic choices based on cultural analysis. The struggle between exploitation and exploited is repeatedly portrayed as a contemporary meditation on the Two Standards.

Surely, McDonough is right that the Jesuits are in the midst of an identity crisis, but it is not for lack of the "macho" in their intellectual life. Rather, it comes of the enormous discrepancy between, on the one hand, threefold reinforcements of profound cultural mandates that go to the quick of all social relationships and institutions and, on the other, the long-envied superior status Jesuits have learned to live with. The crisis as spelled out by Jesuits themselves is a crisis of authenticity versus high social standing and prestige.

Jesuit Authors on the Crisis

A contrasting three-tiered portrayal could summon the thinking of Bernard Lonergan, Don Gelpi, and Dean Brackley to characterize the nature of the crisis. For Lonergan, it is a matter of adaptability. He states:

> There is a crisis of the first magnitude today. For a principal duty of priests is to lead and teach the people of God. But all leadership and all teaching occurs within social structures and through cultural channels. In the measure that one insists on leading and teaching within structures that no longer function and through channels that no longer exist, in that very measure leadership and teaching cease to exist.[18]

Don Gelpi regards the crisis as the need for sociopolitical conversion and thus fundamentally as a matter of authenticity:

As Religious we are called to integrally converted lives; but unless we are willing to advance beyond mere personal conversion to socio-political conversion, we must as Christians and as Jesuits inevitably succumb to inauthenticity in our personal relationship with God and with one another.[19]

Finally, Dean Brackley names the crisis as it has been named throughout this paper, a matter of downward mobility:

First, solidarity means sharing the obscurity of the poor of whom the world takes no account. Second, it means sharing the insults suffered by the poor. Finally, since it implies assuming the cause of the poor, solidarity means enduring misunderstanding, injuries, and rejection from those who oppose that cause. This is the social significance of the desire for insults and humiliations (SpEx 146, 167). Although we do not seek this obscurity and misunderstanding, when we side with the poor it comes inevitably. And, indeed, we do feel bad if our friends suffer these things and we do not.[20]

Prospects for Future Resolution of the Crisis

Adaptability has repeatedly been said to be a characteristic of the Jesuits. In their original conception, the same can be said for Jesuit universities and colleges. In his work on *St. Ignatius' Idea of a Jesuit University,* George Ganss shows that Ignatius did not make the conservation of any tradition the key characteristic of his idea of a university; instead Ignatius considered adaptation and the kind of change that would meet the needs and the culture of his day to be his cardinal principles of Jesuit education.[21]

The settings in which Jesuit schools are situated will one day become more amenable to change. As the consensus of an old-guard power elite becomes increasingly exclusive and restricted, payoffs from allegiance to the "other side" will be a viable option, and legitimation in terms of these minorities will become an effective reality. Gradually the law of diminishing returns will bring about a shift in the burden of proof, and in its wake a change in the major value orientations the universities or colleges would be recognized to have and transmit.

This model of social change rests on values, as the following analysis of a noted American value sociologist states:

Undoubtedly the most comprehensive kind of socio-cultural change is a shift in a major pattern of values or value-orientations. There is a sense in which this is true by definition: if values are generalized criteria of desirability, a basically different set of values (or of emphases and relationships within a given set) necessarily presents a pervasive reordering of social behavior. However, the important non-truistic proposition is that once a new value pattern has come to be accepted as so fully legitimate that the burden of proof is simply assumed to be on the advocate of an opposing pattern, then the dominant pattern continues to attract additional adherents and to extend its coverage into more and more activities across all institutional sectors.[22]

Finally, with compelling strength and gaining effective and creative momentum, there is emerging and being taken seriously as attainable within the culture of the Society of Jesus a new model and contemporary Jesuit idea of a Christian University. The works of Jon Sobrino[23] are being quoted with a force heretofore unseen. The assassination of his six brothers in community leaves few unmoved. The currents that his idea of a Christian university blend are all enunciations of the past General Congregations.

A New Jesuit Idea of a University

The starting point of conversion to the contemporary Jesuit idea of a Christian University is an imperfect world. Once the status quo has been shown to be constituted by exploitative structures and false consciousness, then sinfulness is perpetuated whenever the status quo is perpetuated. *Praxis* as method is undertaken in order to be more a part of the solution than a part of the problem, and being part of the solution requires complementary forces in the first and third worlds. The task of the third world is outlined by liberation theology. The task of the first world would be a kind of sociotheology of letting go.[24]

Jesuits have the effective method for cultural analysis in the discernment of spirits and Two Standards meditation. They have the overlapping array of all the policies of the past twenty years to stimulate cultural reflectiveness and practical deliberations, and they have the blood of martyrs to urge them to the risk of forgoing legitimation and status in favor of relevance and change.

Notes

1. The constitutions of the Society of Jesus specify the purposes of every General Congregation, which is considered its supreme governing body. A General Congregation is ordinarily convoked after the death of a superior general in order to elect a new general. A General Congregation is convoked as an extraordinary measure to legislate on "very difficult matters pertaining to the whole body of the Society" (*Constitutions of the Society of Jesus,* 680). Only seven times has a Congregation been convoked as an extraordinary measure. The outstanding contemporary Jesuit authority on the General Congregations is John W. Padberg, S.J.. Sources of relevance, all by Padberg, include the following: "The General Congregations of the Society of Jesus: A Brief Survey of Their History" in *Studies in the Spirituality of Jesuits* 6 (January and March 1974); "The Society True to Itself: A Brief History of the 32nd General Congregation of the Society of Jesus (Dec. 2, 1974–March 7, 1975)" in *Studies in the Spirituality of Jesuits* 15 (May and September 1983); *Documents of the 31st and 32nd General Congregations of the Society of Jesus,* Saint Louis: Institute of Jesuit Sources, 1977, and *Documents of the 33rd General Congregation of Jesus,* Saint Louis: Institute of Jesuit Sources, 1984. Two older sources duplicated by Padberg's work are: *Documents of the Thirty-First General Congregation: First*

Session: May 7–July 15, 1965/Second Session: September 8–November 17, 1966, ed. Donald R. Campion *et al.* (Woodstock, Md.: Woodstock College, 1967), and *Documents of the Thirty-Second General Congregation of the Society of Jesus: An English Translation* (Washington, D.C.: The Jesuit Conference, 1975). Two other helpful sources from the Thirty-First General Congregation are the following: "Impressions of the 31st General Congregation," George E. Ganss, *Woodstock Letters* 94 (Fall 1965), and "Thirty-First General Congregation: The First Session" and "The Thirty-First General Congregation: Letters from the Second Session," ed. James P. Jurich, S.J., *Woodstock Letters* 95, 97.

2. The distinction made here is that between social structure and culture; the subsequent analysis rests upon this distinction, which underscores the analytic separateness and thorough interdependency of these two concepts. It is particularly emphasized in sociological writings such as the following: Talcott Parsons, *The Social System* (New York: Free Press, 1951), and his *Societies: Evolutionary and Comparative Perspectives* (Englewood Cliffs, N.J.: Prentice-Hall, 1966) and its companion piece, *The System of Modern Societies* (Englewood Cliffs, N.J.: Prentice-Hall, 1971), as well as "On the Concept of Value-Commitments," *Sociological Inquiry* 38 (Spring 1968): 135–60. Also Marvin Olsen, *The Process of Social Organization.* (New York: Holt, Rinehart and Winston, 1978), Karl Mannheim, *Essays on the Sociology of Knowledge* (London: Routledge and Kegan Paul, 1952); and S. N. Eisenstadt, "Social Change, Differentiation and Evolution in *American Sociological Review* 29 (June 1964): 375–86, and his "Transformation of Social, Political and Cultural Orders in Modernization" in *American Sociological Review* 30 (October 1965): 659–73.

3. Padberg, *Documents of the 31st and 32nd General Congregations of the Society of Jesus* and *Documents of the 33rd General Congregation of the Society of Jesus.* These documents will hereafter be referred to by the number of the General Congregation under discussion; all such citations refer to the works edited by Padberg.

4. Document 3, "The Task of the Society Regarding Atheism," *31st General Congregation.*

5. Historical Preface, para. 5, Selection of topics "to be treated first" (pp. 354–55); and Document 4, "Our Mission Today: The Service of Faith and the Promotion of Justice," in *32nd General Congregation.*

6. Decree 1, "Companions of Jesus Sent into Today's World," *33rd General Congregation.*

7. Personal conversation with Rev. Bruce Biever, S.J., former Provincial of the Wisconsin Province.

8. "Companions of Jesus sent into Today's World," para. 44.

9. "Companions of Jesus Sent into Today's World," para. 41.

10. "Companions of Jesus Sent into Today's World," para. 44.

11. "Companions of Jesus Sent into Today's World," para. 48.

12. Thomas P. Faase, *Making the Jesuits More Modern* (Washington, D.C.: University Press of America, 1981); also see the author's "International Differences in Value-Ranking and Religious Style Among Jesuits," *Review of Religious Research* 24 (September 1982), "Making Jesuits More Modern: Changing Values in a Changing Religious Order," *Social Action* 32: (January–March 1982) and "Bulwark-Catholics and Conciliar-Humanists in the Society of Jesus," *The Sociological Quarterly* 21 (Autumn 1980). The nature of the research underlying these studies was first and foremost participatory observation; the author was granted access to the deliberations of the Thirty-Second General Congregation as an observer. Other components of the research were content analysis, voting analysis, and analysis of surveys from the delegates to the Thirty-Second General Congregation. Also see Johannes Schasing, "Soziologie Der Gesellschaft Jesu," *Zietschrift Fur Katholische Theologie,* band

101, heft 3/4 (1979), and David J. O'Brien, "The Jesuits and Catholic Higher Education," *Studies in the Spirituality of Jesuits* 13 (November 1981).

13. "Documents Pertaining to the General Congregation: Address of His Holiness Pope Paul VI to the Members of the General Congregation," 16 November 1966.

14. This information is drawn from the author's observations and from conversations with Congregation delegates. All important pieces of legislation are deliberated upon early in their construction by small groups composed of the delegates from individual assistancies. These assistancy groups share common languages as well. The observation of this delegate's distaste for and resistance to the "priority of priorities" was made at the adjournment of the Italian Assistancy group meeting on this issue.

15. Peter McDonough, "Metamorphoses of the Jesuits: Sexual Identity, Gender Roles and Hierarchy in Catholicism," *Comparative Studies in Society and History* 32, 2 (April 1990).

16. Ibid., pp. 11–12.

17. Walter Ong, S.J., *Rhetoric, Romance and Technology: Studies in the Interaction of Expression and Culture* (Ithaca: Cornell University Press, 1971) and *Interfaces of the World: Studies in the Evolution of Consciousness and Culture* (Ithaca: Cornell University Press, 1977).

18. Bernard J. F. Lonergan, S.J., "The Response of the Jesuit as Priest and Apostle in the Modern World," *Studies in the Spirituality of Jesuits* 2, 3 (September 1970).

19. Donald L. Gelpi, S.J., "The Converting Jesuit," *Studies in the Spirituality of Jesuits* 18, 1 (January 1986).

20. Dean Brackley, S.J., "Downward Mobility: Social Implications of St. Ignatius's Two Standards," *Studies in the Spirituality of Jesuits* 20, 1 (January 1988).

21. Rev. George Ganss, *St. Ignatius' Idea of a Jesuit University* (Milwaukee: Marquette University Press, 1954).

22. Robin M. Williams, Jr., *American Society: A Sociological Interpretation,* 3d ed. (New York: Alfred A. Knopf, 1970).

23. Jon Sobrino, "The University's Christian Inspiration." Paper read at University of Deusto, Bilbao (4 June 1987). And his *Christology at the Crossroads: A Latin American Approach,* trans. John Drury (Maryknoll: Orbis Books, 1984).

24. Marie Augusta Neal, *A Socio-Theology of Letting Go: The Role of a First World Church Facing Third World Peoples* (New York: Paulist Press, 1977).

Jesuit Education in America

JOSEPH A. O'HARE, S.J.

The Jesuit educational mission is an immense topic, one that reminds us not only of the global reach of Jesuit initiatives but also of their complex history: the controversies over Chinese rites and the Paraguay reductions; the cultural challenges of DeNobili's India and Bourdaloue's France; experiments with music, art, and linguistics in Jesuit missions in widely separated parts of the world from the North Pacific to the Southwest of the United States and the deserts of Arabia to the jungles of Peru. Within this international and historical context, this essay will investigate Jesuit education in the United States, a topic of some spirited debate among Jesuits in recent years, leading up to the historic celebration at Georgetown in June 1989 of 200 years of Jesuit education in this republic. Partly as a result of these discussions, I begin with a word on what might be called an Ignatian presupposition of our current discussions. Then I attempt to identify what is distinctive about Jesuit education. Is there a specifically Jesuit philosophy of education? After a review of the history of Jesuit education in the United States, I conclude by suggesting some of the major challenges Jesuit educators in the United States must address in the decades ahead.

An Ignatian Presupposition

First, a word on our presuppositions. What is the spirit in which we should approach the question of the mission and the future of Jesuit education in the United States?

The wide range of topics covered in this volume not only enriches discussions of Jesuit education; it also liberates them. For I think I hear echoes in some of our discussions of an anxiety that can lead to an illusory search for guarantees about the future of Jesuit education in the United States. In a recent discussion at Fordham University about the distinctive character of Jesuit education, one of our most eminent Jesuit sociologists recalled Christopher Dawson's comment, "Happy the nation without a history; thrice happy a nation without a sociology. For when a nation becomes conscious of itself, it has begun to decay." Dawson, we were told, did not mean to dismiss the value of history, much less that of sociology. But he was expressing caution lest an introspective absorption with the past lead to a failure of nerve in responding to the task at hand.

As we talk these days about the distinctive character of Jesuit education, does the question always reflect a confident desire to renew a vital tradition? A distinguished Jesuit scholar, on the eve of retirement, asks, "How can we be sure that this will be a Jesuit university after we are gone?" Does his question express a fear that the investment of a lifetime may be squandered by forces beyond his control? If so, is such a fear, however understandable in human terms, consistent with Ignatian freedom?

At a time of uncertainty and great cultural change, the temptation of fundamentalism can be strong. By this I mean the desire to codify in a more or less rigid formula values that we wish to preserve, when moral and intellectual landmarks are shifting and even disappearing. This desire is understandable, because the sources of anxiety are real. Still, a fundamentalist response to this concern is invariably shortsighted, for the fundamentalist seeks to freeze in a particular form a tradition that needs to be renewed rather than simply rehearsed.

A certain fundamentalism has been at work, I believe, in the discussion over the nature of a Catholic university that has engaged the Vatican Congregation for Higher Education and Catholic educators around the world for the past five years. In the Third International Congress on Catholic Higher Education held in the Vatican in April 1989, the suggestion that a Catholic accreditation committee be established in this country to certify which universities are truly Catholic was roundly rejected by the participants in the Congress. Instead, the Congress voted unanimous approval of the principle that responsibility for maintaining the Catholic identity of the university rested in the university itself.

Yet at Assembly '89, the historic meeting of Jesuits and their colleagues at Georgetown, a similar theme was sounded—namely, that an accrediting association or an accrediting procedure should be established in this country to certify when Jesuit colleges and universities are authentically Jesuit.

Now the accreditation proposal is too impractical and too mischievous in its implications for even Jesuits to consider seriously. The attempt to codify the character of Jesuit education, for purposes of certification, runs the great risk of identifying the Jesuit charism too quickly with one cultural and time-conditioned form it may have taken, for example, the Jesuit high schools and colleges in the United States as they developed from 1945 until 1965—a relatively brief moment in our national, Catholic, or Jesuit history.

The broad range and historical sweep of the essays in this volume provide a powerful antidote to such a parochial view of Jesuit education. Such a liberating perspective can confirm the kind of Ignatian freedom that should be a presupposition of any discussion of Jesuit mission.

A Jesuit Philosophy of Education?

Recognizing then that the Jesuit educational tradition has taken many different forms in the course of history, are there nonetheless distinctive elements of that tradition which define a common identity shared by educational institutions in different cultures and different moments in history? Is there a specifically Jesuit philosophy of education?

Let me begin by stating one of my fundamental assumptions: the most decisive document for defining the character of any Jesuit enterprise is the *Spiritual Exercises* of Saint Ignatius. While other books have been written about more formal issues in Jesuit education—studies of the various editions of the *Ratio Studiorum,* for example—the most powerful and enduring influence on Jesuit education, in all of its variety around the world and through four-and-a-half centuries of history, has been the spirituality of Saint Ignatius, mediated through the instrument of the *Spiritual Exercises* and the constitutions of the Society of Jesus. This spirituality has affected all Jesuit works and ministries, and it is certainly the source of the most distinctive traits of Jesuit education.

Those of us who are asked to define for our colleagues and the general public the meaning of the Jesuit tradition of education here in the United States invariably invoke such themes as the importance of an integrated liberal education that develops habits of mind and powers of expression, both oral and written. We speak of the need to develop the imagination and a sense of history. We recall the Jesuit belief that moral education is as important as intellectual education; our graduates should not be simply successful careerists, but also responsible citizens, concerned especially for the poor and the marginalized. The classic expression of *eloquentia perfecta* was meant to sum up both intellectual and moral qualities. In Robert Harvanek's words, *eloquentia perfecta* implied "rhetorical gifts, combined with political insight, integrity and wisdom."[1]

Education, then, must focus on the whole person. But we also talk of establishing an environment of personal care and attention to individual students. Education must focus not only on the whole person but on each person, we say. More specifically, we insist on the importance of religious thought and experience and the centrality of theology in education. And we have even claimed, or at least some of us have, that a certain openness to innovation and adaptability is also distinctive of the Jesuit approach to education.

Yet every one of these elements can be found in other colleges and universities as well, both Catholic and non-Catholic. What do Jesuit colleges and universities do that other schools do not? Or is this the right question to ask? Should we be more concerned with what is authentically Jesuit, rather than with what is specifically Jesuit?

Father William Rewak, S.J., President of Spring Hill College and formerly

President of Santa Clara University, has suggested that, while the educational values listed above can be found in other institutions, the manner in which these values are combined in a Jesuit institution will be distinctive. Father William McInnes, S.J., has observed that discussions about what is distinctive of Jesuit education are generally more fruitful than the attempt to identify what is unique about Jesuit education.[2]

In any case, even if there is no common curriculum or set of educational standards or procedures peculiar to Jesuit institutions alone, there is nonetheless an identifiable spirit that animates Jesuit institutions. It is a vision of life, a way of proceeding, that has its deepest source in Ignatian spirituality. At the close of his history of the Society of Jesus, William V. Bangert, S.J., with characteristic modesty, attempted to formulate this Jesuit spirit.

Bangert recognized the difficulty of finding a single proposition that could define

> the interior spirit and the external activity of thousands of men through more than four centuries of history who taught Latin and Greek at College Louis-le-grand; composed astronomical tables at the Imperial Court of Peking; . . . lectured on philosophy and theology at the Gregorian University in Rome; died on the gallows at Tyburn in England; adopted the role of the Sanyassi in India; . . . [and] taught in large universities from Boston to San Francisco.[3]

Father Bangert, nonetheless, did offer three specific marks of the Jesuit spirit that set it in contrast to other religious foundations: first, apostolic action; second, a penchant for Christian humanism; and third, a common spiritual ideal, transmitted through the *Spiritual Exercises* and the Constitutions of the Society and defined by Father Bangert as a desire "to be with Jesus—in order to serve."[4]

All three marks of the Jesuit spirit identified in this deceptively modest description have implications for Jesuit education.

For example, the profound and pervasive apostolic orientation of Jesuit life and work can be in tension with the ideal of seeking knowledge for its own sake. Robert Harvanek, in his essay on *The Jesuit Vision of a University,* insists that Jesuit education must be "action-oriented," and Harvanek cites analogies to both Marx and Dewey in the Jesuit emphasis on not only knowing the truth but "doing the truth in love." This Jesuit orientation, he adds, may even be said to anticipate the "new humanism" envisioned in Vatican II, where the human vocation finds its fulfillment not just in the contemplation of God's truth and goodness but also in an active participation in God's creative activity.[5]

But if knowledge is not to be sought for its own sake alone, then are truth and beauty to be subordinated to some higher purpose? In the past, Jesuit teachers have been accused of reducing great works of literature to rhetorical workbooks. Were our students to read the great writers only to learn how to write themselves? This notion of an apostolic purpose, if misunderstood, could also constrict the explorations of pure research. More recently, does the contemporary emphasis on Jesuit education for justice turn the university into an advocate for a certain ideological view of what justice entails?

If there is, indeed, a fear that the Jesuit apostolic orientation could lead to a narrow instrumentalism, the second of Father Bangert's three marks—a full-blooded enthusiasm for Christian humanism—applies its own dynamic corrective. Jesuit humanism in the past has been embodied in Jesuit theater and Jesuit art. Matteo Ricci brought European science and technology to China in the seventeenth century. All of this suggests that, despite the fundamental apostolic orientation of their lives, Jesuits have respected what the Jesuit constitutions call the "natural means" of salvation.

In a very perceptive essay on Ignatian mysticism and liberal education, Father Brian Daley, S. J., speaks of the

> deep correspondence, and inner affinity, between the Christian pedagogy or mystagogy of the Spiritual Exercises, that great vehicle created for communicating the Jesuit spirit, and the effect on the human person of liberal studies at their best. Both are centered, in their own way, on rhetoric: on the laborious process of training the human mind to understand the truth and to speak it powerfully. . . . Wonder at the world, liberation from enclosure in the self, and commitment to service: these traditional goals of classical education became, for Ignatius and his followers—all children of the renaissance—implicitly, if not consciously, the main way-stations in the spiritual education of the Exercises, and allowed them to find in the enterprise of humanistic training for eloquence not only a beneficial secular tradition but a parallel to their own work, a promising prospect for a new and thoroughly Christian ministry.[6]

Father Bangert's third mark of the Jesuit spirit defines the heart of our common spirituality as a desire "to be with Jesus—in order to serve." For all its simple piety, there is an unsettling dynamism contained in this ideal, what Timothy Healy has called "the deadly comparative" of seeking always the *greater* glory of God. This constant search for God's will, this discernment of the signs of the times, can make Jesuits troublesome characters at times. It can lead to some mistaken adventures, to be sure, but it probably explains why developments in Jesuit education in the United States have characteristically been responses to new and changing opportunities, rather than the carefully planned tactics of a comprehensive and clearly elaborated philosophy of education.

Is there, in fact, a specifically Jesuit philosophy of education? Even to raise the question would have seem outrageously perverse when I was a scholastic studying philosophy in the Philippines nearly forty years ago. Once a week, in Cebu City, all forty-four of us (twelve Americans and thirty-two Filipinos) assembled for an evening class on the Jesuit philosophy of education. Our professor, a formidable Boston Jesuit, laid out a series of theses in scholastic form that defined the physical and then the metaphysical essence of Jesuit education. The final thesis asserted, with typical Jesuit understatement, that "not only is Jesuit education the finest system of education ever devised by the mind of man, it is the finest that ever could be devised by the mind of man." And the note given to the thesis was *metaphysice certa.*

This serene self-confidence is missing from a very instructive paper given by William McInnes, long-time President of the Association of Jesuit Colleges and Universities, at Saint Louis University in 1984. After reviewing the history of Jesuit colleges and universities since World War II—a history that Father McInnes neatly divides into a search for academic responsibility in the 1950s; a search for a new citizenship role in the 1960s, and a search for identity in the 1970s—Father McInnes concludes that "there is not and cannot be one canonized philosophy of Jesuit education," that such a philosophy "is formed not only by what philosophers think but by what decision-makers do," and that "the philosophy of Jesuit education is evolving."[7]

But is the search for a Jesuit philosophy of education—even an evolving, tentative, pluralistic philosophy (or philosophies)—another illusion? Might it not be simpler and more creative to recognize that whatever is distinctive about Jesuit education cannot be traced to any philosophy at all but rather to a religious vision?

In 1969 at a workshop in Denver sponsored by the Jesuit Educational Association, William Richardson, S.J., argued that "Jesuit education means a style of maintaining colleges and universities that is-grounded in a certain mode of religious experience—that of Ignatius—and is reinforced by a certain historical, or historically contingent, vision."[8] An important consequence of that religious experience, the delegates to the Denver Workshop concluded, was a "world-affirming spirituality, . . . a secular mysticism, an action-oriented Christian humanism."

Jesuit Education in the United States

If Jesuit education has been characterized in the past by "a certain historical, or historically conditioned vision," how has that historical vision developed here in the United States?

In 1989 we celebrated the Bicentennial of Georgetown University, the first Catholic and the first Jesuit college to be established in the new Republic of the United States. Over the past two hundred years here in the United States the old-world ideal of Jesuit education—a fusion of Ignatian spirituality and renaissance humanism—took on the distinctive forms of the new world, as these developed throughout the nineteenth and twentieth centuries.[9] The American high school gradually took shape as a peculiarly American institution, and today there are forty-six Jesuit high schools here in the United States, where Ignatian images and spirituality are held out to American adolescents at a critical time in their lives.

The American liberal arts college and, eventually, the American research university were also forms that developed in the past two hundred years, and Jesuit institutions developed within those models. As Bangert notes, this adaptation of the European Jesuit college to the evolving structure of American education was the specifically U.S. contribution to the Jesuit tradition of education. "By 1910 they had generally established this division [into high school and college] by the creation of the American Jesuit high school and the American Jesuit college . . . a fresh contribution to the Society's educational tradition."[10]

After Georgetown was founded in 1789, Saint Louis University in 1818 was the first of twenty-one Jesuit colleges founded in the nineteenth century. Six more colleges were established in this century, including Loyola University in Los Angeles in 1914 and the last, Wheeling College in 1954. The story of the development of Jesuit colleges and universities in the United States is part of the larger story of the development of an educational system in this country that has been unique in Catholic communities around the world.[11]

Largely a response to the desires and needs of an immigrant people, Catholic schools represented a way of preserving religious faith and culture in what was perceived to be an indifferent or even hostile environment. Within this system, the success of Jesuit institutions can be measured in many ways. The most obvious, perhaps, is the collective achievement of our more than one million alumni, many of whom enjoy positions of leadership in the corporate world, in public life, and in educational institutions, both Catholic and secular, throughout the country.

For these Jesuit colleges and universities, the years since the close of the Second World War were a period of very rapid growth. Americans, returning from the war, flocked to the campuses of the nation. Throughout the 1950s and 1960s Jesuit institutions expanded in size and complexity. At the same time, along with this institutional expansion, self-criticism about the quality of these schools and their scholarship became a recurrent theme. The essay of John Tracy Ellis on the indequacies of Catholic intellectual life was a landmark in a debate that continued through the 1950s and the 1960s.

Paul Fitzgerald in his book on *The Governance of Jesuit Colleges in the United States 1920–1970* recalls the concern expressed by Jesuit authorities over the rapid development of Jesuit colleges in the 1950s; the pace of expansion, they warned, was outstripping the number of Jesuits available, even though these were still years of bumper crops of Jesuit vocations. Was it wise for Jesuit institutions, Jesuit leaders asked themselves, to expand their graduate programs and develop professional schools, without the resources needed to guarantee the quality of these programs and to preserve their Jesuit character?[12]

The formidable President of the Jesuit Educational Association, Edward Rooney, S.J., relayed the concerns of Rome about the need for greater clarity on the objectives of the rapidly developing Jesuit educational system in the United States. Should Jesuits sponsor university centers? If so, how many?

Robert Harvanek argued at the time that the resources available to the American Catholic community could support only five authentic Catholic universities: the University of Notre Dame, Catholic University of America, and three Jesuit universities.[13] But which three? (One can imagine the twenty-eight Jesuit presidents sitting around together and each one suggesting "you first.")

Father Michael Walsh, in response to Father Harvanek, thought that ten or twelve Catholic universities were possible. In effect, in Fitzgerald's view, Father Walsh was really arguing for the freedom of individual institutions to pursue their own development.

Echoes of that debate can still be heard today, and not only among Jesuits. Frank Rhodes, the President of Cornell, raised the question again in his address to Assembly '89 at Georgetown. "Probably no single Jesuit institution," Rhodes said, "now qualifies as among the very top twenty or so U.S. institutions in terms of scholarly excellence. It is appropriate, I think, to ask why not and also to ask whether an appropriate goal might be one superb Jesuit institution."[14]

For some Jesuits this issue has become all the more urgent because of the decline in Jesuit manpower. For many, however, history has already resolved the issue. Jesuits have never shown much enthusiasm for the national planning necessary for such a concentration of Jesuit resources in a few selected institutions. Does this mean that we have missed a historic opportunity because of a narrow provincial outlook? Or have our instincts been right? Is there something utopian, and to that extent illusory, in the notion that Jesuit apostolic planning can control historical events and regional circumstances to the degree necessary for such national planning to become effective?

In any case, Jesuit education in the United States at the start of this last decade of the century consists of an extraordinary network of forty-six high schools and twenty-eight colleges and universities. Many of these institutions enjoy an enviable reputation for excellence as regional institutions and even as national institutions. Individually and collectively, they must address some difficult challenges in the years ahead, and I would like to conclude these reflections by identifying several of these challenges.

The Challenges Ahead

The most obvious challenge to the future of the Jesuit educational mission in the United States in the years ahead is the declining number of Jesuits. A favored exercise in some of our communities is the continuing recalculation of the actuarial tables. As the pyramid of the Jesuit population becomes more and more inverted, it is clear that the number of Jesuits active in our different colleges and universities will be drastically reduced in the years ahead. This unavoidable reality is one cause of the anxiety about Jesuit identity to which I alluded earlier.

In response, Jesuits have recognized that the distinctive character of our institutions will depend more and more in the years ahead on the interest and commitment of non-Jesuits. The theme of collaboration with non-Jesuits in a common enterprise pervades Jesuit meetings these days.

But perhaps we do not always appreciate how much collaboration involves authentic dialogue, in which both partners listen and learn. Such a process implies change—inevitably continuing change in that "historically contingent idea of Jesuit education." To my mind the desire to certify the content of Jesuit education, reflected in talk of a Jesuit accreditation process, contradicts the promotion of increasing collaboration with non-Jesuits. Collaboration means dialogue, and dialogue means change. I do not believe the implications of this inevitability are fully appreciated by those who are preoccupied with certifying Jesuit identity. For example, is even the term "Jesuit" negotiable? Is it Ignatian to insist that our enterprises must always and conspicuously be labeled "Jesuit"?

Our schools will certainly become more and more laicized in the years ahead, in the sense that the number of Jesuits, priests, and religious working in them will be drastically reduced. Laicization, in this sense, need not mean secularization, but I suspect that the validity of this distinction will depend on issues beyond the campuses of our institutions. To the extent that the American Catholic community remains a vital and coherent community, our Catholic institutions will remain strong in their Catholic identity.

A second challenge that we must face is more internal to the Jesuit community itself. The mandate of the Thirty-Second General Congregation in 1975 on the overall apostolic priority of serving faith and promoting justice has touched off differences of interpretation among Jesuits, particularly between those involved in direct social ministry and those involved in higher education. Frank Rhodes, in his thoroughly sympathetic address in June, 1989 claimed to be puzzled by what he found in reading contemporary Jesuit literature. Rhodes asked,

> Is to serve faith and promote justice—the goal emphasized by the 32nd General Congregation—a valid and adequate mission for Jesuit education? How does one define 'justice'? Is there unanimity or a 'Jesuit' position on what constitutes justice, and how it should be promoted? And if justice is promoted actively, what are the implications of advocacy for scholarly impartiality? Do we end up with something dangerously like dogmatic Marxist economics, which promotes only one point of view?[15]

The Thirty-Third General Congregation in 1983 and Father Kolvenbach in his address in June 1989 at Georgetown insisted on the need to better integrate the apostolic mission to faith and justice with Jesuit ministry in higher education. Father Kolvenbach urged that we invite to our universities those involved in more direct social ministry, so that a healthy exchange between the university and the activist could ensue. The Thirty-Third General Congregation had pointed out that research and understanding are essential to effective social change. If Jesuit colleges and universities in the United States can provide anything distinctive to American higher education in the future years, it will be, I would submit, a successful model of integrating these various concerns.

We have not yet done so. If and when we do, we will be closer to achieving the kind of Jesuit community that must play a critical role on Jesuit campuses. The documents of the Church in recent years have insisted on the Catholic university as a community of faith. If this is an essential element of the contemporary Catholic university, then on Catholic universities in the Jesuit tradition the Jesuit community itself must play a vital role in helping to create this larger community of faith that is the Catholic university community.

Finally, a third challenge is reflected in the theme of this conference. All of American education needs to have a greater international sense. The Jesuit network of schools and ministries around the world should provide a special resource in achieving an international consciousness among our faculty and students. Nonetheless, we recognize that we are frequently more parochial than we should be, and the Jesuit international network is rarely exploited the way it should be.

To sum up:

An important presupposition to any discussion of Jesuit education in the United States must be a sense of Ignatian freedom that does not seek guarantees about the future. Second, what is distinctive about Jesuit education will be found not in a Jesuit philosophy of education, but in a religious vision grounded in the experience of Saint Ignatius and mediated through changing historical circumstances. Third, in the United States national planning for Jesuit education has been limited in its effectiveness, quite probably because the model envisioned for such national planning is more utopian than we may realize and hence not fully consistent with the Jesuit way of proceeding. Finally, the future will depend on a collaboration with non-Jesuits that will inevitably bring change in the character of our institutions, but this change can be healthy and even Ignatian.

If it is true, as I believe it to be, that it is a religious vision that makes Jesuit education distinctive, then it follows that a religious renewal must be at the heart of the future of Jesuit education in the United States. The opportunity for a renewal of this kind of education is very real. We see, for example, a great need in American higher education for models of integrated undergraduate education and for a development of graduate schools and professional schools that keep alive the ethical dimension of the disciplines and the professions. For both of these needs, there are elements in the Jesuit history of education that offer special resources.

There is also great need in our contemporary Catholic Church for models that unite faith and intelligence. We must resist those worrisome watchdogs of orthodoxy who threaten to drain all enthusiasm out of our Catholic humanism. When we think of the nature of a Catholic university, we should not instinctively think of controls and limits. The "world-affirming spirituality," of which the Denver workshop spoke in 1969, needs to be boldly affirmed for contemporary Catholicism.

Finally, if Jesuit education is grounded in this religious vision, then we should not be disappointed that we have not marched as well-rehearsed soldiers in some master strategic plan. Instead, the progress of Jesuit education in this country has looked more like a pilgrimage.

Jesuits, like other Christians, move forward on pilgrimage toward the Kingdom of God. Our march may be more disorderly than many would like; we can appear at times to be a quarrelsome crew as we argue about our response to new needs and new opportunities. Nonetheless, for many of us it is the kind of pilgrimage worth the gamble of a lifetime, and it is very reassuring to realize that so many others have chosen to cast their lives with this disorderly, quarrelsome, but invariably interesting group of pilgrims.

Notes

1. Robert F. Harvanek, S.J., *The Jesuit Vision of a University* (Chicago: Loyola University of Chicago, 1989), p. 10.

2. William C. McInnes, S.J., "The Current State of the Jesuit Philosophy of Education," *Jesuit Higher Education: Essays on an American Tradition of Excellence,* ed. Rolando E. Bonachea (Pittsburgh: Duquesne University Press, 1989), p. 182, n. 28. The attempt to reflect on the Jesuit educational apostolate and to articulate its distinctive character can be a valuable exercise, if understood in a context of a continuing dialectic between action and reflection—a thoroughly Ignatian form of discernment. If such efforts, however, aspire to define in some timeless fashion the normative essence of Jesuit education, then I believe the exercise is built on an illusion. I believe such an illusion is at work in calls for a "Jesuit accreditation process."

3. William V. Bangert, S.J., *A History of the Society of Jesus* (Saint Louis: The Institute of Jesuit Sources, 1972), p. 510.

4. Ibid., p. 512.

5. Harvanek, *The Jesuit Vision of a University,* p. 11.

6. Brian Daley, S.J., " 'Splendor and Wonder': Ignatian Mysticism and the Ideals of Liberal Education," *Splendor and Wonder: Jesuit Character, Georgetown Spirit, and Liberal Education,* ed. William J. O'Brien (Washington, D.C.: Georgetown University Press, 1989), p. 16.

7. McInnes, "The Current State of the Jesuit Philosophy of Education," pp. 44–45.

8. Ibid., p. 34.

9. John W. O'Malley, S.J., has described the tension between the two currents of scholasticism and humanism in the Jesuit educational tradition in a historical essay that enlightens some contemporary dilemmas. "The Jesuit Educational Enterprise in Historical Perspective," in Bonachea, pp. 10–25.

10. Bangert, *A History of the Society of Jesus,* p. 493.

11. "The presence of Jesuit colleges and universities on the American educational

scene testified to one of the most striking instances of adaptation in the history of the Society, comparable to the initial election to embrace the humanism of the 16th Century and place it at the service of the Church." Bangert, *A History of the Society of Jesus,* p. 57.

12. Paul A Fitzgerald, S.J., *The Governance of Jesuit Colleges in the United States 1920–1970* (Notre Dame, Indiana: University of Notre Dame Press, 1984).

13. Ibid., p. 161.

14. Frank H. T. Rhodes, "The Mission and Ministry of Jesuits in Higher Education," *America* (29 July–5 August 1989), p. 58.

15. Ibid., p. 57.

Theology in the Jesuit University: Reassessing the Ignatian Vision

PAUL G. CROWLEY, S.J.

When Jesuit Superior General Peter-Hans Kolvenbach recently visited California, he noted that if we are looking for models of Jesuit universities where the service of faith and the promotion of justice have been institutionally realized, we might turn to El Salvador. The recent murder in El Salvador of six Jesuit priests associated with the Jesuit university there led a few U.S. Jesuits to ask how a U.S. Jesuit university could similarly reflect and advance the call of the entire Society to the service of faith and the promotion of justice.

The answer to this question is tied to the answer to a more fundamental question: "What does it mean to be a Jesuit university?" Father George Ganss's magisterial study of the Jesuit university showed that the issue of theology's role is central to the identity of a university precisely as Jesuit.[1] Therefore, the university's role in the service of faith and the promotion of justice will not become evident apart from a reassessment of theology's role within the Jesuit university as Ignatius saw it. Whereas theology's role was relatively clear in the time of Ignatius, the matter is complicated now by a host of factors unimaginable to Ignatius, not least the development of the modern corporate university and the subsumption of theology within religious studies as a subdiscipline and a requirement for graduation. And the field of theology itself has changed, even within the past twenty-five years.

The question of theology's role in the service of faith and the promotion of justice by a Jesuit university requires a reassessment of three elements of the Ignatian vision: (1) the foundational inspiration of the Jesuit educational mission rooted in Ignatius's vision for the entire Society, (2) the nature and purpose of a Jesuit university, and (3) the nature and role of theology within the Jesuit university. This reassessment will indicate specific directions for Jesuit university theology in the near future. Such a reassessment of the Ignatian vision must take into account the fact that articulations of Jesuit mission by the last two General Congregations of the Society themselves affect the functioning of the university and the direction of theology, that the nature of the university itself affects Jesuit mission and the work of theology, and that theology has a direct relation to and impact upon the nature of the

155

university and Jesuit mission, although in ways significantly different from
the past.

Fundamental Ignatian Vision for Education

As is well known, the *Spiritual Exercises* constitute the foundation of the
Ignatian vision in regard to all things. The summary and climax of the
Exercises, the contemplation of divine love, follows naturally from a love for
the person of Jesus Christ, which leads to an apostolic ardor to remake the
world and be remade ourselves, for the reign of God.[2] Ignatius's is a world-
embracing vision; the entire world and its human inhabitants, not just the
world of one's own culture, are the source of meditation upon and contemplation of God, the theater within which the redemption takes place,
definitively in the humanity of the incarnate Son.[3] Though the world is good
because it is part of creation, it is broken and cries out for redemption. Those
who elect to work with Jesus in companionship are apostles of the redemption.[4] Everything else—the Society of Jesus, its many works, the meaning of
Christian life itself—hinges upon this reading of the Gospel, this particular
Ignatian vision, which is both apostolic and world-embracing.[5]

The first Jesuit universities were founded to further this vision, first by
training Jesuits themselves, and shortly thereafter, by educating non-Jesuits
as well. The purpose of the university was directly tied to the apostolic and
world-embracing vision of Ignatius; education was indispensable to the attainment of that vision.[6] The university was not merely a professional training ground *per se,* nor even primarily a builder of character, virtue, and values
in its students. Rather, it was constituted to advance the evangelical vision
that had so inspired Ignatius and his companions.

Jesuit universities were to function according to the pedagogical ideals of
the University of Paris, where Ignatius had studied, although the Parisian
curriculum was not to be followed slavishly.[7] Like Paris, the Jesuit university
was to be composed of three faculties: humanities and languages, corresponding to the medieval trivium; arts (philosophy) and sciences (including
elements of the medieval quadrivium); and theology. As at Paris, theology
was to be the synthesizing discipline of all other university studies, thus
defining the nature of the entire university. Theology was to be the "architectonic" wisdom of the curriculum, rather than a particular discipline or
science.[8] But in a variation upon the Parisian theme, the nature of theology
within the Jesuit university was to be further specified by the apostolic vision
of Ignatius and the Society. There would thus be a turn away from the
medieval methods of the *Sentences,* which were still being studied even at
Paris, and an adoption of the more cosmopolitan, and in some circles radically new, theology of Thomas Aquinas, so deeply pastoral in its inspiration
and therefore so well-suited to the Ignatian vision.[9]

We can make three observations on the basis of this précis of the Ignatian vision. First, the Ignatian vision, apostolic and world-embracing, is the inspiration of the Jesuit university. Second, the Jesuit university gives theology (though not necessarily the theology department) pride of place because theology is a radically interdisciplinary intellectual wisdom that mediates worldly knowledge and faith; university theology, a university discipline, is foundational and indispensable to achieving the Ignatian vision rooted in the *Exercises,* which is itself highly theological. Third, theology in the Jesuit university is not simply one discipline alongside others; it is rather the discipline that gives coherence and focus to the university. Theology finds its inspiration, discovers its sources, and assumes its mission within the context of the larger apostolic and world-embracing Ignatian vision of the university. The university's identity as a university depends upon theology's role.

Nature and Purpose of the University

The nature and purpose of the Jesuit university, once so clearly tied to the Ignatian vision of advancing the coming of the kingdom of Jesus Christ, even through a curriculum that saw theology as its central and integrating discipline, can no longer be assumed. The fact is that, in the United States, Jesuit universities have adopted the U.S. model of the corporate university and, to a large extent, the standards and values of secular academic culture. While there have been sound reasons for taking this direction, even the most ardent supporters of the current shape of Jesuit higher education would not claim that this has been done without cost, and in some cases, compromise to the essential Ignatian vision, especially as reformulated by recent Congregations.[10] There has been much discussion in recent years about recovering the Jesuit identity of some of our institutions, taking care that faculty hiring reflects this concern, and finding ways of reflecting the reorientation of the Society in the curriculum, in various institutional supports (such as internal funding of research), and through special institutes dedicated to this purpose.

These efforts to maintain the Ignatian vision can be signs of vitality, but they may ultimately serve only as ornaments in the secular academic crown, if the Ignatian vision is not allowed to act as a critical tool in actually refashioning, and even restructuring, basic elements of our universities, at least in changing how Jesuit universities perceive themselves within the larger U.S. academic culture. To become a Catholic Harvard or a Catholic Dartmouth is to be no more faithful to the Ignatian vision than it would have been for the Roman College to have aspired to the heady heights of a Catholic Paris. The recent Congregations suggest that universities are more likely to remain faithful to the Ignatian vision if they ask (1) how their institutions are reflective of the Society's preferential option for the poor,[11] (2) how the university as a whole is enlisted in the Church's engagement with modern atheism in its various forms, and (3) how the university promotes the spiritual advancement of humankind toward the God revealed in Jesus Christ. Such phraseology as "solidarity with the poor" is not intended as high-sounding moralistic rhetoric. But the difficulty for U.S. Jesuit universities has been in moving from rhetoric to reality.[12]

Two Jesuit scholars who have studied the call of these recent Congregations, Michael Buckley and Jon Sobrino, have approached the problem from two different, though in some ways complementary, angles. I address here only their treatment of the meaning for Jesuit universities of "the preferential option for the poor." Buckley approaches it from the history of education. He argues that the constant element connecting the modern corporate Jesuit university with its sixteenth-century forebears is the ideal of humanistic education, an ideal that Jesuit universities are perhaps uniquely equipped to foster in contemporary Western culture.

> . . . [T]he university as such can possess and foster in its faculties and in its students a profound concern for the social order, that this engagement or care for 'the development of peoples who are striving to escape from hunger, misery, endemic disease, and ignorance' emanates from the very nature of the university itself. This attention to the human condition and this corresponding care to develop a disciplined sensitivity to human misery and exploitation, is not a single political doctrine or a system of economics. It is a humanism, a humane sensibility to be achieved anew within the demands of our own times and as a product of an education whose ideal continues to be that of the Western *humanitas*.[13]

Buckley suggests ways in which the university curriculum, including theology, can include as source, subject matter, and aim "the alienation of the student or the institution from the ordinary life of the desperate, the poor and the exploited."[14] Analogous arguments can be made for the university's engagement with atheism and the promotion of spirituality.

Jon Sobrino, working within the context of the University of Central America, finds the link with the Ignatian vision directly in the "preferential option for the poor." Referring to Ignatius's meditation on the Incarnation in the *Spiritual Exercises,* he argues that the Jesuit university is by all appearances more on the road to disaster than to salvation.[15] The Jesuit university is called to advance the reign of God and to do so through a pedagogy of poverty, where the poor (by various definitions—economic, evangelical, spiritual) become integral factors in the program of the institution. In this way, the Jesuit university can begin to counter two tendencies that threaten the integrity of the Ignatian inspiration: a selective incarnation in social reality, and an isolation of university work from the world.[16] He argues that our universities must even ask themselves why they have not questioned, either theoretically (through investigations of various social structures) or through an analysis of their own social influence, those unjust structures that allow sin to persist. To remain isolated from such social realities under the cover of building academic stature or in the interest of preserving some academic sanctuary is to abdicate the fundamental Christian inspiration of a Jesuit university. Transposing the argument to North American terms, such isolation is tantamount to having bought the full basket of secular academic values and to have opted for the false standard of riches, honors, and glory.[17] Sadly, it is also a recipe for a gradual but sure slide by many Jesuit institutions into cultural and even ecclesial dismissal, precisely through abandonment of the Ignatian vision.

Nature and Role of Theology

The lines of this discussion thus far—Ignatian vision and the nature of the university itself—bear upon the role of theology in the Jesuit university, just as they did for Ignatius four hundred fifty years ago. Ignatius himself lived in a time of great theological dislocation. Aquinas had been only recently introduced in some of the universities.[18] The intellectual decadence of late scholasticism was becoming widely recognized, especially within humanist circles, and a critical and historically conscious approach to textual authorities was already emerging, especially in the wake of the Reformation. Already, the ancient unity of theology was collapsing into specializations (biblical, dogmatic, fundamental, moral, mystical, and so forth) that would portend the modern divisions among various theological disciplines and the eventual fissure between theology as an ecclesial (and later, seminary) discipline and religious studies as a science worthy of the academy.[19]

We would be mistaken to imagine that Ignatius was theologically premodern. Although he gave pride of place to theology, much as medieval Paris had done, he realized that this pride of place could not be accorded through simple replication of medieval pedagogy, nor even by adopting the highest medieval notions of theology. Where Ignatius discusses theology in the *Exercises* and *Constitutions* is found an awareness of the emerging complexity of theology itself, corresponding to the needs of the times, to which faith was called to respond. This is evident in the distinction Ignatius makes between "positive" and "scholastic" ideology.[20]

Positive theology, based upon the sources of revelation found in scripture, the fathers, church councils, canon law, and other doctrine, is a theology directed to the immediate pastoral situation of people, a theology engaged with current debates and apologetics. Its aim is "exegetical and explicative," answering especially the needs of humanism and heresies.[21] Scholastic theology, on the other hand, was systematic research into the grounds for discussing the things of God, the warrants of faith, and the meaning of the claims of faith, especially in relation to philosophy and science. For Ignatius, Aquinas was the exemplar *par excellence* of this highly disciplined method of theologizing. Third, Ignatius propounded, through the *Exercises,* a kind of mystical theology, rooted in the scriptures and directed through apostolic service toward the glory of God.[22] He imagined all three types of theology— positive, scholastic, and mystical—as feeding into, informing, and giving final shape to the Jesuit university: positive theology, through its literary method, addressing the secular world into which Jesuit-educated students would be sent to work; scholastic theology addressing in a systematic and reflective fashion the things of faith in conversation with the other arts and human sciences within the university itself; mystical theology, the life of the spirit, imbuing every moment of university life and given thematic expression in the *Spiritual Exercises.*

A correspondence of Ignatius's view of theology to the contemporary theological situation in the Jesuit university is not merely coincidental; it is organic and foundational. To positive theology corresponds the contemporary challenge to draw into theology, through various hermeneutical approaches, the new sources, methods, and aims represented by the church's historic turn to the poor; to scholastic theology corresponds the contemporary commitment of the Society to unfold the inner intelligibility of faith in view of current intellectual challenges; to mystical theology corresponds the Society's original and foundational mission to bring the person of Jesus Christ to all people, that they might be liberated and saved.[23] This set of correspondences is a kind of Ignatian blueprint for theology in the Jesuit university today, and it indicates some specific directions for theology in the Jesuit university.

What are some of these directions for theology?

1. Theology will and should remain within the modern corporate university either a department or a program within a department that takes seriously the tasks given theology in the service of faith and the promotion of justice. While theology will probably remain essentially a research discipline associated with teaching, it will also become much more integrally related to the pastoral situation of the church beyond the university, especially through networks of Jesuits and coworkers. The ends of theological research will thus be consonant with the ends of the Jesuit university itself. Furthermore, because theology is by nature so radically interdisciplinary, it can function, under various rubrics within the university but especially as an academic program, to integrate the intellectual life of the university toward the attainment of its Jesuit mission. Theology was for Ignatius the architectonic integrating discipline of interdisciplinary communication within the Jesuit university; it still can be. While such an integrating function can be accomplished by organs of the university outside the theology program (for example, a high-profile university chaplaincy, not to mention other academic departments, programs, and institutes), theology itself should be named, as Ignatius himself did, the primary bearer of that mission within the university. This would constitute a clear mandate for theology that one would not expect

to find outside the Jesuit university. At the same time, it must not be assumed that theology is any longer a discipline with a unitary method or function;[24] not even Ignatius could make such a blithe assumption. Theology is rather a locus that shares its *raison d'être* with that of the Jesuit university itself: the service of faith and the promotion of justice.

2. As this faith is an ecclesial faith, the university that serves the faith is itself ecclesial. Even though the U.S. Jesuit university follows the corporate university model, as a Catholic university the Jesuit university is still by nature an ecclesial institution, no matter how attenuated the relationship may be to Rome by virtue of the provisions of canon law.[25] This means that the Jesuit university is not merely a private university with a Catholic, much less a Jesuit, veneer. Such was not the understanding of Ignatius, and in this respect his vision needs to be embraced. The implication for theology of the ecclesial nature of the university is that theological research undertaken within a Catholic university is in the interest of not simply pure knowledge, but of knowledge at the service of faith, which includes, in the teaching of the Roman magisterium, the promotion of justice.[26] Loss of this essential ecclesial dimension of the Catholic university is the loss of the soul of theology.[27]

The Ignatian vision is so closely linked to the ecclesial dimension that one cannot let go of one without letting go of the other. This linkage does not mean that theology conducted within the Jesuit university can be narrowly Roman Catholic or apologetic or that a particular systematic theology is the only measure of valuable theological work. All theology today must be conducted within an ecumenical framework and in conversation with the human sciences, especially those that fall under the umbrella of "religious studies." Nor does this linkage mean that the theology conducted in Jesuit universities need only echo Roman doctrine, simply interpret dogmatics, or become retrospective in order to avoid controversy. In speaking of the mandate given to the Society by recent popes to take on the challenges of atheism, Father Kolvenbach has noted:

> Without doubt all the tasks which the church entrusts to us entail risks in their accomplishment. To announce to a world distant from the church the love of God manifested in Jesus Christ; to do this by means of social commitment and in-culturation, dialogue and ecumenism, theological research and pastoral experience—this requires of us initiatives which lay us open to misunderstanding.[28]

What applies to all of the works of the Society applies especially to university theology.

3. Theology is not likely to lose a sense of itself as an activity at the service of faith and the promotion of justice if theologians in the Jesuit university keep before their gaze, as the entire university must, the world for which the university exists. The relation between theology and the world marks one of the most significant shifts in the nature of theology in the past twenty-five years, and in this regard theology differs markedly from the

theology of Ignatius's day. One can find so many points of contact between the world and the tasks of theology at the service of faith: the growth of feminist consciousness, the rise and hegemony of scientific ideology, the legitimation and growth of atheisms, the decline of great religious institutions and values, the growing dialogue and exchange of world religions and spiritualities, the emergence of new gnosticisms, the disappearance of nature and the ruination of the planet, overpopulation and massive starvation, the growing importance of the third world both politically and culturally, the collapse of established political orders on massive scales, the emergence of liberal capitalism as a dominant ideology, and the re-emergence of nationalism, fundamentalism, and racism in many parts of the world. All of these phenomena—some positive, some negative, all problematic—collectively describe the world in which we live and present a mammoth challenge to Jesuit rhetoric about serving faith and promoting justice.

One task for university theology in the face of this massive challenge is to ask how to adopt critically the sources, methods, and apostolic aims of liberation theologies. Liberation theology is not merely an academic fad; it is a valuable tool in the interdisciplinary and theological engagement with the cross-cultural situation in which the Jesuit university finds itself today. Furthermore, liberation theology has become part of the mainstream of Roman Catholic thinking (and indeed of ecumenical theology).[29] Not coincidentally, it springs from those parts of the Catholic world where the preferential option for the poor has been most seriously appropriated, especially by Jesuits. Without abandoning the other well-established streams of Catholic theology, we must nevertheless ask how the strategies of liberation theologies can help Jesuit universities to become both more radically Christian and more radically Jesuit.

A further task for university theology in the face of these challenges from the world is to become critically engaged with the emergence of local theologies within the world church as the faith becomes inculturated, both geographically and socially. The Society of Jesus gave the church the language of inculturation and very possibly the modern idea of it.[30] The hermeneutical task of theology in the Jesuit university today is to further mediate the values of inculturation and catholicity, that the Gospel can be served. This hermeneutical task naturally involves the ongoing traditions of theological activity that are already well-established, but relates them to the cultural situations in which faith finds itself today. Thus, there should certainly be no problem in finding Thomas Aquinas pertinent to the contemporary theological enterprise.[31] The problematic of faith and culture, catholicity and inculturation, is a major locus for theological engagement with the roots of atheism and is thus aptly recommended to Jesuit universities as suited to their theological goals.

A third task for Jesuit university theology is developing models of *praxis*— enabling students and the university as a whole to serve the world in its need for salvation. This is the apostolic moment of the practical mysticism of Ignatius, and it assumes an ultimate concern not for *praxis* itself but for the faith of the practitioner, the faith of which *praxis* is a constitutive moment. Taking theology as a discipline in itself, this is a question of reappraising the sources and the aims of theology.[32] The sources can be the constituent elements of the worlds of the economically, politically, or socially marginalized, the suffering—those who would especially fall within the reach of Jesus' ministry in the Gospels. The aims would be the practical transitions from reflection upon these sources, in light of scripture and the theological tradition, to actual service—an experiential component in education itself that would plant the seeds for a transformation of the world in light of the Gospel. Without confusing theological research with *praxis,* Jesuit university theology must, nevertheless, take with utmost seriousness the importance of *praxis* and the relationship between theory and *praxis,* if it is to remain true to the vision of Ignatius and not to a completely alien set of values.[33] This is perhaps more difficult to accomplish in a first-world situation such as our own, where most of us are somewhat benumbed to the real poverty around us and within us, than in a cultural situation where we are shocked by the scandal of poverty into apostolic action.

Conclusion

Theology continues to have a role to play in Jesuit university education. We must first look to the Ignatian vision itself, understand it as a self-conscious move away from the *status quo* of the sixteenth century, discover its underlying values, and transpose them into our own situation. This requires a reappraisal of the Ignatian vision in light of the new formulation of it by recent Jesuit Congregations and an appropriation of this reformulation not only on the level of rhetoric but on the level of strategies and tasks accomplished. If theology is to spearhead the mission of a Jesuit university, precisely through its radically interdisciplinary nature, then theology must lead the university in the service of faith and the promotion of justice, with a focus upon the preferential option for the poor, an engagement with modern atheisms, and a promotion of the life of the spirit. Within the context of the contemporary world, theology programs within Jesuit universities can begin to accomplish these ends by taking seriously the sources, methods, and aims of liberation theology; by focusing on the mediation of faith and cultures through traditional and new theological strategies; and by stressing *praxis* as an essential moment in theological pedagogy. In these ways Jesuit university theology might remain faithful to the apostolic, world-embracing vision of Ignatius and move the Jesuit university closer to a fulfillment of the Society's mission today.

Notes

1. George E. Ganss, S.J., *Saint Ignatius' Idea of a Jesuit University* (Milwaukee: Marquette University Press, 1954). See Michael J. Buckley's summary of Ganss's work and his own analysis of the relevant parts of the *Constitutions* in "*In Hunc Potissimum* . . . : Ignatius' Understanding of the Jesuit University," *Readings in Ignatian Higher Education* 1/1 (Spring 1989): 19–21. In commenting upon Newman's compatible view, Buckley adds: "It is not merely that theology is present as one branch of knowledge among others. Any presence of Catholic theology does not mean that a university is *Catholic*—and this is Newman's point. It means that it is that much more a *university*, an institution which embodies the universality of significant human discourse and knowledge. What makes a university Catholic for Ignatius is the organic relationship between the other disciplines and theology. Please notice that I am talking about theology, not necessarily about the theology department."

2. See "Christ the King and His Call," otherwise known as the "Kingdom Meditation," in *The Spiritual Exercises of St. Ignatius: A Literal Translation and a Contemporary Reading*, ed. David L. Fleming, S.J. (Saint Louis: Institute of Jesuit Sources, 1978), [91–100], pp. 64–69. The "Contemplation to Gain Love" is situated at the end of the *Exercises*, [230–37], pp. 138–42. All further references to the *Spiritual Exercises* are to this edition.

3. Nowhere is this more evident than in the contemplation on the Incarnation, *Spiritual Exercises* [101–17], pp. 70–76. "The first Point is, to see the various persons: and first those on the surface of the earth, in such variety, in dress as in actions: some white and others black; some in peace and others in war; some weeping and others laughing; some well, and others ill; some being börn and others dying, etc. 2. To see and consider the Three Divine Persons, as on their royal throne or seat of Their Divine Majesty, how They look on all the surface and circuit of the earth, and all the people in such blindness, and how they are dying and going down to Hell. . . . what the Divine Persons are saying, that is: 'Let Us work the redemption of the Human race,' etc. . . . likewise what the Divine Persons are doing, namely working out the most holy Incarnation, etc."

4. This is evident in many parts of the *Exercises*, but especially in the "Kingdom Meditation" [91–100], and the meditation on the "Two Standards" [136–48]. Both meditations invite the exercitant to consideration of an imitation of the pattern of Jesus' own poverty, humility, and rejection—the better to spread the teaching of Jesus "through all states and conditions of persons" throughout the world. See especially [145], p. 88.

5. Brian Daley, S.J., refers to the "practical mysticism" of the *Exercises* and argues that this practical mysticism carries over to the *Constitutions*. "The *Constitutions* of the Society of Jesus, the description of its life and ideals that Ignatius painstakingly wrote and rewrote between 1544 and his death in 1556, makes that fairly clear: the purpose of the organization, in the eyes of its original members, was to be an instrument of active, up-to-date pastoral ministry within the Catholic Church, exercised by those who had been 'converted' to discipleship as Ignatius had been." "Ignatian Mysticism and the Ideals of Liberal Education," in *Splendor and Wonder: Jesuit Character, Georgetown Spirit, and Liberal Education*, ed. William J. O'Brien (Washington, D.C.: Georgetown University Press, 1988), p. 9.

6. See *The Constitutions of the Society of Jesus*, trans. with introduction and commentary George Ganss, S.J. (Saint Louis: Institute of Jesuit Sources, 1970). The nature of the Jesuit university is discussed in Part IV. "Through a motive of charity colleges are accepted and schools open to the public are maintained in them for the improvement in learning and in living not only of our own members but even more especially of those from outside the Society. Through this same motive the Society

can extend itself to undertaking the work of universities, that through them this fruit sought in the colleges may be spread more universally through the branches taught, the number of persons attending, and the degrees which are conferred in order that the recipients may be able to teach with authority elsewhere what they have learned well in these universities of the Society for the glory to God our Lord." [440], pp. 210–11.

7. Michael Buckley has noted how Ignatius pared down the Parisian curriculum, which sometimes spanned some twenty years! See Buckley, *"In Hunc Potissimum . . .,"* p. 20. See also Ganss, on whom Buckley relies here, pp. 46–51, 68–73.

8. Michael Buckley observes, in *"In Hunc Potissimum . . .,"* p. 24: "Theology, then, must not be seen as one science among others, self-contained in its own integrity and adjacent to the other forms of disciplined human knowledge. It is much more like a place, a place within which the arts and sciences are encouraged and their ineluctable movement towards questions of ultimacy taken very seriously, questions not simply of interlocking content but even of the absolute commitments entailed by serious teaching and inquiry. This is theology as an architectonic wisdom rather than as a particular science."

9. See Buckley, *At the Origins of Modern Atheism* (New Haven: Yale University Press, 1978), p. 43, and his notes, p. 377. Also see John F. Farge, *Orthodoxy and Reform in Early Reformation France: The Faculty of Theology of Paris, 1500–1543* (Leiden: E. J. Brill, 1985).

10. We continue to look to Decree 4, "Our Mission Today," of the Thirty-Second Congregation as the *Urtext* from which all further discussion flows: "The mission of the Society of Jesus today is the service of faith, of which the promotion of justice is an absolute requirement. For reconciliation with God demands the reconciliation of people with one another." "Our Mission Today," #2, in *Documents of the 31st and 32nd General Congregations of the Society of Jesus [Documents]*, ed. John W. Padberg, S.J. (Saint Louis: Institute of Jesuit Sources, 1977), p. 411.

11. See, for example, "Prerequisites for Credibility," #48, *Documents of the 33rd General Congregation of the Society of Jesus* (Saint Louis: Institute of Jesuit Sources, 1984), p. 63: "The validity of our mission will also depend to a large extent on our solidarity with the poor. For though obedience sends us, it is poverty that makes us believable. So, together with many other religious congregations, we wish to make our own the Church's preferential option for the poor. . . . Directly or indirectly, this option should find some concrete expression in every Jesuit's life, in the orientation of our existing apostolic works, and in our choice of new ministries."

12. For one of the most thoughtful treatments of the "preferential option," and particularly of how it can be realized within apostolic works, see Thomas E. Clarke, S. J. "Option for the Poor: A Reflection," *America* 158/4 (30 January 1988), pp. 95–99.

13. Michael J. Buckley, S.J., "The University and the Concern for Justice: The Search for New Humanism," *Thought* 57/225 (June 1982): 223.

14. Ibid., p. 229.

15. "Siguiendo a San Ignacio en su meditación de la encarnación, hay que tener ante los ojos a la humanidad entera, en tanta variedad de estados, pero caminando a la perdición. Hoy también, la humanidad real se encuentra más en camino de perdición que de salvación." "Inspiración Cristiana de la Universidad," *Estudios Centroamericanos* 42 (1987): 705.

16. Ibid., p. 696. See entire article, pp. 695–705.

17. The reference is to the "Two Standards" meditation of the *Spiritual Exercises*, [136–48], pp. 84–91. Ignatius applies the same values as those espoused in this meditation and in other parts of the *Exercises* to the spirit in which Jesuits ought to undertake university work. They are expected to perform well, but to refuse honors (regular chairs), as honors are not in keeping with the humility appropriate to the

Society. "En lo que me pedís, si los nuestros que están en Alcalá votarán (como allí usan los estudiantes) por cátedras, no se lo debéis consentir, antes les avisad que en ninguna manera lo hagan, porque así conviene más la seguridad de sus conciencias y quietud, y para nuestro instituto, que es de apartarnos de toda especia de ambición, y tener paz y amor con todos." Letter of Saint Ignatius to Antonio de Araoz, 3 April 1548, in *Obras completas de S. Ignacio de Loyola,* ed. Ignacio Iparraguirre, S.J. (Madrid: Biblioteca de Autores Cristianos, 1963), p. 708.

18. For a discussion of the introduction of the *Summa theologiae* by Ignatius, see Ganss, *Constitutions,* p. 219, n. 1.

19. See Yves Congar, *A History of Theology,* trans. and ed. Hunter Guthrie (Garden City, N.Y.: Doubleday & Co., 1968), pp. 145–65. Congar traces the development of theology as a discipline up to the present day. He notes that after Trent the West witnessed "the death of universities as centers of original thought," even though "the teaching of theology continues in them as it does in the seminaries and the schools of Religious Orders" (p. 177). This development of theology itself as a discipline, up through the current bewildering array of functional specialties, sources, methods, and aims, has to be kept in mind when inquiring into the role of theology in the contemporary Jesuit university.

20. The distinction can be found explicitly stated in *Constitutions* [446], p. 213, and also in the *Spiritual Exercises,* "Rules for Thinking with the Church," #11, [363], pp. 232–35.

21. See Congar, *History,* p. 172, and the entire discussion of the distinction between positive and scholastic theologies, pp. 170–77. Congar more precisely frames the distinction at this stage in the development of theology as a "literary conception, according to which positive theology represents a certain *manner* of working out theology." This literary conception of positive theology is the one Ignatius has in mind, and one can speculate that its apologetic aims are particularly well suited to the apostolic ends of theological training in the Society. The methodological distinctions between positive and scholastic theology were worked out by Cano, for whom "positive theology will mean that part or that function by which theology establishes its principles or works on its foundations or datum." I can find no evidence that this later, more refined rendering of positive theology was evident to Ignatius. Ganss sees positive theology as a methodological distinction—that is, positive theology, like scholastic theology, is concerned with revelation, but treats revelation through a different set of sources than does scholastic theology, the outstanding exemplars of which are Lombard and Aquinas. Thus far, Ganss's view would seem to comport with Congar's interpretation. See Ganss, *Constitutions,* p. 188, n. 5.

22. One might question Congar's view (*History,* p. 166) that the *Exercises,* together with the writings of Francis de Sales and of the reformed Carmel, are to be contrasted with scholastic theology to the point of opposition. "Over against Scholastic theology there will be opposed from now on a mystical or affective theology, which will have its doctors, its works, its sources, and its style." Congar argues that the unity of theology known to the High Middle Ages was thereby broken down. In fact, Ignatius's mystical theology is complementary to the positive and scholastic theologies he so vigorously prescribes. The three together constitute a theological unity; all three approaches are essential to a comprehensive theological enterprise.

23. See "Our Mission Today," #47–48, *Documents,* pp. 427–28. This is a recurring theme in General Congregation 33. In a specific reference to theology in the universities, the Congregation notes: "Of great importance among the ministries of the society are the educational and intellectual apostolates. . . . When carried out in the light of our mission today, their efforts contribute vitally to 'the total and integral liberation of the human person leading to participation in the life of God himself.' [GC 32, "Jesuits Today," #11] Research in theology and philosophy, in the other sciences

and in every branch of human culture is likewise essential if Jesuits are to help the Church understand the contemporary world and to speak to it the Word of Salvation. The opportunities and responsibilities of these apostolates require a change of heart and an openness to human needs around us." GC 33, #44, Documents of the 33rd General Congregation, p. 61.

24. See David Tracy, *Blessed Rage for Order* (New York: Seabury Press, 1975), p. 3: "That the present situation in theology is one of an ever increasing pluralism is by now a truism. . . . The present pluralism of theologies allows each theologian to learn incomparably more about reality by disclosing really different ways of viewing both our common humanity and Christianity."

25. For an analysis of the manifold ways by which a university can be Catholic see Ladislas Orsy, *The Church: Learning and Teaching* (Wilmington, Del.: Michael Glazier, Inc., 1987), especially pp. 109–33.

26. Such language is explicit, for example, in *Evangeli nuntiandi*, by Paul VI: "The Church, as the Bishops repeated, has the duty to proclaim the liberation of millions of human beings, many of whom are her own children—the duty of assisting the birth of this liberation, of giving witness to it, of ensuring that it is complete. This is not foreign to evangelization. Between evangelization and human advancement—development and liberation—there are in fact profound links." *On the Evangelization of the Modern World* (Washington, D.C.: U.S.C.C. Office of Publishing Services, 1975), pp. 22–23. Such themes are endorsed and developed in the subsequent social teaching under the pontificate of John Paul II, notably in *Redemptor hominis* and *Sollicitudo rei socialis*.

27. Congar writes (*A History of Theology,* p. 14): "I cannot exaggerate the importance of the new consciousness which theologians have acquired of their responsibility to the church and to the internal credibility of the faith which the church must offer mankind. There is less question today of technical details derived from standard theological systems; interest in a school's position—so often linked with Religious Orders—continues only in those rare, isolated spots not yet shaken by the great question, 'What is our purpose in the world?' "

28. Such work may involve misunderstanding by elements within the church itself. Kolvenbach continues: "This 'missionary' openness to a world at a distance from the church or allergic to the church will not always be understood by those ecclesiastical movements whose apostolic priority is primarily or exclusively the reinforcement of ecclesiastical structures or the unification of the faithful alone." Peter-Hans Kolvenbach, S.J., "The Jesuits: Perspective on the Future," in *Origins* 14/42 (4 April 1985): 691.

29. Walter Principe traces the path of gradual acceptance of liberation theology by the magisterium of the church, including by Pope John Paul II, who said in a letter to the Brazilian bishops in 1986 that "the theology of liberation is not only timely but useful and necessary." Principe observes: ". . . despite the reservations and warnings and reminders, there is no question that such a text (which also uses the term "praxis" so common in liberation theology) shows a more positive acceptance of liberation theology—undoubtedly the Pope and curia (and Brazilian bishops and liberation theologians themselves) would say acceptance of 'certain kinds' of liberation theology. For me personally this represents quite a change from the five years (1980–85) I served on the International Theological Commission, when 'liberation theology' was a dirty word not to be mentioned." "Catholicity, Inculturation, and Liberation Theology: Do They Mix?" *Franciscan Studies* 47/25 (1987): 41. For a critical appraisal of liberation theologies from a North American perspective, see Schubert Ogden, *Faith and Freedom: Toward a Theology of Liberation* (Nashville: Abingdon, 1979). For a summary of various criticisms of liberation theology and of attempts to appropriate some of the insights of liberation theology see Arthur F.

McGovern, *Liberation Theology and Its Criticisms: Toward an Assessment* (Maryknoll, N.Y.: Orbis Books, 1989).

30. See Robert F. Schreiter, "Faith and Cultures: Challenges to a World Church," *Theological Studies* 50/4 (December 1989): 747.

31. For an example of such an application of Thomas Aquinas see Walter Principe's "The Dignity and Rights of the Human Person as Saved, as Being Saved, as To Be Saved by Christ," *Gregorianum* 65/2–3 (1984): 389–430. Principe prepared this paper while serving on the International Theological Commission. As some indication of the state of theology in the church today, he relates that he had to "make modifications of the section on human rights within the church, which for some was too revolutionary in its suggestions, and whose publication might have caused trouble for the publisher." Principe, "Catholicity, Inculturation, and Liberation Theology," pp. 41–42, n. 26.

32. For an example of such a reappraisal see Micheal Scanlon, "Language and Praxis: Recent Theological Trends," *The Sources of Theology*, Current Issues in Theology no. 3 (The Catholic Theological Society of America, 1988), pp. 80–89. Also see William Hill, "Christian Panentheism: Orthopraxis and God's Action in History," *Proceedings of the Catholic Theological Society of America* 35 (1980): 113: ". . . Christian orthopraxis is indeed the well-spring whence there emerges new meaning in theology. . . . if praxis as such can never be the grounds for the truth of a theory, still Christian faith is always ordered intrinsically to action and the latter safeguards orthodoxy from collapsing into mere ideology."

33. For a discussion of the relationship between theory and *praxis* in theology see David Tracy, *Blessed Rage for Order*, pp. 237–58.

Jesuit Contributions to the Culture of Modernity in Latin America: An Essay toward a Critical Understanding

ALLAN FIGUEROA DECK, S.J.

Introduction

This paper is an interdisciplinary essay on the culture of modernity in Latin America and the role Jesuits have played in the promotion of modernity as well as in its critical understanding. Anyone familiar with the literature on the subject of modernity knows that one is dealing with a vast subject that does not readily lend itself to straightforward analyses.[1] I am not aware of any extensive studies that juxtapose the issue of modernity with Jesuit history as I attempt to do here. My goal in this presentation, then, is rather limited. I propose to raise some questions and pursue some lines of inquiry that may contribute eventually to the development of a framework for addressing this worthwhile but complex issue in a more focused and detailed way.

My method is broadly historical, with concepts taken as well from sociology, anthropology, and theology. Important underlying trends in the social history of Latin America and of the Jesuits are discussed in light of insights from cultural anthropology.

This topic is especially relevant today as we approach the year 1992, the five hundredth anniversary of the evangelization of the New World. As a pervasive cultural force modernity is relevant to the Church's task of evangelization as understood in contemporary church teaching. For evangelization has to do with personal, societal, and, most importantly, cultural transformation.[2] But that conversion, to use the theological term, cannot occur and perdure without an awareness of culture on the one hand and the ability to challenge it on the other.

For the purposes of this study I will use Clifford Geertz's definition of culture:

> Culture denotes an historically transmitted pattern of meanings embodied in symbols, a system of inherited conceptions, expressed in symbolic forms by means of which human beings communicate, perpetuate and develop their knowledge about and attitudes toward life.[3]

169

Culture, then, is understood as the shared values, thoughts, feelings, and customs of a given people or nation. We speak of North American, Spanish, or Chinese cultures. Here I am speaking of modernity as a culture that transcends national, linguistic, and continental barriers. I understand it to be a global and paradigmatic culture, the single most influential of all cultures in today's world.[4]

The issue of modernity, its origins and trajectory in Latin American history, is also a heuristic device for unveiling and interpreting Jesuit history in the Americas. As this paper hopes to suggest, part and parcel of that Jesuit enterprise has been the conscious and unconscious promotion of modern culture. It appears that the Jesuits were specially prepared and positioned to do so. A critical appropriation of Jesuit history in Latin America cannot skirt this fundamental issue.

My Personal Interest in This Topic

Sixteen years ago I completed a doctoral dissertation in Latin American Studies at Saint Louis University on an eighteenth-century Mexican Jesuit scholar by the name of Francisco Javier Alegre.[5] Alegre was one of more than four hundred Jesuits who were exiled from Mexico during the Suppression by order of the king of Spain in 1767. He and his companions settled in the area of Bologna in what were then the Papal States. These Jesuits pursued remarkable careers as writers and teachers—careers they had already begun in Mexico. I discovered that they were in fact the leading intellectuals of New Spain, as Mexico was then called. They were, moreover, among the most articulate modernizers of Mexico.[6] Jesuits from other parts of Latin America were also involved in laying the foundation for a host of attitudes, values, ideas, and institutions that were the first examples of the culture of modernity in the Hispanic American colonies.[7]

As a young Hispanic Jesuit and graduate student I can recall how proud I felt of the intellectual attainments of these Latin American Jesuits. The burden of my dissertation was to show that Alegre was really the first modern literary critic of Mexico. And as I studied his several writings in history, the classics, modern literatures, and theology I marveled at the freshness and urbanity of his methodology and interests. And Alegre was not alone. He was part of the Generation of 1750 that included such Jesuits as Francisco Javier Clavigero, historian and anthropologist of ancient Mexico and of the Californias.[8] This was the group that helped form the subsequent generation of early-nineteenth-century liberals, among them the Father of Mexican Independence, Miguel Hidalgo y Costilla.[9] In my naiveté, I entertained a rather univocal understanding of modernity. I tended to presume that it was a uniformly positive trend and that we Jesuits in being its great promoters were "knights in shining armor." I had not yet been exposed to a critical view of modernity.[10]

Twelve years later I returned to graduate studies—this time in missiology—and had the good fortune of studying under Marcello Azevedo, a Brazilian cultural anthropologist and theologian, author of several books and scores of articles. One of his principal concerns is the culture of modernity. He teaches courses on that subject and on inculturation at the Gregorian University in Rome and at the Pontifical Catholic University of Rio de Janeiro. Building on his extensive reading in modernity in general and on his formation in cultural anthropology, Azevedo provides the beginnings of a critical theory of modernity from a Third-World perspective, one that can be used to evaluate the contributions of Jesuits and other thinkers to the development of Latin American culture over the centuries.

Marcello Azevedo directed my thesis on the evangelization of United States Hispanics. In that work I try to show how the encounter of Hispanic immigrants with the culture of modernity is one of the central issues in their evangelization today. This is true in Latin America and even more crucial in the United States, the paragon of modern culture.[11] I must now specify how I am using the term "modernity" as a pervasive, global form of culture.

What Is Modernity?

Modernity has to do with a process that has been unfolding in Western history for centuries. The progressive application of reason or rationality to human life is one of modernity's most obvious characteristics. A vision of oneself and of the world grounded in religion, faith, or some transcendent norm—something typical of premodern or traditional cultures—is gradually superseded by a fragmented understanding of life characterized by the on-going application of rational and scientific approaches to every sphere of existence—social as well as individual. One of the consequences of this rational approach to the world and oneself is the rise of individualism. Modern cultures form persons who conceive of themselves in isolation from family and community.

Capitalism is also an expression of modernity's drive to transform the world by rationalizing the economy in accord with the laws of the marketplace. The well-being and functionality of the system is viewed as the sum of the success of each person. Modernity has been powerfully linked to the bourgeois or middle socioeconomic classes. These classes have developed attitudes and patterns of life that mirror the rationality, individualism, and entrepreneurial orientation of modern culture.

While less individualistic, socialism, too, is an expression of modernity in its drive to transform the world by rationalizing the economy by means of state control of production and vigorous centralized planning. Marxism purports to give a "scientific" account of human socioeconomic and political realities. Almost every area of life in the Western world and progressively everywhere else can be analyzed in terms of modernity's influences.[12]

It is not difficult to see, then, that the rise and spread of modernity has historically been identified with progress. The Renaissance was one of the earliest expressions of this drive. The Enlightenment was perhaps its greatest moment. The American and French Revolutions are viewed as crucial in modernity's drive to influence the political order by rationalizing government with checks and balances, administrative procedures, establishment of inalienable rights rooted in an enlightened understanding of the individual and of his/her rights and obligations. The Russian Revolution can also be seen as an episode in this modernizing drive, one that now has lost its momentum.

Perhaps the greatest expression of modernity has been the global influence of Americanization, especially after the Second World War. Modernity in the Third World has received a powerful boost through North American technological, commercial, political, and military presence. It has been accompanied by the bombardment of the popular masses with mass media that reflect and inculcate the values, thinking, and feeling characteristic of modernity.

From a strictly theological perspective modernity cannot be viewed as wholly or even mainly negative. Important changes have occurred in the world because of modernity, changes that conform in significant ways to the vision of God's reign—an eschatological vision of Christianity where human rights, self-expression, and human dignity are essential values. Nevertheless, there is need for a critical appraisal of modernity along the lines to be suggested here, a reappraisal inspired by insights from cultural anthropology.

Contemporary Critiques of Modernity

In the past twenty-five years a sustained critique or re-evaluation of modernity has been taking place. There is a great deal of literature on "postmodernity." It speaks of a growing disillusionment with modern rationality and science due to their perceived failure to produce substantial progress in several areas of life, for example, (1) modernity's inability to deal with transcendence, (2) the violence that modern technology has made possible in the form of weapons for mass destruction, (3) the growing ecological crisis, and (4) the apparent inadequacy of both the socialist and the capitalist systems—both children of modernity—to deal with the world's mounting poverty.[13]

The critique of modernity in Latin America implicates the Jesuits, as Octavio Paz and other contemporary Latin American thinkers are suggesting.[14] The underlying vision of Jesuit writers was synthetic and universalist. It was synthetic because it proposed to relate classical culture in its Renaissance forms to the new culture of the Americas and in the process to justify the social status of the *criollo* class (sons and daughters of Spaniards born in the Americas). It was universalist in that it conceived of European culture, especially that of Rome, as providing *the* paradigm for dealing with the encounter with the new hybrid cultures of the Americas. Paz compares the mission project of the Jesuits in China and in Mexico:

> Had the grand plan of the Society of Jesus been realized, a unification of diverse civilizations and cultures would have been achieved under the sign of Rome. What is extraordinary in this enterprise, especially from a religious point of view, is its disconcerting combination of piety and calculation, faith and Machiavellianism. The Jesuits intend to convert the Chinese not through the evangelization of peasants, craftsmen, and merchants but by proselytizing the Emperor and his court. The idea behind this plan for world conversion led not to the kingdom of God, that is to say, to the end of the world, . . . but *to the ascendant movement of universal history.* It is not surprising that in the seventeenth century the chosen site for attempting such an enterprise was that of a great universal empire: China under the Ch'ing dynasty. Nor is it surprising that the other theater of experimentation was the land of the ancient Mexican empire.[15]

Already in the seventeenth century the Mexican Jesuits had become spokesmen for the rising *criollo* class. While there were a large number of Spanish or European-born Jesuits in Mexico, the dominant group was *criollo.* Paz believes that the Jesuits provided a universal, syncretic view that served the *criollo* need to sink roots in Mexican soil and still retain loyalty to the Spanish crown. The erudition and imagination of Jesuit classical humanism provided historical analogies that Romanized New Spain. The Jesuit dream of Christian universalism grounded in reason powerfully influenced Mexican thinkers from the seventeenth through the eighteenth centuries. The emphasis on the ascendant character of history, rooted in a Judeo-Christian heritage and worldview, provided a vision for generations of *criollo* leaders educated by the Jesuits. These leaders, whether liberal or conservative, were working out of a bourgeois, *criollo* ideology, one that reflected important values of modernity and tended to ignore the popular masses, the overwhelming majority of Latin Americans.

This universalism provided a context for the reception of the Enlightenment. Undergirding the Enlightenment was the conviction that reason and science provide a universally valid access to reality. One of the fundamental features of the modern mindset is the idea of progress, whose motor force is functional rationality. Already in the seventeenth century Latin American Jesuits were articulating a syncretic, universal view of the Latin American reality, one that was to be transformed by liberals and nationalists into the dominant ideology of nineteenth-century Latin America. In this project the wisdom of the popular masses, their religiosity and concerns, tended to be systematically ignored if not disdained.

Pedro Morandé, a Chilean sociologist, believes that contemporary Latin

America is experiencing a crisis due to the collapse of this universalist-syncretic concept of modernity that the Jesuits first articulated:

> One of the greatest tasks undertaken by the Jesuits in seventeenth and eighteenth century Latin America was precisely giving the *criollo* socio-economic class an expressive culture. The character of that culture would, naturally, be syncretic given the social group toward which it was aimed. . . . But the Jesuits seemed not to perceive that no syncretism can invent a history for itself, given that it has been made by dissimilar bits and pieces. . . . We consider the Jesuits to be the precursors of that developmentalist mentality which we come to know beginning in the nineteenth century. . . . What is most paradoxical is that those who most promoted their expulsion—the leaders of the Enlightenment in Latin America—ended up inheriting this Jesuit cultural project.[16]

Morandé believes that the contemporary crisis of modernity in Latin America has to do with the fact that this "great universal syncretism without history" has been maintained and fostered in Latin America by progressive and liberal as well as by conservative elites whose social science analyses, whether functionalist or Marxist, have been fundamentally Euro-American and "modern." The originality of Latin America, its indigenous and mestizo masses, have remained marginal as hegemonic groups and various elites, enchanted with modernity's myths, have competed to get and maintain the upper hand. There is a developmentalist logic behind these *criollo,* elitist sociopolitical projects that ignores popular culture. These projects, as the sad history of Latin America demonstrates, often do not succeed.[17] Morandé believes that Latin America has entered a period of "disenchantment" with regard to modernity. It is beginning to see that developmental approaches inspired by the prevailing social-science paradigms of modernity, whether capitalist or Marxist, have failed to deal with the roots of the culture that are found in the indigenous, mestizo, and mulatto masses.[18]

Alegre and Modernity

Alegre is an excellent example of the *criollo* Jesuit thinker singled out by Octavio Paz and Pedro Morandé. Born of Spanish parents, steeped in classical humanism, he and his writings reflect a strong syncretic-universalist orientation. He and many other Jesuits of his time had learned the Nahuatl language. They spoke of the Aztec "empire," comparing it favorably with Rome. Alegre's writings manifest a tension between the universalizing tendencies on the one hand and efforts to deal with particular manifestations of culture on the other. He is neoclassical in that he insists on the didactic character of literature. Yet he is somewhat preromantic in his concern for subjectivity, his respect for originality, and his interest in the literary work's ability to give pleasure as well as to instruct. In order to defend Spanish literature, which has often shown high regard for the popular, the irregular, and the spontaneous, he invokes an inductive, scientifically grounded method of literary criticism.

The point, then, is that Alegre revealed himself to be a truly modern thinker. He firmly believed that reason touches every area of life, confronting all customs, myths, beliefs, and traditions. He shared much in common with Enlightenment thinkers: his devotion to the Greek classics, his insistence on sobriety and clarity of expression, his urbane secularity, and his conviction about the universal accessibility of the message of classical writers. This emphasis on clarity and logic was enhanced by the modern scientific/technological and industrial revolutions that Alegre's eighteenth century was beginning to experience. Alegre and his generation of Jesuits, consequently, can be acknowledged as the first great promoters of modernity in Mexico and elsewhere in Latin America.[19]

Azevedo and Modernity

Two hundred years after Alegre another Jesuit provides an approach for evaluating the modernity of contemporary Latin America, a modernity, as we have just seen, initially fostered by the Jesuits. Azevedo notes that current discussions in Latin America regarding evangelization revolve around the topics of liberation and the role of the popular masses. The theme of liberation stresses socioeconomic and political realities, especially the overwhelming oppression endured by the vast majority of Latin Americans. The theme of *pueblo* or "the people" highlights the need to work for the transformation of society from the grass roots, from *la base,* pointing to the basic ecclesial communities and popular religiosity as key elements in the creation of a truly participative church and society.[20]

In Azevedo's view contemporary Latin American thinkers are correct in giving central importance to the need for structural change, but they have tended to ignore or downplay the relevance of modernity because they mistakenly believed that modernity was and is not really an issue in Latin America, since the peoples of that vast continent are more premodern or traditional than modern. The challenge of modernity, from this point of view, is relevant to the First and Second Worlds but not to the Third. Related to this disregard for modernity is something even more problematic, namely, the disregard for culture. Azevedo explains the disregard for the issues of modernity and culture by pointing out that important writers like João Batista Libanio, Azevedo's fellow Brazilian Jesuit, affirm that the passage from premodernity to modernity was somehow transcended by the events surrounding Medellín and Puebla. The application of the teachings of those two landmark episcopal assemblies put the theme of modernity's impact on the Church in Latin America in second place.[21]

The emphasis on the struggle for social transformation was so clear and convincing in Medellín, Puebla, and subsequent events in Latin America that the thorny question of modernity's influence on the elites, whether Marxist, liberationist, or conservative, was put on hold. Azevedo shows how the liberal-capitalist thinkers used the term modernity or modernization to promote their uncritical understanding of socioeconomic development. He shows how progressive elements in Latin America used the theory of dependency, a Marxist-inspired critique of Latin America's dependent economies, to promote their own, once again uncritical, vision of modernity. Azevedo explains the failure of the contemporary Latin American intelligentsia, especially progressives, to deal adequately with the issue of modernity as a failure to grasp *their own rootedness as elites within the culture of modernity:*

> I am speaking of a kind of inertia that is deeply rooted in the culture and disseminated by academics in a vague and not necessarily militant sort of way: It is a tendency to always disassociate society from culture and to identify modernity exclusively with liberal capitalism. . . . An unequivocal option for socialism (practically never sufficiently specific or qualified) . . . took for granted that the socialist alternative was not itself "modern."[22]

Over against this inadequate understanding of modernity, which onesidedly identifies it with a socioeconomic system disengaged from its cultural underpinnings, Azevedo insists on modernity precisely as a profound *cultural* force operating at the deepest levels of the human. The culture of modernity in Latin America as elsewhere consists of a complex web of meanings, values, and underlying patterns intimately linked to action and communication. The reigning social system may be quite different from the culture. In Latin America this is certainly the case. Modern, democratic, and capitalist socioeconomic patterns are superimposed on a premodern cultural base. In Poland and other states recently emancipated from Soviet control something similar was true: the Marxist project of modernity was superimposed on traditionally Catholic cultures. The fundamental problem in these cases is that the socioeconomic and political projects inspired by modernity are not integral to the culture of the masses. This helps explain why socioeconomic projects of whatever ideological origin are doomed to failure if the issue of culture is not taken into account.

Azevedo proposes a solution to the problem of how lastingly and effectively to transform the Latin American world. The process must seriously deal with *both social and cultural change,* not just with one or the other.

The source of the difficulty is to be found in two complementary conceptions of modernity that can be dichotomized. One is of a philosophical and sociological character and is identified with bourgeois, developmentalist ideology; the other is of a cultural-anthropological character. Those who conceive of modernity in the first way have tended to stress liberation, the transformation of unjust socioeconomic and political structures. Or they have championed market economy "developmentalism." Those who conceive of modernity in a cultural-anthropological manner are stressing the challenges of modernity, its identification with the elites, its difficulty with popular religiosity, and other manifestations of popular culture.[23] They point to the undermining of values, the erosion of solidarity, and a creeping immanentism that undermines transcendence.[24]

Yet the critics of modernity, according to Azevedo, have yet to come up with answers on how the "acids of modernity," to use Ricoeur's expression, can be confronted. Azevedo's writings give some clues as to how to proceed. He gives great importance to inculturation, the process by which the Christian faith is rooted in culture. This process provides a path for promoting change in an organic, wholistic fashion, one that deals with both societal and cultural factors.[25]

In a fascinating little book called *Educación, Sociedad, Justicia* Azevedo proposed the following steps in an inculturated process of leadership formation and education in Latin America: (1) AWARENESS—the acknowledgement of the structural injustice implicit in Latin American society's organizational model, a model replicated in Latin American education a well. But this *structural* injustice is rooted in the human reality, that is, in culture. It cannot be addressed at depth in an anecdotal or synchronic fashion. It must be addressed in terms of its roots, diachronically, appropriating the historical patterns that have given rise to and cemented the current patterns of oligarchical domination that perdure in most Latin American nations. (2) RESTRUCTURING/RETHINKING—there must be a rethinking and restructuring of society from the bottom up. Projects of whatever ideological origin— liberal, progressive, or conservative—that are imposed by an elite uncritical of their modern presuppositions and values will not succeed. They will replicate the now ancient pattern of impositions characteristic of Latin American history. In this connection the *basic ecclesial communities* are of great importance. They represent one of the more valid examples of how rethinking and restructuring of society from the bottom up may occur within an inculturated ecclesial community. (3) CRITICAL CONSCIOUSNESS—the forming and perfecting of a critical consciousness in both individuals and groups. This involves creating interior spaces of freedom, of motivation, evaluation, discernment, and revision. There must be more ability to evaluate what is positive and negative in one's own personal development and in that of one's community. One of the characteristics of this critical consciousness is its reluctance to go to extremes or excesses in emotional moods or in argumentation, in aggressive polemics and polarizations. Critical consciousness seeks whatever is valid in complex and pluralistic realities. This consciousness is more integrating than disintegrating and seeks to make a higher synthesis in a truly analogical fashion.[26]

Azevedo is proposing, then, that the insights of cultural anthropology be taken seriously. He shows how the culture of modernity has unfolded in Latin America like the air one breathes, powerfully present but usually unacknowledged. He shows how that failure to grasp its pervasiveness has impeded evangelization or the transformation of the person and the creation of a more just society.

Azevedo's insights, moreover, provide interesting tools for the critical understanding of the historic influence of Jesuits like Francisco Javier Alegre in Latin America. They, too, were unaware of the culture implicit in their activities, commitments, and concerns. The thinking of Octavio Paz and of Pedro Morandé highlights the formative and still influential character of this Jesuit-propagated modernity. Azevedo shows how it must be critically evaluated lest it continue to be part of the problem rather than of the solution.

Toward a Critical Appraisal of Jesuit History in Latin America

The four hundred fiftieth anniversary of the founding of the Society of Jesus offers the opportunity to appropriate and, I hope, to evaluate the ongoing influence of Jesuits and their collaborators in the development of Church and society in places all over the world. In the case of Latin America that history is truly extraordinary. The scholarly and religious work of Jesuits over those five centuries constitutes a key for understanding some of the most important cultural trends constitutive of that complex continent's identity. Jesuits have been part of the unfolding of that drama. Indeed, some of them like Alegre and his generation of Jesuits were among the main actors. That involvement has been human and for that reason a blend of light and darkness. My juxtaposing of two Jesuits from two seemingly disparate epochs—Alegre and Azevedo—is an effort to reappropriate some important currents in Jesuit history that cut across centuries. Jesuit promotion of the culture of modernity is certainly one of those massive currents that deserves careful study from many different scholarly angles.

In addition, it is worth noting that the martyred Jesuits of El Salvador, especially Ignacio Martín-Baró, were pursuing the relationship of culture to the liberation struggle, using data provided by public opinion surveys. Such an approach stresses the values, feelings, and mindset of the usually silent popular masses. It constitutes a new way, for Latin America at least, to bridge the gap between the modern ideologies of the elites, whether rightist or leftist, and the world of the ordinary citizen.[27] The encounter of premodern and traditional orientations with modern sensibilities is documented in these opinion surveys. The future path of Central America and other oppressed Latin American regions has much to do with confronting the challenges of modernity in an effort to bring about justice. Throughout Latin America, moreover, contemporary Jesuits are seeking and finding ways to be "inserted" in the reality of the poor. This experience of immersion in the context of the poor and powerless is part of the critical reappraisal of the Jesuit apostolate that at other times emphasized the importance of being involved with the rich and powerful. Not only theoretically but also practically, Jesuits are renewing their understanding of their commitments in light of experiences in the context of the poor.[28]

While the four hundred fifty-year history of Jesuits in the Americas is filled with lights and shadows, the ongoing critical reflection of contemporary Jesuits like Azevedo and Martín-Baró suggests that Jesuits and their co-workers will continue to be important contributors to the creation of a more just and human Latin America. Insight into the relationship between the church's mission of evangelization and contemporary cultures, especially the culture of modernity, sheds light on the direction that contribution may take in the years to come.

Notes

1. Marcello Azevedo provides an excellent bibliography with works by the most accomplished writers on the topic of modernity: Max Weber, Jurgen Habermas, S. N. Eisenstadt, Peter Berger, Robert Bellah, and many others in *Inculturation and the Challenges of Modernity* (Rome: Gregorian University, 1982), pp. 57–63.
2. Pope Paul VI's *On Evangelization in the Modern World* (Washington, D.C.: USCC, 1976) comprehensively formulated the issue and promoted the concept of evangelization as foundational to the Church's self-understanding.
3. Clifford Geertz, *The Interpretation of Cultures* (London: 1975), p. 89.
4. Pope Paul VI, *On Evangelization in the Modern World,* no. 20. Pope John Paul II has dramatically stressed the concept of evangelization of culture in his talks and most especially in his travels. See Joseph Gremillion *The Church and Culture Since Vatican II,* (Notre Dame: University of Notre Dame Press, 1985), pp. 187–213.
5. Allan F. Deck, *Francisco Javier Alegre: A Study in Mexican Literary Criticism* (Rome: Historical Institute of the Society of Jesus, 1976).
6. See Bernabé Navarro, *Cultura Mexicana Moderna* (Mexico, D.F.: UNAM, 1964), especially chap. 6, "El Pensamiento Moderno de los Jesuitas," 109–35. Miguel Batllori provides information on other eighteenth-century Jesuits in *La cultura hispano-italiana de los jesuitas expulsos* (Madrid: Editorial Gredos, 1966).
7. Batllori, op. cit., pp. 575–637.
8. B. Navarro, op. cit., p. 119 ff.
9. Hugh M. Hamill, Jr., summarizes Hidalgo's contact with the Jesuits in *The Hidalgo Revolt* (Gainesville: University of Florida Press, 1966), pp. 7, 55–56.
10. In saying this I do not wish to fall into a kind of historicism that condemns people of other times for not sharing in the "enlightened" views of contemporary scholarship. There is no question here about the sincerity of colonial Latin American Jesuits. Nor do I wish to condemn modernity. I agree with Marcello Azevedo's opinion that most of the traits of modernity are positive and in conformity with the Gospel message. See Azevedo, *Inculturation and the Challenges of Modernity,* p. 53.
11. Allan F. Deck, *The Second Wave: Hispanic Ministry and the Evangelization of Cultures* (Mahwah, N.J.: Paulist Press, 1989), pp. 109–13.
12. Langdon Gilkey shows how capitalism and Marxism have developed into the two most powerful "myths" of modernity in his "Modern Myth-Making and the Possibilities of Twentieth-Century Theology," in *Theology of Renewal,* ed. L. K. Skook, (New York: Herder and Herder, 1968), 1: 283–312. He pursues this theme with regard to its impact on Roman Catholicism in *Catholicism Confronts Modernity* (New York: Seabury Press, 1975).

13. Recent examples of the literature on postmodernity are: Huston Smith, *Beyond the Post-Modern Mind* (Wheaton, Ill.: Theosophical Publishing House, 1982); and José María Mardones, *Postmodernidad y cristianismo* (Santander: Editorial Sal Terrae, 1988).

14. Octavio Paz, *Sor Juana* (Cambridge, Mass.: Harvard University Press, 1988), especially part 1, chap. 3, p. 36. Also Pedro Morandé, *Cultura y modernización en América Latina* (Madrid: Encuentro Ediciones, 1978), p. 185.

15. Paz, *Sor Juana*, p. 39.

16. Morandé, *Cultura y modernización en América Latina*, p. 185. The English translation is the present author's.

17. One of the historic reactions to the powerful elitist orientation of Latin American culture is populism. Latin American populism has tended to be opportunistic and swiftly to degenerate into fascism, oligarchism, or narrow nationalism (e.g. Peronismo, Getulio Vargas, the PRI's "indigenismo" in Mexico). Charles A. Reilly gives a definition of Latin American populism that he believes is somewhat exaggerated but still holds a kernel of truth: "Populism is an ideology of the intellectuals who claim to be speaking for the people." See Charles A. Reilly, "Populistas Religiosos en América Latina," *Religión y política en México* (México, D.F.: Siglo XXI, 1985), p. 207.

18. Walker O'Connor, *Mexican Americans in Comparative Perspective* (Washington, D.C.: The Urban Institute, 1985), believes that the promotion or the concept of the mestizo-state in countries like Mexico, Peru and, Guatemala has been ideologically motivated to create the illusion of popular participation in political power. Generally the central authorities have reflected not this indigenous and mestizo presence in the culture, but rather the European, white, and *criollo* elements of the culture. This is true in left-wing as well as in right-wing governments (pp. 3–16).

19. Peter Gay considers the French Jesuits to have been among Europe's most successful modernists. See *The Enlightenment: An Interpretation* (New York: Knopf, 1966), p. 355. *Mutatis mutandis* the same could be said for the Latin American Jesuits of this period. See also Charles E. Ronan, *Francisco Javier Clavigero: Figure of the Mexican Enlightenment* (Rome: Historical Institute of the Society of Jesus, 1977).

20. Marcello Azevedo, "Modernidade e Evangelizacão: Uma Reflexão a Partir da América Latina," in *Síntese*, no. 47, (Sept.–Dec. 1989), 16: 67–68.

21. Ibid., p. 69.

22. Marcello Azevedo, op. cit. Translation from the Portuguese is the present author's. Two suggestive articles relevant to Azevedo's observations about the lack of cultural awareness among some Latin American progressives are: Luis Alberto Gómez de Sousa, "Secularización en declive y potencialidad transformadora de lo sagrado," *Páginas*, no. 84 (July 1987), 112: 8–15; Pedro Trigo, *"Teología de la liberación y cultura,"* *Revista Latinoamericana de Teología* (Jan.–Apr. 1986), pp. 83–93. Both de Sousa and Trigo are respected thinkers identified with liberation theology and are themselves considered progressives writing in progressive theological journals.

23. Morandé, op. cit., considers popular religiosity as the primordial source for understanding the Latin American ethos. See chap. 12, "Hacia una caracterización del ethos latino-americano, pp. 167–87.

24. Azevedo, op. cit., p. 71.

25. Azevedo, *Inculturation and the Challenges of Modernity*, pp. 5–12. Azevedo also discusses the importance of inculturation in the effort to evangelize modern cultures in *Basic Ecclesial Communities in Brazil: A New Way of Being Church*, (Washington, D.C.: Georgetown University Press, 1987), pp. 119–29.

26. Marcello Azevedo, *Educación, Sociedad, Justicia* (Buenos Aires: Ediciones Paulinas, 1987), pp. 58–65. One wonders whether important socioeconomic and

political changes like the one attempted in Sandinista Nicaragua would not have fared better if Azevedo's *culturally*-based process for effecting change had been taken more seriously by the Sandinistas. The same can be said for Violeta Chamorro's coalition. It, too, will experience serious problems if it fails to deal with the profound underlying issues that Azevedo's critique of Latin America's elitist modern culture—whether leftist or rightist—has underscored. U.S. intervention, of course, only exacerbates the problem.

27. See *Interamerican Public Opinion Report,* Memorial Issue in honor of Ignacio Martín-Baró, January 1990. Martín Baró is quoted: "What most Salvadorans really think has been unknown historically, although that did not stop the mass media from making claims about it. . . . This has consisted of a not-too-coherent linking together of fact and fiction, biased interpretations, crude efforts to disguise reality. . . . What I call the 'institutionalized lie' has impeded development of a healthy consciousness about their own daily existence among many Salvadorans, generating a perceptual penumbra or even a schizoid rupture between personal experience and communication." See pp. 2, 13. This affirmation about the Salvadoran situation could be repeated for most Latin American peoples and reflects the history of manipulation at the hands of elites uncritically imbued with the culture of modernity.

28. See Decree 4 of the 32nd General Congregation of the Society of Jesus, "Our Mission Today: "The Service of Faith and the Promotion of Justice," in *Documents of the 31st and 32nd General Congregations,* (Saint Louis: Institute of Jesuit Sources, 1977), p. 411.

The Influence of Ignatian Spirituality on Women's Teaching Orders in the United States

MARGARET GORMAN, R.S.C.J.

When asked to write a paper on the influence of Ignatian spirituality on women's teaching orders, I thought that there would be an abundance of information available. I was wrong. Jesuit after Jesuit said that this was an interesting topic but only one could offer any information on the topic. One well-known Jesuit thought that about one hundred orders of women had been influenced either at their foundation or at renewal when some earlier orders became apostolic. But few facts were forthcoming. So I decided to send out a questionnaire to religious orders in the United States. A list of religious superiors was obtained from the Leadership Conference of Women Religious and mailings were made to all except such orders as the Augustinians, Benedictines, Carmelites, Dominicans, and Franciscans.

My plan in this paper is, first, to indicate the changes in the nature of mission and ministry of women religious brought about by historical conditions. I will then try to present an overview as to how and why Ignatian spirituality can be and has been helpful to women's apostolic congregations. I then will present a broad overview of the results of the questionnaire followed by a deeper examination of certain religious orders who acknowledge their indebtedness to Ignatian spirituality.

Significant Changes in the Forms of Religious Life for Women

I am indebted to Mary Augusta Neal's recent book *From Nuns to Sisters* for clarifying the changes in religious life. Her thesis is that the tension between good works and prayer or between personal sanctification and service of others has resulted in three different forms of religious life emerging in particular socioeconomic conditions.

The first period from the early Christian era to 1600 saw religious women in a contemplative vocation giving primacy to prayer and cloister. The second form, a semicontemplative vocation, was characterized by the doing of good works but with the traditional prayer forms of the earlier type of religious life.

The second type prevailed from around 1600 to 1950. There were required hours for prayer and communal events, and these requirements might well have affected the quality of human services. Then the need for professional competence and the changing conditions in the world led Pius XII in 1950 to advise those still living the contemplative life to earn their living, saying such work would not distract them from their prayer. The Sister Formation Conference initiated the movement to educate the sisters professionally. Since then, Vatican II, especially "Perfectae Caritatis," clarified the need for a lifestyle that did not interfere with the quality of service. There was no longer any need for the early monastic restraints of the second period from 1600 to 1950. In this third period beginning in 1950, religious congregations were urged to rediscover the charism of their foundresses and to emphasize professional competency. As Mary Augusta Neal described it:

> This combination of emphases introduced a slowly accelerating program of formation and education that would culminate, at the time of the Second Vatican Council, with an almost entirely new conception of mission and religious life. This called for a vowed poverty not rooted in the mere security of dependence, but rather opted for responsible stewardship, a sharing with those in need. It demanded a celibate life for mission and a more responsible obedience to the mission of the church as expressed in the gospel.[1]

It is interesting to note that, in the early sixteenth century, Ignatius had realized that the monastic model was not helpful for the service of others needed in his day. Some religious women at that time also realized the need for a genuine apostolic spirituality but were ordered by Roman authorities to adopt a semicloistered rule for their protection. As James Walsh pointed out,

> When Ignatius Loyola founded his Society of Jesus, he won a long hard-fought battle which exempted the new order from rigid enclosure, choral recitation of divine office, and the wearing of a uniform habit. But in all other externals he adopted the life-style of the religious orders of his time, which were of course monastic. And it was inevitable that many congregations, particularly of women, that were founded, like his, with specific apostolic objectives, should find themselves subject to a monastic life style.[2]

He goes on to say that the active orders seem to have the worst of both worlds: ". . . the sweetness of contemplation was denied them because of their preoccupation with the apostolate; and, at the same time, they were forced to live according to a discipline whose only aim and object was the sweetness of contemplation."[3]

A contemporary of Ignatius, Angela Merici, also wanted an uncloistered order to teach and serve the poor, but the Ursulines were soon forced by church authorities to adopt the cloister. Other women founders such as Jeanne de Chantal were also forced to choose between service to the poor and cloister. Jeanne de Chantal chose cloister for her Visitation nuns. The Sisters of Charity chose temporary vows. So the tension between prayer and good works was recognized by Ignatius and religous women as early as the sixteenth century. Ignatius tried in principle to resolve this tension. We must note here, too, that, while Ignatius wrote many letters to women, both in religious orders and "in the world," he himself petitioned the Pope that "in order to be able to live unhampered in accordance with the spirit of their vocation" his Jesuits would "no longer be obliged to undertake the spiritual direction of convents of nuns or female religious nor that of women who, living together in community, wish to place themselves under the obedience of the said priests."[4] This petition arose because of an unfortunate incident with one of the women (Isabel Roser) he was directing at the time. It did not mean that Jesuits *could* not direct women at all, but that they were *not obliged* to. But, as Rahner indicates: "Ignatius, while holding firmly to his principles, nevertheless played a significant role in the reformation of nunneries."[5]

We now need to examine the chief concepts of Ignatian spirituality that can be and have been of help to women religious.

Aspects in Ignatian Spirituality Helpful for Apostolic Mission

It is important to distinguish the type of influence that Ignatian spirituality had on women's teaching orders. I tried to distinguish this in my questionnaire. Were the *Constitutions* directly influenced by the Jesuit *Constitutions* or by the *Spiritual Exercises*? Or was it merely the fact that a Jesuit advised the foundress? Or has there been an influence throughout the existence of the congregation either through contact with individual Jesuits or through retreats? Moreover, since this is a conference on the Jesuits and education, some may think that I should refer directly to the impact of Ignatian spirituality on the educational philosophy and methods of women religious. With few exceptions, I cannot point to a direct impact on the educational philosophy or methods of these congregations of religious women. But since there is considerable evidence of the impact of Ignatian spirituality on the spirituality of these women, I am assuming a powerful indirect influence on their educational ministry, for these sisters are the prime mediators of education. Some religious also emphasize the fact that it was Ignatian, not Jesuit, spirituality that had an influence on their congregations—a notion that may refer to the fact that the *Spiritual Exercises* (written when Ignatius was still a layman), had a greater influence than Jesuit rules or life.

The aspects of Ignatian spirituality that I would like to consider are: the notion of the *single aim* of an apostolic institute; the concept of *the more* or the greater glory of God; the principle of *indifference* or of *availability* for God; the process of *discernment*. Many of the responses in fact referred to these specific elements of Ignatian spirituality.

Although I cannot analyze any of the concepts in depth, in this section I want to discuss what may be the greatest contribution of the vision of Ignatius to Apostolic Institutes: his formulation of the *single aim* of an Apostolic Institute. Caritas MCarthy reflected on the way "that Ignatius of Loyola's Constitutions for his own apostolic order have relevance for apostolic congregations in general."[6] In the Apostolic Institutes of the *first* half of the sixteenth century there were two goals: the perfection of their own soul *and* the salvation of their neighbor. But Ignatius described the end of the Society of Jesus as one—the glory of God and the salvation of souls. No explicit mention of the perfection of the members was made.[7] This is a real shift from the two goals of the older orders to the Ignatian statement of the one end—the glory of God and the service of neighbor.[8] Personal sanctification is the means to this one end. Courel sums up his exposition of the single aim by saying: "In the profound vision of Ignatius, the two are the same thing; and in relation to this single end all the rest is in the order of means to be adapted or directed."[9]

Yet a serious modification occurred, especially after the restoration of the Jesuits in 1814, when religious orders of women tried to base their own Constitutions on Ignatian writings. Their rules were not based on the *Constitutions of the Society of Jesus* but on the *Summary of the Constitutions and Common Rules,* because that was all they were given.[10] Now the *Summary* was what was shown to Jesuit novices. The *Rules* regarded external behavior. These two documents lacked the internal dynamic, the spirit of the *Constitution,* which reiterates the end proper to apostolic life—the greater glory of God and the salvation of men. McCarthy goes on to say:

> The lack of the full ignatian emphasis on the primacy of the law of love in the constitutions of many congregations who sincerely desired to draw on his heritage has been one of the most serious though unintentional misrepresentations of his teaching. . . . the detailed and prescriptive nature of most of the *Summary* seems to have weakened the force of the passage with which the *Summary* begins.[11]

One result of this is that Ignatius has often been invoked by Church authorities in support of a rigid pattern of life. In reality, he desired a firm but flexible way of life in order to respond to the needs of the apostolate.

I will cite below several examples of religious foundresses who wished to adapt the *Constitutions of the Society of Jesus,* yet were limited to the *Summary and Common Rules* and thus deprived of the full riches of Ignatian spirituality.

The second Ignatian concept that has influenced women's religious congregations is the concept of *the more* in choosing ministries: "To proceed more successfully in this sending of subjects one place to another, one should keep the greater service of God and the more universal good before his eyes as the norm to hold oneself on the right course."[12] This principle of the more is also found in the Foundation Exercise of the *Spiritual Exercises,* which influenced many religious women even in those congregations whose constitutions were not based on the *Constitutions* or *Summary of the Society of Jesus.*

The third Ignatian concept that has influenced women religious is the concept of *indifference.* Of course it is also best expressed in the Foundation of the *Spiritual Exercises:*

> As a result, we ought to appreciate and use these gifts of God insofar as they help us toward our goal of loving service and union with God. But insofar as any created things hinder our progress toward our goal, we ought to let them go.[13]

Certainly the returned questionnaires indicated that the *Spiritual Exercises* in directed retreats were considered the greatest source of the influence of Ignatian spirituality.

The last concept of Ignatian spirituality that I wish to discuss is that of *discernment.* In fact, it may well be the greatest help for women in the future as the concept of obedience among women religious is changing. The most general statement of this principle is of course in the *Spiritual Exercises:*

> When we are trying to follow the call of the Lord in our life, we will find that the good spirit tends to give support, encouragement, and oftentimes even a certain delight. The evil spirit generally acts to bring about the opposite reaction.[14]

Caritas McCarthy goes on to show that "ignatian discernment not only helped apostolic religious women develop a patient, mature and efficacious love of the institutional Church, in the face of the obstacles it gave them, but also an efficacious love in better choice of ministries in the face of real needs."[15]

Thus it is the general consensus of many apostolic congregations of women that Ignatian spirituality, especially the notions of *one end, the more or the greater glory of God, indifference,* and *discernment,* could be and has been of help in forming their own spirituality. In fact, a conference was held in Great Britain recently of all apostolic congregations of women influenced by Ignatian spirituality, under the title of *The Ignatian Family.* However, we must remember that such concepts were filtered through three conditions:

1. The perception by church authorities that women religious needed protection and thus semicloister or monastic cloister was imposed.[16]
2. The tension between prayer and human service and the suspicion that active ministry was purely human and secular.
3. The fact that the constitutions of many women religious congregations were based on the dry and more rigid *Summary and Rules* of the Society of Jesus and not on the vital Jesuit Constitutions that emphasized love and flexibility. The Jesuit *Constitutions* say explicitly: "It does not seem expedient to give them any other rule than that which discreet charity dictates to them."[17]

Results of the Questionnaire

We now turn to the results of the questionnaire. Some reservations must be made. These results merely indicated the *perception* of the various superiors who answered, and sometimes members of the same congregation differed in their answers. I will give the quantitative results first and then present some of the interesting comments that were written.

Two hundred and seventy-six questionnaires were sent out to all the Superiors in the United States listed by the Leadership Conference of Religious Women, with the exceptions noted earlier. It was inevitable that questionnaires were sent to many of the same congregation. The end result was that one hundred and forty-two different congregations were contacted, and eighty-four percent responded. Five percent of those who responded were not engaged in teaching.

The greatest influence of Ignatian spirituality was through *retreats* given by Jesuits. Forty percent of those who answered responded affirmatively with many interesting comments. One religous congregation, the Sisters of Providence, sent me the names of the Jesuit retreat directors going back to their foundation in the middle of the nineteenth century. Caritas McCarthy had estimated that individual or small groups of Jesuits have influenced over half of the almost two hundred congregations of women who are engaged in full-time apostolates.[18]

In answer to the question, "Is your *educational mission statement* influenced by the Jesuit philosophy of education or by the spiritual exercises?," twenty-six percent answered affirmatively, but most commented that this influence came about largely through advanced education at Jesuit universities.

An affirmative answer to the question, "Are your constitutions based on Jesuit spirituality?" was given by thirty six congregations or twenty-five percent of those who responded.

Fewer congregations (twenty-five or seventeen percent) answered affirmatively the question, "Was a Jesuit connected with your foundation?" This indicates that some based their constitutions on the Ignatian spirituality without the guidance of a Jesuit. McCarthy[19] estimated that Jesuits have been influential at the founding of about one third of women's apostolic congregations, but I think that her estimates were based on *all* the apostolic congregations of women. I have confined myself to those in the United States. There have been other partial surveys of congregations influenced by Ignatian spirituality, but most of these surveys were written in German and I was unable to procure them.

However, the most interesting responses were in answer to my suggestion, "Any additional comment you may wish to make." After quoting a few comments, I will then go on to analyze in depth several religious congregations who were clearly influenced by Ignatian spirituality, even though today's feminism is lessening this influence.

Two women from the Congregation of the Incarnate Word (founded in France in 1625) wrote somewhat humorously. One member answered:

> As the Jesuits were spiritual directors of Jeanne de Matel, it would seem that the rules of her Order and the Constitutions were developed under Jesuit Philosophy and Theology. In fact, at one time she, the Foundress, was accused for founding and forming of Society of Jesuitesses.

Another wrote in greater detail:

> There were an extraordinary number of Jesuits interested in our Foundress, Jeanne de Matel. Yet she did not seem to "buy into" their spirituality very directly, certainly not slavishly. In her very early letters (which I have just completed translating into English and which we are now studying) she records a conflict with a Jesuit confessor re blind obedience to her mother in even the smallest decisions of her life. Fr. de Villard wanted this; Jeanne de Matel insisted it upset her peace of mind and kept her from praying for herself and for others. And her conclusion was that she was called to greater freedom of spirit than this. When she chose a Rule for her order, she chose the Rule of St. Augustine which has a different "flavor" to Jesuit spirituality. Yet the Jesuits played such an important role in her early spiritual growth that Msgr. Giovanni Papa, the director of the *Positio* for her beautification process, insisted that the Jesuits should be given a special chapter in the study. Jeanne de Matel loved and respected her Jesuit directors and confessors, but she also thought independently and maintained her own personal freedom.

Because I was unaware of the meaning of some of the initials of the religious congregations, I sent a questionnaire to the Sisters of Saint Joseph of the Third Order of Saint Francis (founded in Wisconsin in 1901). This is the somewhat surprising response:

> Already in 1903, the pioneer sister directing activities in the two Detroit schools engaged the Polish Jesuits to preach annual retreats, focusing on how to medi-
> tate. . . .
> I recall vividly that when I made my first retreat before taking the habit in 1935, the Jesuit retreat director asked: What is the spirit of the Sisters of St. Joseph? "Jesuit!" he replied with admiration. Then in the 1940's the superiors general began the movement to Franciscan roots.

A member of the congregation of the Presentation of Mary (founded in 1796) writes:

1) Like the Jesuits, from our very beginnings, we have been called to be CONTEMPLATIVES IN ACTION.
2) Our motto "All for God! All through holy love!" echoes the Jesuit "Ad majorem Dei gloriam"
3) Our Foundress [Blessed Anne Marie Rinier] frequently referred to her congregation as "the Society of Mary," as Ignatius called his order the "Society of Jesus".

The Handmaids of the Sacred Heart of Jesus (founded 1877) made a clear distinction between Jesuit and Ignatian spirituality and reveal the influence of feminism:

> We make that fine distinction between Jesuit spirituality which embraces some things differently from the way Handmaid of "Ignatian-Raphaelan" (foundress) spirituality does—and the Ignatian spirituality of the Spiritual Exercises which is foundational for us.

> Our ministry is to walk with people on their journey of faith. We are particularly invited by our Ignatian/Raphaelan discernment spirituality to

> 1) educate people to make choices for God's greater glory
> 2) promote the dignity and equality of women as an urgent peace and justice issue
> 3) develop lay leadership

The Sisters of Notre Dame de Namur (1804) most clearly indicated the lessening of the Ignatian influence due in part to the careful study of their foundress' charism, in part to the revision of the constitutions, and in part to feminism.

One took the trouble to write:

> Until Vatican II, the dominant tradition of spirituality in our community was that of eighteenth century spirituality, the spirituality that shaped our foundress' vision of God and the world. Although Rodriguez and Verycruss were widely used in our community until the 1950's, the devotional life continued to be that of French spirituality. For this reason, the Exercises as such were never an organic factor. It is equally true, however, that the articles on obedience in our constitutions from 1818 to 1964, were taken directly from the Jesuit articles and thus shaped our understanding of authority and governance for slightly more than 150 years. Yet my own research on our foundress' life and on the history of our congregation in this country convinces me that Jesuit influence on the development of our spirituality was most intense from 1917 through the early 1950's.

Two others of the same congregation write:

> Originally, until Vatican II, our tradition and background was S.J.'s Spiritual Exercises—since then we have come to an awareness of the women's movement and much of our lived experience in today's world has had a strong impact upon us as women religious.

She adds on a card:

> The S.J.'s are very dear to my heart.

Another wrote in answer to the question about the Ignatian influence on her constitutions:

> This would have been answered affirmatively 20 years ago. Jesuit influence now is

more through spiritual direction, principles of discernment and the directed retreat movement.

The Sisters of Providence (1806) sent a book and other documents, but summed up the influence of Ignatian spirituality in these words:

> In essence it seems to be that although the Constitutions in early French communities were based on the Augustinian Rule, later revisions, our retreats, and even changes at the time of Vatican Council II were guided by the Jesuits.

There were many other comments similar to the above. However I wish now to examine in depth several orders where studies have been made of the Ignatian influence. I will discuss them in the chronological order of their foundation: the Ursulines; Loretto Sisters—or the Institute of the Blessed Virgin Mary; the Sisters of St. Joseph; the Religious of the Sacred Heart; the Religious of the Holy Child Jesus; the Sisters of Mercy. The histories of the first four congregations clearly witness to the struggle women had from the sixteenth century on to form truly apostolic congregations, plagued as they were by the imposition of cloister by Roman and/or diocesan authorities. All, with the exception of Saint Angela Merici, who was a contemporary of Saint Ignatius, tried to base their constitutions on Ignatian writings:

> [T]he obstacles and confusions they met with were but the beginning of a long history of ever-multiplying obstacles and confusions which bedeviled apostolic foundresses throughout the period of powerful growth of apostolic life for women after the french revolution and especially after the restoration of the jesuits in 1814.[20]

The Ursulines

Although Angela Merici, twenty years older that Ignatius, could not have been influenced directly by his writings, writers point to the parallel between the Papal Bull of Approbation for the Company of Jesus in 1540 and the Papal approbation by the same Paul III of the Company of Saint Ursula four years later. An Ursuline maintains that the Ursuline Bull of approbation "is visibly modelled on the one granted to the Jesuits three months before." These differences are noted:

> In the bull for the Jesuits exceptional powers are granted to eminent theologians; in the one for the Company of St. Ursula, even greater powers are granted to layfolk without any safeguards and contrary to the rights of the local bishop. The Company, as the text plainly states, is immediately dependent on the holy See. The Ursulines, on the other hand, form a local Company dependent by right upon the Bishop. If he is set aside, they are subject to no one.[21]

But even the early history of the Ursulines in Italy demonstrated both the view of women at that time and the authority of the church. At the outset most of the Ursulines lived at home and taught young women. But toward the end of the sixteenth century, Saint Charles Borromeo invited the Ursulines to the diocese of Milan. He obtained for them the status of a monastic order with enclosure. One Ursuline commented on the shift from the emphasis on the educational apostolate to emphasis on community, which "became an end in itself, sought for its ascetical value and not for an apostolic end. This changed view-point is characteristic of Cardinal Borromeo."[22] Since then, as other Ursuline congregations developed, those who wanted to follow the original plan of a charitable company were called "congregated" Ursulines to distinguish them from the "religious," who had closure and solemn vows.[23]

It was through two French branches of the Ursulines that the Jesuit influence was clearly documented. Both groups wished to give an education to girls that was similar to that given by the Jesuits to young boys. "The first French Ursulines continued to live in their homes, but later on gathered into communities."[24] We know that the tendency to gather into communities was more prevalent in France than in Italy, and the general atmosphere in the Church was for strict reform. The desire to change the Ursulines from a company of women to a religious order with enclosure and vows was evident in a bull from the French cardinals in 1612. At that time, teaching even within the convent was held to be incompatible with the vow of chastity. So the Ursulines like the Visitandines had to choose between giving up religious life or accepting enclosure. Some accepted cloister and some did not.

The influence of the Jesuits on the educational philosophy of the Ursulines in France, especially in Avignon and later in Paris, is well documented in a study by Marie Martin entitled *The Ursuline Method of Education*.[25] The appendix is particularly revealing. The Ursuline foundation in Paris was clearly influenced by Jesuits, who were not only on the Council of Protectors, but also gave retreats and helped in the drawing up of the Constitutions. The author goes on to say:

> As the directors of this first house of Paris brought to the Ursulines the combined influence of the Sorbonne and the Society of Jesus, we may conclude that it was this same influence that shaped the *Règlements*. The *Règlements* were for the Ursulines what the *Ratio Studiorum* was for the Jesuits.[26]

There then follows in column form a comparison of these two documents, indicating the frequent revisions of both. The Ursuline *Règlements* prescribe the same exercises as those prescribed by the *Ratio*, except that the Ursuline plan does not include contests but has emulations chiefly by rewards. The Jesuits seemed to emphasize both rewards and contests. Both documents emphasize discipline and the reading of the rules. Sometimes the very words of the *Ratio* are included in the *Règlements*. Martin clearly indicates the ongoing influence of the Jesuits on the educational philosophy of the Ursulines originating in Paris.

A second group of Ursulines in the sixteenth century who clearly were influenced by Jesuits personally and spiritually was the group founded by Anne de Xainctonge (1567–1621). Having lived next door to a Jesuit school for boys, she felt called to educate girls in a similar way. Anne's first proposal, for a congregation were based on the documents she had procured from the Ursulines in Avignon and in Tournon. These documents did not contain the idea of enclosure. She was already drawing up her own constitutions to be based on the Rule of the Society of Jesus[27] with the help of the Jesuit Father de Villars. Dehey[28] gives the date of her foundation as 1606. Only in 1623 was the definitive Rule of the Society approved, and its status as a noncloistered congregation established. Only then were the three vows specifically mentioned in the formula of profession. In 1900 the Holy See added the name of the Blessed Virgin to the Society of Saint Ursula so that it would be distinguished from the many other groups of Ursulines. "Thus the Ursulines of Dole were the first congregation of women after the Council of Trent who continued to make simple vows and had no rule of cloister with an apostolic purpose in keeping with their vocation: the education of poor little girls."[29]

Despite the many branches of Ursulines, there are, according to Ledochowska, three characteristics that unite them all: first, the educational apostolate and, second, the awareness of the needs of all classes, especially the poor. But it is the third characteristic that gives the deepest insight into the Ursuline vocation—the blending of action and contemplation. "For the Ursulines, God and one's neighbor are the objects of an undivided love and is expressed in service."[30] Clearly this echoes the Ignatian view of the one end of his Society.

Mary Ward and the Institute of the Blessed Virgin Mary

Although Angela Merici was the first woman religious to seek to educate women without enclosure, there were many women in the sixteenth and seventeen centuries whom the Holy Spirit was inspiring to found apostolic congregations to the mystification and confusion of various diocesan and Roman authorities. Many of these women recognized the value of the Ignatian model as a basis for religious congregations of women.

One of the best known and one who suffered the most for her vision is Mary Ward (1585–1645). In her desire to educate young women she recognized that only one Rule matched her vision of a group of women engaged in the active apostolate. In fact, she writes of her own intense experience of an instruction received in prayer: "Take the same of the Society. Father General will never permit it. Go to him."[31] She knew this was true because the Jesuit Constitutions expressly forbade the Jesuits from taking care of an order of women. Soon Mary Ward and her little group formed in Saint Omer, Belgium were to be subject to all kinds of persecution from priests in England who called her Ladies "jesuitesses" (because they actually preached and taught the people) all the way to the dissolution of her group. Throughout her lifetime she persisted in modeling her organization on the Jesuits. In 1621 she presented to the pope her designs, which included:

1 The rules constitutions and manners of life of the Company of Jesus, insofar as the diversity of sex permits;
2. Recognition as religious, with authorization to have probation and profession according to the practice of the Company of Jesus;
3. Special protection under the immediate jurisdiction of the Holy Father without the intervention of bishops.[32]

While some Jesuits collaborated with the Ladies, others were afraid of the damage that might come to the Society from these virgins. Finally, it might be speculated that the opposition of some of the cardinals to Mary Ward's venture may actually have come from their animosity toward the Jesuits themselves.

Since the text of the Jesuit *Constitutions* was not available to Ward at first, the *Spiritual Exercises* formed the foundations of the spiritual structure of her Constitutions. Much of her *Ratio Institutum*—the plan of her Institute— was drawn from the *Formula Instituti* of the Jesuits, which was really the papal bull of approval given in 1540. Actually, in her second plan in 1621 the words of Saint Ignatius and his companions replaced the more feminine formulation of 1615, and she adopted the same sphere of work as that envisaged by the Jesuits. In fact, in her rule on day to day concerns, Mary Ward changes only one word of Ignatius: the members were to "follow the common and approved usage of reputable women." She had changed *honestorum sacerdotum* to *honestarum mulierum*.[33]

It was not until 1703 that the Rules of the Institute were approved. A Bull in 1749 gave tacit approval over one hundred years after the death of Mary Ward. Some of the provisions were:

2. The new Institute of English Virgins is not the Jesuitesses; mention of them is avoided deliberately in the decree of approval.
5. The English Virgins are not true religious; only those with solemn vows and cloister are in that category.[34]

Finally in 1877 Pius IX confirmed the Institute.

In this brief exposition of her vision of religious life for women we can see why Mary Ward has been often seen as one who played a special part among those women who tried in the sixteenth and seventeenth centuries to combine commitment to God with an active apostolate without enclosure but with the three vows. Clearly Ignatian Spirituality and the apostolic form of religious life had the greatest influence on her.[35]

The Sisters of Saint Joseph

Anne Hennessy, C. S. J. wrote *The Influence of Ignatian Spirituality on the Primitive Documents of the Sisters of Saint Joseph*[36] to help the Sisters of Saint Joseph understand the spirituality of the early Sisters by showing their rootedness in Ignatian spirituality, especially in the dynamics of the *Spiritual Exercises* and its resultant practical spirituality. Hennessy admits that she had great difficulty in tracing both the early history of the Sisters of Saint Joseph and the background of the founder and author of the primitive documents, Jean Pierre Medaille, S.J., who, she says,

> initiated this first apostolic congregation of women who made simple profession of the evangelical counsels of chastity, poverty and obedience but whose life was not cloistered.[37]

(I do not wish to be the judge of who was the first noncloistered group of religious women. Anne Xainctonge claims papal approval in 1606 or 1626, whereas the Sisters of Saint Joseph date their foundation from 1650 in LePuy, France.)

While there is no evidence available that Medaille copied the *Constitutions* or *Rules* of *the Society of Jesus*, there is considerable evidence that he relied heavily on the *dynamics* of the *Spiritual Exercises*. Hennessy feels that

> the whole apostolic thrust of the Congregation with its appropriation to women of such a broad and spiritual ministry without cloister, has its foundation in the Contemplation for Attaining Love. Both the portrait of God and the totality of response of the "Suscipe" are the fonts of such an apostolic spirituality.[38]

Because there is in the four Medaille documents given to the Sisters of Saint Joseph no specific reference to the *Spiritual Exercises,* scholars have concluded that Medaille, a very practical person, was more influenced by the ministries of the Society of Jesus. Still, he must also have been affected by the scholarship and devotion of many of the Jesuits at this very complex time in their French history.

Hennessy concludes

> that all of the fundamental Ignatian themes as well as the dynamics of the *Spiritual Exercises* are either stated or presumed in the four Congregational documents written by Medaille. Neither does Medaille introduce any major non-Ignatian elements. At most he re-emphasizes, reinterprets for the sake of his audience. . . .
> In short, in order to understand the spirituality of Jean Pierre Medaille one has to understand the spirituality of his founder, Ignatius of Loyola.[39]

Society of the Sacred Heart (1800)

The influence of Ignatian spirituality and of individual Jesuits is very evident in the early years of the Society of the Sacred Heart—an influence present not only in the spirituality of the religious women but also in their educational philosophy and curriculum. The society was founded in 1800 just after the violence of the French Revolution and during the suppression of the Society of Jesus, which had occurred in 1773. However, both the Fathers of the Sacred Heart and Fathers of the Faith had adopted the customs and rules of Saint Ignatius. Father de Tournely of the Fathers of the Sacred Heart wanted to establish a society for the education of women, but he died at an early age. He had entrusted his vision to Father Varin. Through her brother, Louis, who joined the Fathers of the Faith, Madeleine Sophie Barat met Father Varin, who saw in Sophie the foundation stone for his apostolic society dedicated to the education of women.

The era after the French Revolution saw the development of many religious congregations of women desirous of the apostolic life, but, because of diocesan or papal insistence, they had to retain semicloister and monastic hours of prayer. The Society of the Sacred Heart was based on this model of the "mixed life," as it was called then. Because of the priests present at the foundation, who subsequently became Jesuits when they were restored in 1814, the Constitutions of the Society of Jesus were the basis of the new congregation of women. But there are differences. In referring to the constitutional crisis in 1839, when a Bishop tried to make the Constitutions more like that of the Jesuits, Janet Stuart, the superior general in the early twentieth century, states:

> Blessed Madeleine Sophie always maintained that it could not be done; that an Order of women could not be governed like an order of men. She valued intensely the spirit of the Society of Jesus which pervades the whole Rule and Constitutions, or rather underlies them. She valued the likeness which her Institute had to theirs; but she knew that it was and ought to be the likeness of sister to brother.[40]

Certainly, the broad lines of the *Constitutions* of both Societies are parallel; two sections on certain practices of religious life are reproduced verbatim. The aims are similar: "For the greater glory of God" and "For the greater glory of the Sacred Heart of Jesus." And the letter of Saint Ignatius on obedience was read (out of context) each month at meals to the Religious of the Sacred Heart up until the changes brought about by Vatican II. But one author has pointed out that devotion to the Sacred Heart "adds to rules written for men an affective note for women devoted to a Heart both human and divine."[41] It is also clear that the spirituality of its foundress, while strongly influenced by Ignatian spirituality, is a blend of Carmelite and Jesuit spirituality and devotion to the Sacred Heart.[42] Ignatian retreats were given annually to all Religious of the Sacred Heart until Vatican II, and so the Ignatian influence was very strong, at least up until around 1968.

The same influence is present in the educational tradition of the Society of the Sacred Heart. Madeleine Sophie was educated by her brother, who subsequently became a Father of the Faith. It must be remembered that all schools were closed during the French Revolution and that there were very few schools for girls, with the exception of the schools directed by the Ursulines and Visitandines. The distinctive system of Sacred Heart education has evolved throughout the years, given focus by the Jesuit *Ratio Studiorum,* yet always with the distinctive end of "making the reign of the Heart of Jesus flower in the world." Throughout the development of the *Plan of Studies,* Jesuit educators helped at every step. The most notable influence in the lifetime of Madeleine Sophie was Father Druilhet, a Jesuit who gave conferences in 1827. These conferences were subsequently added to the Plan of Studies of 1852. So, at the very beginning of the Society of the Sacred Heart, the Jesuits both personally and in their writings influenced the educational philosophy of the congregation. But this philosophy was always modified for "the formation of the whole woman with a view to her own vocation in the circumstances and the age in which she has to live."[43]

However, in 1975, the Sacred Heart Schools formed a Network with five goals derived from their own reflection and not directly influenced by the Jesuit emphasis on the work of peace and justice. These goals are to educate to: a personal and active faith in God; a deep respect for intellectual values; social awareness which impels to action; the building of community as a Christian value; and personal growth in an atmosphere of wise freedom.[44] This statement of goals preceded by twelve years the publication of the Characteristics of Jesuit Education that lists twenty-eight characteristics.[45] Both documents indicate the need to adapt their own traditions, which were perhaps very similar in 1852, to the needs of the time and to the growing awareness of social justice.

In summarizing the influence of Ignatian spirituality on the Religious of the Sacred Heart, it is evident that in the early years of the Society, both in spirituality and in philosophy of education, the foundress was decidedly influenced by both the documents of the Jesuits and particular Jesuits themselves. This influence has gradually lessened as the Society of the Sacred Heart has matured and developed its own identity.

Sisters of Mercy

Although nine Sisters of Mercy stated that Jesuit spirituality had *not* influenced their foundress, Mary Sullivan, a Sister of Mercy who has been examining the writings of Catherine McAuley, demonstrates clearly that two key documents for Mercy spirituality, "The Spirit of the Institute" and "The Act of Consecration," long thought to be the original work of Catherine, are actually transcriptions of the work of two Jesuits, Alphonsus Rodriguez and Joseph Dean.[46] "The Spirit" is "regarded as a central document in the self-understanding of Sisters of Mercy throughout the world."[47] In a careful

examination of the first half of Rodriguez's treatise "Of the End and Instuti-
tion of the Society of Jesus" (particularly chapters 5–8) and of Catherine
McAuley's "Spirit of the Institute" Sullivan notes the direct quotations made
by the foundress. But it is important to realize that, as Sullivan says,

> it is unnecessary and probably technically inaccurate to say that Catherine pla-
> giarized Rodriguez's work. She herself never published her essay, and we now have
> no way of knowing what she actually did with it or what she intended to do with it,
> when and if she regarded it as finished.[48]

It can be surmised that some of Catherine's friends and or spiritual directors
passed on to Catherine the 1806 Kilkenny edition of the English translation
of *The Practice of Christian and Religious Perfection.* In parallel columns,
Sullivan shows the identical wording, the same sequence of thought, and
identical citations.

Although Catherine's essay is only seven pages, while Rodriguez's treatise
is eighty printed pages, still the parallel is there, with two significant differences: Rodriguez counsels the Jesuits "to keep their eyes on souls and not
on bodies" while Catherine said in the Rule "great tenderness must be
employed" in the care of the sick. The second adaptation pointed out is the
substitution of "offices of mercy" by Catherine for the "offices of charity" in
Rodriguez.[49] Were the changes made because the new organization consisted
of women?

There is considerable evidence that it was standard practice for Sisters of
Mercy to copy books for community reading. It is evident that Catherine
used as her prayerbook *Devotions to the Sacred Heart of Jesus,* which was
translated from the French and revised by Reverend Joseph Dean. "The Act
of Oblation" in the second Dublin edition is nearly identical to the "Act of
Consecration" long ascribed to Catherine McAuley.

Sullivan points out that Catherine would never have considered herself to
be a theologian but would have "thought it presumptuous of her to compose
from scratch a theological treatise."[50] Her strengths lay in the more practical
area, and therefore she would rely on the greater wisdom of others and would
acknowledge her indebtedness to Rodriguez and the Society of Jesus.

Thus we see that in their two key documents the Sisters of Mercy were
influenced not by Ignatius but by later Jesuits. Can we call the spirituality of
Alphonsus Rodriguez an Ignatian spirituality?.

The Religious of the Holy Child Jesus

The Ignatian influence on the founding and *Constitutions of the Society of
the Holy Child Jesus* has been carefully analyzed and documented in Caritas
McCarthy's excellent book *The Spirituality of Cornelia Connelly.*[51] Papal

approval of her congregation was delayed and complicated by trouble with her former husband, Pierce.

Although Cornelia Connolly herself clearly acknowledged the influence of the constitutions of other religious congregations of women, such as that of the Religious of the Sacred Heart and that of the Figlie del Sacro Cuore di Jesu, she felt that these all sprang from the Constitutions of Saint Ignatius. McCarthy quotes Cornelia toward the end of her life as saying: "The second practice I desire you to keep is fidelity to the rule [Constitutions] and spirit of St. Ignatius, than which nothing could be found more perfect for the spiritual life."[52] McCarthy points out that Cornelia did not consider herself and her sisters as lady Jesuits but recognized the more universal application of the Ignatian charism to other apostolic congregations. Because of the delay in getting approval for her Constitutions, she sent to her convents "the *Jesuit Constitutions,* (with Examen), a volume of Jesuit Rules as a sort of base for the Society's own truncated Constitutions."[53] Of even greater influence was the *Spiritual Exercises,* the "means to the true spirit of the Constitutions." She made prudent use of other classics of western spirituality, although the majority of the authors she read were Jesuits.

In 1877 Bishop Danell imposed a constitution lacking the original charism and the original order of documents, which was to have had Cornelia's First Chapter followed by the Jesuit *Summary, Common Rules, and Rules of Modesty.* Diocesan and Propaganda authorities had never seen the *Summary* in the light of the total Ignatian *Constitutions.* Therefore, as was pointed out earlier, they did not see the vital spirit that underlay Cornelia's use of the *Summary.* Finally a Jesuit, Pierre Cotel, revised the ordering, emphasizing the spirit of the Religious Institute. Like many other foundresses, Cornelia was subjected to authorities who tried to impose on her the more legalistic *Summary of the Jesuit Constitutions* and to ignore the Ignatian spirit as seen in the full *Constitutions.*

Thus throughout the struggles to form the *Constitutions* for her Sisters Cornelia was influenced by Ignatian spirituality, as can be seen in the list of all the documents she consulted, especially the Jesuit *Constitutions* and the *Spiritual Exercises.*

Summary and Conclusions

This paper is but the beginning of an examination of the influence of Ignatian spirituality on women's teaching orders. I examined only the religious congregations in the United States. The religious congregations in other continents remain to be examined.

The clearest insight gained from this study is that the vision Ignatius had of an apostolic congregation with one end—the glory of God and service of others, with personal sanctification as a means to that end—arose in answer to the needs of the times. This vision, many believe, transcends gender distinctions and cultural changes.

Women religious, long restricted by Rome to enclosure and strict orders of day, also recognized the need of the times for service freed from the monastic model. The charism of Ignatius, his *Spiritual Exercises, Rules,* and *Constitutions* seemed to be the model for the new apostolic life, especially for the apostolate of education.

Yet because of the view that women were weak, Rome and various bishops opposed the founding of any congregation of women without enclosure. Angela Merici and the Ursulines illustrate both the apostolic vision and the imposition of enclosure by Rome. Nevertheless, women persisted in trying both to teach young women and to form apostolic congregations, especially in France. And more and more turned to the Jesuit *Constitutions* and to spiritual direction by Jesuits. A few congregations also based their philosophy of education on the Jesuit *Ratio Studiorum,* but the greatest influence mediated to women's teaching orders by Jesuits was through the *Spiritual Exercises.*

However, a few questions need to be asked.

First, with the emergence of feminism—feminist theology and feminist spirituality—will the influence of Ignatian spirituality continue? It is interesting to note that, as a result of their conference this past summer, our religious sisters in England have formed a group entitled "The Ignatian Family." One of the subgroups is "The Enabling Group." In the February 1990 report," The Enabling Group,"[54] indicated that the four topics to be considered are: the formation of those engaged in the *Spiritual Exercises;* communication and network of those involved; the adaptation of the *Spiritual Exercises* to different needs and levels; the reimaging of the *Spiritual Exercises* for women. A publication on Ignatian Identity in Women's Religious Congregations is proposed to discuss of such questions as: What was it that led our founding women to insist that the Ignatian Charism was the only way forward as a response to their particular situation in a given time and context? How has our experience as lay women enriched the Ignatian Charism? How do we locate and explore the activity of this spirit in our present-day search for ways forward?

At least in England there seems to be an effort to adapt the Ignatian charism to the growing influence of feminism or to integrate the two. This might be a healthy development. Is this also possible in North America?

My second question relates to the *perception* of Ignatian obedience and the new understanding of obedience for mission among women religious. Mary Augusta Neal[55] points out that sisters perceive the following characteristics of contemporary obedience "as fundamental to their contemporary mission": 1) learning responsible participation based on interdependency not dependency; 2) a recognition of new authority grounded in apostolically committed competency; 3) a shared use of human skills; 4) other uses of resourceful collegial governance on behalf of the mission of the church.

I emphasize the *perceived* notion of obedience because that perception is probably based on the "Letter of Ignatius on Obedience." The Ignatian process of discernment might be of greater help in formulating responsible models of participation in decision making. I would submit that genuine Ignatian obedience is closer to discernment than to that obedience described in the "Letter on Obedience." The question to be put to Jesuits today is this: Is Jesuit obedience an *obedience to authority* or *discernment* with God and others? Joann Conn[56] already has indicated the appropriateness of discernment for women.

Clearly women's religious congregations owed much in the past to Ignatian spirituality. I hope that the two new movements in these congregations—feminism and participatory decision making—will challenge our Jesuit brothers to indicate how the Ignatian vision can adapt to or absorb these powerful contemporary influences. Is a constructive feminism to enrich the spirituality of those congregations of women whose origins are already deeply rooted in Ignatian spirituality? Or will a more radical feminism tear these congregations from their Ignatian roots and start new growths with new roots? I certainly hope the former.

Notes

1. Marie Neal, *From Nuns to Sisters: An Expanding Vocation,* (Mystic, Conn.: Twenty-Third Publications, 1990), p. 31.

2. James Walsh, "Apostolic Prayer," *The Way* (Summer 1971): 76–77.

3. Ibid., p. 77.

4. Hugo Rahner, *Saint Ignatius Loyola: Letters to Women* (New York: Herder, 1960), p. 155.

5. Ibid., p. 257.

6. Caritas McCarthy, "Constitutions for Apostolic Religious," *The Way,* supplement 14 (1971): 33.

7. Francois Courel, "The Single Aim of the Apostolic Institute," *The Way,* supplement 14 (1971): 49.

8. Ibid., p. 49.

9. Ibid., p. 61.

10. McCarthy, "Constitutions," p. 36.

11. Ibid., p. 41.

12. Ignatius of Loyola, *The Constitutions of the Society of Jesus,* trans. George Ganss, (Saint Louis: Institute of Jesuit Sources, 1970), no. 622.

13. David Fleming, *A Contemporary Reading of the Spiritual Exercises,* 2d ed. (Saint Louis: Institute of Jesuit Sources, 1980), p. 8.

14. Ibid., p. 80.

15. Caritas McCarthy, "Ignatian Charism in Women's Congregations," *The Way,* supplement 20 (1973): 15.

16. Ibid., p. 14.

17. Ignatius, *Constitutions,* 6, 3, 1582, pp. 259–60.

18. McCarthy, "Ignatian Charism," p. 11.

19. Ibid.

20. McCarthy, "Constitutions," p. 35.

21. Teresa Ledochowska, *Angela Merici and the Company of Saint Ursula,* (Rome: Ancora Press, 1967): 2: 301.

22. Ibid., p. 134.

23. Elinor Dehey, *Religious Orders of Women in the United States,* rev. ed. (Hammond, Ind.: W. B. Conkey, 1930).

24. Ledochowska, *Angela Merici,* p. 158.

25. Marie Martin, *Ursuline Method of Education* (Rahway, N.J.: Wuinn and Boden, 1946).

26. Ibid., p. 291.

27. Sister Mary Breslin, *Anne de Xainctonge: Her Life and Spirituality* (Kingston, N.Y.: The Society of Saint Ursula of the Blessed Virgin, 1957), p. 187.

28. Dehey, *Religious Orders.*

29. Ledochowska, *Angela Merici,* 2: 176.

30. Ibid., p. 280.

31. Immolata Wetter, "Mary Ward's Apostolic Vocation," *The Way,* supplement 17 (1972): 78.

32. James Cain, "Cloister and the Apostolate of Religious Women," *Review for Religious* 27 (1968): 668.

33. Wetter, "Mary Ward," p. 86.

34. Cain, "Cloister," p. 669.

35. Wetter, "Mary Ward," p. 69.

36. Anne Hennessy, *The Influence of Ignatian Spirituality on the Primitive Documents of the Sisters of Saint Joseph* (Saint Louis: Sisters of Saint Joseph of Orange, 1983).

37. Ibid., p. 5.

38. Ibid., p. 173.

39. Ibid., pp. 174–75.

40. Janet Stuart, *The Society of the Sacred Heart* (Roehampton, London: Convent of the Sacred Heart, 1923), p. 97.

41. Margaret Williams, *Saint Madelein Sophie* (New York: Herder and Herder, 1965), p. 451.

42. Ibid., p. 501.

43. *Spirit and Plan of Studies in the Society of the Sacred Heart* (Farnborough, Hants: St. Michael's Abbey Press, 1958), p. 13.

44. Sacred Heart Schools in the United States, *Goals and Criteria* (Newton, Mass.: Network of Sacred Heart Schools, 1990).

45. International Commission on the Apostolate of Jesuit Education, "Go Forth and Teach" (Washington, D.C.: Jesuit Secondary Association, 1988).

46. Mary Sullivan, "Catherine McAuley's Theological and Literary Debt to Alonso Rodriguez: The 'Spirit of the Institute' Parallels" *Recusant History* 20 (May 1990): 81–105.

47. Ibid., p. 82.

48. Ibid., p. 83.

49. Ibid., p. 101.

50. Ibid., p. 104.

51. Caritas McCarthy, *The Spirituality of Cornelia Connelly: In God, for God, with God* (New York: Mellon, 1986).

52. Ibid., p. 135.

53. Ibid., p. 136.

54. The Enabling Group, "The Ignatian Family" (London: unpublished manuscript, 1990).

55. Neal, *From Nuns,* p. 95.

56. Joann Conn, "Revisioning the Ignatian Rules for Discernment," in *Women's Spirituality,* ed. Joann Conn (New York: Paulist Press, 1986), pp. 312–16.

Part Two
The Jesuit Tradition: History, Missions, and Cultural Insight

The Peruvian Indian through Jesuit Eyes: The Case of José de Acosta and Pablo José de Arriaga

DR. LUIS MARTÍN

Father José de Acosta, one of the intellectual giants of the Jesuit Order in the sixteenth century, arrived in Peru on 28 April 1572. By that date the heated controversies on the nature of the American Indians that had rocked the Spanish universities, the ecclesiastical intelligentsia, and even the royal court, were a thing of the past. The well-known sermon of Fr. Antonio de Montesinos, delivered on Advent Sunday on the island of Hispaniola in 1511, had ignited the controversy with the affirmation that the Indians were full human beings endowed with rational souls equal to the Europeans. The fiery Bartolomé de Las Casas had clashed in 1550 with Juan Ginés de Sepúlveda in front of a royal commission gathered at Valladolid. He defended the full equality and rationality of the Indians against the Aristotelian theory, held by Sepúlveda, that some men are slaves by nature, destined to serve—because of their inferior nature—the truly developed and civilized human beings. To Sepúlveda, the former were the American Indians and the latter the Spanish conquerors and settlers. To Las Casas, "God's angry man," that was utter nonsense and to him: ". . . all the peoples of the earth are men, and the definition of all men, collectively and severally, is one: that they are rational beings. All possess understanding and volition, being formed in the image and the likeness of God. . . . *Thus all mankind is one, and all men are alike* in what concerns their creation and natural things."[1] The words of men like Montesino and Las Casas had prodded the royal conscience, and the Crown had issued the Laws of Burgos of 1512 and the New Laws of 1542 in a feeble attempt to soften the brutality of the conquest and to recognize the basic human rights of the Indians.[2]

José de Acosta, as a young Jesuit studying at the University of Alcalá from 1559 to 1567, had become familiar with the history of the discovery and conquest of the New World and with the controversy surrounding the nature of the Indians.[3] By the time he arrived in Peru in 1572, Acosta was committed to study the Indian question, not within the polemical and political climate of the previous decades, but with the emotional detachment and intellectual rigor of the scholar and with the profound empathy of the humanist. For fourteen years Acosta crisscrossed the vast territories of the viceroyalty of Peru pursuing an empirical field research among the Peruvian Indians, which by 1590 had blossomed into his massive masterpiece, *Historia Natural y Moral de las Indias.* In this work Acosta provided his fellow Jesuits with the intellectual, rational frame within which the Jesuit Order would operate in Peru until its expulsion in 1767. *The Historia Natural y Moral* is a vast reservoir not just of empirical knowledge, but of reasoned, rationally analyzed, and integrated knowledge, ordered into a cohesive intellectual system. The work exhibits both the philosophical structure of the medieval scholastic *summas* and the empirical, rational methodology of modern scientific thought.

The point of departure for Acosta's study of the Indians, in which he revealed an originality unknown to his predecessors, is his effort to see the Indian not in the abstract or in theological terms as "a soul" to be saved, but as a human being of flesh and blood shaped through the centuries by a unique physical and cultural environment. The New World was, in the mind of Acosta, a twofold reality: the world of physical reality, land and sea, mountains and forest, lakes and rivers, plants and animals; and an invisible, man-made world of language and thought, values and customs, economics, and religion. These two worlds were historically welded together with the physical world of the Americas, the unique stage in which Indian history and culture had been unfolding through the centuries. To understand the Indian fully, Acosta thought, one must understand "su mundo," his physical environment. Thus in the first part of his work, Acosta provided a thorough, scientific description of the new continent led "not so much by the doctrine of ancient philosophers, but by true reason and well-established observation."[4] Let us say parenthetically that in this short quotation we can detect the luminous, breaking dawn of a new, scientific, and empirical approach to the study of the New World. This approach yielded such sterling results in the work of Acosta that, in the late nineteenth century, the German scientist Von Humbold did not hesitate to affirm that "the foundation of what today is called Physics of the earth, if one puts aside the mathematical formulations, is contained in the work of the Jesuit José de Acosta, entitled *Historia Natural y Moral de las Indias.*"[5]

Before turning his attention to the cultural world of the Indian and still seeing him as part of the physical landscape of America, Acosta raised the question of the origins of the inhabitants of the New World. To him, his mind solidly anchored in the doctrine of monogenism like the rest of sixteenth-century Europe, the answer was obvious: they were children of Adam and Eve and, therefore, identical in nature to the Europeans. This bold assertion posed the further question of how the Indians arrived in the New World. As is well known, Acosta's answer was original and unique in the intellectual context of the late sixteenth century. Following only the "thread of reason, no matter how thin," Acosta rejected mythical and miraculous explanations to conclude that the still unknown land mass of the continent extended so far north that it touched Asia or was separated from it by a narrow strait easy to cross. The Jesuit envisioned a slow human migration in search of plants and new hunting grounds. It must have taken centuries, Acosta thought, for those waves of migration to cover the New World and develop their unique ways of life. But there was no doubt in his mind that the Indian had a common origin with the European, and *in nature* was identical to him.[6]

With the Indian placed in his unique physical environment, the Jesuit Acosta turned his attention to that other, invisible world of Indian culture. To him that world was the result of the *libre albedrio,* of the free will of the Indians, and merited respect and thorough, serious study on the part of the European. There was no doubt in Acosta's mind that the Indian was endowed with free will, and that by it he had built his culture, which was not a necessary product of nature, but rather a contingent construction dependent on the mind and will of the Indian himself. Acosta reflected in this view the stubborn Jesuit commitment to the doctrine of free will, a cornerstone of Jesuit ideology and spirituality, and at the same time he provided the intellectual justification for his utter rejection of any kind of force or violence in the preaching of the Christian faith to the Indians. The act of faith *must* be free or it would be worthless religiously and humanly demeaning.[7]

In dealing with the origin of the American Indian early in his work, the Jesuit Acosta already toyed with an idea that would later become a crucial element in his understanding of Indian culture and civilization. To him culture was not a static, but a dynamic, ever changing reality, the product of a long historical evolution. The early Americans were, Acosta speculated, primitive hunters and gatherers, held together by the need for survival, but lacking the economic foundation and the mental sophistication to have gone beyond the social organization of small bands roaming aimlessly the land in search for food. Thousands of years separated them from the splendor of Incan and Aztec cultures. The ascent toward higher levels of culture was, in Acosta's mind, not a process determined by the blind forces of nature, but a product of the mind and will of the Indians. Individuals of courage, knowledge, and wisdom, Acosta thought, must have prodded the rest of the Indians on the road toward cultural growth as the centuries unfolded. Yet not all Indians had attained the same cultural level at the time of contact with the Europeans. We may call inhabitants of the New World Indians, but to Acosta, "va mucho de Indio a Indio, y un bárbaro aventaja mucho a otro" (there is a great cultural distance between Indians, and some barbarians are way ahead of others).[8] Cultural evolution goes on, sometimes by the intrinsic dynamics of a people, sometimes by the shock of extrinsic stimuli.

Acosta knew that what he said about the Indians applied also to the Europeans. The Europe of his day was also the result of a long, at times painful, process of cultural evolution. The Jesuit was fully aware that, without the civilizing power of Rome and the transforming power of Christianity, Europe could not have reached its present level of cultural development. In fact, some Europeans had not yet emerged from barbarism "since it is well known that even in Spain and Italy one can find herds (manadas) of men who, aside from their gestures and countenance, do not have anything else that resemble human beings."[9] Indians may appear to many as simple children not yet blossomed into matured adults, but Acosta stressed that, if so, this was the result not of their different nature or the conditions of the New World, but of education. Culture is "learned" and therefore must be taught by those endowed with "the courage and knowledge" to do so.

By the time that José de Acosta was named Provincial Superior of all the Jesuits of Peru in January 1576, four years after his arrival in the Viceroyalty, he was absolutely convinced that teaching and instruction were the key roles the Jesuit Order had to play among the Indians of Peru. With that conviction he began developing policies that would affect the course of the Jesuits in Peru in the years to come: study of the native languages, acceptance of *doctrinas,* and, most important of all, the development of boarding schools for the sons of *curacas* or *caciques,* the heads of the former Incan *ayllus.*

The study of the Indian languages, Quechua and Ayamara, had been initiated at the Jesuit College of San Pablo in Lima before the arrival of Acosta in Peru, but it was Acosta as Provincial who institutionalized the practice, gave it a new impetus, and brought it to the level of a true academic and scholarly endeavor. The Provincial Congregation of 1576 under the leadership of José de Acosta ordered two grammars, two dictionaries, and two catechisms in Quechua and Ayamara to be written by a team of Jesuit scholars, and the Jesuits Blas Varela, Alonso de Barzana, and others set immediately to the task. The courses in Indian languages were made compulsory, and by the end of the decade about fifty Jesuits and a great number of secular clerics were enrolled in the language courses taught at the Jesuit College of San Pablo. It was clear to Acosta that the Indians could not be brought to an understanding of Christianity unless the European first understood the Indian soul and culture as expressed by, and embodied in, the native languages.[10]

The involvement of Acosta with the study of the Indian languages did not end with the Provincial Congregation of 1576. In 1583 we see him as the intellectual leader of the third Council of Lima persuading the assembled bishops, superiors of religious Orders, and theologians of the need to master the Indian languages. Prodded by Acosta, the Council decreed the writing and publication of two catechisms, two *confesionarios* (manuals for confessors), and two *sermonarios* (collections of sermons) in the two most important languages of Peru—Quechua and Ayamara. In spite of his being occupied with giving final form to the doctrinal and disciplinary decrees and canons of the Council, Acosta plunged with boundless energy into this new linguistic project. He wrote the Spanish version of the catechisms, the *confesionarios,* and the *sermonarios,* and he assembled the team of Jesuit translators—the Spaniard Alonso de Barzana, and the mestizos Jesuits Blas Varela and Bartolomé de Santiago—to prepare under his supervision the Quechua and Ayamara versions of the three works. In about a year the Jesuit linguists had finished the work, and their friend and protégé, the lay printer Antonio Ricardo, published the Quechua catechism in his printshop housed in the Jesuit College of San Pablo. That book, written and translated by a team of Jesuit scholars and published in their college, has the honor of being the first book printed in the South American continent.[11]

The impetus given by Acosta to the scholarly study of the Indian languages would be felt among the Jesuits of Peru even after the return of Acosta to Europe for health reasons. In the same year Acosta returned to Europe, 1586, Antonio Ricardo published the Quechua grammar and dictionary written by the Jesuit Diego Torres Vásquez. The Jesuit grammarian and lexicographer followed the footsteps of the Dominican Domingo de Santo Tomás, who published the first Quechua grammar in Valladolid in 1560, but the Jesuit author was able to incorporate into his work a quarter century of research and, after the work done in the Jesuit College in 1583 and 1584, a deeper and clearer understanding of the language of the Incas. Years later, another Jesuit, Diego Gonzalea Holguín, wrote and published what many scholars considered the definitive linguistic work produced in Peru during the colonial period, *Vocabulario de la lengua general de todo el Peru llamada lengua Quechua o del Inca.* Of him a modern Peruvian scholar has written: "At the head of all the linguistic Quechua movement, as master and leader, invested with the supreme authority of a kind of Academy of the Language . . . stands . . . Diego Gonzalez Holguín."[12]

Once in Europe, José de Acosta several times visited the General of the Jesuit Order in Rome, the Italian Claudio Aquaviva, whom he briefed thoroughly on the status of Peru and the work of the Jesuits among the Indians. General Aquaviva took a keen interest in and read carefully Acosta's works *De Natura Novi Orbis . . . et . . . de Procuranda Indorum Salute,* published in Salamanca in 1589, and *Historia Natural y Moral de las Indias,* published in Barcelona in 1591. The Jesuit General fell under the spell of one of the most brilliant minds Spain produced in the sixteenth century, and he understood and fully shared Acosta's commitment to the study of the Indian languages. In 1596, a year before he appointed Acosta Rector of the Jesuit College of Salamanca, Aquaviva sent orders to Peru decreeing that no Jesuit should be ordained a priest in the Society unless he had first acquired a good command of one of the Indian languages. Once ordained, all the new Jesuit priests should spend three full years working among Indians to perfect their knowledge of the Indian languages before they could be assigned to other ministries of the Society. These guidelines of Aquaviva were still in force in the Jesuit Province of Peru at the end of the seventeenth century, when the Spaniard Thyrsus Gonzalez was General of the Order, and they revealed how deeply the linguistic policies of Acosta had taken root among the Peruvian Jesuits.[13]

Given his evolutionary concept of history and culture, it seems clear that Acosta thought of the Europeans, and specifically of his fellow Jesuits, as agents of change in the ongoing process of the unfolding of human history in the New World. To understand fully the Indian culture and to master the Indian language was for Acosta the condition *sine qua non* for having any kind of positive impact on such change, which historically was unavoidable. Once that condition was fulfilled, there was only one way for Acosta to affect positive and permanent change: education, and that in an atmosphere of freedom avoiding any kind of force and violence. This conviction brought him, as Provincial of the Peruvian Jesuits, to develop his policies on *doctrinas* and boarding schools for Indian children.

The *doctrinas* were Indian parishes headed by a priest or a group of priests, who had the ordinary, pastoral care of the Indians and who lived in the parish in close and daily contact with the Indians. Two years before the arrival of Acosta in Peru, the Jesuit General Francisco de Borja, later canonized by the Church, had send strict orders to Lima forbidding the Peruvian Jesuits to take charge of such *doctrinas*. Borja thought, rightly, that such a pastoral arrangement was clearly against the spirit and the letter of the Jesuit Constitutions and could bring the Jesuits unwittingly under the jurisdiction of the local bishop and of the Viceroy himself in his capacity as vicepatron of the Church in Peru. The Jesuit General favored the traditional Jesuit method of evangelization in Europe—temporary, roving missions with the Jesuit superiors always in control of reassigning or recalling missionaries without interference from bishops or secular authorities.[14]

The Peruvian experience had convinced José de Acosta that the saintly Borja was wrong and out of touch with conditions in the New World. Idolatry, superstitions, and pagan rites were still flourishing in Peru after forty years of evangelization, and Acosta knew that that was due in part to the lack of rational, sustained instruction for the Indians. Permanent *doctrinas* manned by Jesuits were essential to accomplish such a task. As Jesuit Provincial of Peru, Acosta led his fellow Jesuits in the already mentioned Provincial Congregation of 1576 to change the course set by Borja in his orders of 1570. The fathers assembled in the Congregation of 1576 followed the lead of their Provincial and had the intellectual honesty and courage to affirm that temporary missions alone were totally insufficient for the proper instruction of the Indians. If *doctrinas* were against the Jesuit Constitutions, the solution was not to forbid the *doctrinas* but to suspend the Jesuit legislation on that point. Eventually Rome, with a new General at the helm of the Jesuit Order, saw things Acosta's way and allowed the acceptance of *doctrinas* by the Peruvian Jesuits. Without Acosta's strong stand, those controversial laboratories of cultural change that were the *doctrinas* of El Cercado, Huarochiri, Juli, and later Paraguay may have never existed.[15]

The foundation of schools for the children of Indian nobles, the *curacas* and *caciques* of the old Incan *ayllus,* was another idea that Acosta discussed with his fellow Jesuits in the Congregation of 1576. A few Indian boys had been accepted as early as 1570 in the College of San Pablo, founded in Lima by the Jesuits for the children of Spanish settlers, but Acosta must have thought that such a token presence of Indians in the College of San Pablo could not have a significant impact on the Andean Indian communities. He knew that the *ayllus* were the solid foundations of the entire Indian social structure, and that the *curacas-caciques* were the cornerstones of their own *ayllus.* To educate future *curacas* and *caciques* was the key in Acosta's mind to transforming Indian society. After all, the Incas had used the same approach when they brought to Cuzco the children of the chieftains of newly conquered tribes to learn the Quechua language and to be educated in the Inca way of life by the *Amautas* under the shadow of the imperial court. The Peruvian Jesuits, led by Acosta, agreed in 1576 that steps should be taken to establish schools for the children of the Indian nobility, and Acosta was entrusted with the task of writing the rules and guidelines of such future schools.

The overriding principle of those rules and guidelines is Guideline 5, which reveals the wisdom of a Christian humanist and deserves to be quoted in full:

> [The Indian children] should not be deprived of the laws, customs, and methods of governing accepted in their provinces, if they are not contrary to natural and Christian law. It is not suitable to attempt to turn them completely into Spaniards because, besides being very difficult and an occasion of discouragement for the students, it will also be very harmful for their own republic and government.[16]

On the bedrock of this principle José de Acosta built his vision of the future Schools. The students should be between the ages of eight and sixteen at the time of admission, and the "sons of curacas or important Indians so that greater results can be expected of them" as they succeeded their fathers at the head of their communities. They would learn the Spanish language to the point of reading and writing it well, and as a rule "they will speak Spanish among themselves." They will be taught Christian doctrine not by rote, but "to the point . . . of being able to understand and explain it according to their capacity." This should be done both in Spanish and Quechua so that the future *caciques* could bridge the world of the Indian and the world of the Spaniards as fully bilingual persons. Music was also included in the proposed curriculum of instruction. Finally, Acosta mentioned the skills and knowledge needed by those future local rulers to administer their communities in a proper and Christian manner.[17]

Acosta obviously was not rushed by a fanatical zeal for "saving souls" there and then, but rather was concerned with starting the long process of educating minds that could one day become the leaven of a future Indian, Christian society. He even dreamed of locating the first Indian college next to the Jesuit Noviciate in the *doctrina* of El Cercado, where young Jesuit novices and scholastics were already practicing the Quechua language among the Indians. As the young Jesuits absorbed, as much as they could, the Indian culture by studying the native language, Acosta hoped that the Indian young men accepted in the Jesuit School would also absorb a great deal of Spanish, Christian culture by studying Spanish and Christian religion. He never saw his dream realized. In 1586, already in the throes of a profound personal crisis, José de Acosta left Peru to die fourteen years later, in 1600, in the university city of Salamanca.[18]

The dreamer was dead, but his dream was kept alive by his fellow Jesuits. It was finally brought to reality by one of the true intellectual heirs of Acosta, Father Pablo José de Arriaga, who arrived in Lima in 1585, the year before Acosta left for Europe. Arriaga knew well the mind of Acosta and had studied his works. He shared with Acosta the view that the profound cultural change implied in the acceptance of Christianity would be a long evolution-ary process lasting years, perhaps centuries. Christianity took hold of Eu-rope that way, and in Spain itself idolatry and paganism were rampant as late as the end of the seventh century.[19] How could one expect anything else in Peru? Arriaga was also aware of the key role played by the caciques in the social and political system of the Incas:

> They [the *caciques*] do as they please with the Indians, and if they want them to be idolatrous they are idolatrous, if they want them to be Christians they will be Christians. They [the Indians] have no will apart from their caciques, who are a model for them in everything they do.[20]

The consequence of this historical situation was as obvious to Arriaga as it had been to Acosta: "Begin at the beginning" by educating the sons and future heirs of the *caciques*. In 1618 he met several times with the Viceroy, Prince of Esquilache, and with fellow Jesuits, and he was placed in charge of opening the first School of *Caciques* in the *doctrina* of El Cercado in the outskirts of Lima. Arriaga chose the handsome building of the Jesuit Novici-ate and, moving the novices to another location, on 1 January 1619 he accepted the first class of fourteen sons of *caciques* into the new school, named *El Colegio del Príncipe* in honor of Prince Philip, heir to the Spanish throne. Two years later, in 1621, the second school opened in Cuzco with sixteen students and was named *El Colegio San Francisco de Borja.*[21]

The rules and guidelines written by José de Acosta back in 1576 were closely observed in organizing the two new institutions of learning. Acosta's principle of selectivity was followed in recruiting students, and the head-master of San Borja could write that the Jesuits had chosen "the best children and those of greatest nobility, and thus the students we have today in the college are the closest descendants of the Incas, among whom is a grandchild of the Inca himself."[22] No Indian boys were chosen unless they were ready to enter the school "of their own free will." Persuasion and instruction, not force or indoctrination, were the tools to be used in the Indian schools. Several years after the schools were opened, Arriaga could proudly say that they were being run "according to our statutes regarding the care and education of youth" and that "our purpose is to teach them to work and to develop into the kind of men they should be."[23] These were the same educational policies and the same goals the Jesuits were pursuing in their schools for Spanish and *criollo* students.

A reflective and comparative reading of the works of José de Acosta and Pablo José de Arriaga will show that they saw the Indian as a full human type, the result of a distinctive historical process within the peculiar physical environment of the New World. The environment was a thing of nature, but the historical process was the creation of *libre albedrio,* the free will of the Indians themselves. Because history and culture were the products of *libre albedrio,* that is, not of nature but of human will, the two Jesuits perceived history and culture as ever changing and evolving realities. It is the mind and will of men and women that weave the threads of human events into the fabric of culture. Those looms of life, like the looms of Penelope in *The Odyssey,* never stop. The arrival of the Spaniards, of the Jesuits, represented the introduction into America of new threads for a tapestry yet to be woven. In that new cycle of history, *libre albedrio* must also play the main role. The Indians should not be forced to accept Christianity, but rather should be educated to choose it by their own will. Both Acosta and Arriaga were convinced that such a process could not even begin until the European Jesuits would change, first by becoming fluent in the language of the Indians, and then by adapting to their culture. Acosta seemed to be saying to his fellow Jesuits that to Christianize the Indians one must begin by "Indianizing" the Christians.

Notes

1. Benjamin Keen, *Latin American Civilization,* 3d ed. (Boston: Houghton Mifflin Co., 1974), 1:178.

2. Lewis Hanke, *The Spanish Struggle for Justice in the Conquest of America* (Philadelphia: University of Pennsylvania Press, 1949).

3. Jose de Acosta, *De Christo Revelato* (Lyons, 1592), p. 86.

4. P. Francisco Mateos, ed., *Obras del Padre Jose de Acosta* (Madrid: Ediciones Atlas, 1954), p. 39.

5. Quoted by Mateos, *Obras del Padre,* p. xxxix.

6. Mateos, *Obras del Padre,* pp. 26–28.

7. Ibid., 4:429–42.

8. Ibid., p. 38. Leon Lopetegui, *El Padre Jose de Acosta y las Misiones* (Madrid: Consejo Superior de Investigaciones Cientificas, 1942), p. 259.

9. Mateos, *Obras del Padre,* p. 38.

10. Archivo Viceprovincia del Peru (hereafter AVP), *Libro de Congregaciones Ms.,* "Congregacion Provincial del Peru . . . 1576." See also Antonio de Egana, S.J., ed.,

Monumenta Peruana (hereafter *MP*) (Romae: Borgo Santo Spirito, 5, 1954–61) 2:54–102, 133–34, 214–17.

11. Ibid., 3:396–97. Luis Martin, *The Intellectual Conquest of Peru* (New York: Fordham University Press, 1968), pp. 48–50.

12. This is the judgment of the Peruvian scholar Raul Porras Barrenechea in the prologue to Diego Gonzalez Holguin, S.J., *Vocabulario de las Lengua General* (Lima: Universidad Mayor Nacional de San Marcos, 1952).

13. AVP, *Libro de Congregaciones Ms.,* "Congregatio habita Areguipae . . ." no. 4. *Libro de Instrucciones Ms.,* "Ordenes Varios de Ntro. Padre Tyrso Gonzalez," no. 3.

14. Luis Martin, *The Intellectual Conquest of Peru,* pp. 17–18; Egana, *MP* 1:387–400.

15. AVP, *Libro de Congregaciones Ms.,* "Congregacion Provincial del Peru . . . 1576." Latin version given by Egana, *MP* 2:54–102.

16. Luis Martin and JoAnn Pettus, *Scholars and Schools in Colonial Peru* (Dallas: Southern Methodist University School of Continuing Education, 1973), p. 129.

17. Ibid., pp. 127–29.

18. "Anua de la Provincia de Piru" in Mateos, *Obras del Padre,* pp. 290–302.

19. Father Pablo Joseph de Arriaga, *The Extirpation of Idolatry in Peru,* trans. and ed. L. Clark Keating (Lexington: University of Kentucky Press, 1968), pp. 7–8.

20. Ibid., p. 68.

21. Ibid., pp. 16–18, 99, 103, 141–42.

22. Martin and Pettus, *Scholars and Schools,* pp. 131–33.

23. Arriaga, *The Extirpation of Idolatry,* pp. 99, 142.

An Integrated Perspective: Music and Art in the Jesuit Reductions of Paraguay

T. FRANK KENNEDY, S.J.

On 9 July 1717, a convoy of three ships arrived in the port of Buenos Aires after a two-month voyage from Cadiz in Spain. There were more than fifty Jesuits scattered among the three ships, and at least one Jesuit on the expedition claimed that it was the largest Jesuit group ever to arrive at one time in the famous Reductions of the ancient Paraguay Province. Whether this is true or not, it would be difficult to argue that a more talented group of Jesuits had ever arrived previously.[1] Included among the missioners were Jesuits from Spain, Italy, Germany, and Switzerland, as well as one Jesuit from Greece and two from Peru. The long list is graced with names like Sigismund Aperger, a physician, often referred to as the Hippocrates of South America; Johann Wolf and Josef Schmidt, carpenters and architects; Bernard Nusdorffer and Manuel Querini, successive Provincial superiors and zealous defenders of the Indians' rights during the political machinations of the Treaty of Madrid;[2] and, finally, three Italian artists of the highest calibre: Domenico Zipoli, composer and organist; Gianbattista Primoli and Andrea Bianchi, both premier architects.[3]

If it is true, as some philosophers and social scientists claim, that men and women are symbolizers who by their actions tell each other and the world who they are and why they do what they do, then without doubt this particular group of Jesuits who arrived in the Rio Plata basin in the middle of 1717 propounded such an integrated world view and brought it with them to the New World to be shared particularly with the native peoples of what was then known as Paraguay. There have been numerous studies of various aspects of the Jesuit Reductions: politics and history, music, art and architecture, science and medicine, anthropology and economics.[4] All of these have described an exceedingly rich history extending over nearly two hundred years and have revealed a philosophy of man that is noble, partaking of the highest ideals of humankind. By focusing principally on the musical tradition of these ancient Reductions, this study attempts to discuss the integrated vision that the Society of Jesus brought to Paraguay through generations of men who volunteered for that mission, but especially through the very talented group that arrived in the La Plata region in July 1717. This focus has been sharpened by the rediscovery of some of the South American music of Italian-born Jesuit Domenico Zipoli and by its performance in perhaps the greatest of the Reduction churches, La Santisima Trinidad. The art, architecture, music, and even poetic-literary references have combined to reveal an astonishing sense of the unity of humankind—a true Christian humanism. Music, art, architecture, and poetry, then, are means of expression that gather people. The arts reach back to past visions of humankind's identity and reinterpret that past identity in a new way, holding the past and present in a dialectic and pointing toward a future expression that will evolve from the present one. Such was the integrated perspective of the Paraguay Reductions.

The musical tradition of the Reductions was as fascinating as it was outstanding. Almost from the beginning of the mission there were musicians who came to Paraguay. It was Manuel de Nóbrega, sent to Brazil by Saint Ignatius in 1549, who uttered the famous saying, slightly changed in the Hollywood movie *The Mission,* "Give me an orchestra of musicians and I will convert all the Indians for Christ."[5] At an early stage the missioners noticed how attracted the Indians were to both singing and instrumental music, and almost immediately they started the practice of chanting the tenets of Christian doctrine.[6] Once Indian townships were established, Jesuit superiors ordered the establishment of a music school in each town, where not only singing was taught, but also instruction in every type of musical instrument.[7] In 1793 Father Jose Peramás wrote in a biography of several Jesuits of Paraguay, "This missioner was persuaded that the music was working the effects on the soul of the Indian as the lyre of David on the furious Saul, and the lyre of Orpheus on the beasts of the desert, as the legendary myths relate."[8] The quotation interestingly manifests the type of artistic gathering that was common and indeed typical of the whole Jesuit enterprise in Paraguay. Through artistic means the Jesuits symbolized and fused themselves and the Indians with scripture and ancient mythology as well.

The more-than-two-hundred-year history of the Jesuit Reductions actually spans two periods of music history. The first period is characterized by the polyphonic music of the Renaissance, further colored by the Counter Reformation spirit and brought to the New World by the Society of Jesus. The second period, the era of the Baroque, is clearly seen in the Reductions with the arrival of Father Antonius Sepp, S.J., in 1691; the musical tradition continued to flourish throughout the Province for the next sixty-odd years until the Jesuit expulsion in 1767. The musical activity of the Italian-born composer Domenico Zipoli, S.J., (1688–1726) during this period helped to encourage, stabilize, and institutionalize the musical tradition within the various townships of the Paraguay Province.

As early as 1609, two years after the foundation of the Paraguay Province as a juridical entity, the Provincial, Diego de Torres, directed that the Indians learn doctrine by reading and by singing and that they should be taught to construct and play flutes.[9] Father Torres's successor, Pedro de Oñate described how the liturgy was celebrated in San Ignacio Misiones and referred to the beautiful singing of three choirs accompanied by the organ and a band of flageolets—the first such consort in the Province.[10] Wind instruments, including flutes, oboes, and bassoons, were evidently very popular with the Indians. Annual letters from the early years of the missions sent to Rome to describe their musical activities often referred to various wind instruments. These early years of the Province's history record the same stress on music that evidently occurred in other mission lands during the same period. The Franciscans in Mexico taught music to the Indians, as did the Jesuits in other parts of South America and in the Far East. Music was an apostolic instrument to aid conversion.[11] Professional musicians were few in the early years, but one professionally trained Jesuit arrived in Buenos Aires on 15 February 1617—Jean Vaisseau, S.J., from Tournai, Belgium. On the same boat was a Jesuit Brother, Louis Berger, S.J., from Amiens, France, who was described as a painter, musician, and professional dancer.[12] Many, indeed, of the Jesuits who made their way to Paraguay were polymaths. If they were artists, they were most often talented in several distinct fields: art, music, architecture, poetry, rhetoric, and dance.[13]

By 1628 there are references to all kinds of musical instruments. In a letter to the King of Spain, the Governor of the Rio de la Plata basin, Francisco de Céspedes wrote, "More than twenty Indians of San Ignacio Guazú skilled in organ, violin and other instruments have come here to Buenos Aires to perform the music and dances for the feast of the Blessed Sacrament."[14] But by the middle of the seventeenth century, San Ignacio and Loreto, where Father Vaisseau was stationed until his death in 1623, were not any more special in terms of musical activity than the other Reductions, with the exception of Nuestra Señora de los tres Magos at Yapeyú. Each of the towns had its own orchestra and chorus, but of the thirty Reductions that formed the townships of the Guaraní Indians, Yapeyú was the most important musical center by far. At midcentury there was a general conservatory there, where the more talented musicians were sent. At Yapeyú not only were the Indians taught more advanced techniques of musical composition and performance, but here they learned the art of instrument construction. Musical instruments from Yapeyú were sought after and sent all over the far-flung Paraguay Province. The high level of the musical life at Yapeyú can be credited to Antonius Sepp, S.J., an Austrian who studied music at the Imperial Court in Vienna and as a young priest between 1691 and 1695 supervised the formation of Yapeyú into a virtual academy of music.[15]

While Sepp's arrival vastly enriched the musical life of the Reductions and insured the important status of Yapeyú as the training and musical resource center for the whole of the Province, he also set the course of musical life in the townships for the rest of the period of Jesuit involvement with the Indians of Paraguay. Similarly, this kind of consolidation, evident on a musical level at

Yapeyú, also seemed to be happening in the artisan workshops of the Province. As the seventeenth century came to a close, the giant contributions of men like Vaisseau, Berger, and Sepp began to be evident in the development of the system within the Reductions that was now producing indigenous generations of artisans who created musical instruments, statues, ornate retables, and the like, to say nothing of the architectural splendors of the cathedral like churches of the Reductions. Gradually the work was organized around groups of artisans led by *alcaldes* (leaders), who were the most able men within a group.[16] This well-developed organization of the townships, which the Jesuit arrivals of 13 July 1717 encountered, displayed elements of city planning that encompassed all of the arts and dovetailed with Jesuit concerns for evangelization, in consonance with their motto, *Ad Majorem Dei Gloriam*. The culture of the Reductions, in itself transcultural, was the platform for the creation and dissemination of the music of Domenico Zipoli, the architectural wonders of Andrea Bianchi[17] and Gianbattista Primoli, and the countless processions, dramas, dances, and poetry of unknown Jesuit rhetoricians during the last years of Jesuit presence in Paraguay.

In the ruins of the Church of the Most Holy Trinity, La Santisima Trinidad, located about twenty-five miles from the present city of Encarnación in Paraguay, one can sense in stone the vision that motivated the last generation of Jesuits in the Reductions. The settlement was begun in 1706, but the design of the church is credited to Brother Gianbattista Primoli, S.J., (1673–1747), a Milanese and well known as an architect and professor of architecture when he arrived in Paraguay in 1717. Primoli died before the church was finished, so it is not completely his, but a partial signature appears on a stone that belongs to the immense stone polychrome pulpit that stood in and formed part of the nave. The church was fifty-eight meters long and eleven meters high, with three aisles, two sacristies, and an ornate belfry. It is evident that frescoes adorned the walls, as the stone frames are still part of the wall structures, while numerous sculptures of stone and wood decorated the walls and altars. The workshops of Trinidad were famous for their bell foundry and for the manufacture of organs and harpischords.[18] Although the grandeur of Trinidad is overwhelming, even in its ruined state, there are several details in the architecture pointing to the transcultural vision that was obviously part of this "event" that we call Trinidad. While Trinidad is much more like a European church that the Reduction churches of earlier years, there are significant moments that gather the Guaraní people as well as their Jesuit teachers and with them the heritage the Jesuits represented. Three of these "moments" will serve as examples: the sacristy doors, a gravestone in the floor of the church, and a frieze in the church that is dancing with angels playing musical instruments and swinging thuribles.

The doors[19] that link the sanctuary with the two sacristies are at once European Baroque and Guaraní Baroque in style.[20] If Baroque art "enters into the multiplicity of phenomena, the flux of things in their perpetual process of becoming," as some art historians suggest, and if the Baroque tries "to transcend the limits of matter and space by mobility of line and a restless striving after infinity,"[21] then a careful view of the Trinidad sacristy doors would note a correspondence with this concept of Baroque. In addition though, one must note not only a European statement of Baroque, qualities, but also a native one. The doors are intensely ornate, perhaps even "restless," but characterized by flora that are typically Paraguayan. They reflect the natural surroundings and communicate a *genius loci* thoroughly Paraguayan, Guaraní, and Baroque.

The gravestone in the floor of the church marked MEDIUM TENUEBE BEATI is both more curious, not to say mysterious, and more profound as another "moment" of gathering.[22] *Tenuebe* catches the eye first, because it is obviously bad Latin. If one looks carefully at the carving, one notices that the "r" of *tenuere* was changed to a "b." So the Latin form was originally correct, but then changed to its present incorrect form. Whoever carved the inscription had a sense that *tenuebe* was more Guaraní-sounding than the proper poetic form *tenuere*. After acknowledging the curiosity, one focuses on the meaning of the marking, and the mystery deepens. "The Blessed ones held the middle," is the literal translation of the inscription, and yet it seems a rather paltry sentiment to mark for memory the graves of the Fathers and Brothers who accomplished such incredible feats as the Church of Trinidad. Could it be that holding the middle way in all things—*modus in rebus*—was the key to the vision of the Reductions? The phrase *medium tenuere beati* has a poetic ring, resembling almost the measure, or rather half-measure, of a dactylic hexameter. Part of the answer to this mystery may lie in the opening line of the fifth book of Virgil's *Aeneid,* where Aeneas and his men leave Dido and the flames of Carthage to continue their journey to Latium: "Interea medium Aeneas iam classe tenebat / certus iter fluctusque atros Aquilone secabat."[23] Here, and only here, Virgil uses both *medium* and *tenere* idiomatically to mean to set out into the deep and to hold the course that is the duty of Aeneas and his companions—to found Rome. It could well be that this gravestone marking is a reference to Virgil and to those sentiments expressed in the opening of book 5. Blessed are they who persevere, who set out into the deep, who hold the course, who do the will of the gods. Put in Jesuit terms, blessed are they who do the will of the Father. That allusion from Virgil is possible, even probable, because of the classical training the Jesuits brought with them to Paraguay; it is even more likely since the quotation not only gathers classical antiquity into the ambit of Reduction life in a marvelous way, but helps reflect the missionary spirit in a more meaningful manner. It is not unlike the 1793 quotation from Father Peramás noted above, comparing the mission music's effects with those of the lyres of David and Orpheus. The gravestone then is a symbol that is transcultural, and one with various levels of meaning.

Perhaps the most delightful architectural view in the Church at Trinidad is the frieze of thirty angels playing musical instruments and swinging thuribles filled with incense.[24] From a musicological viewpoint the Indian angels, set in stone in high relief, are an iconographic historical record of the musical instruments that were used in the Reductions. There are violins, flutes, guitars, oboes, flageolets, maracas, and harps. There is even a charming relief of a positive organ, with one angel playing the instrument and the other pumping the bellows. That particular image reconfirms the research of musicologists who have suggested that the organs of the New World were often of Spanish origin, and lacking in pedalboards.[25] What appears to be a single manual, Italian harpsichord also appears on the frieze with an angel harpsichordist merrily performing. The angels in relief also represent something more than a historical record. There is no doubt, especially since the restoration of Trinidad that took place after 1981, that the angels are "Indian" angels, not Italian *putti* or European angels of any description. While Trinidad in many respects represents a stage of building that is even more European in inspiration than previous constructions, the decoration and blending is unmistakable. The statement that Trinidad makes is a statement about European Christian and cultural values, but one that happily meets and incorporates the myth and ritual of the Guaraní. Like the Middle Ages, then, the sacred and the secular blend in harmony so that "transcendent meaning affects everything."[26]

The iconography of the musical instruments suggests that music may have been the string through time that connected, and in some manner held together, this vision of life that the Jesuits helped themselves and the Guaraní discover and appropriate. In a sense, listening to music is akin to hearing your life pass before you, and music seems to have a special ability, when used in conjunction with the other arts, to define, organize, and symbolize the unity of human experience on a very deep level. According to archive records music and dance were so incorporated into the everyday world of the Guaraní that the Indians began their workday schedules in the fields accompanied by drums and flutes.[27] The evangelization of the Guaraní was accomplished partially through art and music that was composed in the full spirit of the Counter Reformation, which gathered all the Baroque techniques used in Europe, but also created in the Reductions a new interpretation of the medieval monastic concept of the *Opus Dei,* where not only was time marked and oriented toward living in the presence of God, but all things and events within time revealed that transcultural identity of humans which is the image of God.

Music, then, holds a special place in the history of the Reductions. With the arrival of Domenico Zipoli in July 1717 the Reductions procured a musician who as a composer and performer was the musical equivalent of the architects and colleagues Primoli and Bianchi who accompanied him on the voyage from Cadiz. Born 17 October 1688 at Prato, very near Florence, the young Zipoli studied organ and music theory with Giovanni Francesco

Becatelli before moving first to Florence, and then to Naples in 1708 to study with the famous Alessandro Scarlatti. Domenico stayed only a year in Naples, and many have speculated why he studied for so short a period with the great Scarlatti. The eighteenth-century music theorist Padre G. B. Martini (1706–84) wrote that it was "on account of strong differences of opinion."[28] Whatever the case, in 1709 Zipoli was in Bologna studying with the monk Felice Lavinio Vanucci, and by 1710 was in Rome studying with the renowned composer and theorist Bernardo Pasquini. From 1711 until his departure for Seville to enter the Society of Jesus in July 1716, Zipoli was a significant figure in Roman musical circles. Through two oratorios, "Oratorio in honor of Saint Anthony of Padua" and "Oratorio in honor of Saint Catherine, Virgin and Martyr," he became associated both with Santa Maria in Vallicella, the famous church of the Oratory of Saint Philip Neri, and with San Girolamo della Carità, perhaps Rome's second most noted site for oratorio performance.[29] In 1715 Zipoli became organist and choirmaster for the Church of the Gesù, but remained in that post only until the middle of 1716. In addition to the two oratorios, Zipoli published a set of Vesper Psalms, a Mass for the Feast of San Carlo, and his most famous work—the two-volume *Sonate d'Intavolatura per Organo e Cimbalo* of January 1716.

Domenico Zipoli arrived in Buenos Aires in July 1717 and, after a short rest period, moved to the Jesuit house of studies in Cordoba, where he was to remain for the rest of his short life, dying in January 1726. Annual letters written to the Jesuit Curia in Rome, as well as diaries and histories of the period, often mentioned Zipoli and the great work that he accomplished during his years in Cordoba; but very little of his music from the New World seemed to have survived. Some years ago Professor Robert Stevenson of the Music Department at the University of California at Los Angeles discovered the *Mass in F* by Zipoli in the National Archives of Bolivia in Sucre, formerly the archives of the Cathedral.[30] Professor Samuel Claro of the Catholic University of Santiago, Chile also discovered some of Zipoli's music in a remote corner of Bolivia—the former Reduction of San Ignacio, among the Moxos Indians.[31] A dedicated Zipoli scholar, Professor Francisco Curt Lange of the National Library of Caracas, has published much of the archival research concerning Zipoli and has noted several references to existing scores of Zipoli's music.[32] An important moment in recent Zipoli scholarship occurred in the summer of 1986. A cache of manuscripts numbering about five thousand pages as discovered in Concepción, Bolivia, dating to the era of the Reductions. While most of the manuscripts are anonymous, a certain number of them are ascribed to Zipoli, and others that are anonymous are certainly by him as well.[33]

To date, the following works in the Concepción Collection have been attributed to, or recognized as, the music of Domenico Zipoli: the Divine Office invitatory *Domine ad adiuvandum me;* the Confitebor, Psalm 110; the *Beatus Vir,* Psalm 111; the *Laudate Pueri,* Psalm 112; the *Laudate Domi-*

num, Psalm 116; the Marian hymn *Ave Maris Stella;* the eucharistic hymn *Tantum Ergo;* the *Mass in F,* referred to in the Concepción Collection as the *Mass of the Holy Apostles;* the *Mass of Saint Ignatius;* a second setting of the *Laudate Dominum;* an instrumental piece entitled *Introducción;* and several pieces from the *Sonate d'Intavolatura,* published first in Rome in 1716—the *Canzona in C,* the *Canzona in F,* the *Offertorio in C,* and the *Partita in C* (partially combined with his *Suite in C*). The collection is not well preserved. Not all the part books have survived, and so some of these pieces are whole and others are not. The three pieces that were performed at the 1990 conference, Casassa—the *Beatus Vir, Laudate Dominum,* and *Tantum Ergo*—are more or less whole. Some reconstruction of the *Tantum Ergo* has been necessary, but, as this piece is the same one that Samuel Claro discovered among the Moxos, his score has facilitated a reconstruction. The rest of the reconstruction has been necessary because of the poor condition of the manuscripts, often worm-eaten.

The style of Zipoli's choral music is similar to other Italian Baroque composers of the period, such as Alessandro Scarlatti or Antonio Vivaldi. The music is governed by the basso continuo, the ever present emphasis on the harmonic motion within the music represented by the effective underpinning of that motion by the harpsichord. At the same time the musical texture is principally polyphonic, where a number of musical lines compete for the attention of the listener's ear in a very delightful cavalcade of sound. A very common compositional procedure during the Baroque era, the *ritornello,* where a recognizable section of musical material is repeated in whole or in part throughout the structure of a piece to give it a sense of unity, is evident in these pieces. Perhaps this form is most clearly heard in the *Beatus Vir,* which is the longest of the three pieces, but also it is quite clear in the *Laudate Dominum.* Without calling attention to itself, the *ritornello* form created a sense of unity that reflected in part the total fabric of meaning for Reduction life. The meaning of the music, which is partially created by the sense of form that the listener appropriates throughout the use of memory as the musical work unfolds, reinforces the meaning that the art, architecture, and poetry have created within a particular space, like the Reduction Church of Trinidad. In his article on Domenico Zipoli for the *New Grove Dictionary of Music and Musicians,* Professor Robert Stevenson wrote of the beauty of Zipoli's music and suggested that Zipoli was careful in "timing his modulations exquisitely, never belaboring any imitative points, making of conciseness a cardinal virtue, and writing tunes instead of dry contrapuntal lines."[34] This music forms part of a story that has been told by all of the arts of the Paraguay Reductions.

While there are no particularly Indian elements in the music of Zipoli that would compare with the Indian faces of the angels and statuary of Trinidad— for his music belongs squarely to the glorious sound of the Italian Baroque— could it be that music, more easily than other arts, can cross the cultural lines that separate people and can instead create understanding?[35] Antonio Sepp introduced the harp to Paraguay, and today it is the national instrument. Is this an example of acculturation or of cultural imposition? In the art of music the Jesuits were definitely more givers than receivers and in that sense were paternalistic. An ethnomusicologist might lament this fact, but, until a thorough and complete study of the music of Concepción is finished, along with a study of the other great Latin American collections of music from the Colonial era, we cannot make a final judgement. The Indians were certainly not kept *in statu pupillari,* as the growth and development of the generations of artisans in the Reductions have clearly shown. In addition, there are many letters written to the Spanish governor by the *caciques* (leaders) of the seven Reductions evacuated by the Treaty of Madrid in 1750 that reveal a maturity and independence of mind that belie the charge of paternalism. Several key passages are as follows:

> Lord Governor: we have received your letter but cannot believe that these are the words of our King. For they go against what King Philip V promised us: that if we are faithful vassals and defend his land, he will never surrender it to another king. The king, our king, cannot break his promise made to our forefathers and to us. . . . We are all creatures of one and the same God. Can it be that He loves Spaniards more than us Indians? Why, then, would he want to deprive us of our lands and homes? . . . Even wild animals love their dens and attack anything and anyone that threatens them. How much more do we Christians love the town God has given us and our great, beautiful church, all built of stone by our own hands and sweat. . . . In this land of ours have died our holy teachers, priests who wore themselves out for us and who suffered so much for God and His love. Surely, if the present king understood all this he would not want us to leave our land, but would be full of anger against those who do. . . . We do not want war. But if war comes, trusting in Jesus Christ we say: Let's save our lives, our lands, all our property! If God wills that we die, then this is the land where we were born and baptized and where we grew up. Only here do we wish to die. And you, Lord Governor, will pay for this eternally in hell![36]

What then is the ultimate meaning of this story, a story that represents the noblest aspirations of mankind? If we allow the various modes of Reduction art to speak to us, the ultimate meaning of this story resides in the linking of all people of all periods with one another in a transcendent reality.

Notes

1. I am indebted and immensely grateful to my mentor and colleague Clement J. McNaspy, S.J., of Loyola University in New Orleans for his close collaboration, valuable advice, and suggestions throughout our study of this material. Guillermo Furlong, S.J., *Arquitectos Argentinos durante la dominacion hispanica* (Buenos Aires, 1946), 149.
2. For the best study of the Treaty of Madrid see Wilhelm Kratz, S.J., *El Tratado*

Hispano Portugues de Limites de 1750 y sus consecuencias (Rome: Jesuit Historical Institute, 1954).

3. In the Reductions Bianchi was known as Andrés Blanqui. See Furlong, *Arquitectos,* 149.

4. For a general bibliographic survey see Philip Caraman, S.J., *The Lost Paradise: The Jesuit Republic in South America* (New York: The Seabury Press, 1976). See also Guillermo Furlong, S.J., *Misiones y sus pueblos de Guaranies* (Posadas, Argentina, 1978).

5. Guillermo Furlong, S.J., *Musicos Argentinos durante la dominacion hispanica* (Buenos Aires, 1945), 45.

6. The chanting of Christian doctrine was not a new invention, but seemingly a standard Counter Reformation practice of the Jesuits in Europe. See T. Frank Kennedy, S.J., "Jesuits and Music: Reconsidering the Early Years," *Studi Musicali* 17 (1988): 81–83.

7. Furlong, *Musicos,* 47.

8. Furlong, *Misiones,* 576.

9. Furlong, *Musicos,* 52.

10. Ibid., 53.

11. Robert Stevenson, *Latin American Colonial Music Anthology* (Washington, D.C.: General Secretariat, Organization of American States); 1975) and Gerard Béhague, *Music in Latin America: An Introduction* (Englewood Cliffs, N.J.: Prentice Hall, 1979). For a preliminary discussion of how Jesuits used music in mission lands see Thomas D. Culley, S.J., and Clement J. McNaspy, S.J., "Music and the Early Jesuits (1540–1565)," *Archivum Historicum Societatis Jesu,* 40 (1971): 213–45.

12. Furlong, *Musicos,* 58, 60.

13. The Jesuit historian José Cardiel, writing from Europe after the expulsion of 1767, mentions the educational spirit that prompted the Jesuits to teach the best students to read in their own language, in Spanish, and in Latin. At the same time they learned music and dancing in order to celebrate the holy days. See Pablo Hernandez, S.J., *Declaracion de la verdad, obra inedita del P. José Cardiel* (Buenos Aires, 1900), 276.

14. Ibid., 53. For a description of the dances of the Blessed Sacrament, see n. 70, p. 178, taken from Francisco Xarque, *Insignes Missioneros* (Pamplona, 1687), 344–46. The incensing of the Blessed Sacrament and the multiple genuflections that formed part of the dances were all performed in time with the music.

15. Artur Rabuske, S.J., *P. Antônio Sepp, S.J., O Gênio das Reduções Guaranís* (São Leopoldo, Brazil, 1979), 41.

16. Josefina Plá, "The Missionary Workshops (1609–1767), Organization and Operation, Labor and Achievements," *Paradise Lost: The Jesuits and the Guaraní, South American Missions 1609–1767* (New York: Americas Society, 1988). See sections 6 and 7.

17. See Clement McNaspy's interview with Dalmacio Sobron, S.J., in *The National Jesuit News* (May, 1983), 16. In that interview Father Sobron discusses his unpublished doctoral dissertation from the University of Rome on Andrea Bianchi. The most astonishing and least known fact about the great Jesuit architect is his designs were used to complete the eighteenth-century restoration of the Basilica of Saint John Lateran in Rome after the death of Borromini.

18. Paul Frings and Josef Übelmesser, *Paracuaria: Die Kunstschätze des Jesuitenstaats in Paraguay* (Mainz: Matthias-Grünewald-Verlag, 1982), 108.

19. See figure 1.

20. Clement J. McNaspy, S.J., *Lost Cities of Paraguay* (Chicago: Loyola Press, 1982), 77.

21. Ibid., 136.

22. See figure 2.

23. "Aeneas and his fleet were now far out to sea. He set course resolutely and ploughed through waves ruffled to black by a northerly wind," W. F. Jackson Knight, trans., *The Aeneid* by Virgil (New York: Penguin, 1980), 119.

24. See figures 3 through 7.

25. See Peter Williams, "Organ," *The New Grove Dictionary of Music and Musicians,* (London: Macmillan, 1980), 13: 750–53.

26. Ramón Gutiérrez, "The Jesuit Missions: City Planning, Architecture and Art, Evangelization and the Baroque," in *Paradise Lost: The Jesuits and the Guaraní, South American Missions, 1609–1767* (New York: Americas Society, 1988), 5.

27. Ibid., 5.

28. Luigi Fernando Tagliavini, ed., *Sonate d'Intravolatura per organo e cimbalo,* 2 vols. (Heidelberg: Süddeutscher Musikverlag, 1957).

29. For a history of the oratorio in Italy see Howard Smither, *A History of the Oratorio, Vol. 1: The Oratorio in the Baroque Era, Italy, Vienna, Paris* (Chapel Hill, 1977).

30. For a modern edition of the work, edited by Professor Stevenson, see the Inter-American Music Review 19, no. 2 (1988): 35–89.

31. Samuel Claro, "La música en las misiones jesuitas de Moxos," *Revista Musical Chilena* 17, no. 108 (1969): 22–30.

32. See especially "Domenico Zipoli: storia di una riscoperta," *Nuova Rivista Musicale Italiana* 19, no. 2 (1985): 203–26.

33. See T. Frank Kennedy, S.J., "Colonial Music from the Episcopal Archive of Concepción, Bolivia," *Latin American Music Review* 9, no. 1 (1988).

34. Robert Stevenson, "Domenico Zipoli," *The New Grove Dictionary of Music and Musicians,* (London: Macmillan, 1980), 20: 696–697. Also quoted in McNaspy, S.J., *Lost Cities,* 132.

35. Some of these ideas about meaning in music are discussed in a more thorough and technical manner in a provocative and thoughtful book by Jonathan D. Kramer, *The Time of Music, New Meanings, New Temporalities, New Listening Strategies* (New York: Schirmer Books, 1988).

36. Francisco Mateos, "Cartas de Indios Cristianos del Paraguay," Missionalia Hispanica (Madrid, 1949), 547–72. The translation here is by Clement J. McNaspy, S.J.

Figure 1

Figure 2

Figure 3

Figure 4

Figure 5

Figure 6

Figure 7

Kino: On People and Places

CHARLES W. POLZER, S.J.

This essay will not reach stimulating and stratospheric heights because history is forever grounded in dirt and documents. It is not my purpose to expound here on theories of Jesuit education or to delve into the inner psychomechanics of I-Thou, Self, or the role of imagination in mysticism. Since this volume is focused on Jesuit education, I have questioned the propriety of my essay here as an historian of the Jesuit missions of northern New Spain because those missions did not embody "Jesuit education" in any formal sense—that is, as educational institutions. Yet in a very real way the Jesuit missions at the time of Padre Kino were deeply involved in the process of education, which occurred at a much more primary level due to the nature of the contacts with the native peoples of northwestern New Spain.

Before I deal with the life and personal characteristics of Padre Eusebio Francisco Kino, it would be beneficial to probe into the meaning of "mission," which has become so badly stereotyped today that few people really have a correct understanding of what a mission was historically or theologically. For some, the concept of a mission is almost sacrosanct—the idea of foreign service, total sacrifice, but as an activity closely linked to the Church and not the State. The modern concept of mission, molded by years of pious propaganda, is forced upon the missions of history so that their final interpretation is as ill-fitting as a badly cast bicuspid. Our first task is to demythologize the concept of mission, to "unromanticize" it, because life in those missions was a tremendously difficult task.

Let me digress a moment to become somewhat Scriptural. At the end of His mission on earth, Christ was reputed to have said to His disciples, "Go forth and teach all nations." And we quickly tumble on, "Baptizing them in the name of the Father, the Son, and the Holy Spirit." I have never been terribly certain that Christ came up with that particular doxology, but there is no doubt that He said, "Go forth and teach—all nations." It was easy for Christ to tell His followers to teach others what He Himself had taught them. Unfortunately, in the twentieth century, and probably in the twenty-first, twenty-second, and beyond, we are still trying to interpret that directive in terms of Magisterium, in terms of a doctrine, in terms of ascetical practices. Those words fall so quickly from our lips that I wonder if we ever really contemplate their meaning. We insist that we are going to involve ourselves in Faith and Justice; we never ask ourselves what that Faith is. When we attempt to define Faith, we submit a list of decrees, a set of propositions that we affirm, a gaggle of assertions that must be taught. We carefully construct an unassailable, institutional framework of principles that are really quite far removed from the all-embracing simplicity of Christ's faith. In working on the history of the Society of Jesus and especially its early missions, I have learned that its missionaries were not preoccupied with questions of orthodoxy and refinements of the Magisterium. They were much more radical; they were really doing what Christ asked us to do—that is, to teach the Way, to teach Christian living. They were not worried about making certain that their neophytes were doctrinally precise. As a matter of fact most converts had no clue about what they were being taught—at least in the beginning.

These observations compel one to become critical about what the mission of a missionary is, what the mission of the Church is, what the mission that Christ has given is—to those who were to follow Him and teach as He did. When I look at the life of Padre Kino and the other missionaries with him, this is precisely what I see. This may be a misreading, a misinterpretation, but I do not think so. When Christ said, "Go and teach all nations," we were thrust on a course of contacting peoples that would seek in some way to transform them. But the question is, what do you transform? Are people to be transformed according to what they think? Or how they act? Or perhaps both? What is the interaction to be expected? We can even more basically ask: what is the goal of mission? What is the final causality? Sometimes a nominalistic answer is offered: "Well, one converts them from being pagan to being Christian, to being believers in Christ, obviously." But how do you know there has been conversion? Here we find ourselves confronted with the same question that Saint John asked: how do you know they are Christians? And he answered better than anyone, ever—better than Bishops, councils, congregations, or encyclicals. "You shall know them by their love." For Saint John, it was not a question of what they thought; it was a question of what they did. It was a question of interpersonal conduct. It was a question of outreach in a sense of giving, in a sense of community, in a sense of sharing. In fact, in the earliest days of the Church, its members were not known as "Christians," but as "Followers of the Way." They were doers, although we can presume they were not exactly inept at theology either.

If this is historically accurate, then a mission really attempts to reach out to others and asks for *metanoia,* a change of life; this clearly becomes the goal and option of our contact. Our educational efforts, then, focus on bringing this change about, and we naturally attempt to shore our efforts up with rational argument and example. Put yourselves in the shoes, boots perhaps, of a man like Padre Kino, who was young, vital, and a dreamer of almost impossible dreams, somewhat like Don Quixote—well, not exactly, because Kino came from the Italian Tyrol and not La Mancha. Imagine yourself, like Kino, being sent to the New World to contact people whose language you do not speak. He was contacting people who did not understand his language either. How do you educate? How do you communicate? What can you do under these circumstances to change their lives? How can you preach or teach *metanoia*? This is not an easy task, but this is what the foreign missionary faced. He came without tools to communicate and was expected to construct those very tools. Arriving in a totally foreign culture, bereft of the means of communication, he was expected to transform native peoples from being pagans to being Christians. He was to build Christian community among peoples whose concept of God bore little resemblance to the Hellenic biases of Christian dogma. This was no mean feat. But this is exactly what a man like Padre Kino set out to accomplish. So when we look at the problematic situation that faced Jesuit missions world-wide, we can only be amazed at their foolhardy faith—and even more at God's grace-ous generosity.

In my own historical work I have seldom concentrated on the Jesuit missions of the Orient; I have spent my time studying missions in the New World—the Western hemisphere—particularly North America. One of the elements that has caught my attention is the enormous discrepancy between the cultural presuppositions of Western culture and those of the Americas. One sees that the Western mind has considered itself far advanced over these "primitive, savage, backward, unenlightened, and dull peoples." But when one pays honest attention to Indian cultures, none of these judgments rings true. Perhaps the cultures of the Americas did not display the kinds of scientific sophistication with which we credit ourselves, but the Indians' knowledge and integration of nature with their way of life, with their sense of morality, were remarkable. As a matter of fact, it is only today that the West is coming to understand the immense sacredness of nature that cries for respect, a respect that long since characterized Indian cultures in the New World—which many Christians deigned to call paganism. Interestingly enough, Indian peoples began to contact Christianity through the resonances of their natural beliefs—not, for heaven's sake, with the Trinity. As a matter of fact, in the numerology of most Indian tribes the primacy of three is unacceptable. Consider the Trinitarian sign of the cross: "In the name of Father, and of the Son, and of the Holy Spirit." This was acceptable not because it enumerated the Persons of the Holy Trinity, but because the sign was made in the *four* cardinal directions, a wholly appropriate symbol. This was the summation of God's presence in all the world. Obviously, these Christians understood something correctly and deserved to be listened to. The point I wish to emphasize here is that the penchant to impose our European concepts requires an ability to communicate far in excess of language alone. We seldom reflect that the Church's Magisterium is buried in Judeo-Hellenic presuppositions that cloak the teachings of Christ in cultural clothing that is out of style in other parts of the world.

We have touched on the idea of the Trinity, but there are other difficult concepts that shape our dogma. Take a case that puzzled Padre Kino when he was in Baja California—how to teach the Resurrection. Not knowing any words in the Pericue vocabulary to express the idea, Kino reverted to an old childhood trick of stunning a fly. He caught a fly and stunned it with a clap of air in the hollow of his hand. The Indians viewed the apparently dead fly, and, when it revived, they uttered an exclamation which Kino took to be their word for resurrection—and so it became a part of their creed. What this example suggests is the irony that faced every missionary who came from Europe. They were sophisticated, college-educated men from the universities; they were theologians, mathematicians, scientists, cartographers, physicists, and agriculturalists. With all their erudition they were coming into direct contact with peoples who lived very simple, basic, and confined lives. Daily they faced the problem of communicating the complexities of their knowledge to people who could only absorb so much at any one time. One is immediately reminded of the example in "The Gods Must be Crazy II" when the Bushman laments that the Heavy People's heroine is illiterate because she cannot read signs in the sand. These were wholly different cultures scraping against each other in the darkness of mutual ignorance. One can expect, then, that only so much will be able to be communicated and absorbed over any given period of time.

What is it that the missionary must teach? What are the basics? Are they the rudiments of doctrine? Are they the ABCs of the Magisterium? Are these the propositions of the Faith? Is this a question of knowledge or something more? I suggest the issue is a holistic one and that the task of the missionary was not, and is not, that of communicating knowledge alone. The missionary's task is one of sharing knowledge, the basic appraisal of nature, and the fundamental appreciation of peoples, their interaction, and their relationships. After all, I must recognize, no matter who I am, what culture I represent, what skin color I have, what bone structure I have, that that "other" out there is a person like me. If that is not seen or accepted, we are locked into a racism of the most destructive kind. The missionary was someone who reached out to the Indian peoples as persons; he tried to move them to discover a better vision of themselves. Often the missionary learned as much from the Indian with whom he worked as he taught them. There is a beauty and wisdom that exists among communities of people that has to be respected. Sometimes we, as communities of people, no matter what may be our origins, can concoct systems that are unjust and unwise. It is then that we must sit down among ourselves to interact and reconcile our aberrations so that we can devise something more beneficial to all. To impose law, morality, and authority on another community solely from the outside is pious folly. Such a process does not create, invite, or engender *metanoia* in anyone. *Metanoia* is an interchange, a complete transformation of the person. When we look at the teachings of the Church, when we review the paradigms of doctrine, they are only valid as metaphors that reinforce, that communicate some richer, higher notion to people who are on a quest for truth, understanding, and ultimately love.

But enough of abstract reflections. Let us return to the concrete historical realities of Padre Kino. The Jesuit missions of northwestern New Spain are so familiar to me now that I often forget how little they are known to a California audience, and most especially the missionaries themselves. Eusebio Kino [Chini] was born in Segno in the Italian Tyrol in 1645. He was educated at the Jesuit colleges of Trento and Hall. When he was finishing his studies, he fell seriously ill and vowed to enter the Society of Jesus if he should recover. Recover he did, and he added the name of Francis in gratitude to his special patron, Xavier. He was destined to spend his life in the missions of New Spain until his death in Magdalena, Sonora, in 1711.

Kino was indisputably one of those highly sophisticated, highly educated men of his time. In 1676 he was invited by the Duke of Bavaria to take a chair of mathematics at Ingolstadt. But nearly at the same time he was to accept a "tenure-track" position in the German university system, he received word from Giovanni Paolo Oliva, Father General of the Society of Jesus, that his petitions for an assignment to the missions were granted and that he was being sent to the missions of the Spanish Crown. Kino was thrilled because the new assignment fulfilled a childhood dream of following in the footsteps of his Tyrolese cousin, Martino Martini, a renowned Jesuit missionary to China.

Of course, Kino's highest hope was for an assignment to China; he had even rejoiced when his college room had an eastern exposure. Since he was a Jesuit in the Upper German Province, he came under the political jurisdiction of the Hapsburgs, which meant that he would be sent to the Spanish missions. This presented a problem because he would have to go East by going West through New Spain and the Philippines. And as luck would have it, during the transatlantic crossing he lost a bet with Antonio Kerschpamer, his companion from Germany. It was Kerschpamer who would go on to the Orient, and Kino would have to remain humbly behind to seek his fortunes in America.

Kino had been delayed in leaving Spain. First, by just missing the fleet; second, by experiencing shipwreck in the Bay of Cádiz; third, by seeing his passport expire. During the year he spent in Spain, he witnessed a bright comet that caused much comment in Europe, and, on arriving in New Spain, Kino was quickly engaged in a war of words with Carlos Sigüenza y Gongora, a savant of the new sciences. They battled over the physical influence of the comet, which Kino held responsible for plagues and illnesses that had spread over Europe in 1680. Kino's arrival in New Spain in 1681 coincided with the Viceroy's need for a cosmographer to accompany a major colonizing expedition to the Californias under the direction of Don Isidro Atondo y Antillón, the Governor of Sinaloa.

The expedition set sail in January 1683 for the Bay of La Paz on the southeastern coast. Kino was named the Rector of the new missions and was accompanied by Padre Matias Goñi; the task before them was almost overwhelming. Although the welfare of the Guaicuro Indians was foremost in the minds of Kino and Goñi, the terrain was inhospitable and progress very slow. As Royal Cosmographer, Kino remained very much the scientist and mathematician, observer, empiricist, and mapmaker. With all of that, however, he was still a seeker of the truth who applied all he knew to the world around him; he observed and respected the people with whom he dealt. The Indians saw this and received him with loving trust. But there was a serious problem lurking in the expedition, which Kino's lack of experience led him to overlook. All human relations were being affected by Spanish policies harshly applied by military men for personal gain. One tragic incident must be mentioned.

A readily believed rumor had spread about the murder of a mulatto drummer boy, and so when a band of Guaicuro Indians wandered into the Spanish camp at La Paz, they were invited to a generous meal where reconciliation was the theme. Atondo then ordered the soldiers to fire a small cannon into their midst. Three men lay dead and the others, who were wounded, fled. The Spaniards had their day, but soon war clouds, driven by the traditional laws of vengeance, loomed over the fragile beach head. Since the supply ships had returned to the mainland, there was no avenue of escape for the expedition. Cut off from the interior by gathering bands of Indians, desperation grew in the Spanish camp. But as the Indians massed to attack, the sails of the mainland ships pushed over the horizon. The survivors frantically paddled away in fragile canoes and left the missionary efforts of Kino and Goñi in shambles.

The Atondo expedition was a major effort, and so the failure at La Paz could not be allowed to be the last attempt. The expedition regrouped, resupplied, and returned to California, but this time two hundred miles north, immediately east of the Gigantea Mountains. A suitable defensive site was found along the high banks of the Río San Bruno where a low stone fortification was built. Again, Kino and Goñi tried mightily to evangelize a completely new Indian nation; the task was more gigantic than the mountains that towered over the villages. This time the effort met with somewhat greater success, especially in the exploration of the "island"—Kino was able to reach the Pacific shores by New Year's day, 1685. But drought gripped the fragile community, and Atondo ordered the final abandonment of the *real*; it was all over for Spain and California—except in the mind and heart of Padre Kino, who would never accept leaving the destitute Indian peoples.

Reading about Kino's feats of exploration and mapping, one might be drawn to the erroneous conclusion that he would have been a more effective missionary if he had engaged in building chapels and teaching catechism in a protected compound. On the contrary, Kino was always on the trail living with and learning about the people he had come to serve. He rode among the cactus and elephant trees and sat on the sprawling roots of the strangler fig, just as his neophytes did. He really began to absorb the Indian way of life by being in the open with the Indians; this was the door to understanding them—the door to their culture, the door to their theology. He found it very early on and opened it wide, which explains why he was always so effective with various Indian nations.

With Atondo's decision to leave California Padre Kino was left with a difficult decision because he was still charged with the missionary care of those people. He yearned to return to the barren and desolate island to keep "the most abandoned peoples on earth"—a possible precursor to today's preferential option for the poor. Kino was like most of his Jesuit companions of the time; they did not talk and speculate about apostolates; they acted. They lived in the most austere circumstances imaginable, and yet they stood back, laughed, and made the most of impossible situations. They were always trying to make the lives of the persons they served better than they found them. Although Kino gained permission to return, finances and material assistance dried up so completely that he had to accept a change in assignment—this time to the untested mission field of the Pimería Alta, the area of modern day Sonora and Arizona.

The Pimas Altas were a nation that had not been evangelized, except for an occasional contact by a missionary accompanied by a military patrol. No one had yet lived and worked among them, and so it was a new apostolate. However, it was not unspoiled, because the Spaniards had been raiding Piman villages for nearly two decades to capture pagan prisoners to enslave in the mines in the foothills of the Sierra Madre. The general assessment was that the Pimas were lazy, unreliable, and hostile; it was better to aggravate them to the point of skirmishes so that prisoners could be justifiably taken. Slavery, to be sure, was not openly permitted; Indians could not be rounded up like so many wild cattle. But the enslavement of a nonbeliever was permissible, following hostile action.

When Padre Kino arrived in the Pimería Alta in March 1687, he carried with him a recent *cédula* (decree) of the King that proclaimed freedom from slavery or servile labor for any Indian for twenty years if he accepted Christianity. Given the recent history, that was a most attractive edict. While it is clear that this *cédula* acted as a powerful incentive to conversion, one must not lose sight of the fact that Kino used it less for making converts than to establish his clear intent to protect Indian peoples in all their rights—which is exactly what he proceeded to do throughout his missionary career. He moved freely among the desert villages, making friends of leaders and learning the language. The rumor that Kino was not able to speak the Piman language is sheer nonsense. I suspect he talked with a heavy German-Spanish accent, but it is very clear he communicated well with all the desert peoples he met.

By the way, Jesuit missionaries did not ride over the horizon to discover some idyllic site for a church, there to erect a bell and call the Indians to their chapel on a hill. Such romantic nonsense, unfortunately, still resides in the modern mind, untrammeled by fact or reason. Missionaries rode into established Indian towns; they built small ramadas in the villages; they lived and worked among the Indians all the time. They did not enter a country with a military escort to round up Indians, to tie them up in a mission compound like mustangs in a corral. As a matter of fact, Jesuit missionaries in northwest New Spain—as in other areas of the world—were often accused of "going native." They were so isolated and so involved with native languages that they often lost their proficiency in Spanish.

During Kino's twenty-four years in the Pimería Alta, he established twenty-seven missions and visitas, many of which have survived to this day as desert communities. Some have crumbled and succumbed to changes in trade routes due to the coming of the railroads and high-speed highways; some, like San Xavier del Bac near Tucson, have undergone major architectural changes, but the memory of Kino remains strong and vibrant.

Do not be misled by Kino's fervor in expanding the mission frontier in his charge. He was not a brick-and-mortar cleric, but a missionary on the move. He was not dubbed "the Padre on Horseback" by Herbert E. Bolton for lack of a better description. No, he recognized in the Pima Alta a vigorous, docile, industrious, and loyal people. He also saw that the religious and economic integration of this whole region could become the springboard for a return to California, whose abandoned peoples he never forgot. But any return would require a solid support base. So all of Kino's actions were geared to create the kind of interactive communities that would be able to cope with the unpredictable vagaries of weather and harvests. As he wove the scattered rancherías together, he spent days and weeks in the saddle. It was a commonplace for Kino to ride thirty miles and more every day. He would be received with crosses and arches of flowers in all the villages he visited. Often arriving at night, he sat before a small mesquite fire under the brilliant stars of the desert sky. He spoke of sun, moon, and stars; he drew world maps in the dirt to explain the relations of peoples and nations. He related his teachings to the things of nature that they understood and respected because he knew this was the door to deeper truths. There have been many missionaries whose mysterious piety has driven them to build compounds and chapels into which "converts" were herded to see Jesus in a draped box. But this was not Kino. He was a man of the outdoors; he built splendid churches only as symbols of community, as meeting places. But he found God everywhere, just as the Indians did. Let the high winds of the Magisterium blow where they will; Kino remained humble on the earth with his eyes to the heavens.

Kino's success with the Pimas threatened failure with the colonials who witnessed their labor pool diminishing as the missions expanded. Within three years of his arrival rumors circulated that Kino was a catastrophe; the

Provincial even dispatched a special visitor to determine if the missions should be closed. The inspection was conducted by Juan María Salvatierra, an Italian Jesuit from Milan who knew Indian dialects similar to those of the Pimería. Salvatierra was amazed by the vigorous mission system he found. Not only did he recognize the importance of Kino's accomplishments, but he also caught Kino's enthusiasm for integrating the mainland missions for a return to the Californias.

Salvatierra returned to Mexico City with a glowing report on the new missions of the northwest, and more men were found to assist Kino in their development. This led to another important incident that affected the course of history. One of the young men sent to help Kino was Francisco Javier Saeta, a Sicilian. He had hardly been on the mission six months when an embittered malcontent convinced some relatives to attack the isolated Jesuit mission at Caborca. Saeta was murdered in April 1695, and the Spanish reaction that ensued unleashed the same kind of military brutality Kino had seen at La Paz. The Indian leaders assembled at the small ranchería of El Tupo to hand over the murderers. During the course of the summary trial the chief culprit was beheaded; frightened by the sudden and savage "justice," the leaders bolted, only to be cut down by withering musket fire from the mounted cavalry. It took the whole summer before Kino was able to placate the Pimas and arrange a peace between them and the Spanish regional commanders.

The Pima revolt of 1695, as this incident has been called, rekindled the criticisms some colonials had levelled against Kino and the Pimería missions. There now seemed to be sufficient cause to recall Kino to Mexico and place him in one of the universities where his energies would be less likely to upset the establishment. In the meanwhile, Kino was requesting a return to argue the case for more missionaries. So in December 1695 Kino set out for the distant capital—reaching there in fifty-two days, an average of thirty miles a day. Two things happened immediately on his arrival: 1) Salvatierra unexpectedly met him at the Casa Profesa, and 2) the Provincial received a letter from the Jesuit General praising Kino and assigning him and Salvatierra to California for at least six months a year. So much for the colonial nay-sayers.

The two dreamy-eyed Jesuits approached the Viceroy of New Spain for permission to return to the Californias, but the bitter experience of one hundred and fifty years of expensive failures was adequate for him to refuse. Sensing the reason for the refusal and remembering the deep commitment they had for the "most abandoned people on earth," Kino and Salvatierra proposed that they return at their own expense. Here was the ultimate irony: two Jesuits with vows of poverty were asking to undertake a massively expensive expedition to California that even the King's vicar found too costly. Eventually the Viceroy relented, but not before the help of Juan Ugarte, the Jesuit Paul-Bunyan-to-be of Baja California, was enlisted and pledges of money and ships were confirmed. These ambitious ideas of Kino and Salvatierra and the genius of Ugarte were the seeds of the famous Pious Fund of the Californias—a kind of Spanish-colonial Ford Foundation. Bequests, sunken boats, and run-down haciendas were reshaped into shrewd investments, refurbished sailing vessels, and efficient, profitable farms. The Pious Fund paid for the California missions and their needs; in turn, the California missions purchased food and cattle from the mainland missions, who spent their earnings on supplies from Mexico. The "most abandoned peoples" eventually brought prosperity to hundreds of families throughout the northwest. And the Pious Fund was destined to become the largest private foundation in Spanish-colonial North America.

The Kino-Salvatierra plan did not stop with the innovation of the Pious Fund. Experience had taught that success on the desolate "island" depended on careful screening and control of personnel. So a part of the agreement with the Viceroy stipulated that the Jesuit Rector would approve of all persons coming to or staying in the Californias. Every priest, brother, soldier, sailor, and merchant served under the direct approbation of the Rector. It was as if the Society were running a novitiate at the end of the world. Effectively the Rector was governor of the land and admiral of the sea. Without this firm control it is doubtful that the Jesuit missions would have succeeded, but the Society paid dearly in a way because the California missions were one of the contributing factors to the expulsion of the Jesuits from the Spanish empire in 1767. The insistence of the Society regarding the exercise of authority in California conjured up wild fictions in the minds of the Bourbon court. When Visitor General José de Gálvez led his expedition to the peninsula in 1768, he was searching for a secret Jesuit mission that was reputed to have twenty-five thousand elite Indian troops being trained to seize the empire. (In Gálvez's defense it must be noted that he frequently suffered from mental derangement to the extent he had to be tied down on a bed or in a litter).

Californians generally know little about Father Kino. The mere mention of California missions will trigger visions of a Junípero Serra or a Gaspar de Portolá. But without Kino and Salvatierra there would probably never have been a California as you know it. Why? Because their insight and bravado created the Pious Fund, shaped the mission policies, and sustained the commitment to the "most abandoned peoples on earth." And all of those missions that Serra has been credited with were paid for by Jesuit money. The colonizing expedition of Juan Bautista de Anza? Paid for by Jesuit money. Costanso's scientific expedition? Paid for by Jesuit money—confiscated to be sure but existing because of the trust that benefactors had in Jesuit abilities and good will. The Pious Fund was brought into existence by Kino and Salvatierra because of their seventeenth-century vision of expanding this whole region—not to increase the size of the empire but to better the lives of the people. Kino is a historical figure of staggering proportions; his role in the development of northern New Spain and the West is immensely important. Kino stands in deep contrast to the figure of Serra and to what happened in this region long years after. In my opinion, Franciscan entry into the Californias was not to expand a mission frontier for the sake of the people, but to establish religiously operated compounds to supply the military needs of the Bourbons. Alta California's missions were each situated at strategic points, not at Indian towns. Serra championed the military priorities of Spain even against the opposition of his own subjects. These policies were aimed at money and power at the expense of people.

The goal of the men of the Society was always faith and justice—although they may have used different terminology a few centuries ago. When one studies the history of the Jesuit missions of yesteryear, one cannot help but discover the rich, complete, unrelenting commitment to genuine faith and equal justice. Those Jesuits were dedicated to their Indian peoples. They did not bemoan them as dumb and benighted peoples; rather they joined with them in their struggling quest for truth—which brings me back to what I said in the beginning about "going forth to teach all nations." The task of the Society has always been one in my estimation, and that is to quest for truth—everywhere it can be found, in every way it can be reformulated, every time we penetrate deeper into mathematics, deeper into science, deeper into computers, deeper into chemistry, deeper into nuclear physics, deeper into space, deeper into philosophy, deeper into anything wherein truth resides. For we shall never exhaust the discovery of truth because God is truth. It is a quest for the Divine. It is not a question of being rationalists; it is not a question of being voluntarists. It is a question of being holistic. It is a question of simplifying what faith really is—and communicating that to people.

"Going out and teaching all nations and baptizing them" is to search for truth, to bring life, hope into the hearts of all humankind—into all our hearts: man, woman, Black, Yellow, Red, Indian, any way a person is to be found. That is the faith we find in Padre Kino. This is why I titled this essay, "Kino: On People and Places." I could have recounted his expeditions, his mapmaking, his church-building, with an impressive array of historical statistics. One might then have misunderstood in thinking he came to do these things. No, Kino came to all these places and recorded them because of people. And in finding people in the places he visited and explored and in doing the brave things he did, he found God. He found God in the people he served, and together they joined in the quest of the recreation of the world, which we like to call salvation. We are engaged in something more than just saving our souls; we are engaged in making a newer world, a better world. And we are just barely set out on that path, even though Kino rode those trails more than three centuries ago.

Reference List: Works by Charles W. Polzer, S.J.

Father Eusebio Francisco Kino and His Missions of the Pimeria Alta. Book 1: The Side Altars. Tucson: Southwestern Mission Research Center, 1982.

Father Eusebio Francisco Kino and His Missions of the Pimeria Alta. Book 2: The Main Altars. Tucson: Southwestern Mission Research Center, 1983.

Father Eusebio Francisco Kino and His Missions of the Pimeria Alta. Book 3: Facing The Missions. Tucson: Southwestern Mission Research Center, 1983.

A Kino Guide: His Missions and Monuments. Tucson: Southwestern Mission Research Center, 1968.

Pedro de Revera and the Military Regulations for Northern New Spain, 1724–1729. Tucson: University of Arizona Press, 1988.

The Presidio and the Militia on the Northern Frontier of New Spain: A Documentary History. Tucson: University of Arizona Press, 1987.

Rules and Precepts of the Jesuit Missions of Northwestern New Spain. Tucson: University of Arizona Press, 1976.

"Faith Enters by the Ear": Missionary Linguistics in the Pacific Northwest

GERALD McKEVITT, S.J.

One aspect of Jesuit intellectual activity that has received little attention from historians has been the learning of Native American languages by Jesuit missionaries.* Despite the supreme importance that language study held for the missionaries, their attempts to learn native idioms remain relatively unexplored by scholars. Untrained or uninterested in linguistics, historians have often neglected the topic or ignored the generous store of data already gathered by anthropologists that could facilitate their work. Whatever the cause, with the exceptions of works by Victor Hanzeli, James Axtell, and a few others, only passing mention is made of linguistics in most histories of Catholic and Protestant missionary activity among Native Americans.[1] A systematic analysis of that process—its methods, problems, and achievements—is yet to be written.

Missionaries themselves recognized that the ability to speak aboriginal tongues was crucial for successful evangelization. Paul Le Jeune, a seventeenth century Jesuit who served among the Montagnais of New France, stated the case for language learning most succinctly in 1633 when, quoting Saint Paul, he declared "faith enters by the ear."[2] The centrality of linguistics in the daily lives of Le Jeune and other seventeenth century Jesuits has been ably described by linguistic scholar Victor Hanzeli. His conclusions can be applied to missionaries of almost every church and every generation:

> The most precious gift a missionary could have was, humanly speaking, his gift of languages. The whole success of his work depended on how he would exploit his linguistic talents in language learning and use. As for the mission itself, the efficiency of its operation depended, in the long run and especially during the early years, on the linguistic documentation it could accumulate.[3]

One area rich in possibilities for beginning a study of missionary language

---

*A more comprehensive version of this study is copyrighted by the Western Historical Association. Portions of it are reprinted here by permission. It first appeared as "Jesuit Missionary Linguistics in the Pacific Northwest: A Comparative Study," *Western Historical Quarterly*, 21 (August 1990): 281–304.

learning is the nineteenth-century Pacific Northwest, where abundant sources are available on the learning of Indian languages by Protestant and Catholic missionaries. This study focuses on one of those groups—Jesuits who served in the order's Rocky Mountain Mission, a vast enterprise embracing the modern states of Washington, Oregon, Idaho, and Montana. Based on an analysis of the careers of missionaries who were active there from the 1840s until the turn of the century, it poses fundamental questions. What methods did the missionaries (who lacked textbooks and teachers) employ to learn native idioms? How well did they learn them, and what difficulties did they encounter? Although concentrating primarily on Jesuits, the study also briefly compares their language work with that of Protestant missionaries in the same region. Did the clergy of the various churches manifest similarities or differences in their approach to linguistics? Conclusions will also be drawn about the quality of the missionaries' grammar books and dictionaries of Indian languages and about their contributions to the field of linguistics.

Historians have ascribed a variety of causes to the success of the Jesuits' Rocky Mountain Mission. One of the missionaries' most important assets was their linguistic skill. While studying in Italy, Gregory Mengarini was selected for missionary work precisely because of his aptitude for languages. Mengarini, Philip Canestrelli, Anthony Morvillo, and John Post also authored useful dictionaries and grammars of Pacific Northwest languages. Most of the priests in the Northwest could express themselves in one or more native dialects. Edward Griva, the "premier Jesuit linguist among the Salish tribes," managed to communicate—although certainly not with anything approximating equal fluency—in twelve Indian languages. Joseph Cataldo, one of the most accomplished linguists, knew ten.[4]

It is not easy, however, to draw clear conclusions about the degree of skill attained by individual missionaries. The scarcity of evaluations about them by native speakers, the most qualified and best judges, renders definitive judgments difficult, and the historian must be cautious in accepting uncritically non-Indian estimates of their abilities, especially subjective assessments made by fellow missionaries or by biographers whose grasp of the languages was weak or nonexistent. It should be noted, too, that not all Jesuits were good linguists. Notwithstanding their skill in Latin and Greek, some missionaries could not master Indian languages. Cataldo complained that the well-known missionary-historian, Lawrence Palladino, "never learned enough of the Indian language to be able to hear confession or teach a little catechism to boys."[5] Peter Barcelo's inability to learn Crow provoked Indian ridicule and exasperated his more gifted coworker, Peter Paul Prando. Thus, individual ability, the paramount factor in language learning, was not a gift universally possessed.

Nonetheless, an impressive number of missionaries were proficient linguists. What accounts for the Jesuits' relative success? Although their approach to language study was similar to that of their Protestant counterparts, it also differed in significant details. One distinguishing factor was the priority that the order gave to the study of languages. In 1843, Oregon minister Daniel Lee outlined a portrait of the ideal Methodist missionary; such a person, he declared, "should be at the very foundation, a thorough linguist. . . . He should be well acquainted with Hebrew, Greek, and Latin, and the grammatical construction of French, Spanish, and German languages." However, one historian has observed, "Few men, and fewer Methodist ministers, could have met those requirements." The only person who matched Lee's description of the "perfect missionary" was the hated Jesuit.[6] Most of the priests had not only studied classical and European languages before taking up missionary careers; they had also taught them. Although Indian languages were strikingly different from those of the Indo-European family and although the Jesuits' linguistic training was, from a modern point of view, limited in its technical aspects, their Old World experience did facilitate their study of the languages of the New.

The order's missionary tradition was also a benefit. The founder of the Society of Jesus, Saint Ignatius of Loyola, urged his missionaries to learn the language of the countries to which they were sent. Thus, the Jesuits of the Pacific Northwest were heirs to three centuries of practice that stressed language study and included time-tested methods for achieving proficiency.

Circumstances peculiar to religious orders also helped Jesuits surmount linguistic barriers. Married Protestant missionaries, struggling with the challenge of feeding and clothing families and educating their children, frequently complained about the amount of time they had to spend on manual work and other secular activities. "I feel that it is a great calamity that we are under the necessity of spending so much time in providing for our temporal wants," complained Asa Smith, a companion of the Whitmans at Waiilaptu in 1839.[7] A missionary wife recorded that "our still winter evenings . . . [are] often almost the only time husband can secure for close and uninterrupted study."[8] Celibate Jesuits, on the other hand, were not only free from family obligations, but they were aided in manual work by lay brothers of the order. Men of varied vocational training, these nonpriests performed the tasks of carpenter, infirmarian, cook, gardener, thus freeing the priest for language study and other directly ministerial activities.

Another characteristic that distinguished the Northwestern Jesuits from their Protestant counterparts was that the vast majority of the Jesuits were foreigners. Only four of the fifty priests working in the Rocky Mountain Mission at the turn of the century were born in the United States. The remainder were from Italy, France, Holland, Belgium, Germany, and other European countries.[9] The international composition of the order in the Northwest had important implications for language learning. Most of the missionaries were from small nations, and since childhood they had been exposed to a multiplicity of languages. As Europeans they were not intimidated by the prospect of learning a new tongue, but recognized it as a necessity of life. As Jesuits, most of them had not only taught languages, but during their long Jesuit training many of them had lived in international houses of study in which learning new idioms was a necessity. The breadth of that experience, consequently, freed them from the psychological barriers that sometimes impede effective mastery of new languages.

The Jesuits' European origin had other far-reaching repercussions. Many missionaries arrived in the Northwest knowing little or no English. At one time, Italian was spoken so extensively by the Jesuit community at De Smet Mission that Father Aloysius Parodi thought he was back in Italy when he visited there on one occasion.[10] Many newcomers to the Northwest had, simultaneously, to learn both English and an indigenous language. This unusual circumstance slowed learning in many instances, but in others it provided an added incentive for trying to subdue native dialects. Unable to speak with Indians in English, the missionary, if he hoped to communicate, was compelled to tackle the Indian idiom as soon as possible.

Priority was clearly given in some cases to acquiring the Native American language. Philip Canestrelli, professor at Rome's Gregorian University, emigrated to America in 1878 knowing little English. From Fort Colville the new missionary wrote to Joseph Cataldo, then superior of the Mission, informing him of his safe arrival and stating his assumption that English was the most important and first language that he should learn. The reply came back from Cataldo: "No. Kalispel." Ten years later Canestrelli still did not know much English, but he had authored thirteen publications in Kalispel.[11]

The linguistic traditions of Native American cultures also influenced language learning by missionaries, Catholic and Protestant equally. Communication between natives and missionaries was not a one-sided relationship whose outcome depended solely on missionary background and skill. The natives' tolerance of the whites' imperfect ability to speak, for example, encouraged the missionary effort. Some tribes were especially patient with the outlanders' attempts at communication, no matter how infelicitous.

Another factor that historians have frequently overlooked was Indian linguistic ability and willingness to learn new languages. This tendency was "not unusual among the Pacific Northwest Coast Indians," one authority notes.[12] The flexibility of native speakers enabled Christian missionaries to cope with the linguistic diversity they encountered. The Cayuses allowed Presbyterian missionary Marcus Whitman to instruct them in the Nez Perces' language. Native adaptability also enabled Jesuits to transfer dialects from one tribe to another. In 1902, missionary Edward Griva encountered bands living near Saint Francis Regis Mission, Washington, who spoke the Colville dialect in ordinary discourse, but conducted their religious services in the Kalispel tongue. He discovered the reason: ". . . they have all been taught to pray in Kalispel by the old Fathers, who were formerly at the mission of St. Paul near Kettle Falls."[13]

Another variable that aided Jesuit entry into the Indian world, especially in the first half of the century, was the usefulness of French in many parts of the Indian Northwest. Pierre De Smet, founder of the Jesuits' Rocky Mountain Mission, although he never learned a Native American language, was able to communicate with many tribes in French when he arrived in the 1840s. The second language of some Indians and the principal language of most métis in the employ of the Hudson's Bay Company, French remained an important medium of communication even after American acquisition of Oregon country. The fact that many Native Americans and European Jesuits were fluent in that tongue was no small advantage to the latter—both to their missionary work and to their learning of Indian tongues from French-speaking natives.

What specific means did the missionaries take to learn new languages? The Jesuit system—in their missions as well as in their colleges—employed what modern educators call learning through immersion. Although procedures were complex, varying from time and place, the missionaries realized that the more students were exposed to situational experiences and the more they interacted with others in the new speech, the faster they would acquire it. "The best way to learn the Indian language," Cataldo believed, "was to go live in the Indian camp."[14] Protestant missionaries also sought total immersion in the target language, but the necessity of supporting a family often discouraged prolonged sojourns in the field. Field study also demanded a willingness to accommodate oneself to the unfamiliar vagaries of the native diet and housing. When frontier conditions disappeared at the end of the century and as Jesuits sought to promote more traditional ways of living religious community life, the Jesuit practice of dwelling with Indians came to an end. But the principle of cultural insertion itself was still operative in the 1890s when Cataldo founded seminaries for future missionaries on reservations so that young Jesuits would have immediate and frequent contact with the tribes early on in their career.

The preferred procedure was to put a newcomer in touch with an experienced missionary teacher, particularly if the target languages were still unwritten. In cases where no Jesuit teacher was available—as in the earliest days of the Mission or when it extended into new linguistic areas—bilingual Indian or métis instructors were hired for elementary instruction. Persons of mixed racial ancestry, who had long assisted the fur companies as interpreters, also aided missionaries. Historian Robert Loewenberg's observation that the "half-breeds" were the Methodist missionaries' entrée into the Indian world applies to all missionary groups in the Northwest.[15]

But reliance on interpreters was ideally only a temporary expedient. Paid help proved undependable, as a Protestant missionary learned after he hired two traders of French-Indian descent to help translate the Gospel of John into Sioux. "By the time we had reached the end of the seventh chapter," he lamented, the relations between the two Frenchmen "were such as to entirely stop our work."[16] Jesuits made similar discoveries. "Do not neglect the study of the language," one priest advised another in 1848, "for the peace of our residence depends mainly upon our being independent of the Canadians and the interpreters. Believe me, no good will ever come to us from those men." It costs too much to keep them in gunpowder, lead, food, and tobacco, he complained; besides, they waste too much time "eating and sleeping."[17] Thirty-five years later, Father Prando voiced similar reservations about the man whom he and a fellow Jesuit paid to teach them the Crow language:

> Our interpreter is a busy do-nothing who takes little interest in us. He sleeps late every morning and then works until late at night, not eating supper until nine o'clock. Consequently, he doesn't say a word to us all day long. After supper he stretches out on his bed or on the ground, where he gives us a lesson that lasts a quarter of an hour.[18]

One of the most formidable challenges was creating an orthographic system, while one also labored to learn the language itself. "To learn an unwritten language, and to reduce it to a form that can be seen as well as heard," declared a Protestant minister, "is confessedly a work of no small magnitude."[19] Cataldo, who had learned Nez Perce under similar circumstances, concurred. "The difficulty of studying an Indian language without a grammar is something no one can appreciate who has not actually sat down and tried it," he wrote. "It was only after three years that I began to grasp the genius of the Nez Perce language, whose active verb has a million inflections."[20] Progress in learning was inevitably slow. Fathers Barcelo and Prando painstakingly compiled their Crow dictionary "by showing objects to the son and wife of the interpreter."[21] Griva, a turn-of-the-century Jesuit missionary, improved his vocabulary by acquiring the help of "a full blood Moses Indian" who pronounced the Indian names for articles pictured in a Sears and Roebuck catalog.[22]

Given these difficulties, it is not surprising that the Jesuits' preferred method was to rely on linguists of their own. Once the first missionaries arrived in a new area, they began writing word lists, dictionaries, and grammars that would eventually be used by their successors. Father Urban Grassi's manuscript of Okanagan Valley language passed from hand to hand, as did Mengarini's Salish grammar and Kalispel dictionary, before their eventual publication. This practice greatly eased the difficulty and increased the rate of learning between the first missionaries and the later ones. As a young man, Joseph Cataldo began his study with Mengarini at Santa Clara College, in California, even before arriving in the Northwest. He declared, "I know from my own experience that I learned more Flathead in three months from studying Fr. Mengarini's writings than I did in three years' study of Nez Perce" on my own.[23]

So convinced was Cataldo of the importance of such scholarship that in 1890 he temporarily set aside his duties as Superior of the Rocky Mountain

Mission and travelled to Saint Francis Xavier Mission, Montana, where he remained for two months in order to help Prando write a Crow grammar.[24] Throughout his long career Cataldo remained a sort of polyglot trouble-shooter, whom superiors sent to rescue fellow Jesuits in linguistic distress. The Society was fortunate in having skilled members who, having learned a language the hard way, created grammars and dictionaries that, however imperfect by modern standards, alleviated the labor of succeeding generations.

Protestant work in Indian languages of the Northwest paralleled, in many ways, that of the Jesuits. Both groups followed similar methods of study; both possessed a handful of talented individuals who served as master teacher for other missionaries. Both found themselves "greatly handicapped in their attempts to communicate with the Indians without written works in the Indians' own tongue."[25] Consequently, both churches established printing presses for the publication of works in native languages.

There were, however, some significant contrasts between them. Protestants, who began their evangelization before the advent of Jesuits, were the first to actually publish Indian texts, beginning with Henry Spalding's Nez Perce translation of a portion of the Gospel of Matthew, which was produced at the Lapwai Mission in 1839. The first Jesuit imprint, a collection of Biblical narratives in Kalispel, was printed by the Saint Ignatius Mission Press in 1876. The two groups also published different types of materials. Protestants "were primarily interested in getting their writings into the hands of the Indians themselves," one authority notes. Hence production focused on readers, primers, calendars, and other Indian-English works devised for Indian use. Although the Jesuits, too, published hymnals, catechisms, and prayer books in indigenous languages, their aims were less ambitious. They were chiefly interested in printing works—such as the grammars and dictionaries—"intended to help succeeding missionaries learn the language." Moreover, Jesuit publications were "designed primarily for the use of missionaries whose native tongues were many." Consequently, because English was a relatively new language for most of the priests, the classic grammars—Mengarini's Kalispel, Morvillo's Nez Perce, and Canestrelli's Kootenai—were all printed with the explanatory text in Latin.[26]

Missionaries are sometimes accused of having found Indian languages "incapable of expressing Christian truths."[27] That charge can be somewhat mitigated in the case of the Northwestern Jesuits, who generally sought native equivalents for theological concepts. According to missionary dictionaries, the Crow word for *baptize* meant "pouring of water on top of the head"; a *church* was "where they pray"; *eucharist* translated "the eating of the heavenly bread." *Hell* was simply rendered "big fire" in Crow, and *heaven* was in Nez Perce "the home of joy." Other concepts were more elusive, and thus the missionaries discovered that evangelization involved some formidable linguistic challenges. Seeking to translate *sacrament,* Belgian Jesuit Aloysius Vrebosch drew on his knowledge of patristic theology: he used a word in Crow meaning "medicine of the soul."[28] Cataldo wrestled with Crow words for "confession of sin." A phrase meaning "I make the sin seen" would be acceptable, he concluded, but he worried on hearing it that "the carnal Crow would understand *ostendo genitalia* [show my genitals]".[29]

In view of the religious purpose of missionary study, it should come as no surprise to learn that the published writings, in native idioms, of both Protestants and Catholics had practical, rather than theoretical or speculative aims. Aboriginal languages were rarely studied for their own sake. Jesuits would have concurred with Protestant missionary Stephen Riggs, who wrote that the "labor of writing the language was undertaken as a means to a greater end," namely, evangelization.[30] Unlike twentieth-century anthropologists, who seek to preserve bodies of aboriginal text and folklore, nineteenth-century missionaries probed the mysteries of native languages in order to translate the Bible, to preach, and to write prayer books and doctrinal tracts needed for Christian instruction and liturgy. Missionaries in their ignorance also imposed upon Indian speech the familiar paradigms of European grammar. Jesuit dictionaries and grammars were not only usually written in Latin, but also used the classical language as a framework for their Indian studies.

Missionary scholarship mirrored its historical context in other ways. Not only was grammatical and syntactic analysis unconsciously linked to Latin, but field work was primitive. Phonetics, the area in which linguistics has since made some of its greatest progress, was still in its infancy. Consequently, missionary grammars and dictionaries are phonetically dated and inadequate by today's standards. Bombarded by a host of entirely new sounds, the missionaries could not capture the uniqueness of what they heard. "There are many sounds" in Indian languages, admitted a French-born Jesuit, "that a European can never catch or articulate."[31]

Despite shortcomings, missionaries did contribute to knowledge about Indian languages. In some cases, they preserved data that might otherwise have been lost. Morvillo's Nez Perce grammar, though cast in a Latin mold, is significant because it is among the earliest primers of the language. Giorda and Mengarini's works were standard references for the Kalispel language until a modern grammar appeared in 1940.[32] The value of the missionaries' publications is also attested by the use modern scholars have made of them. Linguistic scholar Gladys Reichard's research on Coeur d'Alene grammar drew on the earlier work of Giorda and Mengarini.[33] Perhaps the greatest testimony to the value of Father Canestrelli's Kootenai grammar is the fact that in 1927 Franz Boas, the dominant figure in Native American linguistics in the first half of the twentieth century, published an edition of that scarce volume. Although critical of Canestrelli's phonetic system, Boas concluded that the missionary "had a very intimate knowledge of the language" and that his remarks on the syntactic use of forms were "particularly valuable."[34] Father John Post's little-known manuscript, "Kalispel Grammar," with its "extraordinary number of Kalispel examples" was edited and reprinted as recently as 1980.[35]

Consequently, although intended chiefly as tools of the missionary trade, missionaries' Indian grammars have not been without lasting value. "The work of priests and missionaries, Protestant as well as Catholic," one anthropologist writes, "has accounted for ninety percent of the material available on American Indian languages."[36] Missionaries in the Pacific Northwest not only taught Native Americans to read and write their own languages, but they also preserved data about Pacific Northwest idioms that have proved useful to scholars.

The heyday of Jesuit Indian-language study and grammar writing ended with the turn of the century. In succeeding decades, a combination of causes led to declining use of Native American languages in the churches and classrooms of the order's missions. Government policies that discouraged the use of Indian languages in federally subsidized mission schools, increasing native facility in English, and the gradual disappearance of missionaries skilled in native idioms all contributed to the shift. Indian speech continued to be spoken and sung in Jesuit churches during religious services, but with decreasing frequency. The death in 1916 of Father Stephen De Rougé marked the end of an era at Saint Mary's Mission on the Colville Reservation. "The non-English speaking Indians were passing," recorded Indian leader Pascal Sherman, "and the English speaking generation was rising." De Rougé's Jesuit successors "did not stop to learn Indian, at least to the extent of its use in the confessional, on the grounds that all Indians used English well enough" for the priests to be understood.[37]

Seventy-five years passed between De Smet's 1841 founding of the Jesuit ministry in the Northwest and the changed circumstances symbolized by the death of De Rougé in 1916. During that interval, European clerics and Native Americans created bilingual societies on many reservations and missions throughout the Pacific Northwest. The story of their linguistic encounter sheds light on a little-understood aspect of Jesuit education. It also offers a unique and important perspective on Indian-white relations in the nineteenth century. Since language is the key to a culture, any study of the cultural confrontation that occurred between Indians and Christian missionaries must begin with an understanding of their attempts to cross linguistic bridges. The problems that arose when missionaries struggled to learn native speech were formidable, and the methods used to meet that challenge evidenced a high degree of resourcefulness, on the part of all parties. The consequences of breaking the linguistic barrier were far-reaching. Language was the door that gave missionaries entrée into the Indian world and, eventually, enabled them to alter that world. But it is ironic that clerics, who viewed language as a tool of cultural conquest, helped codify and conserve the languages of the very societies they strove to transform.

The struggle to communicate also sheds light on the religious history of the Northwest, the early development of which, including its acquisition by the United States, was shaped and molded by missionary activists. If the linguistic encounter provides insights into the spiritual odyssey of Native Americans, it also illuminates a little-appreciated aspect of missionary activity. Although the Jesuits of the Rocky Mountain Mission may not have possessed the "uncanny ability" to learn native languages ascribed to their seventeenth-century predecessors in New France, an impressive number of them made significant contributions to Indian evangelization and to linguistic scholarship.[38] Jesuits and Protestant missionaries responded in strikingly similar ways to the challenge of mastering native idioms, but they also evidenced significant differences. Perhaps the greatest contrast stemmed from the advantages that their European origins gave to the Jesuits in that struggle. Thus, a comparison of Protestant and Catholic learning of native tongues in the Pacific Northwest not only clarifies a neglected aspect of the confrontation between Indians and missionaries, but it also underscores the significance that ethnic diversity played in the religious history of the Pacific Northwest.

Notes

1. Victor Egon Hanzeli, *Missionary Linguistics in New France: A Study of Seventeenth- and Eighteenth-Century Descriptions of American Indian Languages* (The Hague: Mouton, 1969); and James Axtell, *The Invasion Within: The Contest of Cultures in Colonial North America* (New York: Oxford University Press, 1985). Informative analyses of the role that linguistic ability played in the careers of individual missionaries are found in Clyde A. Milner II and Floyd A. O'Neill, eds., *Churchmen and the Western Indians, 1820–1920* (Norman, Oklahoma: University of Oklahoma Press, 1985).

2. LeJeune's reference to Romans 10:17 is found in Ruben Gold Thwaites, ed., *The Jesuit Relations and Allied Documents: Travels and Explorations of the Jesuit Missionaries in New France, 1610–1791* (New York, 1959), 5:191.

3. Hanzeli, *Missionary Linguistics*, 53–54.

4. Eleanor Carriker and others, *Guide to the Microfilm Edition of the Oregon Province Archives of the Society of Jesus Indian Language Collection: The Pacific Northwest Tribes* (Spokane, Washington: Gonzaga University, 1976), 10, 13.

5. Joseph Cataldo (De Smet, Idaho) to [Turin Provincial], 3 January 1888, Turin Province Archives of the Society of Jesus, Turin, Italy (located at Villa San Maurizio, Strada comunale di Superga, 70, Turin). Hereafter the Archives is cited as TPA.

6. Robert J. Loewenberg, *Equality on the Oregon Frontier: Jason Lee and the Methodist Mission, 1834–43* (Seattle, Washington: University of Washington Press, 1976), 94, 96.

7. Clifford M. Drury, *Marcus and Narcissa Whitman and the Opening of Old Oregon,* (Glendale, California: A. H. Clark Co., 1973), 1: 339.

8. Stephen R. Riggs, *Mary and I: Forty Years with the Sioux* (Chicago, Illinois, W. G. Holmes, 1880), 74.

9. Statistical data derived from "Catalogus Primus, 1889, Rocky Mountain Mission," Oregon Province Archives of the Society of Jesus, Crosby Library, Gongaza University, Spokane, Washington (hereafter cited as OPA).

10. Aloysius Parodi, S.J., "Reminiscences and Reflections of Rev. Al. Parodi, S.J.," Aloysius Parodi, S.J., Papers, OPA.

11. Charles Mackin, S.J., "The Wanderings of Fifty Years [An Autobiography]," Charles Mackin, S.J., Papers, OPA. See also Carriker, *Guide to Microfilm,* 9.

12. Robert H. Ruby and John A. Brown, *Indians of the Pacific Northwest: A History* (Norman, Oklahoma, University of Oklahoma Press, 1981), 77.

13. Edward M. Griva, S.J., "History of the 50 Years of My Missionary Life Among the Indians and Whites, from the 7th of July 1894 till the end of September, 1944," 33–34, Edward M. Griva, S.J., Papers, OPA.

14. Cited in Parodi, "Reminiscences," OPA.

15. Loewenberg, *Equality,* 123.

16. Riggs, *Mary and I,* 52–53.

17. John Nobili, S.J., (Fraser River) to Anthony Goetz, S.J., 6 June 1848, quoted in *Woodstock Letters* 18 (1889): 77–79.

18. Peter Prando, S.J., (Crow Agency) to Joseph Cataldo, S.J., 4 August 1883, Peter Prando, S.J., Papers, OPA.

19. Riggs, *Mary and I,* 35.

20. Joseph Cataldo, S.J., (Saint Francis Xavier Mission, Fort Custer, Montana) to Fr. General, 31 January 1891, OPA.

21. Prando (Crow Agency) to Cataldo, 4 August 1883, Prando Papers, OPA.

22. Griva, "History," 30–31, OPA.

23. Cataldo (Saint Francis Xavier Mission) to Fr. General, 31 January 1891, OPA.

24. Ibid.

25. Wilfred P. Schoenberg, S.J., *Paths to the Northwest: A Jesuit History of the Oregon Province* (Chicago: Loyola University Press, 1992), 100–101.

26. Philip Canestrelli, S.J., *A Kootenai Grammar,* ed. Wilfred Schoenberg, S.J., (Santa Clara, 1894), 3.

27. Henry Warner Bowden, *American Indians and Christian Missions: Studies in Cultural Conflict* (Chicago: University of Chicago Press, 1981), 81.

28. [Joseph Cataldo, S.J.], "Dictionary: English-Crow Dictionary, Volume II, Covering Words 'Christian' to 'Dust'," OPA; [Joseph Giorda, S.J., and others], *A Dictionary of the Kalispel or Flathead Indian Language Compiled by Missionaries of the Society of Jesus* (Saint Ignatius, Montana: Saint Ignatius Mission Print, 1877–79). Citations from Nez Perce are found in Anthony Morvillo, S.J., *A Dictionary of the Numípu or Nez Perce Language* (Saint Ignatius, Montana: Saint Ignatius Mission Print, 1895). The Belgian priest was Aloysius Vrebosch, S.J., author of "A Vocabulary of Absaroki or Crow Language," OPA. See also Aloysius Vrebosch, S.J., "Dictionary of the Crow Indian Language," OPA.

29. [Cataldo], "Dictionary: English-Crow," 2, OPA.

30. Riggs, *Mary and I,* 37.

31. Victor Garrand, S.J., *Augustine Laure, S.J., Missionary to the Yakima,* ed. Edward J. Kowrach (Fairfield, Washington: Ye Galleon Press, 1977), 12. For a study of the evolution of the science of phonetics in the United States, see Franklin Edgerton, "Notes on Early American Work in Linguistics," *Proceedings of the American Philosophical Society* 87 (1943): 25–34.

32. See Hans Vogt, *The Kalispel Language: An Outline of the Grammar with Texts, Translations, and Dictionary* (Oslo: Norske Videnskaps-Akademie I Oslo, 1940).

33. Gladys Reichard, "Coeur d'Alene: Handbook of American Indian Languages Smithsonian Institution, Bureau of American Ethnology, Bulletin 40, Part 3, No. 5 (Washington, D.C.: Government Printing Office, 1938): 517–707.

34. Philip Canestrelli, "Grammar of the Kutenai Language, Pater Philippo Canestrelli, S.J., Annotated by Franz Boas," *International Journal of American Linguistics* 4 (1927): 1.

35. See Brenda J. Speck, ed., "An Edition of Father Post's Kalispel Grammar," University of Montana Occasional Papers in Linguistics, no. 1 (Missoula, 1980), 2–3.

36. Mary R. Haas, *Language, Culture, and History* (Stanford, California: Stanford University Press, 1987), 176.

37. Quoted in Maria Ilma Raufer, O.P., *Black Robes and Indians on the Last Frontier* (Milwaukee, Wisconsin: The Bruce Publishing Co., 1966), 374.

38. Jay P. Dolan, *The American Catholic Experience: A History from Colonial Times to the Present* (Garden City, New York: Doubleday and Co., Inc., 1985), 56.

The Jesuits in Africa

JOHN ORR DWYER

I promise special obedience to the Holy Father regarding the missions.
—Fourth solemn vow in the Society of Jesus

Shortly before the dissolution of their Order, the Peking Jesuits built a monument to their extinct brotherhood in the cemetery where so many of their great dead lay. The Latin inscription on the monument ends with the words: ABI, VIATOR, CONGRAT- ULATORE MORTUIS, CONDOLE VIVIS, ORA PRO OMNIBUS, MIRARE ET TACE (Depart, traveller, congratulate the dead, mourn for the living, pray for everyone, marvel and be silent).
—Felix A. Plattner, *Jesuits Go East*

As historians have been recently reminded,[1] inspiration to missionary history was given by Professor John K. Fairbank in his presidential address to the American Historical Association in December 1968. Fairbank decried the "general neglect" of the field and called the "missionary in foreign parts . . . the invisible man of American history." "Few academic studies of foreign missions seem to have been made," Fairbank continued, and "mission archives have not been used for monographic studies. Mission history is a great and underused research laboratory for the comparative observation of cultural stimulus and response in both directions."[2]

Since 1968 much has been done by missiologists, social scientists, and historians. But much needs to be done.[3] One of the great gaps is the absence of a general account of one of the great missionary thrusts in modern history—that of the men of the Society of Jesus who have moved about the world for the last 450 years. These Jesuits, dedicated to spreading the message of Christ through education, have been sent to Africa, Asia, and North and South America. Voluminous records exist in the form of letters, diaries, reports, and statistics to support such a general study.

This paper will describe the origins of Jesuit missionary activity in the sixteenth century and the arrival of the first Jesuit in Africa—Francis Xavier in Mozambique in 1541. Concentrated activities of the Jesuits will be described for four separate regions in Africa over the four-hundred-and-fifty-year period; Abyssinia (Ethiopia), the Congo (Zaire, Kwango, Angola), the Zambezi (Zimbabwe), and the Sudan. Significant Jesuit activity in Egypt, Madagascar, and other areas is omitted from this account.

The Origins

Ignatius of Loyola had a severe disappointment soon after surrendering his career as a soldier. During his recovery from wounds suffered in battle, he was inspired by his reading about Christ and the lives of the saints. Converting to a life of devotion, he made his way from Spain first to Rome and then to the Holy Land in 1523. There he attempted to preach to the "infidels," but members of missionary orders there would not allow him to continue because of his lack of training. He left the Holy Land vowing to return to continue his mission. Thus the dedication to the missionary spirit was a part of Ignatius before Ignatius became a part of the Society of Jesus.

More than a decade later, when Ignatius gathered with his companions in the chapel of St. Denis in Montmartre on 15 August 1534, they pronounced, along with their private vows of poverty, chastity, and obedience to the Pope, a vow to return to Jerusalem for an "apostolic undertaking." From the earliest moment of its existence, the Society of Jesus was dedicated to the conversion of "the infidels."[4]

These brothers of the faith followed through on their commitment just after their ordinations in 1537. Ignatius and his nine first companions reunited in Venice, where they hoped to secure passage to the Holy Land. There was turmoil in the eastern Mediterranean at the time, however, and passage through the war-torn sea was uncertain at best. The nascent Jesuits were not deterred by danger; they simply wanted to serve Jesus in His own land. In the end it was impossible. No ship came, though they waited a whole year. "Taking this disappointment as a sign from heaven, Ignatius widened their mission; Jesuits were soon to travel the world and settle in any place where the service of God and the good of souls might be achieved."[5]

The Jesuits were not the first Europeans to take the word of Christ to other continents. As early as A.D. 635, shortly after the death of Mohammed, the monk Alopen was received at court by the Chinese emperor. Numerous Christian communities soon grew up near the capital of Ch'ang-an, and over the following centuries members of many orders made their way to the east.[6] The goal for Ignatius, as for others, was to compete with the Muslims for the conversion of souls in Asia and Africa.

Even before Pope Paul III granted final and official approval of the Society of Jesus in 1540, he sought Ignatius's help in responding to a request he had received from John III, King of Portugal. The King wanted to send Jesuits to his colony of Goa on the west coast of India.[7] Thus the Jesuits were linked from their earliest days in service to both the Church and the state.

Francis Xavier, Ignatius's closest companion in the Society, was selected for the task. When the two men parted, even before Ignatius was selected and had accepted the office of general of the Society, it was to be forever. Francis Xavier would not return from the east.

Voyages in the sixteenth century were not anticipated with pleasure. Indeed, the ceremonies attending the departures of ships from Lisbon were funereal. Looking back at the sailing of the fleet of Vasco da Gama in 1497, Luis de Camoens included the following verses in his *Lusiads:*

> The multitude already deemed us lost
> In the long mazes of a barren chase.
> The wails of women saddened all the coast,
> Mixed with the groans of men, a dismal base.
> Brides, mothers, sisters, as they loved the most,
> With deepest anguish sought a last embrace. . . .
>
> Old men that creep as if they read the ground,
> And little children, tottering as they go,
> In imitation of the mourners round
> Lament for sorrows deeper than they know.
> The neighboring mountains murmered back the sound,
> As if to pity moved for human woe,
> Uncounted as the grains of golden sand
> The tears of thousands fell on Belem's strand.[8]

Francis Xavier sailed from Lisbon on his thirty-fifth birthday, 7 April 1541. Several months later he became the first Jesuit in Africa. The voyage involved many hardships, especially during the forty days they were becalmed off the Guinea Coast of West Africa. The heat there, we are told, was so intense that it melted the candles on board.[9]

The ship carrying Xavier arrived at Mozambique Island in August, 1541, just a few weeks too late to continue on to India on the southwest monsoon. There they waited until the favorable winds would blow again in February. Mozambique Island lies on the coast of southeast Africa, just fifteen degrees below the equator. Because of the difficulty Europeans had in adjusting to the climate, the island was known as "the cemetery of the Portuguese." Francis himself reported eighty deaths during his five months there.[10]

Although it is certainly true to say that Francis Xavier was the first Jesuit missionary to set foot in Africa, it is not possible to say that he ministered much to Africans. His efforts at Mozambique Island were an extension of those he had offered to his shipmates during the voyage around the Cape. He cared for the sick and even gave over to the needs of others the private cabin that had been assigned to him in recognition of his rank. (Among other things, Xavier held the commission of John III of Portugal to Abyssinia; it was never used.) He provided the sacraments and indulgences—the province of any priest. He taught Christian doctrine. And, in spite of his own ill health and occasional bouts of delirium, "he always looked happy—*alegre*—no matter what his sufferings and burdens." There was certainly no limit to the tasks he was willing to perform: washing clothes, feeding patients, emptying and cleaning commodes.[11]

The only recorded meeting between Francis Xavier and an African is described in his own letter from Goa to his brothers of the Society at Rome dated 18 September 1542. Sailing north along the Swahili coast of what is now Tanzania and Kenya, Francis was moved by the sight of the *padrao,* or Portuguese cross, placed by da Gama on a promontory during his voyage almost a half-century earlier. One of Xavier's more imaginative biographers speculates that "during his free moments—few as ever—on the voyage north, Francis must have looked west across a sea smooth and transparent as the Apocalyptic sea of glass to the palm-fringed coast, and thought of the millions beyond it waiting in darkness for the coming of Christ."[12] Well, maybe.

In what must have been a fascinating conversation between Francis and a leading citizen of the Muslim community in Malindi (north of the now-larger Kenyan city of Mombasa), the two devouts lamented the fact that "piety was growing cold" in their respective religious communities.

> "We had a great deal of conversation about this," Xavier writes, "and I told him that God, most Faithful and True, held the misbelievers and their prayers in abomination, and so willed that their worship, which He rejected altogether, should come to nought. . . . One sees in such cases in what anxiety and despair the life of unbelievers and wicked men is so often passed: and indeed this in itself is a blessing sent them by God, that they may be thereby warned of their state and led to conversion."[13]

In short, Francis Xavier ended this first sustained conversation between a Jesuit and an African in Africa with the assertion that "Christians are right and all others are wrong." This was not an auspicious beginning. Fortunately, Xavier went on to more productive missionary work in India and the east.

Abyssinia (Ethiopia)

There was a country in Africa whose Christianity predated all these missionary activities. It was, of course, Abyssinia, known to Ignatius and his Jesuit brothers through the writings of Alvares and from Piedro, an Ethiopian monk residing in Rome since 1540.[14]

Ignatius was personally involved in the preparations to send the first Jesuit missionaries to Abyssinia. As noted above, Francis Xavier himself held King John's commission to the Ethiopians when he left Lisbon in 1541. In about 1546, John of Portugal received a letter from the Negus Claudius asking his fellow monarch to intercede with the Pope to send a patriarch to Abyssinia, as his people were eager for a union with Rome. John suggested that a Jesuit be consecrated. Ignatius did not dissent, even though the office was episcopal, because the "dignity was one of toil and hardships only."[15] The reputation of the Jesuits must have been well established with the Holy See, because Pope Julius III agreed to select members of the Society of Jesus to constitute his delegation to remote and inaccessible Abyssinia. Three Jesuits were consecrated in 1555: Nunez Baretto as patriarch, Oviedo and Camero as suffragan bishops.[16] Ignatius died in the following year before the work that he had inspired could begin.

Ignatius Loyola had a clear vision of the missionary effort he designed for his Jesuit brothers. Although the Muslims were always an important "target"—as they were also for Francis Xavier in East Africa in 1541 and for the Detroit Province Jesuits in the Southern Sudan in the 1980s—the first Jesuit general recognized the role of *accommodation* in missionary activities. In preparing priests to go the Ethiopia, for instance, he urged toleration of the Jewish inheritance of the ancient Christian church, for this was to be missionary work among an already Christian people. He advised his priests not to challenge local customs like circumcision and other "minor abuses." Then, he suggested, the needed changes could be gradually introduced to replace practices unacceptable to Roman Christianity.[17] Ignatius also recognized the necessity for missionaries to provide care for the temporal as well as the spiritual welfare of the people. Thus his vision for the missions included not only those who could act as priests, but construction workers who could build bridges and churches and schools, agricultural experts, physicians, surgeons, and nurses. He also knew that the missionary activity of the Society would benefit the metropole, because his well-educated Jesuits would play their roles as explorers, geographers, astronomers, historians, linguists, and teachers and would bring back detailed knowledge of the rest of the world to Europe. He would not have been disappointed, for Fathers Paez, D'Almeida, Mendez, and Lobo brought scholarly information back to Europe on the customs, usages, and traditions of Abyssinia.[18]

Sadly, this early mission to Abyssinia failed miserably. Bishop Baretto died in Goa in 1562 without ever visiting his diocese. Turkish military activity in the Red Sea area prevented any subsistence from reaching the few Jesuits isolated in Abyssinia. The Negus had turned hostile to their presence in any case, and their ministry was restricted to the small Portuguese community in the country. The Society considered withdrawing its members from the country, but Pope Gregory XIII, anxious not to lose a "Christian country" to the Muslim world, insisted that the mission be maintained.[19]

By 1580 the situation seemed hopeless. Only one Jesuit, Father Lopez, remained in the country in 1583, and, when he died in 1597, the days of the Society of Jesus in Abyssinia were numbered.[20]

This was not from a lack of trying, however. In 1589, Fathers Antonio Montserrat and Pedro Paez, en route to Abyssinia, were captured by "Mussulmans" and "doomed to the slavery of the galleys."[21] In 1595 a Maronite

Jesuit, de Georgiss, had landed at Massawah in the hopes of relieving Lopez, but he was soon slain.[22]

The mercurial status of the Jesuit mission to Abyssinia is reflected by the new developments in the early seventeenth century. In 1603, Father Paez was, remarkably, released from the galleys and was able to enter Abyssinia with five other Jesuits, one a converted Brahmin from India.[23] Paez was a man of many talents; one writer has even compared him with Lawrence of Arabia.[24] He was a priest, a physician, an architect, and an explorer; in 1616 he became the first European to reach Lake Tana, the source of the Blue Nile. Paez was obviously an effective diplomat as well, for at last he won the confidence of the Negus. Paez built the royal palace at Gondar, taught the catechism to members of the royal family and others, engaged in disputations with local clergy of the monophysite persuasion, established a college, and even placed mission stations in tribal villages remote from the capital. Just before Paez's death in 1623 he was able to receive the Negus himself into the church.[25]

Though there were still dangers from the Turks, who beheaded two Jesuits, Machado and Pereira, conversions continued, and by 1625 it was reported that twenty-five thousand people had been baptized in Abyssinia. In the following year, the Negus declared Roman Catholicism to be the "state religion." By 1632, however, a new Negus had succeeded, and the Jesuit misson to Abyssinia was destroyed.[26]

The story of Abyssinia in this period comes to us from a variety of sources. One of the most interesting begins with a book about the country written by Father Jerome Lobo, S. J., who served there in the early seventeenth century. Some time later the book was translated from Portuguese to French. In the eighteenth century, the great English lexicographer, Doctor Samuel Johnson, translated it from French to English and published it as *A Voyage to Abyssinia* (1733). Johnson's more popular dramatic version, *The History of Rasselas, Prince of Abyssinia* (1759), takes its name from that of the Prince, Ras Sella, of Father Lobo's narrative.

Congo and Angola

The first Jesuit mission in all of Africa was established near the mouth of the Congo (now Zaire) River. Two priests, a scholastic, and a lay brother went there in 1547 and worked with sufficient success so that King John III of Portugal could report to Pope Julius III in 1552 that the Congo "was Catholic."[27] This is certainly an overstatement by any measure. Perhaps a few chiefs and their followers had converted in those early years, and one source states unequivocally that three thousand four hundred Africans were baptized during the first six months the Jesuits were on the scene in 1548.[28] But lack of cooperation by local chiefs or "les mauvais vouloir des tyranneaux indigenes," as one Jesuit writer put it, caused the Jesuits to withdraw in 1553.[29]

The Jesuits had more success in nearby Angola during the latter part of the sixteenth century. Four members of the Society accompanied the Portuguese ambassador to the Angolan capital in 1560 with the intention of converting the king. They failed, but they were allowed to leave one of their number there, one Father Gouvea, who remained until his death fifteen years later. Further Jesuit efforts followed in 1584, when the Angolan king and a thousand of his subjects were baptized. By 1590, our Jesuit source continues, there were twenty thousand Christians in the country, and one thousand five hundred were being baptized annually. By 1599 authorities were able to announce that, in Angola, "Christianization was completed."[30]

By the mid-seventeenth century the Jesuits had been joined at Loando by other religious orders. Four monasteries had been established there, one each for the Jesuits, the Franciscans, the Capuchins, and the Carmelites.[31]

Some Jesuit historians argue the the Society's most significant achievement in the Congo-Angola region during the sixteenth and seventeenth centuries was the protection they provided to the African people from the ravages of the slave trade.[32] They did this, however, by owning slaves themselves.[33]

The suppression of the Society of Jesus by Pope Clement XIV in 1773 led to an interruption of Jesuit missionary activity throughout the world. The society was restored in 1814 by Pope Pius VII.

Late in the nineteenth century, when the European powers were preparing to carve up the continent of Africa and divide it among themselves, missionary societies were doing much the same thing. By 1885 the Congo region was under the control of King Leopold of the Belgians, and the political unit was styled l'Etat indépendant du Congo (E. I. C.). Although Leopold had urged many Catholic orders to evangelize the Africans of the Congo, he appealed directly to the Pope, Leo XIII, for Jesuit participation. The Society responded, and the Belgian Jesuits were assigned to the Kwango basin in the west of the E. I. C. In 1893, seven Jesuits, four priests and three brothers, went out, followed in the next year by the sisters of Notre Dame.[34]

Although several missionaries died from illness in the first year or so, the mission itself was remarkably successful in the years 1893 to 1906. Particular attention was given to education for the young. This task was carried out according to an organizational structure similar to the Reductions of Paraguay in the seventeenth and eighteenth centuries. They were called *fermes-écoles-chapelles,* a combination of farms, schools, and chapels. These "secondary posts," built on land donated by local chiefs or secured from them with bribes, allowed the influence of the priests to be extended to the people in the villages. The most intelligent of the youth, sometimes catechists, would be appointed heads of the posts. Instruction in reading, writing, and arithmetic would be alternated with prayerful devotion and practical training in agriculture and cattle raising. They were visited often by a priest who would provide "counsel, encouragement, or reprimand."[35] The progress of the priests through the riverain districts was made easier when some generous benefactors provided them with "le petit steamer," the "Saint-Pierre Claver," a vessel about forty feet long with a covered deck and enclosed quarters.[36]

By 1906 the Kwango mission at Kisantu had a church measuring forty feet by one-hundred-and-twenty feet plus twenty-six other buildings. The priests' house had eighteen private rooms, each about ten feet by fourteen feet, a chapel, a refectory, a library, and a recreation room. The house was surrounded by covered verandas.[37]

Among the many activities supervised by the Jesuits on this thriving mission station was agriculture. Priests and brothers worked with Africans to produce such crops as rice, manioc, sorghum, potatoes, maize, beans, bananas, cabbage, and sugar beets. Significant contributions in this area were made by individual Jesuits such as Brother Gillet, an agricultural economist. He studied various species and their methods of cultivation, identified and categorized them, and even introduced new crops that became staple foods.[38]

Other Jesuits devoted themselves to different forms of scholarship, such as translating scripture and compiling dictionaries of local languages. A printing press was in place at the mission that allowed Jesuits and Africans working together to publish prayer books, catechisms, manuals for various projects, and articles on a variety of topics.

Females were very much involved in the activities of the Kwango mission. The nuns taught the girls, often in an outdoor setting. One photograph shows an imperious sister on a stool, dressed in full habit with a pith helmet atop it—all for protection from the brutal sun. Seated around her on the ground were the attentive girls she was preparing to be good Christian spouses for the young students of the Jesuit priests.[39]

Records report success also in the number of baptisms carried out during the thirteen years under investigation. They averaged about six hundred per year, for a total of seven thousand eight hundred between 1893 and 1906. During the same period the mission was served by a total of forty-six Jesuits, thirty-one priests and fifteen brothers.

The sad aspect of this generally successful missionary experience in Kwango was the mortality rate. Twelve missionaries died in the thirteen years, eleven in the Congo itself and one in Belgium after returning home.[40]

Zambezi (later Rhodesia, now Zimbabwe)

Ignatius Loyola played an indirect but important role in the beginning of

Jesuit missionary activity on the Zambezi: he personally received into the Society of Jesus Father Gonçalo da Silveira, pioneer missionary and "Protomartyr of Rhodesia."[41]

In 1559, three years after the death of Ignatius, word came to the Jesuit station at Goa that the Zambezi River area in southeast Africa was "favorable for the introduction of the gospel."[42] Local African chiefs, perhaps even "kings" and "princes," were requesting baptism. Gonçalo da Silveira, a former provincial, was chosen for the task and went from India to Africa with two other Jesuits, a Father Fernandez and one brother.[43]

In 1560, the party proceeded up the Zambezi River as far as Tongue, where they baptized King Gamba of Inhambane and four hundred of his subjects. They proceeded onward past Sena and Mabate, also baptizing in those places, until they reached the kingdom of Monomatapa itself. There they baptized the "God Emperor" himself, together with all his court.[44]

These accomplishments of the first year of the Zambezi mission constituted its zenith. Soon there were implications of a vague "Mohammedan" conspiracy, in which Father Gonçalo was slandered for "alleged political machinations" with the Portuguese. A sentence of death was soon passed upon him. The accounts reveal that Father Gonçalo was spiritually prepared for martyrdom, a fact that must have intimidated his executioners, for they were unable to approach him when he was awake and resorted to strangling him in his sleep. His corpse was then thrown into the Zambezi, down which it floated until it was caught on a small island. There, we are told, wild beasts and birds guarded the body day and night, "evidently taking watches in turn, as by superior direction, so as to prevent any mutilation or desecration."[45]

These and other difficulties convinced Father Fernandez to return to the station at Goa, which he did in 1562.

The Jesuits made another series of missionary efforts on the Zambezi in the seventeenth century, and these were somewhat more successful. By 1624 there were eight stations in the region with twenty missionaries, and four year later there were twenty-five Jesuits there, fifteen in the field and ten on the faculty of "Mozambique College."[46]

Intense Jesuit activity did not resume in the area for another two-and-a-half centuries. In 1875, at the request of Bishop James Richards, a party of Jesuits was sent to Grahamstown, South Africa, to take over Saint Aidan's College there. In 1879, a portion of this group, under the leadership of Father Henry Depelchin, S. J., set out for the north to extend Catholicism once again into the Zambezi region. His goal was Lobengula's Matabeleland, which he wanted to prevent from becoming an exclusively Protestant area of missionary activity. The work was extremely difficult, the territory vast, the Africans not receptive, and the threat of disease ever present. One of the brightest and most promising members of Depelchin's team, an English Jesuit named Augustus Law, became a "bloodless martyr" during the first year of the mission, "a victim of the chief's indifference and the climate."

Law died before the mission established any permanent settlement or made any converts.[47]

The struggle went on for more than a decade, during which time hardly any progress was made. At one point, in 1889, the Jesuits were offered the choice of leaving Matabeleland or restricting their teaching to agriculture. Naturally, they accepted the restriction so that they could stay, and then they went right on with their mission of converting the Africans.

The arrival of the British in the country that was to become Rhodesia intensified the political rivalries among the Europeans and the religious competition among the Christians. When Lobengula failed to secure a holding in Mashonaland from the British, he responded by ordering all Europeans out of Matabeleland. The Jesuits, along with others, left as ordered and continued their efforts in other parts of the Zambezi basin, including Mashonaland, where the British Company made a concession to them. Farther to the east, toward Portuguese East Africa, there was a series of struggling stations managed by Polish Jesuits.[48]

The Jesuit experience on the Zambezi raises several interesting questions about their activities. Their links with colonial governments—with the French on Madagascar as well as with the British, the Boers, and the Portuguese in southern Africa—were never understood by the Africans and thus were always suspect. In addition to natural opposition from the Protestant missionaries, particularly the London Missionary Society, the Jesuits provoked the hostility of European traders in the area. This may have been an animosity founded in morality, as the Jesuits objected to the European traders taking African wives and mistresses.

A bewildering aspect of the behavior of the Jesuits on the Zambezi in the late nineteenth century is their apparent naïveté about health hazards. Their letters and reports, particularly those involving Father Augustus Law, indicate that they took hardly any precautions against fever or other illnesses. One writer suggests that the explanation is the ignorance of the Jesuit authorities in Rome regarding conditions in Africa's interior. But this seems unlikely, because the Society's efforts were allegedly inspired by the message of Doctor David Livingstone, whose fate illustrated and whose writings warned against the dangers of disease. The Jesuits would certainly have known that quinine was the appropriate prophylactic to combat malaria, but their letters reveal that they rarely used quinine carefully or took the necessary rest when stricken. This is all the more bewildering in the light of so many diary entries of Jesuits who devoted many hours to giving health care to Africans.

The story of the Zambezi mission is filled with tales of devotion, dedication, hard work, and tenacity among the Jesuit missionaries. It also contains testimony about their hostility to some African customs and traditions, the insensitivity of their political alliances, and their indifference to their own health and well-being.

The Southern Sudan

In 1989, there were 1,240 Jesuits working in twenty-nine African countries. More than one-third of that total, 450 Jesuits, were African. The remaining two-thirds came from twenty different nations in Asia, Europe, North and South America. These Jesuits are involved in parish work, directing the Spiritual Exercises, running social centers, training their own novices, and teaching at seminaries, secondary schools, universities, and institutes of higher education.[49]

The experience of one Jesuit school in Africa in the 1980s might serve as an example of the persistence of the Jesuit missionary spirit, the focus on the education of African youth, the international dimension of support and supply for relatively small projects, the ability to "carry on" in the midst of political and military turmoil, and the courage of individual priests and brothers in the face of physical danger.

Loyola Secondary School in Wau, Southern Sudan, was a mission enterprise undertaken by the Detroit Province of the Society of Jesus in cooperation with the Province of East Africa (Nairobi). A chronicle of the experience was kept by Father Norman Dickson, S.J., who participated in the mission during its entire operation. Father Dickson's account is supplemented by appendices containing correspondence, reports, diagrams, photographs, and other information.

Wau is the capital of the Bahr-el-Ghazal, one of the three administrative districts of the Southern Sudan. It is also the seat of the Catholic diocese of Wau, whose Bishop since 1981 has been Joseph Nyekindi.

The chief Catholic missionaries in the southern Sudan from 1881 to 1964 were the Italian Verona Fathers, also known as the "Combonis." They were forced out by a hostile Muslim regime in 1964. The first Jesuits to arrive in the Wau area were from India; they came in 1971. These Jesuits paid tribute to the work of the Combonis, noting that they provided "models for religious activity" and "Catholicism of the Italian brand."[50]

During a 1981 visit by the Detroit Provincial, Father Mike Lavelle, S.J., to his men who were teaching at Saint Paul's Major Seminary in Bussere, nine miles from Wau, Bishop Nyekindi asked him about the possibility of the Jesuits founding a secondary school there. Father Lavelle's response was positive, but he insisted on the precondition that the school "would have to be overwhelmingly Christian." Also, no matter what relation existed with the diocese or the government of the Sudan, the Society of Jesus would have to have *de facto* jurisdiction over the school.[51]

Father Lavelle and his fellow Jesuits had two fundamental goals in establishing the school. First, they hoped to meet the needs of the Sudan, for there were hardly any competent African teachers in the southern part of the country. Second, they believed that the students of the school might provide the future clergy of the area. Father Lavelle thought the school could be established relatively inexpensively—perhaps for less than $20,000. (This proved to be optimistic. By the time the school opened in the fall of 1983, $212,000 had been spent.)[52]

Basic intruction was first offered in English and mathematics; in 1984 religion, geography, and general science were added. Sixty-two students were accepted for the term beginning in March of that year.

Loyola Secondary School was born in the midst of a revolution. The Sudan People's Liberation Army (SPLA), under the leadership of John Garang, was in revolt against the Muslim government in Khartoum. Conditions in April and May of 1984 can be discerned from the following entry in Father Dickson's chronicle:

> Thus the time of April and May, 1984 was a difficult period. To carry on construct- ing several buildings and to launch a new school in a foreign country which was then on the brink of a disastrous civil war demanded constant and prayerful dedication and much mutual tolerance and support. Given the pretty grim political circumstances, and despite more than a few moments of community tension, Loyola did make remarkable early progress.[53]

Remarkably, as external conditions worsened—through the institution of traditional Muslim Law (the *sharia*), the intensification of the fighting, the restrictions on travel and on the transport of supplies, and the overthrow of the Numieri government—attendance, punctuality, and retention at Loyola Secondary School remained strong. Indeed, 7 September 1985 was Parents' Day. "More than forty parents of Loyola's sixty students walked, biked, or drove up to Loyola for an effective two hour program which included talks by the Bishop and Fr. Dickson, a tour of the facilities, and a tea social with the staff."[54]

Inevitably, such bliss could not continue in the context of war. By mid-1986, conditions were such that the Provincial in Detroit ordered the Jesuits out of Wau. It was too dangerous. True to their independent spirit, however, the Wau Jesuits appealed the order on the grounds that two funda- mental conditions for withdrawal had not yet been met: (1) a general break- down in law and order, and (2) a direct threat to them as missionaries or as citizens of a foreign country. The leadership relented, and they stayed.[55] Both the teaching of the students and the construction of the buildings continued for the remainder of 1986, even in the context of famine in the countryside and occupation by government forces of the hill upon which the school was built. This soon became too much for the students and their families, how- ever, and attendance dwindled to such a low level that teaching at the school had to be terminated on 30 January 1987. Later that year, the Jesuits decided to pull out of Wau completely, leaving the building and the property under the care of the Bishop. To prevent a takeover of the property by Government troops, however, one Detroit Province Jesuit, Father Dick Cherry, remained on the site when Father Dickson completed his chronicle in mid-1988.[56]

Afterword

An interesting echo of a common Jesuit missionary concern throughout the centuries was heard in the context of the Wau Jesuits' "discernments" in 1986 and 1987 as they made lists of the pros and cons of withdrawal. Number 7 on the list of reasons why the Jesuits *should* continue the operation of Loyola Secondary School was: "Loyola offers the people of Southern Sudan a resource for resisting Islamization."[57]

Notes

1. Noel Q. King, "Of God and Maxim Guns: Presbyterianism in Nigeria, 1846–1966," *American Historical Review* 95.1 (February 1990): 226.

2. John K. Fairbank, "Assignment for the '70s," Presidential Address to the American Historical Association, December 1968, *American Historical Review* 74.3 (February 1969): 870–71.

3. Noel Q. King, "Of God and Maxim Guns," p. 226.

4. Joseph N. Tylenda, S.J., *Jesuit Saints and Martyrs* (Chicago: Loyola University Press, 1984), p. 449.

5. Ibid., in foreword by Bernard Bassett, S.J., p. xx.

6. Felix A. Plattner, *Jesuits Go East* (Dublin: Clonmore and Reynolds, 1950), p. 10.

7. Joseph N. Tylenda, S.J., *Jesuit Saints and Martyrs,* p. 450.

8. Luis de Camoens, *Lusiads,* quoted in James Broderick, S.J., *Saint Francis Xavier* (New York: Wicklow, 1952), p. 97.

9. James Broderick, S.J., *Saint Francis Xavier,* pp. 101–2.

10. Margaret Yeo, *St. Francis Xavier, Apostle of the East* (London: Sheed and Ward, 1931), p. 94.

11. James Broderick, S.J., *Saint Francis Xavier,* pp. 102–6.

12. Margaret Yeo, *St. Francis Xavier, Apostle of the East,* p. 94.

13. Ibid., p. 94.

14. Philip Caraman, S.J., *The Lost Empire: The Story of the Jesuits in Ethiopia, 1555–1634* (London, 1985), pp. 10–11.

15. Martin P. Harney, S.J., *The Jesuits in History: The Society of Jesus through Four Centuries* (New York: The America Press, 1941), p. 98.

16. Ibid., p. 98.

17. Philip Caraman, S.J., *The Lost Empire,* p. 11.

18. Thomas J. M. Burke, S.J., *Beyond All Horizons: Jesuits and the Missions* (New York: Hanover House, 1957), p. 138.

19. Martin P. Harney, S.J., *The Jesuits in History,* p. 153.

20. Philip Caraman, S.J., *The Lost Empire,* p. 16.

21. Martin P. Harney, S.J., *The Jesuits in History,* p. 220.

22. Ibid., p. 220.

24. Ibid., p. 220.

24. Edward D. Reynolds, S.J., *Jesuits for the Negro* (New York: The America Press, 1949), p. 5.

25. Martin P. Harney, S.J., *The Jesuits in History,* pp. 220–21.

26. Ibid., pp. 220–21.

27. Edward D. Reynolds, S.J., *Jesuits for the Negro,* p. 5.

28. *Au Congo et aux Indes: Les Jesuites Belges aux Missions* (Bruxelles: Charles Bulens, 1906), pp. 13–14.

29. Ibid., pp. 13–14.

30. Edward D. Reynolds, S.J., *Jesuits for the Negro*, pp. 6–7.

31. Ibid., pp. 6–7.

32. Ibid., pp. 6–7.

33. Roland Oliver, *The Cambridge History of Africa*, (Cambridge: The University Press, 1977), 3: 555.

34. *Au Congo et aux Indes*, p. 15.

35. Ibid., p. 24.

36. Ibid., p. 35.

37. Ibid., p. 43.

38. Edward D. Reynolds, S.J., *Jesuits for the Negro*, pp. 9–10.

39. *Au Congo et aux Indes*, pp. 82, 93.

40. Ibid., p. 125.

41. Edward King, S.J., *Black Robes and Black Skins* (London: Catholic Truth Society, 1920), p. 2.

42. Edward D. Reynolds, S.J., *Jesuits for the Negro*, p. 10.

43. Ibid., p. 10.

44. Ibid., p. 10.

45. Ibid., p. 10.

46. Ibid., p. 10.

47. Edward King, S.J., *Black Robes*, pp. 3–6.

48. Ibid., p. 21.

49. Jesuit Province of East Africa, *Newsletter*, September 1989.

50. Norman Dickson, S.J., *Chronicle, Loyola Secondary School, Wau, Sudan* (unpublished typescript, 1988), p. 6.

51. Ibid., p. 11.

52. Ibid., p.14.

53. Ibid., p. 19.

54. Ibid., p. 29.

55. Ibid., p. 36.

56. Ibid., p. 43.

57. Ibid., appendix.

Translating the Good: Roberto de Nobili's Moral Argument and Jesuit Education Today

FRANCIS X. CLOONEY, S.J.

It is an essential component of Jesuit education today that we, lay and Jesuit alike, challenge and help students to live the moral life—to become "men and women for others." In this challenge the goals of education and our religious faith converge. But it is also true that it is a complex task to explain how religion, and specific religions, relate to living the moral life, in the religiously plural world of the late twentieth century. We need to ask: when we maintain schools in the Jesuit tradition and thereby seek to offer an education system that brings religion and morality together, are we saying that there is a special link between being Christian and being moral, or that being religious (in some way or another) is an important part of being moral, or simply that believers, like unbelievers, need to be morally responsible? Does it matter today whether one is Christian, or Hindu, or Lakota, or none or these, when confronted by moral challenges?

Even if our students do not formulate these questions explicitly, their experience implies such questions. The modern world places them in frequent contact with people of religions very different from their own, and from an early age they begin to notice the similarities and differences among religions; they grow up at least implicitly aware of the religious pluralism of the much smaller world of the late twentieth century. As Jesuit educators we need to ask: how does this new situation change the way we teach the moral values learned in the Christian tradition, but now in relation to a much wider variety of religious and nonreligious values than was hitherto the case?

This essay travels a circuitous path in order to respond to these basic, urgent questions. I will travel to south India in the seventeenth century, in order to reflect on the moral and religious argumentation of Roberto de Nobili, an early Jesuit expert in the problems of education and pluralism. If we understand how his project compares with ours, our task as educators will be helpfully clarified.

Roberto de Nobili and the Limits on Openness to Other Religions

Roberto de Nobili (1577–1656) is rightly taken as a model of the Jesuit who takes seriously the problem of rethinking Christian truth and values in a new context.[1] His experience and achievements were remarkable. At the beginning of the seventeenth century in Madurai, south India, he presented himself to the local Hindus[2] as a "holy man," or renouncer *(saṁnyāsi),* who had come from the West; he dressed in the very simple fashion adopted by Hindu renouncers and lived an austere and pure lifestyle—even to the extent or respecting caste restrictions and avoiding the lower castes (leaving work with them to other missionaries); he became fluent in Tamil and perhaps in Sanskrit and acquired great familiarity with Hindu beliefs and customs. In his Latin works he defended the principle of "adaptation": just as Christianity legitimately adopted many of the local customs and even religious practices of the Greco-Roman world and successfully endowed these with "Christian significance," it is equally legitimate to practice this adaptation when Christianity encounters other great civilizations beyond the boundaries of Europe.

My limited examination of de Nobili's Tamil treatises—I have read portions of a number of them, but none completely—suggests that a profound faith in the unversality of human experience, in the universality of reason, and in the goodness of creation underlies de Nobili's practical argumentation. His critique always distinguished between what he considered to be the basic soundness, humanity, and potential for salvation that he felt were inherent in Indian culture, and the overlay of superstition and wrong ideas, which he condemned. He avoided sweeping attacks on the culture he saw around him and always maintained the confidence that people can be persuaded, no matter how different they are from the missionary.

But despite his openness and pioneering achievements in learning about the Hindu religion, he remained always a highly educated and committed European Christian who carefully assessed, and then assimilated only in modified form, bits and pieces from the religious environment around him. He was not tolerant in a modern sense. In his Tamil treatises, which ranged from catechetical expositions of the faith to a theoretical treatise on Christian doctrines and their presuppositions and to directly apologetic works in which he would refute Hindu doctrines such as rebirth and the Hindu image of the divine in general,[3] de Nobili presented the truths of the Catholic Faith with admirable clarity, defended them vigorously against a variety of criticisms, and devoted considerable energy to the project of criticizing corresponding Hindu practices and theories.

In the remainder of this essay I ask how we should go about locating ourselves vis-à-vis de Nobili the adapter of the Christian message and de

Nobili the zealous apologist. I will argue that we have to negotiate carefully
and intelligently the distance between his world and ours, recognizing much
of his task as our own, but also making distinctions that he did not make. On
the one hand, if Jesuit education is to have a purpose, we need to share his
confidence in reason, in the possibility of normative moral claims, and in the
rightness of the Christian religion; on the other, if Jesuit education is to be
successful, we must be responsibly informed about the religions that flourish
around us, take them seriously in their specificity, and argue differently than
did de Nobili about how religions and morality relate. I will illustrate these
points by a critique of a single example, de Nobili's demonstration of the
immorality and hence unreality of the Hindu gods in his Tamil *Catechism,*
the *Ñānōpatēcam.*[4]

God, Goodness, and the "Right Religion"

De Nobili devotes the fifth and sixth chapters of the first part of the
Catechism to a consideration of the moral and ontological goodness of God
and the application of this truth in the south Indian context. The two chapters
are an exercise in apologetics, and chapter 6 is particularly polemic in tone.

In chapter 5, he argues that there is a correlation between the degree of
goodness of God/gods and the goodness of religious and moral behavior, and
that this correlation is correctly represented in the Christian religion. The
very idea of God includes the idea of perfect (ontological and moral) goodness; God is metaphysically good, in the sense of being perfect in every way,
and therefore is not deficient, and is liable neither to improvement and
decline, nor to any of the wants or weaknesses that provoke evil behavior in
humans.[5] Finally, since God is perfect and beyond the grasp of our imperfect
minds, which know only through their engagement in a world of imperfect
realities, God is not imaginable in terms of our ordinary projections of what
intelligent beings are like. God ought not to be imagined as behaving in the
ways that humans do, nor as satisfying even good desires in the way that
humans do. God is perfect and without need.

Given this nature of God as good and the implied features of a religion
appropriately directed to the true God, de Nobili goes on to argue in chapter
6 that the Hindu gods are not real gods and that the Hindu religion is neither
morally acceptable nor conducive toward making people morally better. He
martials evidence to the effect that the Hindu gods do not warrant the name
"God," because they are neither ontologically nor morally good. His evidence is based on the accounts of the gods in Hindu myths, on the religious
practice of Hindus and, as a corollary to the latter, on the condition and
function of Hindu temples. Since he invests great energy in showing that the
gods can be shown not to measure up to the standard of divine goodness, let
us consider his evidence and estimate its relevance for us.[6]

De Nobili's Evidence against the Goodness of the Hindu Gods

First, the myths recounted in the ancient stories (the *purāṇas*) show the vile character of the gods. We learn all kinds of scandalous details: the evil deeds and dispositions of Rudra, Viṣṇu, Brahmā; another god lusts after his own daughter; another is not satisfied after a thousand years "with a woman," and so scatters his semen everywhere, finally into fire; another lives with women resting on his head, his chest, and other parts of his body; the gods continually appear in undignified forms, such as those of the boar, the fish, and so forth; they are immersed in the mire of infatuation; they abuse one another and commit all kinds of improper deeds.

Second, the worship in their honor is evil: devotees spurn marriage with women who are suitable to their families and seek satisfaction elsewhere; they care nothing about sin; devoid of all shame, they go about totally naked, drinking in public, performing the worship of Śiva; they perform horrible rites, such as ripping a fetus out of a mother's womb, cutting its throat, and finally walking in the blood; they kill people of certain castes in the worship of certain gods; they commit suicide at the command of their gods. They do all of this to please their gods, who must surely be evil if they are thus pleased.

Third, even their temples are foul and immoral. Hindus carry on sinful practices in them, such as the practice of maintaining *devadāsis* (who have been termed variously "temple dancers" or "prostitutes") right inside their temples. This is so despite the evident fact that places of worship should be purer than ordinary places, so as to be conducive to the improvement of the worshippers. The filth of the temples exemplifies vividly the nature of the gods who dwell in them.

De Nobili insists that it is clear from this evidence that the Hindu gods do not fit the definition of God. Unsurprisingly, given the falseness of its gods, the Hindu religion is shown to serve a purpose just the opposite of what true religion is meant for: it corrupts rather than edifies its members by persuading them to act immorally in order to please immoral gods. Therefore, he concludes, anyone who understands properly the nature of God and the purpose of religion should turn away from Hinduism and seek salvation in Christianity.

Thus far his argumentation. It is not my purpose here to attempt a historical reconstruction of the setting in which the arguments were posed and (possibly) responded to.[7] Rather, I am interested in exploring the implications of de Nobili's arguments for our late-twentieth-century educational project.

On the one hand, we can readily admit that, though he was working in circumstances quite different from ours, de Nobili was engaged in a project we should be loath to abandon—the investigation of the relationship of religion and morality, and the construction of convincing religious arguments in favor of moral behavior. On the other hand, we must find de Nobili's arguments rather unconvincing. We know too much about religion and the Hindu religion, and we know what we know too differently for it to be possible for us simply to adopt his apologetic. Let us now distinguish the underlying principles, which we should be reluctant to abandon, from those theoretical and practical arguments which we cannot responsibly maintain today; and at the same time let us identify some skills that we need to acquire today.

Some Basic Principles Underlying de Nobili's Apologetics

First let us consider de Nobili's presuppositions, which I summarize as follows:

1. Reason is universal, at least in the sense that communication and some conclusive arguments across cultural boundaries are possible.
2. There are universal norms, at least in the sense that persuasive claims about right and wrong are possible across cultural boundaries.
3. Religion, reason, and morality are deeply connected: morality functions fully, in theory and in practice, only when located within the horizon of religious meaning; conversely, when religious meaning is deficient, morality too will suffer.
4. It is possible to show that there is a strong positive connection between being a Christian, being reasonable, and being moral: the Christian experience and understanding of God support the theory and practice of the moral life.[8]

I see no reason why we should abandon these presuppositions. As theologians and educators, we are challenged to follow de Nobili in the project of connecting the reasonable, the moral, and the religious, if we wish to make convincing crosscultural and crossreligious arguments about how to live the moral life. For de Nobili, however, there is a fifth presupposition, which is at stake in chapter 6 of the *Catechism:*

5. It is possible to demonstrate that non-Christian religions, such as Hinduism, are inherently lacking the adequate, comprehensive basis for morality.

This is where the evidence from de Nobili's personal learning and observation becomes relevant, and it is here that problems arise. As it stands, this fifth presupposition fails to persuade, for it is difficult to accept the evidence de Nobili offers us as contributing to the conclusion that he intends. In the following pages I will consider three reasons why we cannot simply borrow his arguments—reasons related to the understanding of myth, to the evaluation of moral behavior, and to the role of theology in religion.

The Problem of Reading Myths

We have seen that de Nobili argues from the images of the gods presented in the myths he was familiar with to conclusions about the nature of the gods thus portrayed. But today we know that myths—or the texts that recount myths previously passed down in oral form—are not intended to inform us directly of the real nature of gods and supernatural realities. In a complex fashion myths signify a supernatural realm, but without a one-to-one correspondence of elements in the myth and elements in reality. We are ill advised to read myths as if they intend to tell us about real participant persons or real historical events, either celestial or terrestrial. Surely, too, we ought not impose on other religions' texts the unexamined referentiality we have largely abandoned regarding the Bible.

Today we cannot move as comfortably as did de Nobili from the depicted events in myths to the implied nature of the gods or to deductions about the fundamental claims of the religions that remember these myths.[9] Hindu myths in particular further dissuade us from his mode of interpretation. As they are now available to us, they are shown to be literarily sophisticated texts (or oral discourses and practices) that inscribe the pantheon of ancient deities from the Vedic period (from before 1000 B.C.E.) and to a certain extent later Hindu deities as well in a frame of reference that indicates that gods and humans both are constrained by the same rules. Instead of being detached, perfect models for human activity, the gods are often presented as examples of what happens when one violates the boundaries of acceptable behavior. Moreover, in the course of the theological shifts that mark the transitions and sectarian developments in Indian religion as a continually growing and shifting set of beliefs and practices, the retelling of myths is often a device for marking the downfall of some gods and the rise of others. We cannot take at face value everything that is said; we have to understand what is meant.

For example, when de Nobili refers to the story of the god who lusts after his daughter, he is probably referring to an ancient myth of Prajāpati, one of the early creator gods. De Nobili thinks that this myth clearly illustrates the depravity of the god and the Hindu religion connected with it. But from the several versions of the myth we have today we can see that the successive retelling of the story condemn the portrayed incest, as the other gods reprehend Prajāpati's flawed urge toward creation and then take steps to punish him and to make ritual amends. The tradition actually uses the continually reworked story as the basis for a critique of Vedic polytheism and for a positive exposition of ritual and the ritual paradigm of creativity.[10]

The project of gleaning moral values and claims from information in myths is, then, not as straightforward a task for us as it might have been for a seventeenth-century Jesuit. We cannot simply decipher the story line of a text and on that basis assess the validity of the thought intended or the pattern of life implied. If we wish to move from myth to judgments about the moral values of a religion, this cannot be done in a direct leap from plots to corresponding patterns of real or ideal behavior. Rather, we need to learn to read myths in their literary and lived context(s).[11] The texts—myths, but then also practices, images, and, in short, everything that is related to a religion's worldview—do reflect and constitute ways of looking at the world, but not simply by reporting merely available, out-there realities that can grasped one by one. As educators we are therefore challenged to teach students to read their own and other peoples' religions in a sophisticated manner.

Assessing the Relationship between Reported Moral Behavior and Religious Worldviews

If, as de Nobili charges, (some) Hindus in Madurai indulged in practices such as ritual murder and incest, we cannot condone the practices just because they belong to a foreign culture—any more than we should be inclined to forgive a foreign government today for the practice of torture or terrorism, or a religious group for the slaughter of its heretics. However respectful we want our students to be toward religions and their cultures, our schools will quickly lose their relevance if we are unable to argue for some normative standards for moral behavior. Hence, in assessing de Nobili's arguments, we cannot dismiss the charges he makes as simply irrelevant.

Of course, we need to ascertain the facts before we judge, and here we are in a difficult position regarding de Nobili's actual charges. In general, we do not have readily available sufficient and detailed evidence on actual religious practices in Madurai in de Nobili's time. Much primary research still needs to be done, and I do not believe that we have evidence that would support his harsh claims. Since he does not base his charges on larger structural and systemic considerations (such as caste distinctions) that are still in evidence today and that could, mutatis mutandis, be weighed, it is difficult for us to assess particular charges about practices that are no longer current.

But let us suppose for a moment that his charges are accurate, in the sense that they are based on what de Nobili actually saw in Madurai; after all, we have no reason to believe he was simply making up his examples. But we are obliged to interpret the charges correctly, locating them in the apologetic discourse composed around them. Even real cases of immoral behavior still require description in some manner and location within a narrative that weaves the individual cases together, so as to use them to the greatest rhetorical effect as convincing materials in the indictment of the opposing religious position. We need to take into account the style of apologetic literature, wherein it is a frequent strategy to associate wrong ideas with bad morality.

De Nobili presumedly argued his cased against the Hindus with an awareness of the long Christian tradition of apologetics. An interesting parallel is book 2 of Saint Augustine's *The City of God,* wherein the immorality of the Roman gods and their permissive attitude toward immoral human behavior are identified as causes for many of the troubles experienced by Rome before the coming of Christ. The tone and procedure of Augustine's and de Nobili's texts are strikingly alike, as are some of the conclusions; it would not be surprising if de Nobili were familiar with Augustine's text and used it as a model for his own.[12] If there are such literary and theological precedents, it is all the more important to read the set of charges, however damning, as a carefully composed literary document and not simply as a report on what is really the case.

But let us further suppose that the rhetorical presentation of the charges does not obscure their basis in fact. We will still not have reached the point where we can conclude that these immoral activities are inherent in Hinduism, so as to be able to make a decisive judgment about the religion. For we still have to think about the kind of conclusions that can be drawn from these facts: for example, these instances of evil behavior may be characteristic of Hinduism, or prevalent (or occasional) in a culture in which Hinduism flourishes, or merely disparate instances of human divergence from ideal religious norms.

It is by no means clear how one is to make these arguments.[13] Even if we suppose that there are universal moral norms and so feel confident in judging certain kinds of behavior universally immoral, it is difficult, especially since we now know a great amount about Hinduism and its complex mix of the ideal and the practiced, to draw conclusions about whether the apparent flaws are inherent in the religion or not. Certainly, the history of the Christian West has made it necessary for us to distinguish between what happens in a culture and what is inherent in the dominant religion of that culture; we need to be likewise cautious in judging other peoples' religions by the worst behavior of persons who belong in some way to those religions.

If we are thus compelled to be very cautious about making de Nobili's claims our own, we also need to avoid lapsing into an embarrassed silence where we simply stop making claims. It is no solution simply to concede that one can never claim a connection between religions and the practice of good behavior. Even if we are correctly hesitant about trying to prove that religions other than our own are inherently morally flawed, we should not go so far as to concede that no connections can be made or that religions can never be criticized for what happens in cultures they helped form and still dominate. We need to be able to argue moral claims in theory and practice, if education for the moral is to be religious in any meaningful sense.

Our task is then twofold. We need to be able to teach students how to think in terms of a true crossreligious moral normativity, while yet learning also how to read this morality as insiders do, within the larger horizon of each religion. The necessary skills include the ability to disabuse ourselves of baseless stereotypes of the other, a sensitivity as to how religions go about recognizing and confronting the evidently immoral vis à vis their core values, and the ability to be as fair in judging other religions as we are in judging our own.

The Comparative Theological Component of Crosscultural Moral Argument

When de Nobili juxtaposes his discussion of the inherent goodness of God (chapter 5) with his critique of Hinduism (chapter 6), he legitimately bridges the gap between theology and observed religious practice. But another problem then arises. De Nobili was undoubtedly a sophisticated and learned Christian theologian, but, although he was probably more familiar with Hinduism than any European in the early seventeenth century, we cannot avoid the impression that he was only partially successful in getting inside information about Hinduism and that he was therefore not in a position to balance his Christian theological training with a sophisticated grasp of Hindu theological tradition.[14]

By contrast, it is very clear that *we* have access to a great number of sophisticated Hindu treatises in theology and morality—far more than we have assimilated into our theological reflection. We now know that, even in de Nobili's time, the Hindus had well-worked-out systems that intended, at least, to present the Hindu religion(s) of Kṛṣṇa, Śiva, and others at its (their) best and so to support moral behavior. They took moral issues seriously and even argued about whether the great Gods—such as Kṛṣṇa and Śiva (who were thought to be superior to the old Vedic gods and not necessarily subject to the same rules and sanctions as they were)—would be constrained in their moral behavior. For instance, the well-known account of Kṛṣṇa's daliance with the married cowherd women (the *gopis*) in the *Bhāgavata Purāṇa* occasioned a commentarial debate about the propriety and significance of Kṛṣṇa's apparent violation of the accepted norms of sexuality.[15]

But even apart from direct considerations of moral and theological problems, south Indian Hindu communities developed important theological systems such as the Śaiva Siddhānta, which constituted a comprehensive theology for the Śaiva religion—including an understanding of scripture; supporting epistemological, cosmological, and metaphysical arguments; and developed doctrines of grace, sin, and soteriology. Like Christian theologians, the Śaiva Siddhānta theologians located discussions of right and wrong human behavior in broader, comprehensive theological perspectives.

My point is not simply that Hindus have theology, nor do I wish to argue here that one or another Hindu theological idea might be equal to or better than a corresponding Christian theological idea. Rather, my point is that, if we make ambitious claims about the universality of reason and morality and about the strong relation of religion to both, we are making complex theological claims. If so, we are *necessarily* involved in crossreligious theological conversation. We need to read and even to talk to our theological counter-/parts in other religions before we assess their moral practices.

The available knowledge about Hindu theology makes it all the less legitimate for us to compare their practice, in all its imperfections, with our theology, in all its ideal correctness. De Nobili might be excused for not having access to Hindu reasoning as systematized as his own, but we have no excuse for examining only the practices of other religions and not the theologies and strategies of doctrine by which the various communities tried to order and explain right behavior.

So too, the expansion of our knowledge about Hindu theology means that we have to make our judgments about morality and religions differently than did de Nobili and thereafter to teach them differently. Our efforts to assess similarities, to adjudicate differences, and to condemn what we judge to be unacceptable have to be responsibly informed by traditions' theological positions as well as the religions' lived, popular versions. This is so even if we want to focus on how people act in today's world; however practical our concerns, as theologians and educators we need to be as sophisticated in connecting their theology and practice as we are in connecting Christian theology and practice.

Consequently, when we teach students how to think about morality in the context of religious pluralism, we need to teach them how to take into account the specifically theological argumentation of those religions and not simply their primary religious language or remarkable instances of moral or immoral behavior. This broader theological contextualization will of course require that we introduce our students to theological reasoning in general, since we cannot presume their familiarity with Christian or any other theological reasoning. If the students are Christian, we need to introduce them to examples of theological thinking in the Christian tradition and, in the same introductory courses, to theological thinking as practiced in other traditions and then, finally, to possible ways of thinking theologically in a pluralistic, comparative context. Then we will be able to explain more convincingly how the religious traditions under discussion link moral behavior with their specific theological traditions; ultimately, we will be better able to help students understand how religion and morality relate.

Conclusion

Unlike de Nobili, we live in a world that questions the universality of reason and morality or that at least doubts whether we can talk about either in any specifiable, practical fashion.[16] Our age questions strongly whether a claim linking any given religion with any given moral or immoral behavior is possible; it certainly doubts very strongly the notion that Christianity—or any religion—possesses a basis for the morally good that is demonstrably superior to all others.

There is much in this change in modern sensibility that is for the better. We will certainly all be better off if we learn to compare, contrast, and debate religiously without falling back into notions of superiority and competition, and if we likewise encourage our students to think about religious pluralism without looking simply for a clean winner in the competition of religions.

Nevertheless, some version of de Nobili's seventeenth-century claims needs to be retrieved and preserved in the late twentieth century, if Jesuit education is to retain its distinctive character. We too need to argue that it is possible to communicate rationally across cultural and religious boundaries and that, despite many loose ends and ambiguities, it is possible to identify certain behavior as unacceptable, no matter whose behavior it is. We must still claim that there is a link among the religious, the rational, and the moral and that there is a strong, significant relationship between being Christian and being good.

But we are 350 years distant from him, and we do not speak the same language. We can be his heirs—defenders of continuity, right behavior, and truth in a context of diversity—*only* if we do not imitate him directly. As I have indicated, we know too much, and we know what we know differently. So we have to teach differently, too.

Before we teach, we ourselves have to rethink our views on religion in light of the vast store of new information readily available to theologians and scholars of religion, especially on the nature of rationality and its contexts and on the functions and meanings of myths and ritual. If we are serious about having coherent theological underpinnings to our educational process, we need also to become better informed about the theologies of other religions and more skilled in the intelligent assessment and negotiation of similarities, differences, and contradictions between their theologies and ours.

Then, with this knowledge and skill at least incipiently in place, we can rethink how morality is to be taught in an educational context that retains a religious filiation. We can begin to devise strategies by which to show students how to negotiate the distance between what is universal—rational, moral, religious—and the local particularity of the religion(s) and culture(s) within which they and other people live rationally and morally.

This challenge clearly pertains in a global context, where our Jesuit schools usually have students bodies that are primarily or even entirely non-Christian. If we take seriously the link of religion to morality, we should not venture to teach morality while passing in silence over the religious traditions to which the students belong—unless we have and can articulate some convincing reasons why a particular religious tradition is not a suitable starting point for talking about morality.

The challenge pertains also in countries like the United States, where the majority of our students are usually still Catholic, particularly on the high school level. Much more than our generation, our students already live in a religiously plural culture and are not prepared to think about religion except in a pluralistic context. We need to be able to help them deal with this diversity, to read properly the complexity of the world, and to imagine the multiple possibilities of how reason, morality, and religion relate to one another—without losing a sense of what being a Christian has to do with it all. If we can succeed in re-educating ourselves and then in revising the course of studies in our schools, the 350 years that separate us from de Nobili will perhaps no longer seem so great a distance.

Notes

1. See Vincent Cronin, *A Pearl to India* (New York: E. P. Dutton and Company, 1959,) and S. Rajamanickam, S.J., *The First Oriental Scholar* (Tirunelveli: de Nobili Research Institute, 1972).
2. Throughout I refer loosely to Hinduism and Hindus when speaking of the religious practices, theologies, sects, etc., that flourished in south India in de Nobili's time. However, it is important to remember that these are terms of convenience, and do not indicate one organized religion.
3. As he perceived these; below, I will discuss the constraints of partial knowledge under which he probably worked. In brief, we can say that he had more immediate, everyday experience of Hinduism and less knowledge of it as expressed in sophisticated Hindu writings. Modern research and communications have made it possible for us to reverse this situation.
4. The *Ñāṇōpatēcam* (literally, "The Instruction in Knowledge") has been published in Tamil by S. Rajamanickam, S.J., in four vols.: vol. 1 (1966), vol. 2 (1966), vol. 3 (1968), and vol. 4 (1963). Vol. 5 is not extant. The entire work, however, is available in an early Portugese translation. Rajamanickam says that de Nobili dictated the five volumes of the *Catechism* in his old age, after going blind; it reflects de Nobili's teaching over the forty years before that dictation. I wish also to note here that I refer to the Hindu gods instead of to the Hindu Gods, since de Nobili's argumentation presumes a polytheistic context in which there are many such deities in the genus god. Of course, many important religions within what we conveniently label Hinduism in effect treat one of these gods as God.
5. De Nobili thus moves directly from the notion of the metaphysical good to that of the moral good without discussing the possibility that a perfect being could simply choose to be evil by free will.
6. The following paragraphs summarize major points from his more extended exposition in chap. 5.
7. Even though that reconstruction is desired, since we know very little about

how Hindus responded to de Nobili's arguments, written or oral. See Rajamanickam, for materials that can be used in this reconstruction.

8. This claim is implicit in chap. 5 of the *Catechism,* where it is shown that God—as understood properly, and so in conformity with the Christian tradition—is the perfect model of good moral standards. In the *Tūṣaṇa Tikkāram,* de Nobili presents Christ as the divine teacher come down on earth and stresses the moral exemplarity of his behavior. See my "Christ as the Divine Guru in the Theology of Roberto de Nobili," in *One Faith, Many Cultures,* Boston Theological Institute Series, vol. 2, ed. Ruy O. Costa (Maryknoll, New York: Orbis, 1988), pp. 25–40.

9. The nature of myth of course involves many complex questions that cannot be introduced here; and, although the view I sketch here is a predominant one, I do not mean to suggest that today we have progressed to *the* right view of myth. For overviews of the current discussion of myth, one can begin with the articles "Myth: An Overview" by Kees Bolle and "Myth and History" by Paul Ricoeur in *Encyclopedia of Religion,* ed. Mircea Eliade (New York: Macmillan Publishing Company, 1987) and "Myth" by Heinrich Fries in *Encyclopedia of Theology,* ed. Karl Rahner (New York: Crossroad, 1982).

10. See Wendy D. O'Flaherty, *Hindu Myths* (Nw York: Penguin, 1975), pp. 28–35 for several versions of the Prajāpati story.

11. On the treatment of evil in Hindu myth, see Wendy D. O'Flaherty, *The Origins of Evil in Hindu Mythology* (Berkeley: University of California Press, 1976).

12. Just as the *Tūṣaṇa Tikkāram* consciously evokes Aquinas's *Summa contra Gentiles.*

13. The field of comparative religious ethics is a complex one, still in formation. For indications of how it can proceed responsibly, see *Cosmogony and Ethical Order,* ed. Robin Lovin and Frank Reynolds (Chicago: University of Chicago, 1985) and Lee Yearly, *Aquinas and Mencius* (Albany: State University of New York, 1990). See also my "Finding One's Place in the Text: A Look at the Theological Treatment of Caste in Traditional India," *Journal of Religious Ethics* 17/1 (1989): 1–29.

14. More research is required before we can say anything definitive about what de Nobili knew of Hindu theology. He seems to have had some knowledge of Hindu myths and, as we have seen, he accumulated a great deal of first-hand observations about Hindu practices. He probably had some access, at least by way of debate, to more systematic and theological arguments. When he introduces adversarial voices in objection to what he says, presumably many of these at least recall arguments that actually took place. But it is not clear to me that he had access to actual theological texts or a clear idea of whole theological systems that were comparable to his own. Although he quotes occasionally from theological treatises—for example, in chap. 5 he cites the first verse of a very important Śaiva Siddhānta text, the *Śivajñānasiddhiyār,* in support of his definition of God—even this does not indicate conclusively that he read the whole texts, since quotations might have been learned in discussion.

15. See James Redington, *Vallabhacarya on the Love Games of Krsna* (Delhi: Motilal Banarsidass, 1983), pp, 295–306, for a good illustration of how a classical Hindu commentator raises and argues the problems connected with Kṛṣṇa's behavior. We can also note here that commentators on occasion interpret myths in the realist-referential sense I have disputed above.

16. On the distance between our world and de Nobili's on the issue of the role of reason, see my "Roberto de Nobili, Adaptation and the Reasonable Interpretation of Religion," *Missiology* 18/1 (January 1990): 25–36.

Contributors

FRANCESCO C. CESAREO is Assistant Professor of History at John Carroll University in Cleveland. He is author of several articles on Catholic reform and of the book *Humanism and Catholic Reform: The Life and Work of Gregorio Cortese.*

CHRISTOPHER CHAPPLE, the editor, is Associate Professor of Theology at Loyola Marymount University. He is author of several articles on Asian religious traditions and of the book *Karma and Creativity.*

FRANCIS X. CLOONEY, S.J., is Associate Professor of Theology at Boston College. He is the author of numerous articles on Hinduism and comparative theology, and of two books, *Thinking Ritually: Recovering the Purva Mimamsa of Jaimini* and *Theology after Vedanta: An Experiment in Comparative Theology.*

PAUL G. CROWLEY, S.J., is Assistant Professor of Religious Studies at Santa Clara University. He has published in the area of philosophical theology and the relationship between science and religion.

ALLAN FIGUEROA DECK, S.J., is Coordinator for Hispanic Pastoral Programs at the Center for Pastoral Studies at Loyola Marymount University. He has written extensively on Hispanic ministry issues and is the author of *The Second Wave: Hispanic Ministry and the Evangelization of Cultures.*

ANTONIO T. DENICOLAS is Professor Emeritus of Philosophy at the State University of New York at Stony Brook. He has published several articles and over a dozen books, including *Ignatius of Loyola: Powers of Imagining* and *Habits of Mind: The Philosophy of Education.*

JOHN ORR DWYER is Vice President for Academic Affairs and Dean of the College at Thiel College, Greenville, Pennsylvania. He has held deanships at the Universities of San Francisco and Detroit. His publications include articles on African history and on issues of higher education.

THOMAS PHILIP FAASE is Associate Professor of Sociology at Saint Norbert College in DePere, Wisconsin. He is author of *Making Jesuits More Modern.*

MARGARET GORMAN, R.S.C.J., teaches psychology and theology at Boston College. She is the author of numerous articles on moral education and development, as well as the book *Contemporary Semantics and Contemporary Thomism*.

T. FRANK KENNEDY, S.J., is Associate Professor of Music at Boston College. An expert on Jesuits and music, he has published several articles on colonial period music in Latin America. In 1991 he produced and edited the Jesuit opera *Apotheosis sive Consecratio SS. Ignatii et Francisci Xaverii*, a 1622 work by Johannes Hieronymous Kapsberger.

PETER MCDONOUGH is Professor of Political Science at Arizona State University. He has published extensively on Latin American politics and is the author of *Power and Ideology in Brazil* as well as of *Men Astutely Trained: A History of the Jesuits in the American Century*.

GERALD MCKEVITT, S.J., is Associate Professor of History at Santa Clara University. He has published *The University of Santa Clara: A History, 1851–1977* and several articles on the Catholic presence in the West and is currently researching the history of Italian Jesuits in the United States.

LUIS MARTIN is Edmund and Louise Kahn Professor of History at Southern Methodist University. His books include *Daughters of Conquistadores: Women of the Viceroyalty of Peru* and *The Kingdom of the Sun: A Short History of Peru*.

JOSEPH A. O'HARE, S.J., President of Fordham University, spent many years studying and teaching in the Philippines. Father O'Hare served as editor of *America*, the weekly journal of opinion published by the Jesuits of the United States and Canada, from 1975 to 1984. He is currently Chairman of the Association of Jesuit Colleges and Universities and in 1990 became Chair of the Association of Catholic Colleges and Universities.

REV. CHARLES W. POLZER, S.J., is Curator of Ethnohistory at the University of Arizona's Arizona State Museum. He has published over fifteen books and monographs in English and Spanish on the history of the American Southwest and on Eusebio Kino. His publications include *A Kino Guide: His Missions and Monuments* and *The Militia on the Northern Frontier of New spain*.

JOHN D. WILLIS is Senior Minister at the Rockville Christian Church (Disciples of Christ) in Rockville, Maryland. He has published several articles. His current research compares first-generation Jesuits and Protestants on the topics of faith and justification. His dissertation (University of Chicago, 1989) compared the Biblical exegeses of Salmerón, Erasmus, Luther, and Menno Simons.

LAWRENCE WOLFF is Associate Professor of History at Boston College. He has published several articles on the Enlightenment and Eastern Europe and is author of two books: *The Vatican and Poland in the Age of the Partitions* and *Postcards from the End of the World: Child Abuse in Freud's Vienna.*

Index